SIDE by SIDE
THIRD EDITION

BOOK 3

Steven J. Molinsky
Bill Bliss

Contributing Authors

Sarah Lynn
Mary Ann Perry

with

John Kopec

Correlation and Placement Key

Side by Side correlates with the following standards-based curriculum levels and assessment system score ranges:

	Side by Side 1	Side by Side 2	Side by Side 3	Side by Side 4
NRS (National Reporting System) Educational Functioning Level	Low Beginning	High Beginning	Low Intermediate	High Intermediate
CASAS (Comprehensive Adult Student Assessment System)	181–190	191–200	201–210	211–220
BEST Plus (Basic English Skills Test)	401–417	418–438	439–472	473–506
BEST Oral Interview	16–28	29–41	42–50	51–57
BEST Literacy	8–35	36–46	47–53	54–65

For correlations to other major curriculum frameworks, please visit: www.longmanusa.com/sidebyside

Side by Side, 3rd edition
Teacher's Guide 3

Copyright © 2002 by Prentice Hall Regents
Addison Wesley Longman, Inc.
A Pearson Education Company.
All rights reserved.
No part of this publication may be reproduced,
stored in a retrieval system, or transmitted
in any form or by any means, electronic, mechanical,
photocopying, recording, or otherwise,
without the prior permission of the publisher.

Pearson Education, 10 Bank Street, White Plains, NY 10606

Vice president, director of publishing: *Allen Ascher*
Editorial manager: *Pam Fishman*
Vice president, director of design and production: *Rhea Banker*
Director of electronic production: *Aliza Greenblatt*
Production manager: *Ray Keating*
Director of manufacturing: *Patrice Fraccio*
Digital layout specialists: *Kelly Tavares, Paula Williams, Wendy Wolf*
Interior design: *Wendy Wolf*
Interior art: *Judy A. Wolf*
Cover design: *Elizabeth Carlson*
Cover art: *Richard E. Hill*
Copyediting: *Janet Johnston*

The authors gratefully acknowledge the contribution
of Tina Carver in the development of the original
Side by Side program.

ISBN 0-13-512612-6
ISBN 978-0-13-512612-7

Printed in the United States of America

2 3 4 5 6 7 8 9 10 – QWD – 12 11 10 09

CONTENTS

Guide to Multilevel Resources	iv	Chapter 8	252
Introduction	vi	*Side by Side* Gazette	290
Chapter 1	2	Chapter 9	298
Chapter 2	34	Chapter 10	336
Chapter 3	64	*Side by Side* Gazette	367
Side by Side Gazette	97		
Chapter 4	104	**APPENDIX**	
Chapter 5	150	*Side by Side* Picture Cards	374
Side by Side Gazette	179	Glossary	377
Chapter 6	186		
Chapter 7	218		

Guide to Multilevel Resources

The *Side by Side Teacher's Guides* provide valuable resources for effective multilevel instruction. Easy-to-use strategies help teachers preview and pre-drill lesson objectives for students who need extra preparation. Hundreds of dynamic expansion activities offer reinforcement and enrichment for students at three different ability-levels:

- *Below-level* students who need extra support and some re-teaching of skills and content to master basic objectives;
- *At-level* students who are performing well in class and can benefit from reinforcement;
- *Above-level* students who want and deserve opportunities for enrichment and greater challenge.

Getting Ready sections are ideal lesson-planning tools. They provide a careful sequence of instructional steps teachers can use during the warm-up, preview, and initial presentation stages of a lesson—especially helpful for *below-level* students who need careful preparation for a lesson's new vocabulary, grammar, topics, functions, or language skills.

The Getting Ready section is an "on-ramp" that allows students to get up to speed with lesson content so that they comprehend the lesson and master its learning objectives.

 Text Page 3

💬 **TALK ABOUT IT!** *What Do They Like to Do?*

FOCUS

- Review: Simple Present Tense, Past Tense, Present Continuous Tense, Future: Going to
- Daily Activities

GETTING READY

1. Write the following on the board:

2. Point to *Bill* on the board and tell the class that this is your friend Bill, and he really likes to study.

   a. Point to *every day* on the board and ask: "What does he do every day?" (Students answer: "He studies.")
   b. Point to *yesterday* on the board and ask: "What did he do yesterday?" (Students answer: "He studied.")
   c. Point to *right now* on the board and ask: "What's he doing right now?" (Students answer, "He's studying.")
   d. Point to *tomorrow* on the board and ask: "What's he going to do tomorrow?" (Students answer: "He's going to study.")

3. Point to *Jane* on the board and tell the class that this is your friend Jane, and she really likes to drink milk.

   a. Point to *every day* on the board and ask:

   "What does she do every day?" (Students answer: "She drinks milk.")
   b. Point to *yesterday* on the board and ask: "What did she do yesterday?" (Students answer: "She drank milk.")
   c. Point to *right now* on the board and ask: "What's she doing right now?" (Students answer: "She's drinking milk.")
   d. Point to *tomorrow* on the board and ask: "What's she going to do tomorrow?" (Students answer: "She's going to drink milk.")

INTRODUCING THE PEOPLE

1. Have students read silently or follow along silently as the description of the characters is read aloud by you, by one or more students, or on the audio program.

2. Ask students if they have any questions. Check understanding of vocabulary. Introduce the irregular past tense form *swam*.

CONVERSATION PRACTICE

There are two sets of questions at the bottom of the page. The questions on the left are singular. The questions on the right are plural.

1. Have pairs of students use these questions to talk about the people on the page. This can be done as either Full-Class Practice or Pair Practice.

2. Then, have students ask and answer questions about other people they know.

3. If you do the activity as Pair Practice, call on pairs to present their conversations to the class.

WORKBOOK

Page 3

8 CHAPTER 1

Multilevel Expansion Activities include games, tasks, brainstorming, discussion, movement, drawing, miming, and role playing—all designed to reinforce and enrich instruction in a way that is stimulating, creative, and fun! Activity levels are indicated through a three-star system:

★ **One-star activities** are designed for *below-level* students. These activities typically present students with a single task, such as listening for particular vocabulary words or grammar, repeating words or phrases, or pantomiming actions. These activities are highly structured with very defined answers. Often the direction of input is from the teacher, rather than the student.

★★ **Two-star activities** are for *at-level* students. These activities usually present dual tasks—such as categorizing while taking dictation, listening to a partial sentence and completing it, or speaking and finding a student with a matching line. These are moderately structured activities, with some open answers and room for interpretation. They can be teacher-directed or student-directed, so these activities require that students have some control of language and some independence.

★★★ **Three-star activities** are for *above-level* students. These activities often include several steps and multiple language tasks, such as role plays, discussions, debates, and creative writing based on lesson themes. These activities are highly unstructured, with much room for student input, interpretation, and control. Since most input comes from students, these activities require mastery of vocabulary and student independence.

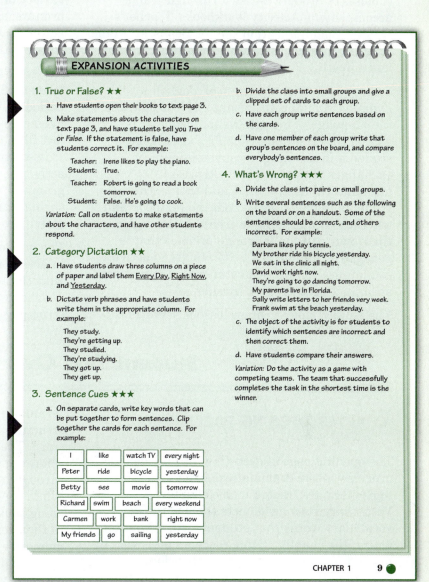

Here's an at-a-glance summary of how *Side by Side* expansion activities are differentiated by the nature of the tasks, their structure, and the extent of teacher/student input.

	★ Below-level	★★ At-level	★★★ Above-level
Tasks	Single task	Dual tasks	Multi-tasks
Structure	Highly structured	Moderately structured	Less structured/Unstructured
Input	Teacher-directed	Teacher-directed/Student-directed	Student-directed

GUIDE TO MULTILEVEL RESOURCES

INTRODUCTION

Side by Side is an English language program for young-adult and adult learners from beginning to high-intermediate levels. The program consists of Student Books 1 through 4 and accompanying Activity Workbooks, Teacher's Guides, Communication Games Books, an Audio Program, a Video Program, a Picture Program, and a Testing Program.

Side by Side offers learners of English a dynamic, communicative approach to learning the language. Through the methodology of guided conversations, *Side by Side* engages students in meaningful conversational exchanges within carefully structured grammatical frameworks, and then encourages students to break away from the textbook and use these frameworks to create conversations on their own. All the language practice that is generated through the texts results in active communication between students . . . practicing speaking together "side by side."

The Guided Conversation lessons serve as the "anchor" for the presentation of the grammatical and functional language core of the program. These lessons are followed by a variety of reading, writing, listening, pronunciation, role-playing, and discussion activities that reinforce and expand upon this conversational core.

A special feature of this third edition are the "*Side by Side* Gazette" pages that appear periodically throughout the texts. These magazine-style pages contain feature articles, fact files, interviews, vocabulary expansion, cross-cultural topics, authentic listening activities, questions and answers about English grammar, e-mail exchanges, and cartoon springboards for interactive role-playing activities.

The goal of *Side by Side* is to engage students in active, meaningful communicative practice with the language. The aim of the *Side by Side* Teacher's Guides is to offer guidelines and strategies to help achieve that goal.

Student Text Overview

CHAPTER OPENING PAGES

The opening page of each chapter provides an overview of the grammatical structures and topics that are treated in the chapter. A Vocabulary Preview depicts some of the key vocabulary words that students will encounter within the chapter. Some teachers may wish to present and practice these words before beginning the chapter. Other teachers may prefer to wait until the words occur in the particular lesson in which they are introduced.

GUIDED CONVERSATION LESSONS

Grammatical Paradigms

A new grammatical structure appears first in the form of a grammatical paradigm, or "grammar box"—a simple schema of the structure. (Grammar boxes are in a light blue tint.) These paradigms are meant to be a reference point for students as they proceed through a lesson's conversational activities. While these paradigms highlight the structures being taught, they are not intended to be goals in themselves. Students are not expected to memorize or parrot back these rules. Rather, we want students to take part in conversations that show they can *use* these rules correctly.

Model Guided Conversations

Model conversations serve as the vehicles for introducing new grammatical structures and many communicative uses of English. Because the model becomes the basis for all the exercises that follow, it is essential that students be given sufficient practice with it before proceeding with the lesson.

Side by Side Exercises

In the numbered exercises that follow the model, students pair up and work "side by side," placing new content into the given conversational framework. These exercises form the core learning activity of each conversation lesson.

FOLLOW-UP EXERCISES AND ACTIVITIES

- **Reading** selections offer enjoyable reading practice that simultaneously reinforces the grammatical and thematic focus of each chapter.

- **Reading Check-Up** exercises provide focused practice in reading comprehension.

- **Listening** exercises enable students to develop their aural comprehension skills through a variety of listening activities.

- **Pronunciation** exercises provide models of authentic pronunciation and opportunities for student listening and speaking practice.

- **How to Say It!** activities expose students to key communication strategies.

- **Talk About It!** and **Think About It!** activities offer additional opportunities for conversational practice.

- **In Your Own Words** activities provide topics and themes for student compositions and classroom discussions in which students write about their friends, families, homes, schools, and themselves.

- *Side by Side* **Journal** activities provide the opportunity for students to write about things that are meaningful to them.

- **Role Play**, **Interactions**, and **Interview** activities provide opportunities for dynamic classroom interaction.

- **On Your Own** and **How About You?** activities give students valuable opportunities to apply lesson content to their own lives and experiences and to share opinions in class. Through these activities, students bring to the classroom new content based on their interests, their backgrounds, and their imaginations.

SIDE BY SIDE GAZETTE

- **Feature Articles** provide interesting and stimulating content.

- **Fact Files** present facts about the world for class discussion.

- **Interviews** offer students an in-depth look into people's lives.

- **Fun With Idioms** sections introduce students to common idiomatic expressions.

- **Around the World** photo essays offer rich opportunities for cross-cultural comparison.

- **We've Got Mail!** sections provide clear, simple explanations of key grammatical structures.

- **Global Exchange** activities give students experience with online communication.

- **Listening** sections offer students authentic listening opportunities.

- **What Are They Saying?** cartoons serve as springboards for interactive role-playing activities.

SUPPORT AND REFERENCE SECTIONS

- The **Chapter Summary** at the end of each chapter provides charts of the grammar structures presented in the chapter along with a listing of key vocabulary words. This summary is useful as a review and study guide after students have completed the chapter.

- An **Appendix** contains Listening Scripts, a Thematic Vocabulary Glossary, and a list of Irregular Verbs.

- An **Index** provides a convenient reference for locating grammatical structures in the text.

Ancillary Materials

ACTIVITY WORKBOOKS

The Activity Workbooks offer a variety of exercises for reinforcement, fully coordinated with the student texts. A special feature of the Activity Workbooks is the inclusion of GrammarRaps for practice with rhythm, stress, and intonation, and in Levels 1 and 2 GrammarSongs from the *Side by Side TV* videos. Periodic check-up tests are also included in the workbooks.

AUDIO PROGRAM

The Student Text audios are especially designed to serve as a student's speaking partner, making conversation practice possible even when the student is studying alone. In addition to the guided conversation models and exercises, the audios contain the vocabulary preview words at the beginning of each chapter, the listening and pronunciation exercises, the reading selections, and the *Side by Side* Gazettes.

The Activity Workbook audios contain the listening and pronunciation exercises, along with the GrammarRaps and GrammarSongs.

VIDEO PROGRAM

The *Side by Side TV* videos and accompanying Video Workbooks are designed to serve as a video accompaniment to Levels 1 and 2 of the series. These innovative videos offer original comedy sketches, on-location interviews, rap numbers, music videos, and other popular TV formats. The *Side by Side TV* videos are fully coordinated with the *Side by Side* student texts.

COMMUNICATION GAMES BOOKS

This innovative teacher resource provides a wealth of interactive language games designed to serve as enjoyable and motivating reinforcement of key grammatical structures presented in the student texts. All of the games are accompanied by reproducible activity masters for ease of classroom use.

PICTURE PROGRAM

Side by Side Picture Cards illustrate key concepts and vocabulary items. They can be used for introduction of new material, for review, for enrichment, and for role-playing activities. Suggestions for their use are included in the Teacher's Guide. Also, the Appendix to the Teacher's Guide contains a triple listing of the Picture Cards: numerically, alphabetically, and by category.

TESTING PROGRAM

The *Side by Side* Testing Program consists of a placement test and individual chapter tests, mid-book tests, and final tests for each level of the program.

Format of the Teacher's Guide

CHAPTER OVERVIEW

The Chapter Overview provides the following:
- Functional and grammatical highlights of the chapter
- A listing of new vocabulary and expressions

CHAPTER OPENING PAGE

The Teacher's Guide offers suggestions for presenting and practicing the words depicted in the Vocabulary Preview.

viii   INTRODUCTION

STEP-BY-STEP LESSON GUIDE

Conversation Lessons

Included for each conversation lesson are the following:

- **FOCUS:** the grammatical and topical focus of the lesson
- **CLOSE UP:** short grammar explanations accompanied by examples from the lesson
- **GETTING READY:** suggestions for introducing the new concepts in the lesson
- **INTRODUCING THE MODEL:** steps for introducing model conversations
- **SIDE BY SIDE EXERCISES:** suggestions for practicing the exercises, as well as a listing of new vocabulary
- **LANGUAGE NOTES, CULTURE NOTES,** and **PRONUNCIATION NOTES**
- **WORKBOOK:** page references for exercises in the Activity Workbook that correspond to the particular lesson
- **EXPANSION ACTIVITIES:** optional activities for review and reinforcement of the content of the lesson

Reading Lessons

Included for each reading lesson are the following:

- **FOCUS** of the reading
- **NEW VOCABULARY** contained in the reading
- **READING THE STORY:** an optional preliminary preview stage before students begin to read the selection, along with suggestions for presenting the story and questions to check students' comprehension
- **READING CHECK-UP:** answer keys for the reading comprehension exercises
- **READING EXTENSION:** additional questions and activities that provide additional skill reinforcement of the reading selection

Other Follow-Up Lessons

Included for other follow-up lessons are the following:

- **LISTENING** scripts and answer keys for the listening exercises
- Strategies for presenting and practicing the *How to Say It!*, *How About You?*, *On Your Own*, *In Your Own Words*, *Role Play*, *Interactions*, *Interview*, *Talk About It!*, *Think About It!*, *Pronunciation*, and *Side by Side Journal* activities

Chapter Summary

Included for each Chapter Summary are the following:

- **GRAMMAR SUMMARY** tasks
- **KEY VOCABULARY** reinforcement and expansion activities
- **END-OF-CHAPTER EXPANSION ACTIVITIES** that review and reinforce the grammar structures and vocabulary presented in the chapter

Side by Side Gazette

Included for the *Side by Side* Gazette pages are the following:

- Strategies for introducing, practicing, and expanding upon the *Feature Articles*, *Fact Files*, *Interviews*, *Fun with Idioms*, *Around the World*, *Global Exchange*, *We've Got Mail!*, *Listening*, and *What Are They Saying?* sections of the Gazette

WORKBOOK ANSWER KEYS AND LISTENING SCRIPTS

Answers and listening scripts for all exercises contained in the Activity Workbooks are provided at the end of each chapter of the Teacher's Guide.

General Teaching Strategies

VOCABULARY PREVIEW

You may wish to introduce the words in the Vocabulary Preview before beginning the chapter, or you may choose to wait until they first occur in a specific lesson. If you choose to introduce them at this point, the Teacher's Guide offers these suggestions:

1. Have students look at the illustrations and identify the words they already know.

2. Present the vocabulary. Say each word and have the class repeat it chorally and individually. Check students' understanding and pronunciation of the words.

3. Practice the vocabulary as a class, in pairs, or in small groups. Have students cover the word list and look at the pictures. Practice the words by saying a word and having students tell the number of the illustration and/or giving the number of the illustration and having students say the word.

GUIDED CONVERSATION LESSONS

Introducing Model Conversations

Given the importance of the model conversation, it is essential that students practice it several times in a variety of ways before going on to the exercises.

This Teacher's Guide offers the following comprehensive 8-step approach to introducing the model:

1. Have students look at the model illustration. This helps establish the context of the conversation.

2. Set the scene.

3. *Present the model.* With books closed, have students listen as you present the model or play the audio one or more times. To make the presentation of the model as realistic as possible, you might draw two stick figures on the board to represent the speakers in the dialog. You can also show that two people are speaking by changing your position or by shifting your weight from one foot to the other as you say each speaker's lines.

4. *Full-Class Repetition.* Model each line and have the whole class repeat in unison.

5. Have students open their books and look at the dialog. Ask if there are any questions, and check understanding of new vocabulary.

6. *Group Choral Repetition.* Divide the class in half. Model line A and have Group 1 repeat. Model line B and have Group 2 repeat. Continue with all the lines of the model.

7. *Choral Conversation.* Have both groups practice the dialog twice, without a teacher model. First Group 1 is Speaker A and Group 2 is Speaker B; then reverse.

8. Call on one or two pairs of students to present the dialog.

In steps 6, 7, and 8, encourage students to look up from their books and *say* the lines rather than read them. (Students can of course refer to their books when necessary.)

The goal is not memorization or complete mastery of the model. Rather, students should become familiar with the model and feel comfortable saying it.

At this point, if you feel that additional practice is necessary before going on to the exercises, you can do Choral Conversation in small groups or by rows.

Alternative Approaches to Introducing Model Conversations

Depending upon the abilities of your students and the particular lesson you're teaching, you might wish to try the following approaches to vary the way in which you introduce model conversations.

- **Pair Introduction**

  Have a pair of students present the model. Then practice it with the class.

- **Trio Introduction**

  Call on *three* students to introduce the model. Have two of them present it while the third acts as the *director*, offering suggestions for

INTRODUCTION

how to say the lines better. Then practice the dialog with the class.

- **Cloze Introduction**

    Write a cloze version of the model conversation on the board for student reference as you introduce the model. For lessons that provide a skeletal framework of the model (for example, Book 3 pp. 24, 48, 63, 87, 89, 91, 104, 106, 122), you can use that as the cloze version. For other lessons, you can decide which words to delete from the dialog.

- **Scrambled Dialog Introduction**

    Write each line of the dialog on a separate card. Distribute the cards to students and have them practice saying their lines, then talk with each other to figure out what the correct order of the lines should be. Have them present the dialog to the class, each student in turn reading his or her line. Have the class decide if it's in the correct order. Then practice the dialog with the class.

    Warning: Do a scrambled dialog introduction *only* for conversations in which there is only one possible sentence order!

- **Disappearing Dialog Introduction**

    Write the dialog on the board and have students practice saying it. Erase a few of the words and practice again. Continue practicing the dialog several times, each time having erased more of the words, until the dialog has completely *disappeared* and students can say the lines without looking at them.

- **Eliciting the Model**

    Have students cover up the lines of the model and look only at the illustration. Ask questions based on the illustration and the situation. For example: *Who are these people? Where are they? What are they saying to each other?* As a class, in groups, or in pairs, have students suggest a possible dialog. Have students present their ideas and then compare them with the model conversation in the book. Then practice the dialog with the class.

Side by Side Exercises

The numbered exercises that follow the model form the core learning activity in each conversation lesson. Here students use the illustrations and word cues to create conversations based on the structure of the model. Since all language practice in these lessons is conversational, you will always call on a pair of students to do each exercise. Your primary role is to serve as a resource to the class — to help students with new structures, new vocabulary, intonation, and pronunciation.

The Teacher's Guide recommends the following three steps for practicing the exercises. (Students should be given thorough practice with the first two exercises before going on.)

1. **Exercise 1:** Introduce any new vocabulary in the exercise. Call on two students to present the dialog. Then do Choral Repetition and Choral Conversation practice.

2. **Exercise 2:** Same as for Exercise 1.

3. For the remaining exercises, there are two options: either Full-Class Practice or Pair Practice.

    Full-Class Practice: Call on a pair of students to do each exercise. Introduce new vocabulary one exercise at a time. (For more practice, you can call on other pairs of students or do Choral Repetition or Choral Conversation.)

    Pair Practice: Introduce new vocabulary for all the exercises. Next have students practice all the exercises in pairs. Then have pairs present the exercises to the class. (For more practice, you can do Choral Repetition or Choral Conversation.)

The choice of Full-Class Practice or Pair Practice should be determined by the content of the particular lesson, the size and composition of the class, and your own teaching style. You might also wish to vary your approach from lesson to lesson.

- **Suggestions for Pairing Up Students**

    Whether you use Full-Class Practice or Pair Practice, you can select students for pairing in various ways.

    - You might want to pair students by ability, since students of similar ability might work together more efficiently than students of dissimilar ability.

    - On the other hand, you might wish to pair a weaker student with a stronger one. The slower student benefits from this pairing, while the more advanced student strengthens his or her abilities by helping a partner.

You should also encourage students to look at each other when speaking. This makes the conversational nature of the language practice more realistic. One way of ensuring this is *not* to call on two students who are sitting next to each other. Rather, call on students in different parts of the room and encourage them to look at each other when saying their lines.

- **Presenting New Vocabulary**

  Many new words are introduced in each conversation lesson. The illustration usually helps to convey the meaning, and the new words are written for students to see and use in these conversations. In addition, you might:

  - write the new word on the board or on a word card.
  - say the new word several times and ask students to repeat chorally and individually.
  - help clarify the meaning with visuals.

  Students might also find it useful to keep a notebook in which they write each new word, its meaning, and a sentence using that word.

- **Open-Ended Exercises**

  In many lessons, the final exercise is an open-ended one. This is indicated in the text by a *blank box*. Here students are expected to create conversations based on the structure of the model, but with vocabulary that they select themselves. This provides students with an opportunity for creativity, while still focusing on the particular structure being practiced. These open-ended exercises can be done orally in class and/or assigned as homework for presentation in class the following day. Encourage students to use dictionaries to find new words they want to use.

General Guiding Principles for Working with Guided Conversations

- *Speak*, not *Read* the Conversations

  When doing the exercises, students should practice *speaking* to each other, rather than *reading* to each other. Even though students will need to refer to the text to be able to practice the conversations, they should not read the lines word by word. Rather, they should scan a full line and then look up from the book and *speak* the line to the other person.

- **Intonation and Gesture**

  Throughout, you should use the book to teach proper intonation and gesture. (Capitalized words are used to indicate spoken emphasis.) Students should be encouraged to truly *act out* the dialogs in a strong and confident voice.

- **Student-Centered Practice**

  Use of the texts should be as student-centered as possible. Modeling by the teacher should be efficient and economical, but students should have every opportunity to model for each other when they are capable of doing so.

- **Vocabulary in Context**

  Vocabulary can and should be effectively taught in the context of the conversation being practiced. Very often it will be possible to grasp the meaning from the conversation or its accompanying illustration. You should spend time drilling vocabulary in isolation only if you feel it is absolutely essential.

- **No "Grammar Talk"**

  Students need not study formally or be able to produce grammatical rules. The purpose of the texts is to engage students in active communication that gets them to *use* the language according to these rules.

Relating Lesson Content to Students' Lives and Experiences

- **Personalize the Exercises**

  While doing the guided conversation exercises, whenever you think it is appropriate, ask students questions that relate the situations in the exercises to their own lives and personal experiences. This will help make the leap from practicing language in the textbook to using the language for actual communication.

- **Interview the Characters**

  Where appropriate, as students are presenting the exercises to the class, as a way of making the situations come alive and making students feel as though they really *are* the characters in those situations, ask questions that students can respond to based on their imaginations.

READINGS

If you wish, preview the story by having students talk about the story title and/or illustrations. You may choose to introduce new vocabulary beforehand, or have students encounter the new vocabulary within the context of the reading.

Have students read silently or follow along silently as the story is read aloud by you, by one or more students, or on the audio program. Ask students if they have any questions and check understanding of new vocabulary. Then do the Reading Check-Up exercises.

How to Say It!

How to Say It! activities are designed to expose students to important communication strategies. Present the conversations the same way you introduce model guided conversations: set the scene, present the model, do full-class and choral repetition, and have pairs of students present the dialog. Then divide the class into pairs and have students practice other conversations based on the *How to Say It!* model and then present them to the class.

How About You?

How About You? activities are intended to provide students with additional opportunities to tell about themselves. Have students do these activities in pairs or as a class.

 ON YOUR OWN

On Your Own activities offer students the opportunity to contribute content of their own within the grammatical framework of the lesson. You should introduce these activities in class and assign them as homework for presentation in class the next day. In this way, students will automatically review the previous day's grammar while contributing new and inventive content of their own.

These activities are meant for simultaneous grammar reinforcement and vocabulary building. Students should be encouraged to use a dictionary when completing the *On Your Own* activities. In this way, they will use not only the words they know but also the words they would *like* to know in order to really bring their interests, backgrounds, and imaginations into the classroom.

As a result, students will teach each other new vocabulary as they share a bit of their lives with others in the class.

 IN YOUR OWN WORDS

Have students do the activity as written homework, using a dictionary for any new words they wish to use. Then have students present and discuss what they have written, in pairs or as a class.

 ROLE PLAY

Have pairs of students practice role-playing the activity and then present their role plays to the class.

 INTERACTIONS

Divide the class into pairs and have students practice conversations based on the skeletal models. Then call on students to present their conversations to the class.

 INTERVIEW

Have students circulate around the room to conduct their interviews and then report back to the class.

TALK ABOUT IT!

Call on a few different pairs of students to present the model dialogs. Then divide the class into pairs and have students take turns using the models to ask and answer questions about the characters and situations depicted on the page. Then call on pairs to present conversations to the class.

THINK ABOUT IT!

Divide the class into pairs or small groups. Have students discuss the questions and then share their thoughts with the class.

PRONUNCIATION

Pronunciation exercises provide students with models of natural English pronunciation. The goal of these exercises is to enable learners to improve their own pronunciation and to understand the pronunciation of native speakers using English in natural conversational contexts.

Have students first focus on listening to the sentences. Say each sentence in the left column or play the audio one or more times and have students listen carefully and repeat. Next, focus on pronunciation. Have students say each sentence in the right column and then listen carefully as you say it or play the audio. If you wish, you can have students continue practicing the sentences to improve their pronunciation.

JOURNAL

The purpose of the *Side by Side Journal* activity is to show students how writing can become a vehicle for communicating thoughts and feelings. Have students begin a journal in a composition notebook. In these journals, students have the opportunity to write about things that are meaningful to them.

Have students write their journal entries at home or in class. Encourage students to use a dictionary to look up words they would like to use. They can share their written work with other students if appropriate. Then as a class, in pairs, or in small groups, have students discuss what they have written.

If time permits, you may want to write a response in each student's journal, sharing your own opinions and experiences as well as reacting to what the student has written. If you are keeping portfolios of students' work, these compositions serve as excellent examples of students' progress in learning English.

CHAPTER SUMMARY

- **Grammar**

  Divide the class into pairs or small groups, and have students take turns forming sentences from the words in the grammar boxes. Student A says a sentence, and Student B points to the words from each column that are in the sentence. Then have students switch: Student B says a sentence, and Student A points to the words.

- **Key Vocabulary**

  Have students ask you any questions about the meaning or pronunciation of the vocabulary. If students ask for the pronunciation, repeat after the student until the student is satisfied with his or her own pronunciation.

- **Key Vocabulary Check**

  When completing a chapter, as a way of checking students' retention of the key vocabulary depicted on the opening page of the chapter, have students open their books to the first page of the chapter and cover the list of vocabulary words. Either call out a number and have students tell you the word, or say a word and have students tell you the number.

xiv   INTRODUCTION

Side by Side Gazette

FEATURE ARTICLE

Have students read silently or follow along silently as the article is read aloud by you, by one or more students, or on the audio program. You may choose to introduce new vocabulary beforehand, or have students encounter it within the context of the article. Ask students if they have any questions, and check understanding of vocabulary.

FACT FILE

Present the information and have the class discuss it.

INTERVIEW

Have students read silently or follow along silently as the interview is read aloud by you, by one or more students, or on the audio program.

FUN WITH IDIOMS

Have students look at the illustrations. Say each expression or play the audio and have the class repeat it chorally and individually. Check students' understanding and pronunciation of the expressions. Then have students match the expressions with their meanings.

AROUND THE WORLD

Divide the class into pairs or small groups and have students react to the photographs and answer the questions. Then have students report back to the class.

WE'VE GOT MAIL!

Have students read silently or follow along silently as the letters are read aloud by you, by one or more students, or on the audio program.

GLOBAL EXCHANGE

Have students read silently or follow along silently as the message is read aloud by you, by one or more students, or on the audio program. For additional practice, you can have students write back to the person and then share their writing with the class. You may also wish to have students correspond with a keypal on the Internet and then share their experience with the class.

WHAT ARE THEY SAYING?

Have students talk about the people and the situation in the cartoon and then create role plays based on the scene. Students may refer back to previous lessons as a resource, but they should not simply reuse specific conversations. You may want to assign this exercise as written homework, having students prepare their role plays, practice them the next day with other students, and then present them to the class.

Multilevel Expansion Activities

This Teacher's Guide offers a rich variety of Multilevel Expansion Activities for review and reinforcement. Feel free to pick and choose or vary the activities to fit the particular ability-levels, needs, and learning styles of your students. Activity levels are indicated through a three-star system:

★ **One-star activities** are designed for *below-level* students who need extra support and some re-teaching of skills and content to master basic objectives;

★★ **Two-star activities** are for *at-level* students who are performing well in class and can benefit from reinforcement;

★★★ **Three-star activities** are for *above-level* students who want and deserve opportunities for enrichment and greater challenge.

See pages iv–v for a complete description of these ability-levels.

We encourage you to try some of the teaching approaches offered in this Teacher's Guide. In keeping with the spirit of *Side by Side*, these suggestions are intended to provide students with a language learning experience that is dynamic . . . interactive . . . and fun!

Steven J. Molinsky
Bill Bliss

CHAPTER 1 OVERVIEW: Text Pages 1–10

GRAMMAR

PRESENT CONTINUOUS TENSE

(I am)	I'm	
(He is)	He's	
(She is)	She's	
(It is)	It's	eating.
(We are)	We're	
(You are)	You're	
(They are)	They're	

Am	I	
Is	he / she / it	eating?
Are	we / you / they	

TO BE: SHORT ANSWERS

		I	am.
Yes,		he / she / it	is.
		we / you / they	are.

	I'm	not.
No,	he / she / it	isn't.
	we / you / they	aren't.

SIMPLE PRESENT TENSE

I / We / You / They	eat.
He / She / It	eats.

Do	I / we / you / they	eat?
Does	he / she / it	

	I / we / you / they	do.
Yes,	he / she / it	does.

	I / we / you / they	don't.
No,	he / she / it	doesn't.

Subject Pronouns	Possessive Adjectives	Object Pronouns
I	my	me
he	his	him
she	her	her
it	its	it
we	our	us
you	your	you
they	their	them

FUNCTIONS

ASKING FOR AND REPORTING INFORMATION

Are you busy?
  Yes, I am. I'm *studying*.
What are you *studying*?
  I'm *studying* English.

Who are you calling?

What are you doing?
  I'm *practicing the piano*.

What *are George and Herman* talking about?

What *are you* complaining about?

What's *your teacher's* name?
What are their names?

What do you do?

When do you *go to class*?

Where are you from?
Where do you live now?
Where do you *work*?

How often do you *watch TV*?

Do you *practice* very often?
  Yes, I do.

Is *she* a good *tennis player*?
  Yes, *she* is.

Are you married?
Are you single?

Her tennis coach says *she's excellent.*
Her friends tell *her she plays tennis better than anyone else.*

INQUIRING ABOUT LIKES/DISLIKES

Do you like to *ski*?

What do you like to do *in your free time*?

EXPRESSING INABILITY

I'm not a very good *skier*.

2 CHAPTER 1

NEW VOCABULARY

Occupations and Agent Nouns

ballet dancer
ballet instructor
coach
cook
instructor
music teacher
skater
soccer coach
swimmer
tennis coach
typist
violinist

Verbs

compose
stay after

Miscellaneous

army
Beethoven
bill
interests (n)
Little Red Riding Hood
Madagascar
Orlando
professional
Scrabble
talk show
telephone bill
whenever

once *a day*
twice *a day*
three times *a day*

Text Page 1: Chapter Opening Page

VOCABULARY PREVIEW

You may want to introduce these words before beginning the chapter, or you may choose to wait until they first occur in a specific lesson. If you choose to introduce them at this point, here are some suggestions:

1. Have students look at the illustrations on text page 1 and identify the words they already know.

2. Present the vocabulary. Say each word and have the class repeat it chorally and individually. Check students' understanding and pronunciation of the words.

3. Practice the vocabulary as a class, in pairs, or in small groups. Have students cover the word list and look at the pictures. Practice the words in the following ways:
   - Say a word and have students tell the number of the illustration.
   - Give the number of an illustration and have students say the word.

Text Page 2: They're Busy

FOCUS

- Review: Present Continuous Tense

CLOSE UP

RULE: The present continuous tense is used to express events that are happening right now.

EXAMPLES: What's she doing?
　　She's reading.
　　What's she reading?
　　She's reading the newspaper.

GETTING READY

1. Review Yes/No questions and affirmative short answers. Form sentences with the words in the left and center boxes at the top of text page 2. Have students repeat chorally. For example:

    Am I eating?　　Is he eating?
    Yes, I am.　　　Yes, he is.

2. Use *Side by Side* Picture Cards or your own visuals to practice short answers.

    a. Point to each visual and ask:

        Is ___ _____ing?

    Have students respond with the affirmative short answer. For example:

        A. Is she eating?
        B. Yes, she is.

        A. Are they studying?
        B. Yes, they are.

    b. Point to each visual and call on pairs of students to ask and answer as above.

3. Review the present continuous tense.

    a. Form sentences with the words in the right-hand box at the top of the page. Have students repeat chorally. For example:

        I'm eating.
        He's eating.

    Check students' pronunciation of the final *s* sound in *He's*, *She's*, *It's*.

    b. Use your own visuals or *Side by Side* Picture Cards for verbs.

    Ask students: "What ___ doing?" and have students answer individually, then chorally. For example:

        A. What's he doing?
        B. He's cooking.

        A. What's she doing?
        B. She's reading.

        A. What are they doing?
        B. They're studying.

    c. Have students role-play people in the visuals. Ask students: "What are you doing?" For example:

        A. What are you doing?
        B. I'm cooking.

        A. What are you and (*Jim*) doing?
        B. We're cooking.

INTRODUCING THE MODEL

1. Have students look at the model illustration.

2. Set the scene: "A daughter is talking to her father."

CHAPTER 1　　5

3. With books closed, have students listen as you present the model or play the audio one or more times.

4. **Full-Class Repetition:** Model each line and have students repeat.

   Pronunciation Note

   The pronunciation focus of Chapter 1 is **Reduced *are*** (text page 10). You may wish to model this pronunciation at this point (*What are you studying?*) and encourage students to incorporate it into their language practice.

5. Have students open their books and look at the dialog. Ask students if they have any questions. Check understanding of vocabulary.

6. **Group Choral Repetition:** Divide the class in half. Model line A and have Group 1 repeat. Model line B and have Group 2 repeat, and so on.

7. **Choral Conversation:** Groups 1 and 2 practice the dialog twice, without teacher model. First, Group 1 is Speaker A and Group 2 is Speaker B. Then reverse.

8. Call on one or two pairs of students to present the dialog.

   (For additional practice, do Choral Conversation in small groups or by rows.)

SIDE BY SIDE EXERCISES

Examples

1. A. Is Alan busy?
   B. Yes, he is. He's baking.
   A. What's he baking?
   B. He's baking cookies.
2. A. Is Doris busy?
   B. Yes, she is. She's reading.
   A. What's she reading?
   B. She's reading the newspaper.

1. **Exercise 1:** Call on two students to present the dialog. Then do Choral Repetition and Choral Conversation practice.

2. **Exercise 2:** Same as above.

3. **Exercises 3–9:**

   New Vocabulary
   9. compose

   Culture Note

   Exercise 9: Ludwig van Beethoven (1770–1827) was a German composer of classical music.

Either

Full-Class Practice: Introduce the new vocabulary before doing Exercise 9. Call on a pair of students to do each exercise.

(For more practice, call on other pairs of students, or do Choral Repetition or Choral Conversation.)

or

Pair Practice: Introduce all the new vocabulary. Next have students practice all the exercises in pairs. Then have pairs present the exercises to the class.

(For more practice, do Choral Repetition or Choral Conversation.)

WORKBOOK

Pages 2–3

EXPANSION ACTIVITIES

1. What Are They Doing? ★

Use *Side by Side* Picture Cards for verbs and community locations or your own visuals to review the present continuous tense.

Hold up each visual and call on students to ask and answer as many questions as possible about what the person or people in the visual are doing. For example:

A. What's she doing?
B. She's cleaning her apartment.

A. What's he doing?
B. He's playing the piano.

A. What are the other people doing?
B. They're listening to the concert/music.

2. Dictation ★

Dictate the following sentences to your students. Read each sentence twice.

1. She's painting the kitchen.
2. What's he doing?
3. He's baking cookies.
4. They're studying.
5. We're cooking dinner.
6. He's knitting.
7. What are you doing?
8. I'm composing a song.

3. Can You Hear the Difference? ★

a. Write on the board:

①
I am studying.
You are ironing.
He is cooking dinner.
They are watching TV.
She is composing music.
We are painting the house.

②
I'm studying.
You're ironing.
He's cooking dinner.
They're watching TV.
She's composing music.
We're painting the house.

b. Choose a sentence randomly from one of the two columns and say it to the class. Have the class listen and respond "One" if the sentence is not contracted, and "Two" if the sentence is contracted.

c. Have students continue the activity in pairs. One student says a sentence, and the other identifies its form. Then have students reverse roles.

d. Write other similar sentences on the board and continue the practice.

4. Telephone ★

a. Divide the class into large groups. Have each group sit in a circle.

b. Whisper the following message to one student:

"Billy is sitting, Willy is knitting, Eve is reading, and Steve is eating."

c. The first student whispers the message to the second student, and so forth around the circle. The student listening may ask for clarification by saying, "I'm sorry. Could you repeat that?"

d. When the message gets to the last student, that person says it aloud. Is it the same message you started with? The group with the most accurate message wins.

5. Miming ★

a. Write on cards the following activities:

bake a cake	paint a wall	read a newspaper
knit a sweater	iron a shirt	eat ice cream
study mathematics	make a pizza	ride a motorcycle
listen to rock music	put on mittens	feed the dog

b. Have students take turns picking a card from the pile and pantomiming the action on the card.

(continued)

CHAPTER 1

EXPANSION ACTIVITIES (Continued)

c. The class must guess exactly what the person is doing—both the verb and the object.

Variation: This can be done as a game with competing teams.

6. Role Play: I'm Sorry, But I Can't ★★

a. Write the following conversation model on the board:

> A. Hi, _____. This is _____. Do you want to come over and visit?
> B. I'm sorry, but I can't. I'm _____ right now.
> A. Oh, well. Maybe some other time.
> B. Sure. Thanks for calling.

b. Call on pairs of students to role-play the telephone conversation, using any vocabulary they wish. For example:

> A. Hi, Tom. This is Paul. Do you want to come over and visit?
> B. I'm sorry, but I can't. I'm studying right now.
> A. Oh, well. Maybe some other time.
> B. Sure. Thanks for calling.

7. Describe the Pictures ★★★

a. Bring in several pictures or ask students to bring in pictures of interesting scenes or events.

b. In pairs, have students select a picture and write a description of what's happening in the picture.

c. Have students read their descriptions aloud as the class listens and tries to identify the correct picture.

8. Information Gap: Alan's Family ★★★

a. Tell students that Alan's family is home today. Make up a map of his house with his family members placed in each room and a description of what they are doing, but divide the information between two different maps. For example:

House Map A:

Living room	Kitchen	Basement
_____ _____	Alan's mother baking a cake	_____ _____
Yard		Dining room
Alan's grandparents planting flowers		Alan's younger brother doing his homework
Attic	Bedroom	Bathroom
_____ _____	Alan's sister listening to the radio and cleaning her room	_____ _____

Questions:
Who's in the *living room*?
What's he doing?
What's she doing?
What are they doing?

House Map B:

Living room	Kitchen	Basement
Alan's aunt and uncle watching videos	_____ _____	Alan's older brother playing the guitar
Yard		Dining room
_____ _____		_____ _____
Attic	Bedroom	Bathroom
Alan's father looking for old photographs	_____ and _____	Alan's cousin brushing her hair

<u>Questions:</u>
Who's in the *kitchen*?
What's he doing?
What's she doing?
What are they doing?

b. Divide the class into pairs. Give each member of the pair a different map. Have students ask each other questions and fill in their house maps. For example:

  Student A: Who's in the living room?
  Student B: Alan's aunt and uncle.
  Student A: What are they doing?
  Student B: They're watching videos.
  Student A *[writes the information in House Map A]*

c. The pairs continue until each has a filled map.

d. Have students look at their partner's map to make sure that they have written the information correctly.

Text Page 3: What Are They Doing?

FOCUS

- Contrast: Simple Present and Present Continuous Tenses
- Review of Question Formation

CLOSE UP

RULE: The simple present tense expresses habitual activity.

EXAMPLES: **Do** you **practice** the piano often?
Yes, I **do**. I **practice** the piano whenever I can.

GETTING READY

1. Review the simple present tense by talking about habitual activities.

   a. Write the following adverbs on the board: *always, often, sometimes, rarely, never.* Review the pronunciation. Say each word and have students repeat chorally.

   b. Make a statement about yourself, such as:

   I always see a movie on the weekend.
   I never worry about things.
   I sometimes drive too fast.
   I usually sing in the shower.
   I never dance at parties.

   After each statement, ask students: "How about you?" Have students respond with statements about themselves. For example:

   Teacher: I always see a movie on the weekend. How about you?
   Student A: I rarely see a movie on the weekend.
   Student B: I usually see a movie on the weekend.

2. Review *he, she,* and *they* forms in the simple present tense.

   a. Put the following cues on the board:

   b. Set the scene: "Bob and Betty are happily married. They like each other very much, but they're very different." Then tell the story:

   Bob and Betty both work.
   He works in a bank.
   She works in a museum.

   They both study in the evening.
   He studies math.
   She studies business.

   They both like to eat in restaurants.
   He likes to eat in Italian restaurants.
   She likes to eat in Mexican restaurants.

   They both do exercises every day.
   He does exercises in the morning.
   She does exercises at night.

   c. Put the following guide on the board and call on pairs of students to create conversations about Bob and Betty.

10   CHAPTER 1

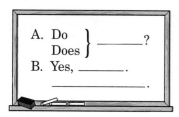

For example:

A. Do Bob and Betty work?
B. Yes, they do.
   Bob works in a bank, and Betty works in a museum.

A. Does Betty study in the evening?
B. Yes, she does.
   She studies business.

INTRODUCING THE MODEL

1. Have students look at the model illustration.
2. Set the scene: "Two people are talking."
3. Present the model.
4. Full-Class Repetition.
5. Ask students if they have any questions. Check understanding of the word *whenever*.
6. Group Choral Repetition.
7. Choral Conversation.
8. Call on one or two pairs of students to present the dialog.

   (For additional practice, do Choral Conversation in small groups or by rows.)

SIDE BY SIDE EXERCISES

Examples

1. A. What's Carol doing?
   B. She's watching the news.
   A. Does she watch the news very often?
   B. Yes, she does. She watches the news whenever she can.

2. A. What's Edward doing?
   B. He's swimming.
   A. Does he swim very often?
   B. Yes, he does. He swims whenever he can.

1. **Exercise 1:** Call on two students to present the dialog. Then do Choral Repetition and Choral Conversation practice.
2. **Exercise 2:** Same as above.
3. **Exercises 3–8:** Either Full-Class Practice or Pair Practice.

New Vocabulary

5. Scrabble

Culture Note

Scrabble is a popular game in which players have to create words using letter blocks.

4. **Exercise 9:** Have students use the model as a guide to create their own conversations, using vocabulary of their choice. (They can use any names and activities they wish.) Encourage students to use dictionaries to find new words they want to use. This exercise can be done orally in class or for written homework. If you assign it for homework, do one example in class to make sure students understand what's expected. Have students present their conversations in class the next day.

WORKBOOK

Pages 4–5

CHAPTER 1   11

EXPANSION ACTIVITIES

1. He or They? ★

a. Put on the board:

b. Have students listen as you read each of the following sentences with blanks:

___ goes to school every day.
___ play baseball every weekend.
___ practice the piano often.
___ reads at night.
___ always studies English.
___ always go to the movies after work.
___ never drive carefully.
___ usually speaks very slowly.
___ usually take the bus to school.
___ always cleans the apartment.

c. Have students choose the correct pronoun on the board, say it, and then repeat the entire sentence chorally and individually. For example:

Teacher: ___ goes to school every day.
Student: He. He goes to school every day.

2. Pronunciation Practice ★

Write pairs of verbs on the board with and without the final -s. Have students practice saying these words chorally and individually. For example:

```
cook – cooks
read – reads
fix – fixes
study – studies
write – writes
go – goes
take – takes
watch – watches
swim – swims
exercise – exercises
```

3. That's Strange! ★★

a. Put the following conversation model on the board:

A. What _____ doing?
B. _____ing.
A. That's strange! ___ never _____!
B. Well, _____ing today!

Use *Side by Side* Picture Cards for verbs, your own visuals, or word cues on the board. If you use word cues, include a name and a verb. For example:

| Mrs. Murphy | Howard |
| dance | roller-blade |

b. Point to a visual or word cue and call on a pair of students to create a conversation based on the model. For example:

(Side by Side Picture Card 44: play cards)

A. What are they doing?
B. They're playing cards.
A. That's strange! They never play cards!
B. Well, they're playing cards today!

4. How Many Sentences? ★★★

a. Write the following on the board:

```
bake      -s
cook      -ing
chicken   the
kitchen   is
clean     in
chef      are
```

b. Divide the class into pairs or small groups.

c. Tell students that the object of the game is to see how many sentences they can think of based on these words. Explain that *-ing* can be added to verbs (for example: *cooking, baking*), and *-s* can be added to verbs (*cooks,*

12   CHAPTER 1

bakes) and to nouns (*chickens, chefs*). Students can say their sentences or they can write them.

Some possible sentences:

> The chicken is cooking in the kitchen.
> The chefs are cleaning chickens in the kitchen.
> The chickens are clean.
> Clean the kitchen!
> The chef's kitchen is clean.
> The chicken is baking in the kitchen.
> The chef bakes chickens in the clean kitchen.

Variation: You can do this activity as a game in which the pair or group of students who comes up with the most sentences wins.

5. Class Story: The Brown Family ★★

a. Begin the following story:

> The Brown family is always busy on the weekend. For example, today is Saturday. Mr. Brown is washing his car. He washes his car every Saturday morning.

b. Have each student continue the story by telling about another member of the Brown family. For example:

> Mrs. Brown is vacuuming the living room rug. She vacuums the living room rug every Saturday morning.

c. The story continues until each student has added similar sentences about other family members to the story.

Note: If your class is large, you might want to divide the class into groups of 6 to 8 students and have each group create its own story. Have the groups compare their stories after they have completed them.

6. Dictate and Discuss ★★★

a. Divide the class into pairs or small groups.

b. Dictate sentences such as the following:

> He never listens to the radio in the basement, but he's listening to the radio in the basement today.
>
> They never walk to work, but they're walking to work today.

> She never washes her clothes in the sink, but she's washing her clothes in the sink today.
>
> We never eat spaghetti for breakfast, but we're eating spaghetti for breakfast today.

c. Have students discuss possible reasons for the strange behavior. For example:

> He's listening to the radio in the basement because he wants to the listen to the baseball game, and his teenage children are listening to music on the radio in the living room.

d. Call on students to share their ideas with the rest of the class.

7. What Do You Think They're Doing Now? ★★★

a. Write the names of some famous people on the board. For example:

> the president
> the queen
> the prime minister
> (popular entertainment star)

b. Ask about these famous people. For example:

> Teacher: It's midnight in Washington, D.C. What's the president doing?
>
> Student 1: He's sleeping.
> Student 2: He's probably talking on the hot line.
> Student 3: I think he's meeting with the secretary of state.
>
> Teacher: It's 4 P.M. in London. What's the queen doing?
>
> Student 1: She's probably having tea.
> Student 2: She's working in her office.
> Student 3: Maybe she's playing with her dogs.

Encourage students to be imaginative when thinking about possible answers to your questions.

CHAPTER 1

Text Page 4: Do You Like to Ski?

FOCUS

- Review:
  - *Don't* and *Doesn't*
  - *Like to*
  - Agent Nouns
  - Negative forms of *To Be*

CLOSE UP

RULE:	The simple present tense is used to express a fact.
EXAMPLE:	I **don't like** to skate.

RULE: In the simple present tense, the verb *to be* can contract with *not* or with the subject. In this lesson, the following negative forms are presented:

    he isn't   we aren't
    she isn't   you aren't
    it isn't   they aren't

Equally correct alternatives are:

    he's not   we're not
    she's not you're not
    it's not   they're not

GETTING READY

1. Review short answers with *don't* and *doesn't*.

   a. Have students look at the left-hand box at the top of the page as you ask questions about people in the class, using each pronoun and the simple present tense. Have students respond with negative short answers. For example:

Teacher	Student
Do you speak (*German*)?	No, I don't.
Do you and (*Mary*) wear glasses?	No, we don't.
Do I live in (*Tokyo*)?	No, you don't.
Do (*Bill*) and (*Bob*) drive too fast?	No, they don't.
Does (*Barbara*) live in (*London*)?	No, she doesn't.
Does (*Tom*) like to cook?	No, he doesn't.

   b. Call on students to make up other questions such as those above, and have other students answer.

2. Review short answers with the verb *to be*.

   a. Have students look at the right-hand box at the top of the page. Ask questions about people in the class, using each pronoun and the verb *to be*. Have students answer with negative short answers. For example:

Teacher	Student
Are you married?	No, I'm not.
Are you and (*Carol*) sisters?	No, we aren't.
Am I a student?	No, you aren't.
Are (*Tom*) and (*Jim*) teachers?	No, they aren't.

Is (*Ted*) a truck driver?   No, he isn't.
Is (*Betty*) a doctor?   No, she isn't.

b. Call on students to make up other questions such as those above, and have other students answer.

INTRODUCING THE MODEL

1. Have students look at the model illustration.
2. Set the scene: "Two people are riding on a ski lift. They just met each other."
3. Present the model.
4. Full-Class Repetition.
5. Ask students if they have any questions. Check understanding of vocabulary.
6. Group Choral Repetition.
7. Choral Conversation.
8. Call on one or two pairs of students to present the dialog.

(For additional practice, do Choral Conversation in small groups or by rows.)

SIDE BY SIDE EXERCISES

Examples

1. A. Does Richard like to sing?
   B. No, he doesn't. He isn't a very good singer.

2. A. Does Brenda like to swim?
   B. No, she doesn't. She isn't a very good swimmer.

3. A. Do Mr. and Mrs. Adams like to skate?
   B. No, they don't. They aren't very good skaters.

1. **Exercise 1:** Call on two students to present the dialog. Then do Choral Repetition and Choral Conversation practice.
2. **Exercise 2:** Introduce the word *swimmer*. Same as above.
3. **Exercise 3:** Introduce the word *skater*. Same as above.
4. **Exercises 4–9:** Either Full-Class Practice or Pair Practice.

New Vocabulary
5. typist
9. cook

WORKBOOK

Pages 6–8

CHAPTER 1

EXPANSION ACTIVITIES

1. **Chain Game** ★

   a. Start the chain game by asking Student A: "Do you like to swim?"

   b. Student A answers and asks Student B, who then continues the chain. For example:

   Student A: No, I don't.
   (to Student B): Do you like to ski?

   Student B: Yes, I do.
   (to Student C): Do you like to . . . ?

2. **Is That True?** ★★

   a. Write on cards statements such as those below, using names of students in your class if you wish:

   - (Rita) dances beautifully.
   - (Richard) doesn't ski very well.
   - (Michael) and (Maria) type very quickly.
   - You're a very good skier.
   - (Peter) doesn't act very well.
   - (Carol) skates very badly.
   - I sing beautifully.
   - You and (Jane) cook very well.
   - (Sam) writes very interesting stories.
   - (Thomas) drives very carelessly.
   - (Shirley) swims very badly.

   b. Put this conversation model on the board:

   A. Everybody says _____. Is that true?

   B. { Yes, it is. / No, it isn't. } _____ a/an { great / fantastic / wonderful / terrible / awful / very bad } _____!

   c. Give the cards to pairs of students. Have students create conversations, using the model on the board, and then present them to the class. Students may choose to agree or disagree with the first speaker. For example:

   A. Everybody says (Rita) dances beautifully. Is that true?
   B. Yes, it is. She's a wonderful dancer!
   or
   No, it isn't. She's an awful dancer!

3. **What's the Occupation?** ★★

   a. Put the following on the board:

   He's a/an _____.
   She's a/an _____.
   They're _____s.

   b. Have students listen as you read the following job descriptions. After each description, have students tell the occupation, using the sentence models on the board. If you wish, you can do the activity as a game with competing teams.

   Walter plays the violin in concerts.
      (He's a violinist.)

   Carla types for a company downtown.
      (She's a typist.)

   Michael and his brother fix broken sinks.
      (They're plumbers.)

   Alice drives a truck between Chicago and Denver.
      (She's a truck driver.)

CHAPTER 1

Tom plays tennis all around the world.
(He's a tennis player.)

Barbara paints houses for a living.
(She's a painter/house painter.)

David acts in plays and movies and on TV.
(He's an actor.)

His girlfriend also acts.
(She's a actress.)

Brian repairs televisions.
(He's a TV repairperson.)

Tony and Greta repair cars and trucks.
(They're mechanics.)

Boris plays chess in countries all around the world.
(He's a chess player.)

Diane cleans people's chimneys.
(She's a chimneysweep.)

Bob takes pictures at weddings and other special occasions.
(He's a photographer.)

Olga translates from English into Russian.
(She's a translator.)

Frank and his brother cook in a very good restaurant downtown.
(They're cooks/chefs.)

Barbara designs beautiful clothes.
(She's a designer.)

Joe bakes bread, cakes, and special desserts.
(He's a baker.)

George and Paul plant flowers in people's yards.
(They're gardeners.)

Betty helps doctors and takes care of people in the hospital.
(She's a nurse.)

Peter takes care of sick dogs and cats.
(He's a veterinarian.)

c. Find out what other occupations your students are interested in. Have students use their dictionaries to find out the names of these occupations and tell what the people do.

4. Tell About Yourself! ★★

a. Set the scene by telling about yourself or about a person on the board. For example:

"This is Mary. Mary likes to swim, and she's a good swimmer. She likes to type, but she isn't a very good typist. She doesn't like to cook because she isn't a very good cook. She likes to play the piano, and she plays whenever she can."

b. Divide students into pairs.

c. Have students interview each other to find out about their likes and dislikes and related abilities.

d. Then have each student tell the class about the person he or she interviewed.

Variation: You can do this as a writing activity. For homework, have students write about themselves: their likes, dislikes, and related abilities.

5. Common Interests ★★★

a. Put the following on the board:

> I like to _____.
> He/She likes to _____.
> He's/She's a good _____.
> We both like to _____.
> We're both good _____.

b. Divide the class into pairs.

c. Have students interview each other about what they like to do. The object is for students to find things they have in common and then report back to the class. For example:

(continued)

CHAPTER 1   17

EXPANSION ACTIVITIES (Continued)

I interviewed Maria. I like to ski. She likes to skate. She's a good skater. We both like to dance. We're both good dancers. Also, we both like to sing. We're both good singers.

6. **Classroom Interviews** ★★★

   a. On an index card, have each student write three things that he or she likes to do. For example:

   > I like to swim.
   > I like to watch TV.
   > I like to play tennis.

   b. Collect the cards and distribute them randomly to all the students in the class.

   c. Have students interview others in the class to match the correct person with each card, that is, to find out which student likes to do the three activities written on each card.

   d. When the interviews are completed, call on students to tell about the others in the class, based on their interviews. For example:

   > Alexander likes to swim.
   > He likes to watch TV.
   > And he likes to play tennis.

Text Pages 5–6

READING *Practicing*

FOCUS

- Review:
  - Simple Present Tense
  - Present Continuous Tense
  - Subject Pronouns
  - Possessive Adjectives

NEW VOCABULARY

ballet dancer
ballet instructor
coach (n)
instructor
music teacher
professional
soccer coach
stay after
tennis coach
violinist

READING THE STORY

Optional: Preview the story by having students talk about the story title and/or illustrations. You may choose to introduce new vocabulary beforehand, or have students encounter the new vocabulary within the context of the reading.

1. Have students read silently or follow along silently as the story is read aloud by you, by one or more students, or on the audio program.
2. Ask students if they have any questions. Check understanding of vocabulary.
3. Check students' comprehension, using some or all of the following questions:

   What am I doing?
   How often do I practice?
   What does my soccer coach tell me?
   What do my friends tell me?
   What do I want to be when I grow up?

   What's Anita doing?
   How often does she practice?
   What does her tennis coach tell her?
   What do her friends tell her?
   What does she want to be when she grows up?

   What's Hector doing?
   How often does he practice?
   What does his music teacher tell him?
   What do his friends tell him?
   What does he want to be when he grows up?

   What are Jenny and Vanessa doing?
   How often do they practice?
   What does their ballet instructor tell them?
   What do they want to be when they grow up?

✓ READING *CHECK-UP*

Q & A

1. Call on a pair of students to present the model.
2. Have students work in pairs to create new dialogs.
3. Call on pairs to present their new dialogs to the class.

READING EXTENSION

1. **Question the Answers!**

   a. Choose one of the four paragraphs. Dictate answers such as these to the class:

      Every day after school.
      Her tennis coach.
      Her friends.
      A professional tennis player.
      Because she wants to be a professional tennis player.

   b. Have students write questions for which these answers would be correct. For example:

CHAPTER 1   19

Answer: Every day after school.
Question: How often does Anita practice?

Answer: Her tennis coach.
Question: Who tells her she's an excellent tennis player?

Answer: Her friends.
Question: Who tells her she's better than anyone else in school?

Answer: A professional tennis player.
Question: What does she want to be when she grows up?

Answer: Because she wants to be a professional tennis player.
Question: Why does she practice every day?

c. Have students compare their questions with each other.

Variation: Write the answers on cards. Divide the class into groups and give each group a set of cards as cues for the activity.

2. Pair Discussion

Have pairs of students discuss the following questions and then report back to the class:

Do you have a hobby? Do you play sports or a musical instrument?
What do you play?
How often do you practice?
Do you want to be a professional player?
Did you practice when you were a child?
When you were a child, what did you want to be when you grew up?

 **LISTENING**

Listen and choose the correct answer.

1. What are you doing?
2. Do you watch the news very often?
3. Are you a good swimmer?
4. What's Cathy reading?
5. Who cooks in your family?
6. Do they like to skate?
7. Does your sister want to be a ballet dancer?
8. Do you and your friends play basketball very often?
9. Are your parents good dancers?
10. What does Peter want to be when he grows up?

Answers

1. b
2. b
3. a
4. b
5. a
6. b
7. b
8. a
9. a
10. b

 IN YOUR OWN WORDS

1. Make sure students understand the instructions.
2. Have students do the activity as written homework, using a dictionary for any new words they wish to use.
3. Have students present and discuss what they have written, in pairs or as a class.

Text Pages 7–8: How Often?

FOCUS

- Pronoun Review
- Contrast: Simple Present and Present Continuous Tenses

CLOSE UP

RULE:	In spoken English, **who** is used to refer to both a subject and an object.
EXAMPLES:	**Who** are you calling? (I'm calling *my brother*.)
	Who is calling your brother? (*I* am calling my brother.)
	Who are you arguing with? (I am arguing with *my neighbor*.)

RULE:	In formal and written English, **whom** is used to refer to an object.
EXAMPLES:	**Whom** are you calling?
	With **whom** are you arguing?

GETTING READY

1. Review pronouns.

   a. Write on the board:

   > My {friend / friends} _____ {likes / likes} to visit me here in _____.
   >
   > When _____ {comes / come} to visit, I always take _____ to _____ favorite {museum / restaurant / theater}.

   b. Set the scene: "My friend Bob likes to visit me here in (*name of your city*). When he comes to visit, I always take him to his favorite restaurant."

   c. Have students use this model to review other pronouns. Ask students: "What about your friend(s) _____?" Students can refer to the box at the top of text page 7 for the pronoun. For example:

   A. What about your friend Maria?
   B. My friend Maria likes to visit me here in _____. When she comes to visit, I always take her to her favorite museum.

   A. What about your friends Dave and Donna?
   B. My friends Dave and Donna like to visit me here in _____. When they come to visit, I always take them to their favorite theater.

CHAPTER 1   21

d. Change *my* to *our* in the model on the board. Have students make all the necessary changes as they tell about *our friend(s)* _____ and _____.

2. Review time expressions.

    a. Write on the board:

    ```
    study English              play soccer
    clean your house           watch the news
    call your grandparents     read poetry
    read the newspaper         iron clothes
    ask questions in class     exercise
    do your homework           chat online
    ```

    b. Ask students a few questions based on the cues on the board, and have students respond, using the expressions with *every* in the chart on text page 7. For example:

    > Teacher: How often do you study English?
    > Student: I study English every day.

    c. Introduce the new expressions with *once, twice*. Ask students: "How often do you play soccer?" Have students respond, using the time expressions with *once, twice,* and *(three) times,* which are presented in the chart on text page 7. For example:

    > Teacher: How often do you play soccer?
    > Student: I play soccer twice a week.

    d. In pairs, have students ask and answer *How often* questions, using the cues on the board.

INTRODUCING THE MODELS

There are two model conversations. Introduce and practice each separately. For each model:

1. Have students look at the model illustration.
2. Set the scene:

    > 1st model: "Two friends are talking. One of them is making a phone call."
    > 2nd model: "Two friends are sitting and talking in the park."

3. Present the model.
4. Full-Class Repetition.
5. Ask students if they have any questions. Check understanding of vocabulary.
6. Group Choral Repetition.
7. Choral Conversation.
8. Call on one or two pairs of students to present the dialog.
9. After the 1st model:

    a. Go over the alternative vocabulary at the top of the page.

    b. Have several pairs of students present the dialog again, using alternative vocabulary in place of *every Sunday evening*.

10. After the 2nd model, have several pairs of students present the dialog again, using alternative vocabulary in place of *all the time*.

SIDE BY SIDE EXERCISES

Students can use any time expression they wish to complete these conversations.

Examples

1. A. Who is Mr. Tanaka calling?
   B. He's calling his son in New York.
   A. How often does he call him?
   B. He calls him (*every week*).

2. A. Who is Mrs. Kramer writing to?
   B. She's writing to her daughter in the army.
   A. How often does she write to her?
   B. She writes to her (*once a month*).

1. **Exercise 1:** Call on two students to present the dialog. Then do Choral Repetition and Choral Conversation practice.

2. **Exercise 2:** Introduce the word *army*. Same as above.

3. **Exercises 3–9:** Either Full-Class Practice or Pair Practice.

New Vocabulary
7. telephone bill
8. talk show

Whenever possible, after each exercise ask students to compare their own experiences with that of the people in the exercise. For example, after Exercise 4 ask: "How about you? Do you argue with your landlord?" After Exercise 5 ask: "How about you? How often do you send e-mail messages to friends and family members?" After Exercise 6 ask: "Do you know someone who shouts a lot?" After Exercise 7 ask: "Do you get large telephone bills? Do you make many long-distance phone calls?" After Exercise 8 ask: "How often do you watch TV talk shows? Which is your favorite?" After Exercise 9 ask: "How often do you visit your grandparents?"

Culture Note

Exercise 9: *Little Red Riding Hood* is a well-known folk tale about a little girl wearing a red hood who goes to visit her grandmother in her house in the woods. In the story, a clever wolf pretends to be the grandmother and nearly succeeds in eating Little Red Riding Hood.

4. **Exercise 10:** Have students use the model as a guide to create their own conversations, using vocabulary of their choice. Encourage students to use dictionaries to find new words they want to use. This exercise can be done orally in class or for written homework. If you assign it for homework, do one example in class to make sure students understand what's expected. Have students present their conversations in class the next day.

WORKBOOK

Pages 9–11

EXPANSION ACTIVITIES

1. **Pronoun Review: A Story About Peggy and John** ★

   a. Put the following on the board:

   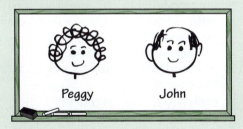

   b. Set the scene: "I want to tell you about my friends Peggy and John."

   c. Read each sentence below while pointing to the faces on the board. Have students listen and repeat each sentence, changing all the nouns to pronouns.

   Example: Peggy and John are married.
   (They're married.)

   Peggy likes John.
   (She likes him.)

   John likes Peggy.
   (He likes her.)

   Peggy and John live in Canada.
   (They live in Canada.)

   Peggy and John's last name is Jones.
   (Their last name is Jones.)

   Peggy met John at a party.
   (She met him at a party.)

   John liked Peggy right away.
   (He liked her right away.)

   John and Peggy got married at Peggy's parents' house.
   (They got married at her parents' house.)

   On Peggy's last birthday, John gave Peggy a watch.
   (On her last birthday, he gave her a watch.)

   On John's last birthday, Peggy gave John a new coat.
   (On his last birthday, she gave him a new coat.)

   (continued)

CHAPTER 1   23

EXPANSION ACTIVITIES (Continued)

2. Mystery Word ★★

a. Divide the class into pairs.

b. Give each pair a card with a *mystery word* on it. Possibilities include:

granddaughter	complain	shout
army	bill	argue
landlord	employees	practice

c. Have each pair create a sentence in which that word is in final position. For example:

> My son's daughter is my _____.
> (granddaughter)
> Before you leave the hotel, don't forget to pay the _____. (bill)

d. One student from the pair then reads aloud the sentence with the final word missing. The other pairs of students try to guess the missing word.

Variation: This can be done as a game in which each pair scores a point for identifying the correct *mystery word*. The pair with the most points wins the game.

3. Expand the Sentence! ★★

Tell students that the object of the activity is to build a long sentence on the board, one word at a time.

a. Call on a student to write a pronoun or someone's name on the far left side of the board. For example:

George

b. Have another student come to the board and add a word. For example:

George likes

c. Have a third student add a third word. For example:

George likes to

d. Continue until each student in the class has had one or more turns to add a word to expand the sentence into the longest one they can think of. For example:

> George likes to talk to his brother on the telephone every Sunday night because his brother lives in Russia, and George doesn't see his brother very often.

4. Grammar Chain: How Often? ★★

a. Write the following activities on the board:

see a movie	argue with someone
write a letter	visit your grandparents
bake cookies	paint your house
iron your shirts	pay bills
play baseball	play the piano
knit a sweater	watch the news
read poetry	play tennis
cook dinner	read the newspaper
chat online	watch a talk show
compose music	send e-mail messages

b. Start the chain game by saying:

> Teacher (*to Student A*): How often do you see a movie?

24 CHAPTER 1

c. Student A answers truthfully and then makes a new question, using another verb phrase on the board. Student A asks the new question to Student B, who then continues the chain. For example:

> Student A: I see a movie every weekend.
> (to Student B): How often do you write a letter?
>
> Student B: I write a letter once a week.
> (to Student C): How often do you read poetry?

5. Find the Right Person! ★★

a. Collect some information about students' habits.

b. Put the information on a handout in the following form:

> Find someone who . . .
> 1. watches talk shows every night. _____
> 2. bakes bread once a week. _____
> 3. knits sweaters. _____
> 4. chats online every evening. _____
> 5. reads a novel once a month. _____

c. Have students circulate around the room, asking each other questions to identify the above people. For example:

> How often do you watch talk shows?
> Do you bake bread? How often?

d. The first student to find all the people, raise his or her hand, and tell the class who they are is the winner of the game.

6. Role Play: At the Doctor's Office ★★

a. Put the following conversation model on the board:

> A. How often do you _____?
> B. I _____ { all the time.
>   every _____.
>   once a _____.
>   twice a _____.
>   _____ times a _____. }
> A. I see. And how often do you _____?
> B. I _____.
> A. Well, you don't have any serious medical problems. I'll see you next year.

b. Also put these word cues on the board:

> exercise
> take vitamins
> eat rich desserts
> go to bed late
> listen to loud music
> go to the dentist
> eat fatty foods
> eat healthy foods

c. Set the scene: "You're at the doctor's office for your annual physical examination."

d. Call on pairs of students to role-play the conversation. Speaker A is the *doctor*. Speaker B is the *patient*. For example:

> A. How often do you exercise?
> B. I exercise once a week.
> A. I see. And how often do you take vitamins?
> B. I take vitamins every morning.
> A. Well, you don't have any serious medical problems. I'll see you next year.

Encourage students to expand the conversation in any way they wish.

7. Interview the Characters ★★★

Have students pretend to be the different characters from this lesson. *Interview* them to find out more about their situations. For example:

> Model 1: Tell us, what do you and your sister usually talk about?
> Model 2: George and Herman, tell us about your grandchildren.
> Exercise 1: Mr. Tanaka, what do you usually talk to your son about?
> Exercise 2: Mrs. Kramer, what do you write to your daughter about?
> Exercise 3: What are you saying about your teachers?
> Exercise 4: Lenny, what's the problem? What are you arguing about with your landlord?

(continued)

CHAPTER 1

EXPANSION ACTIVITIES (Continued)

Exercise 5: Martha, tell us about your granddaughter. What do you write to her about?

Exercise 6: Mr. Crabapple, why are you shouting at your employees? (Also interview some employees: Why is Mr. Crabapple shouting at you? How often does that happen? What kind of a boss is he?)

Exercise 7: What's the problem with your telephone bill?

Exercise 8: George, what's your favorite talk show? Why is it your favorite? Tell us about it.

Exercise 9: Little Red Riding Hood, does your grandmother look a little different today?

8. Role Plays ★★★

a. Divide the class into pairs.

b. Have each pair choose one of the situations in the lesson—either of the models or any of the exercises—and create a role play based on that situation.

c. Have the pairs present their role plays to the class and compare their interpretations of the situation.

9. Little Red Riding Hood ★★★

Little Red Riding Hood appears in Exercise 9 in the student text. If you think your students would be interested, go to the library or look on the Internet, find the story of Little Red Riding Hood, and read it to the class. Possible follow-up activities:

a. Call on students to retell the story.

b. Read the story and have students write it as best they can remember it.

c. Have students tell the class famous folk tales from their countries.

Text Page 9

How to Say It!

> **Asking for and Reacting to Information:** *Tell me* is a common way to preface a question. There are many ways to react to new information. "Oh," "Really?" "Oh, really?" and "That's interesting" are four common phrases. The intonation rises to indicate interest in what the other person has just said.

1. Set the scene: "Two diplomats at the United Nations are talking."
2. Present the conversation.
3. Full-Class Repetition.
4. Ask students if they have any questions. Bring a world map to class and point out the location of Madagascar.
5. Group Choral Repetition.
6. Choral Conversation.

 INTERACTIONS

There are three topics of conversation, with suggested questions under each. For each topic:

1. Go over the questions and introduce the new vocabulary: *What do you do?, interests*.

    Culture Note

    The question *What do you do?* is commonly asked to find out what someone's profession is. The importance of this question in U.S. culture reflects the value of work as a means of establishing one's identity.

2. Divide the class into pairs. Have students interview each other, using the questions on student text page 9. Remind students to use the phrases in **How to Say It!** to express interest in what the other person is saying. Have students take notes during their interviews in order to remember each other's answers.

3. Call on several students to report back to the class about the people they interviewed.

    Option: As the class changes topics, have students change partners so they may get to know many different people in the class.

4. For homework, have students write several sentences about each person they interviewed.

EXPANSION ACTIVITIES

1. Silent Letters ★

Write the words below on the board. Have students try to find the silent letter or letters in each word:

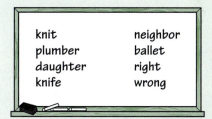

knit neighbor
plumber ballet
daughter right
knife wrong

2. Who Is Your Favorite? ★★

Have students talk about their favorite writers, singers, painters, actors, actresses, and composers.

a. Put on the board:

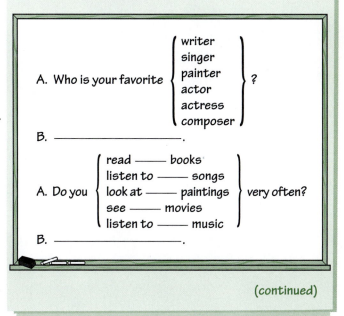

(continued)

CHAPTER 1   27

EXPANSION ACTIVITIES (Continued)

b. Have pairs of students create conversations based on the model. This can be done as Full-Class Practice or Pair Practice. Examples:

A. Who is your favorite singer?
B. *(Timmy Martin.)*
A. Do you listen to his songs very often?
B. Yes, I do. I listen to them every day.

A. Who is your favorite actress?
B. *(Julie Richards.)*
A. Do you see her movies very often?
B. Yes. I see them whenever I can.

JOURNAL

Have students write their journal entries at home or in class. Encourage students to use a dictionary to look up words they would like to use. Students can share their written work with other students if appropriate. Have students discuss what they have written as a class, in pairs, or in small groups.

Text Page 10

 PRONUNCIATION

Reduced *are*: When the word *are* is in the middle of a question or sentence, it is reduced to an /er/ sound.

Focus on Listening

Practice the sentences in the left column. Say each sentence or play the audio one or more times. Have students listen carefully and repeat.

Focus on Pronunciation

Practice the sentences in the right column. Have students say each sentence and then listen carefully as you say it or play the audio.

If you wish, have students continue practicing the sentences to improve their pronunciation.

 CHAPTER SUMMARY

GRAMMAR

1. Divide the class into pairs or small groups.
2. Have students take turns forming sentences from the words in the grammar boxes. Student A says a sentence, and Student B points to the words from each column that are in the sentence. Then have students switch: Student B says a sentence, and Student A points to the words.

KEY VOCABULARY

Have students ask you any questions about the meaning or pronunciation of the vocabulary. If students ask for the pronunciation, repeat after the student until the student is satisfied with his or her own pronunciation.

EXPANSION ACTIVITIES

1. **Do You Remember the Words?** ★

   Check students' retention of the vocabulary depicted on the opening page of Chapter 1 by doing the following activity:

   a. Have students open their books to page 1 and cover the list of vocabulary words.
   b. Either call out a number and have students tell you the word, or say a word and have students tell you the number.

   Variation: You can also do this activity as a game with competing teams.

2. **Student-Led Dictation** ★

   a. Tell each student to choose a word or phrase from the Key Vocabulary list on text page 10 and look at it very carefully.
   b. Have students take turns dictating their words to the class. Everybody writes down that student's word.
   c. When the dictation is completed, call on different students to write each word on the board to check the spelling.

3. **Beanbag Toss** ★

   a. Call out the topic: *Actions*.
   b. Have students toss a beanbag back and forth. The student to whom the beanbag is tossed must name an action. For example:

   Student 1: argue
   Student 2: bake
   Student 3: shout

   c. Continue until all the words in the category have been named.

   Variation: You can also do this activity as a game with competing teams.

4. **Letter Game** ★

   a. Divide the class into two teams.
   b. Say: "I'm thinking of a family member that begins with *d*."

   (continued)

CHAPTER 1   29

EXPANSION ACTIVITIES (Continued)

   c. The first person to raise his or her hand and guess correctly [*daughter*] wins a point for his or her team.

   d. Continue with other letters of the alphabet.

   The team that gets the most correct answers wins the game.

5. **Miniming Agent Nouns** ★

   a. Write on cards the agent nouns on text page 10.

   b. Have students take turns picking a card from the pile and pantomiming the agent noun on the card.

   c. The class must guess what word the person is miming.

   Variation: This can be done as a game with competing teams.

6. **Who Is It?** ★★

   Divide the class into teams and quiz them with the following clues:

your mother's mother	(grandmother)
your mother's brother	(uncle)
your father's sister	(aunt)
your father's father	(grandfather)
your daughter's son	(grandson)
your son's children	(grandchildren)
the man you married	(husband)
the woman you married	(wife)
your parents' son	(brother)
your parents' daughter	(sister)

END-OF-CHAPTER ACTIVITIES

1. Board Game ★★★

a. On poster boards or on manila file folders, make up game boards with a pathway consisting of separate spaces. You may use any theme or design you wish.

b. Divide the class into groups of 2 to 4 students and give each group a game board and a die, and each student something to be used as a playing piece.

c. Give each group a pile of cards face-down with sentences written on them. Some sentences should be correct and others incorrect. For example:

> Are you busy?
> Yes, she's.
> Does they eat?
> Who does she sending an e-mail to?
> Are you married to?
> What do you do?
> I'm swimming whenever I can.
> How often do you practice soccer?
> I'm calling my brother. I call her every Friday.
> They watch a movie on TV one a week.
> How often she visits her grandparents?
> I talk to them every month.
> What they are complaining about?
> Does he like to swim?
> She's not very good skater.
> Why he shouting at those people?

d. Each student in turn rolls the die, moves the playing piece along the game path, and after landing on a space, picks a card, reads the sentence, and says if it is *correct* or *incorrect*. If the statement is incorrect, the student must correct it. If the response is correct, the student takes an additional turn.

e. The first student to reach the end of the pathway is the winner.

2. Question the Answers! ★★

a. Dictate answers such as the following to the class:

> Yes, she is.
> No, they aren't.
> Yes, I do.
> No, we don't.
> I'm an actor.
> Her name is Alice.
> I read the newspaper every morning.
> I'm from El Salvador.
> She lives in New York.

b. Have students write questions for which these answers would be correct. For example:

> Answer: Yes, she is.
> Question: Is your sister married?
>
> Answer: No, they aren't.
> Question: Are they good skiers?

c. Have students compare their questions with each other.

Variation: Write the answers on cards. Divide the class into groups and give each group a set of cards.

3. Dialog Builder ★★★

a. Divide the class into pairs.

b. Write several lines on the board from several conversations such as the following:

> Yes, I am.
> Do you like to _____?
> How often do you _____?
> No, he doesn't.
> Really?
> That's interesting.

c. Have each pair create a conversation incorporating those lines. Students can begin and end their conversations any way they wish, but they must include those lines in their dialogs.

d. Call on students to present their conversations to the class.

WORKBOOK ANSWER KEY AND LISTENING SCRIPTS

WORKBOOK PAGE 2

A. WHAT'S HAPPENING?

1. What's, reading, She's reading
2. Where's, going, He's going
3. What's, watching, She's watching
4. What are, cooking, I'm cooking
5. Where are, moving, We're moving
6. Where are, sitting, They're sitting
7. What's, composing, He's composing
8. What are, baking, I'm baking

WORKBOOK PAGE 3

B. ON THE PHONE

1. are
   I'm watching
   Is
   she is, She's taking
2. Are
   They're
   are they
   is doing
   is playing
   What are you
   I'm cooking
3. Is
   he isn't, He's exercising
   She's, She's fixing

WORKBOOK PAGE 4

C. YOU DECIDE: Why Is Today Different?

1. clean, I'm cleaning, . . .
2. irons, he's ironing, . . .
3. argue, we're arguing, . . .
4. worry, I'm worrying, . . .
5. watches, she's watching, . . .
6. writes, he's writing, . . .
7. take, I'm taking, . . .
8. combs, he's combing, . . .
9. gets up, she's getting up, . . .
10. smiles, he's smiling, . . .
11. bark, they're barking, . . .
12. wears, she's wearing, . . .

WORKBOOK PAGE 5

D. WHAT ARE THEY SAYING?

1. Do you recommend
2. Does, bake
3. Does, get up
4. Do, complain
5. Does, speak
6. Does, live
7. Do you watch
8. Does she play
9. Does he practice
10. Do you plant
11. Does he add
12. Do you wear
13. Does she ride
14. Does he jog
15. Do we need
16. Does he iron
17. Do they have

WORKBOOK PAGE 6

E. PUZZLE

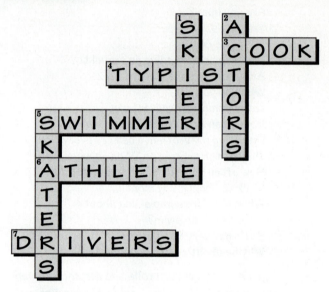

F. WHAT'S THE ANSWER?

1. b
2. c
3. b
4. c
5. b
6. c
7. a
8. b

WORKBOOK PAGE 7

G. WHAT ARE THEY SAYING?

1. don't, doesn't
   isn't, cook
2. don't, I'm
   drive
3. Do you
   don't, I'm
   You're, type

32 CHAPTER 1

4. composes, he's
5. isn't, doesn't
   swimmer
6. don't
   speak, speaker

H. LISTENING

Listen to each question and then complete the answer.

1. Does Jim like to play soccer?
2. Is Alice working today?
3. Are those students staying after school today?
4. Do Mr. and Mrs. Jackson work hard?
5. Does your wife still write poetry?
6. Is it raining?
7. Is he busy?
8. Do you have to leave?
9. Does your sister play the violin?
10. Is your brother studying in the library?
11. Are you wearing a necklace today?
12. Do you and your husband go camping very often?
13. Is your niece doing her homework?
14. Are they still chatting online?
15. Do you and your friends play Scrabble very often?

Answers

1. he does
2. she isn't
3. they are
4. they do
5. she doesn't
6. it is
7. he isn't
8. I do
9. she doesn't
10. he is
11. I'm not
12. we do
13. she is
14. they aren't
15. we don't

WORKBOOK PAGE 9

J. WHAT'S THE QUESTION?

1. What are you waiting for?
2. Who is he thinking about?
3. What are they ironing?
4. Who are you calling?
5. Who is she dancing with?
6. What's he watching?
7. What are they complaining about?
8. Who is she playing baseball with?
9. Who are they visiting?
10. What are you looking at?
11. What are you writing about?
12. Who is he arguing with?
13. Who is she knitting a sweater for?
14. What are you making?
15. Who are you sending an e-mail to?
16. What are they worrying about?
17. Who is she talking to?
18. Who is he skating with?

WORKBOOK PAGE 10

K. WHAT ARE THEY SAYING?

1. your
   We're, them
2. his
   He, them, his
3. they, me
4. her
   She, them
5. your
   I, my
6. your
   I'm, her
7. They, them
8. us, it
9. he, it
10. your
    She, my

WORKBOOK PAGE 11

L. WHAT'S THE WORD?

1. with
2. —
3. at
4. 2
5. about
6. —
7. —, with
8. for
9. —

CHAPTER 1   33

CHAPTER 2 OVERVIEW: Text Pages 11–20

GRAMMAR

Simple Past Tense

| What did | I / he / she / it / we / you / they | do? |

| I / He / She / It / We / You / They | worked. |

| Did | I / he / she / it / we / you / they | fall asleep? |

| Yes, | I / he / she / it / we / you / they | did. |

| No, | I / he / she / it / we / you / they | didn't. |

| I / He / She / It | was |
| We / You / They | were | tired. |

| I / He / She / It | wasn't |
| We / You / They | weren't | tired. |

Past Continuous Tense

| I / He / She / It | was |
| We / You / They | were | working. |

FUNCTIONS

Asking for and Reporting Information

Who *did you meet*?

What did you *buy*?
What did *she do yesterday*?
What were you doing?
What happened?
What language *did you speak*?
What kind of *hotel did you stay in*?

Where were you?
Where did you *go*?

Why?

How did *John break his arm*?
How did you feel?
How did you get there?
How many *pictures did you take*?
How long were you there?

Did *Robert shout at his dog*?
  Yes, *he* did.
  No, *he* didn't.
Did you have a good time?

Admitting Poor Performance

I didn't *teach* very well *this morning*.
I *taught* very badly.

Initiating a Topic

You know . . .

Tell me about . . .

Making a Deduction

I bet *that was a difficult experience for you.*

Reacting to Bad News

What a shame!
What a pity!
That's a shame.

NEW VOCABULARY

Travel and Tourism

boat
Colosseum
Mediterranean
souvenir
take pictures
tourist
Vatican

Verbs

bet
fight
hike
prepare
realize
rip

snowboard
sprain
wave

Miscellaneous

ankle
audience
black eye
daily
daily exercises
demonstrator
experience
kid
lines
magic trick
magician
prepared

EXPRESSIONS

at the back of
get around by taxi/by bus
I bet
look over *his* shoulder
sleep well

PAST TENSE VERB FORMS

Irregular

am/is – was
are – were
break – broke
buy – bought
come – came
cut – cut
do – did
drink – drank
eat – ate
fall – fell
feel – felt
fight – fought
forget – forgot
get – got
go – went
have – had
hurt – hurt

keep – kept
lose – lost
meet – met
ride – rode
see – saw
shake – shook
sing – sang
sit – sat
sleep – slept
speak – spoke
stand – stood
swim – swam
take – took
teach – taught
tell – told
write – wrote

Regular

burn
chop
cover
cry
deliver
finish
growl
hike
jump
look
paint
play
poke
practice
prepare

realize
rip
shave
shout
snowboard
sprain
stay
study
talk
trip
type
wash
watch
wave
work

CHAPTER 2   35

Text Page 11: Chapter Opening Page

VOCABULARY PREVIEW

You may want to introduce these words before beginning the chapter, or you may choose to wait until they first occur in a specific lesson. If you choose to introduce them at this point, here are some suggestions:

1. Have students look at the illustrations on text page 11 and identify the verbs they already know.

2. Present the vocabulary. Say each word and have the class repeat it chorally and individually. Check students' understanding and pronunciation of the verbs.

3. Practice the vocabulary as a class, in pairs, or in small groups. Have students cover the word list and look at the pictures. Practice the words in the following ways:

   - Say a verb in its present or past form and have students tell the number of the illustration.

   - Give the number of an illustration and have students say the verb in its present and past forms.

Text Page 12: Did They Sleep Well Last Night?

FOCUS

- Past Tense Review:
    Regular and Irregular Verbs
    To Be
    Was/Were
    Questions with *Did*
    Affirmative Short Answers

CLOSE UP

The simple past tense is used to express events that happened in the past.

RULE:	The simple past tense describes events that occurred at a particular point in time.
EXAMPLE:	**Did** you **sleep** well last night? Yes, I **did**.
RULE:	The simple past tense also describes events that took place over a period of time.
EXAMPLES:	I **studied** English all day. She **taught** all day.
RULE:	When a verb ending with *t* or *d* takes the regular past tense *-ed* ending, an additional syllable is formed at the end of the word.
EXAMPLE:	He **painted** his apartment all day.

GETTING READY

Review the past tense.

1. Practice listening for the *-ed* ending.

   a. Write on the board:

   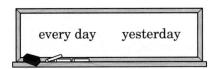

   every day   yesterday

   b. Read statements such as the following one or more times:

   She works.
   He worked.
   They worked.
   They work.
   We study.
   I bake a cake.
   He studied.
   She plays the piano.
   We played cards.
   They need some books.
   I study.
   She needed some bread.

   c. Have students respond by saying "every day" when they hear a verb in the present tense and "yesterday" when they hear a verb in the past tense. For example:

Teacher	Students
I work.	every day
I worked.	yesterday

CHAPTER 2   37

2. Practice forming sentences that contrast verb endings in the simple present and simple past tenses.

   a. Write on the board:

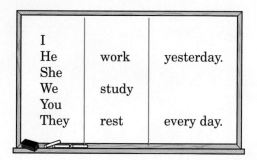

   b. Call on students to form sentences with these words. For each student, point to one word in each column. The student then makes a sentence using these words. For example:

   (She) (work) (every day)   She works every day.

   (He) (study) (yesterday)   He studied yesterday.

   (They) (rest) (yesterday) They rested yesterday.

3. Review a few irregular verbs in the past tense.

   a. Using the same columns on the board from 2 above, change the verbs to *teach*, *write*, and *meet people*.

   b. Review the past tense forms *taught*, *wrote*, and *met*.

   c. Again, have students form sentences, using one word from each column.

4. Review the past tense of the verb *to be*.

   a. Write on the board:

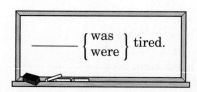

   b. Say each pronoun and have students form sentences using the correct verb. Have students respond chorally and individually. For example:

   (He):   He was tired.
   (They): They were tired.

INTRODUCING THE MODEL

1. Have students look at the model illustration.
2. Set the scene: "Two people are talking about Emma."
3. Present the model.
4. Full-Class Repetition.

   Pronunciation Note

   The pronunciation focus of Chapter 2 is **Did you** (text page 20). You may wish to model this pronunciation at this point (*What did you do yesterday?*) and encourage students to incorporate it into their language practice.

5. Ask students if they have any questions. Check understanding of the expression *sleep well*.
6. Group Choral Repetition.
7. Choral Conversation.
8. Call on one or two pairs of students to present the dialog.

   (For additional practice, do Choral Conversation in small groups or by rows.)

SIDE BY SIDE EXERCISES

Examples

1. A. Did you sleep well last night?
   B. Yes, I did. I was VERY tired.
   A. Why? What did you do yesterday?
   B. I studied English all day.
2. A. Did Rick sleep well last night?
   B. Yes, he did. He was VERY tired.
   A. Why? What did he do yesterday?
   B. He painted his apartment all day.

1. **Exercise 1:** Call on two students to present the dialog. Then do Choral Repetition and Choral Conversation practice.
2. **Exercise 2:** Same as above.
3. **Exercises 3–8:** Either Full-Class Practice or Pair Practice.

4. **Exercise 9:** Have students use the model as a guide to create their own conversations, using vocabulary of their choice. (They can use any names and activities they wish.) Encourage students to use dictionaries to find new words they want to use. This exercise can be done orally in class or for written homework. If you assign it for homework, do one example in class to make sure students understand what's expected. Have students present their conversations in class the next day.

WORKBOOK

Pages 12–13

EXPANSION ACTIVITIES

1. **Can You Hear the Difference?** ★

    a. Write on the board:

    > I study English. I studied English.
    > You work all day. You worked all day.
    > They wash windows. They washed windows.
    > They deliver pizzas. They delivered pizzas.
    > We paint the We painted the
    >   apartment.   apartment

    b. Choose a sentence randomly from one of the two columns and say it to the class. Have the class listen and identify whether the sentence is *present* or *past*.

    c. Have students continue the activity in pairs. One student says a sentence and the other identifies its time frame. Then have students reverse roles.

    d. Write other similar sentences on the board and *continue the practice.*

2. **Tell More About Situation 8** ★★

    Have students look at the illustration for Situation 8. Ask students the questions below. These questions allow students to use their imaginations to tell you more about the people in the situation.

    > Did the president sleep well last night?
    > What did he do yesterday?
    > Who did the president meet?
    > What did they talk about?

3. **Interview** ★★

    a. Write the following on the board:

    > What did you do yesterday?

    b. Have pairs of students interview each other about what they did yesterday and then report back to the class.

    Option: Have the class decide who had *the most interesting day* yesterday.

4. **Find the Right Person!** ★★

    a. From the prior activity, write down information about what students did yesterday.

    b. Put the information on a handout in the following form:

    > Find someone who . . .
    > 1. cleaned the house. _____
    > 2. wrote a letter. _____
    > 3. worked late. _____
    > 4. rode her bicycle. _____
    > 5. studied math. _____

    c. Have students circulate around the room, asking each other information questions to identify the above people. For example:

    > What did you do yesterday?
    > Where did you go?

    (continued)

CHAPTER 2   39

EXPANSION ACTIVITIES (Continued)

d. The first student to find all the people, raise his or her hand, and identify the students is the winner of the game.

5. Sense or Nonsense? ★★

a. Divide the class into four groups.

b. Make four sets of split-sentence cards with beginnings and endings of sentences. For example:

She worked	in the office all day.
He washed	windows all day.
I met	a professional soccer player yesterday.
We rode	our bicycles all day.
They taught	English all day.
I studied	for the English test.
She painted	the living room.
We delivered	mail all morning.
He wrote	letters all afternoon.

c. Mix up the cards and distribute sets of cards to each group, keeping the beginning and ending cards in different piles.

d. Have students take turns picking up one card from each pile and reading the sentence to the group. For example:

I washed	mail all morning.

e. The group decides if the sentence makes *sense* or is *nonsense*.

f. After all the cards have been picked, have the groups lay out all the cards and put together all the sentence combinations that make sense.

6. Miming: Why Am I So Tired? ★★

a. On cards write activities such as the following:

paint my apartment	cook	wash clothes
ride my bicycle	write letters	vacuum my rugs
plant flowers	play soccer	bake a cake
clean my apartment	rearrange furniture	do exercises
pay bills	rake leaves	fix my car
work	study	type letters

b. Have students take turns picking three cards from the pile and pantomiming the actions on the cards in succession.

c. The class must guess what the person did yesterday. For example:

You studied, you painted your apartment, and you washed clothes.

Variation: This can be done as a game with competing teams.

7. Sequencing ★★

a. Dictate the following sentences to students:

He was late for an important meeting.
Then he quickly ate breakfast and left the house.
He took a shower and got dressed.
He arrived at work at ten o'clock.

He took the bus to the office.
Henry got up late this morning.

b. Have students then sequence these sentences from *one* to *six*, with *one* being the first thing that happened to Henry:
  1. Henry got up late this morning.
  2. He took a shower and got dressed.
  3. Then he quickly ate breakfast and left the house.
  4. He took the bus to the office.
  5. He arrived at work at ten o'clock.
  6. He was late for an important meeting.

c. As a class, in pairs, or in small groups, have students compare their sequences.

8. What's New in the News? ★★★

Have students look in the newspaper for an article that tells about a recent local, national, or international event. Have them take notes on the article and come to the next class prepared to tell the class about it. Encourage the rest of the class to ask questions.

Text Page 13: Did Robert Shout at His Dog?

FOCUS

- Past Tense Review:
    Regular and Irregular Verbs
    Yes/No Questions and Short Answers with *Did*
    Negative Statements with *To Be*

GETTING READY

Contrast *did* and *was/were*.

1. Write on the board:

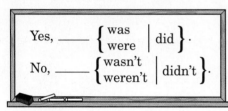

2. Make up questions, such as those below, that will pertain to your students' experience. Pick questions that will allow students to practice all the forms on the board. Read each question and have students respond chorally and/or individually.

> Was it (*sunny*) yesterday?
> Did it (*rain*) yesterday?
> Were (*Bob*) and (*Jane*) late for class today?
> Did (*Mary*) miss class last week?
> Were (*you*) on time this morning?
> Did (*Alice*) and (*George*) ride their bicycles to class today?
> Were we at school last (*Wednesday*)?
> Was (*Gloria*) at the beach yesterday?
> Did you sleep for (*15*) hours last night?
> Was (*John*) tired this morning?
> Did we study (*French*) in class last week?

INTRODUCING THE MODELS

There are two model conversations. Introduce and practice each separately. For each model:

1. Have students look at the model illustration in the book.

2. Set the scene:
    1st model: "Two people are talking about Robert."
    2nd model: "Two people are talking about Helen."

3. Present the model.
4. Full-Class Repetition.
5. Ask students if they have any questions.
6. Group Choral Repetition.
7. Choral Conversation.
8. Call on one or two pairs of students to present the dialog.

    (For additional practice, do Choral Conversation in small groups or by rows.)

SIDE BY SIDE EXERCISES

Examples

1. A. Did Howard fall asleep in class?
   B. Yes, he did. He was bored.
2. A. Did Amy take the plane to Rio?
   B. No, she didn't. She wasn't on time.

1. **Exercise 1:** Call on two students to present the dialog. Then do Choral Repetition and Choral Conversation practice.
2. **Exercise 2:** Same as above.
3. **Exercises 3–8:** Either Full-Class Practice or Pair Practice.

New Vocabulary

4. prepared
5. lines

WORKBOOK

Pages 14–17

EXPANSION ACTIVITIES

1. What Did They Do? ★

Use your own visuals or *Side by Side* Picture Cards 36–67, 141–148, and 158–162 to review verbs in the past tense.

a. Hold up a visual and ask a student:

   What did _____ do (yesterday/last night . . .)?

   You can use any appropriate time expression or name in your questions. For example:

   What did (*Bill*) do last weekend?
   What did (*your friends*) do yesterday?
   What did (*Sally*) do this morning?
   What did (*you*) do today?
   What did (*we*) do last week?

b. Give the visuals to students and have them ask and answer questions in the past tense.

2. Finish the Sentence! ★

a. Write the following words on the board:

| angry | hungry | on time | scared | tired |
| bored | nervous | prepared | thirsty | upset |

b. Say the sentences below. Have students complete each sentence with the appropriate word on the board.

   He drank two bottles of soda because he was very . . .
   I didn't know the answers on the test because I wasn't . . .
   Kathy didn't want to go into that dark room herself because she was . . .
   It rained all day yesterday. I stayed home and didn't do anything. I was . . .
   I didn't have any lunch today, and now I'm . . .
   Class began at nine. I arrived at nine thirty. I wasn't . . .
   My little brother cried because he was . . .
   Bob fell asleep in class because he was . . .
   Your big exam is tomorrow. Are you feeling . . . ?
   Paul had an accident with his father's car. His father was very . . .

3. Tic Tac Adjective! ★★

a. Have students draw a tic tac grid on their papers and fill in the grid with any nine of the ten adjectives in the previous activity.

b. Read the sentences from Activity 2, and tell students to cross out any word on their grids that finishes the sentence.

c. The first person to cross out three words in a straight line—either vertically, horizontally, or diagonally—wins the game.

d. Have the winner call out the words to check the accuracy.

4. Question the Answers! ★★

a. Dictate answers such as the following to the class:

   Yes, she did. She was prepared.
   No, he didn't. He wasn't on time.
   Yes, they did. They were very angry.
   No, he didn't. He wasn't hungry.
   Yes, we did. We were tired.
   No, she didn't. She wasn't nervous.

b. Have students write questions for which these answers would be correct. For example:

   Answer: Yes, she did. She was prepared.
   Question: Did Betty do well on her English exam?

   Answer: No, he didn't. He wasn't on time.
   Question: Did your husband take the bus to Denver this morning?

c. Have students compare their questions with each other.

Variation: Write the answers on cards. Divide the class into groups and give each group a set of cards.

5. Match the Conversations ★★

a. Make a set of matching cards. For example:

| Did you enjoy yourself? | No, I didn't. I was bored. |

(continued)

EXPANSION ACTIVITIES (Continued)

Did you drink that whole glass of water?	Yes, I did. I was thirsty.
Did you do well on the test?	No, I didn't. I wasn't prepared.
Did you miss the bus?	No, I didn't. I was on time.
Did you finish the apple pie?	Yes, I did. I was hungry.
Did you shout at those people?	Yes, I did. I was angry.
Did you cry at the play?	No, I didn't. It wasn't sad.
Did you laugh during the movie?	No, I didn't. It wasn't funny.
Did you bite your nails?	Yes, I did. I was nervous.

b. Distribute a card to each student.

c. Have students memorize the sentences on their cards, and then have students walk around the room saying their sentences until they find their match.

d. Then have pairs of students say their matched sentences aloud to the class.

6. Extend the Conversations ★★★

a. Review the following verb forms from student text page 13:

> Model Conversations
> shout–shouted
> sleep–slept
>
> Exercises
> 1. fall–fell
> 2. take–took
> 3. cry–cried
> 4. do–did
> 5. forget–forgot
> 6. cover–covered

b. Divide the class into pairs and have each pair prepare a short role play to present to the class. Use both model conversations and Exercises 1–6. Have students pretend to be the people in the situations and create a possible 4- to 6-line dialog based on the situation. Encourage students to use their imaginations to embellish the dialogs. Suggest that students begin their dialogs like this: "Hi, _____ What's new?" For example:

> (Model 1)
>
> A. Hi, Robert. What's new?
> B. Well, I'm very upset.
> A. What happened?
> B. My dog ate today's newspaper. I was so angry that I shouted at him.
> A. Hmm. Maybe you should feed your dog more often.

7. Pronunciation Story: The Boys at Dover Academy ★★

Use the story below to have students practice past tense verbs in -ted and -ded.

a. Put on the board:

Peter	Sam	Nick	Paul
painted	started	went needed	planted

Walter	Richard	Frank
went wanted	didn't feel well rested	went fainted

b. Set the scene: "The boys at Dover Academy are always very busy."

44 CHAPTER 2

c. Point to the appropriate cue as you tell each part of the story below.

"Last Saturday afternoon, . . .
   Peter painted his room.
   Sam started to study for a history exam.
   Nick went to the store because he needed a new notebook.
   Paul planted flowers in front of the school.
   Walter went to the library because he wanted to be by himself.
   Richard didn't feel very well, so he rested in bed.
   Frank went jogging in the hot sun and fainted."

d. Ask questions about the story. You can pause as you tell it and ask questions, or you can wait until the end. Then call on one or two students to retell the whole story.

e. As an optional writing assignment, have students write the story, using only the cues on the board.

8. Guess How They're Feeling! ★★★

a. Write the following words on the board:

| angry | bored | hungry | nervous |
| scared | thirsty | tired | |

b. Divide the class into pairs.

c. Give each pair a situation card. Possibilities include:

> You're at the movies, and you're talking about the movie you're watching.

> You and a friend are at a restaurant, and the service is very slow tonight.

> You and a friend are at a lecture.

> You and a friend are sitting in the waiting room at the doctor's office.

> You and a friend are talking before English class.

d. Give each pair a card with one of the *feeling* words from the board written on it.

e. Have each pair prepare a short role play based on their situation and then act it out for the class, according to the *feeling* on their card.

f. The rest of the class has to guess what was on the card:

   They're angry.
   They're nervous.
      Etc.

9. Tell About a Time . . . ★★★

a. Write the following words on the board:

In the lesson on student text page 13, some people were *angry, bored, sad, nervous,* and *scared*.

b. Divide the class into pairs and have students talk with each other about a time *they* were angry, bored, sad, nervous, or scared.

c. Call on students to share their experiences with the class.

Text Pages 14–15: How Did Marty Break His Leg?

FOCUS

- Review: Past Continuous Tense

CLOSE UP

RULE: The past continuous tense is commonly used to show a past activity that was in progress when another event happened.

EXAMPLES: He **broke** his leg while he **was snowboarding**.
She **sprained** her ankle while she **was playing** volleyball.

GETTING READY

1. Use your own visuals or *Side by Side* Picture Cards for verbs to review the past continuous tense.

   a. Hold up visuals and ask students questions in the past continuous tense. For example:

      (*Side by Side* Picture Card 44)
      A. What were they doing last night?
      B. They were playing cards.

      (*Side by Side* Picture Card 36)
      A. What was she doing last night?
      B. She was reading.

   b. Hold up visuals and have pairs of students ask and answer, using the past continuous tense.

2. Review the irregular past forms of the following verbs: *lose–lost, cut–cut, fall–fell, get–got, hurt–hurt.*

   a. Write the following verbs on the board:

   b. Call on students to pantomime actions with those verbs and have the class tell what the person just *did*.

INTRODUCING THE MODEL

1. Have students look at the model illustration.
2. Set the scene: "Two people are talking about Marty's accident."
3. Present the model.
4. Full-Class Repetition.
5. Ask students if they have any questions. Check understanding of the word *snowboard*.
6. Group Choral Repetition.
7. Choral Conversation.
8. Call on one or two pairs of students to present the dialog.

   (For additional practice, do Choral Conversation in small groups or by rows.)

SIDE BY SIDE EXERCISES

Examples

1. A. How did Greta sprain her ankle?
   B. She sprained it while she was playing volleyball.
   A. That's too bad!

2. A. How did Larry lose his wallet?
   B. He lost it while he was hiking in the woods.
   A. That's too bad!

46 CHAPTER 2

1. **Exercise 1:** Introduce the words *sprain, ankle*. Call on two students to present the dialog. Then do Choral Repetition and Choral Conversation practice.
2. **Exercise 2:** Introduce the words *hike, woods*. Same as above.
3. **Exercises 3–10:** Either Full-Class Practice or Pair Practice.

> **New Vocabulary**
>
> 4. prepare
> 5. rip
>   daily exercises
> 9. black eye
>   fight
>   kid
> 10. magician
>   magic trick

WORKBOOK

Pages 18–19

EXPANSION ACTIVITIES

1. **Do You Remember?** ★
   a. Divide the class into pairs.
   b. Show the class a picture for two or three minutes of a scene with many people engaged in many activities.
   c. Put the picture away and have students write down what the characters in the picture *were doing*.
   d. Have the partners compare their sentences and then look at the picture again to see how much they remembered.

2. **Find the Right Person!** ★★
   a. Find out what students were doing last night at 8:00.
   b. Put the information on a handout in the following form:

   > Find someone who . . .
   > 1. was cleaning the house. _____
   > 2. was watching TV. _____
   > 3. was listening to music. _____
   > 4. was studying for a math exam. _____
   > 5. was preparing dinner. _____

   c. To identify the above people, have students circulate around the room, asking each other information questions about their activities yesterday. For example: "What were you doing last night at 8:00?"
   d. The first student to find all the people, raise his or her hand, and identify the people is the winner of the game.

3. **What Were They Doing?** ★★★
   a. Divide the class into pairs or small groups.
   b. Dictate sentences such as the following:

   > He fell off the train while he was . . .
   > She sprained her ankle while she was . . .
   > They burned their hands while they were . . .
   > I lost my glasses while I was . . .
   > He hurt his finger while he was . . .
   > We met the president while we were . . .
   > She ripped her jacket while she was . . .

   c. Have students write possible endings for the sentences.
   d. Call on students to share their ideas with the rest of the class.

   (continued)

CHAPTER 2

EXPANSION ACTIVITIES (Continued)

4. I Saw You! ★★

Have pairs of students role play the conversation below. Use your own visuals or *Side by Side* Picture Cards as cues for community locations. Students can use any vocabulary they wish to finish the dialog as long as the verb is in the past continuous tense.

a. Briefly review some or all of the locations in the community below, using visuals if possible. Say each word and then have students tell what people usually do in that location. For example:

   library: read/study/borrow books

airport	hospital
bakery	laundromat
bank	library
bus station	movie theater
butcher shop	museum
cafeteria	park
candy store	pet shop
clinic	playground
concert hall	police station
courthouse	post office
department store	school
doctor's office	shopping mall
drug store	supermarket
gas station	train station
hardware store	zoo

b. Write on the board:

   A. Were you at the _____ yesterday?
   B. Yes, I was. How did you know?
   A. I was there, too. I was _____. I saw you, but I guess you didn't see me.
   B. I'm sorry I didn't see you. I was _____, and I was in a hurry.

c. Call on pairs of students to role play the dialog. For each pair, signal a location in the community with a visual or word card. For example:

   Cue: *department store*

   A. Were you at the department store yesterday?
   B. Yes, I was. How did you know?
   A. I was there, too. I was (*looking for a new coat*). I saw you, but I guess you didn't see me.
   B. I'm sorry I didn't see you. I was (*buying a birthday present for my brother*), and I was in a hurry.

5. Chain Story ★★

a. Begin by saying: "Henry had a bad day today. He fell while he was getting out of bed."

b. Student 1 repeats what you said and continues the story. For example:

   Henry had a bad day today. He fell while he was getting out of bed. Then he cut himself while he was shaving.

c. Continue around the room in this fashion, with each student repeating what the previous one said and adding another sentence.

d. You can do the activity again, beginning and ending with different students.

   If the class is large, you may want to divide students into groups to give students more practice.

6. A Bad Day ★★

a. Write the following conversation model on the board:

   A. I had a bad day today.
   B. Why? What happened?
   A. I _____ while _____.
   B. That's too bad!

b. Write the following cues on the board or on word cards:

burn	forget
cut	lose
fall asleep	rip
fall down	spill

48 CHAPTER 2

c. Have pairs of students create conversations based on the word cues and the model on the board. For example:

> A. I had a bad day today.
> B. Why? What happened?
> A. I cut myself while I was cooking dinner.
> B. That's too bad!
>
> A. I had a bad day today.
> B. Why? What happened?
> A. I lost my homework while I was walking to school.
> B. That's too bad!

7. Student Discussion: Accidents ★★★

   a. Write on the board:

   > Were you ever in an accident?
   > What happened?
   > What were you doing when the accident happened?

   b. In pairs or small groups, have students share their stories and then share them with the class.

8. How Did You Meet? ★★★

   a. Put the following on the board:

   > How did you meet your boyfriend/ girlfriend/ best friend/husband/wife?
   > Where were you?
   > What were you doing?
   > What was he/she doing?

   b. Divide the class into pairs and have students discuss the questions on the board. Have them tell how they met their boyfriend, girlfriend, best friend, husband, or wife. Where were they? What were they doing? What was the other person doing?

   c. Have students share their stories with the class.

How to Say It!

Reacting to Bad News: There are many ways to respond with sympathy to bad news. "That's too bad!" "That's a shame!" "What a shame!" "What a pity!" and "I'm sorry to hear that" are five common sympathetic responses.

1. Set the scene: "Someone just heard some bad news."
2. Present the expressions.
3. Full-Class Repetition.
4. Ask students if they have any questions.
5. Group Choral Repetition.
6. Have students practice the conversations in the lesson again, reacting to the bad news with any of these five expressions.
7. Call on students to present their conversations to the class.

CHAPTER 2　　49

Text Pages 16–17

READING Difficult Experiences

FOCUS

- Review:
    Simple Past Tense
    Past Continuous Tense

NEW VOCABULARY

at the back of	look over *his* shoulder
audience	principal
demonstrator	realize
experience	wave

READING THE STORY

Optional: Preview the story by having students talk about the story title and/or illustrations. You may choose to introduce new vocabulary beforehand, or have students encounter the new vocabulary within the context of the reading.

1. Have students read silently or follow along silently as the story is read aloud by you, by one or more students, or on the audio program.

2. Ask students if they have any questions. Check understanding of vocabulary.

    Culture Note

    Demonstrators often go to listen to a politician's speech. During the speech, they shout and disrupt the politician because they disagree and are angry with what the person has to say.

3. Check students' comprehension, using some or all of the following questions:

    Did Ms. Henderson teach well this morning?
    How did she teach?
    Why?
    Why was it a difficult experience for Ms. Henderson?
    Why couldn't she do anything about it?

    Did Stuart type well today?
    How did he type?
    Why?
    Why was it a difficult experience for Stuart?
    Why couldn't he do anything about it?

    Did the Baxter Boys sing well last night?
    How did they sing?
    Why?
    Why was it a difficult experience for the Baxter Boys?
    Why couldn't they do anything about it?

    Did the president speak well this afternoon?
    How did he speak?
    Why?
    Why was it a difficult experience for the president?
    Why couldn't he do anything about it?

✓ READING CHECK-UP

Q & A

1. Call on a pair of students to present the model. Check understanding of the expression *I bet*.

2. Have students work in pairs to create new dialogs.

3. Call on pairs to present their new dialogs to the class.

MATCH

1. f
2. c
3. h
4. a
5. g
6. d
7. e
8. b

50 CHAPTER 2

READING EXTENSION

1. ***Class Discussion***
   a. Have students discuss the following:

   In each situation, the character was too upset to do a good job. What advice can you give each of these people? What are some simple ways to relax?

   b. Call on students to share their thoughts with the class.

2. ***Stories Alive!***
   a. Divide some of the students into pairs, and have them choose either the story about Ms. Henderson or the story about Stuart, and then create a dramatization of the situation.

   b. Divide the rest of the class into groups. Have them choose either the story about the Baxter Boys or the story about the president, and then create a dramatization of the situation.

   c. Call on students to present their *dramas* to the class.

How About You?

Have students answer the questions, in pairs or as a class. If you do it as pair practice, call on students to report to the class about their conversation partner.

LISTENING

Listen and choose the correct answer.

1. Did you do well at your job interview yesterday?
2. Were your children tired last night?
3. What was he doing when he broke his leg?
4. Did you finish your dinner last night?
5. How did your husband lose his wallet?
6. What was your supervisor doing?
7. Did you do well on the exam?
8. What happened while you were preparing lunch?

Answers

1. a
2. b
3. b
4. a
5. b
6. b
7. a
8. a

CHAPTER 2

Text Pages 18–19: Tell Me About Your Vacation

FOCUS

- Past Tense Review:
    Regular and Irregular Verbs
    Information Questions

GETTING READY

Review the irregular past forms of the following verbs: *get–got, eat–ate, speak–spoke, take–took, buy–bought, swim–swam, see–saw, meet–met, come–came.*

1. Write the following cues on the board:

    get up
    eat
    speak
    take the bus
    buy
    swim
    see
    meet
    come home

2. Call on students to pantomime actions with those verbs, and have the class tell what the person just *did*.

INTRODUCING THE MODEL (Exercise 1)

1. Have students look at the illustration at the top of the page and then the illustration for Exercise 1.
2. Set the scene: "One neighbor is telling the other about her vacation."
3. Present the introductory conversation and Exercise 1.
4. Full-Class Repetition.
5. Ask students if they have any questions. Check understanding of vocabulary.
6. Group Choral Repetition.
7. Choral Conversation.
8. Call on one or two pairs of students to present the dialog.

    (For additional practice, do Choral Conversation in small groups or by rows.)

SIDE BY SIDE EXERCISES

Examples

1. A. Did you go to Paris?
   B. No, we didn't.
   A. Where did you go?
   B. We went to Rome.
2. A. Did you get there by boat?
   B. No, we didn't.
   A. How did you get there?
   B. We got there by plane.

1. **Exercise 2:** Introduce the expressions *get there, by boat*. Call on two students to present the dialog. Then do Choral Repetition and Choral Conversation practice.
2. **Exercise 3:** Same as above.
3. **Exercises 4–12:** Either Full-Class Practice or Pair Practice.

New Vocabulary

6. take pictures
7. souvenir
8. Mediterranean
9. Colisseum
   Vatican
10. get around by taxi/by bus
11. tourist

Culture Note

Exercise 9: Each year many people in Rome visit the Vatican, the seat of the Roman Catholic church and home of the pope. The Roman Colosseum, an ancient amphitheater, is a major tourist attraction in the city.

WORKBOOK

Pages 20–23

  52   CHAPTER 2

EXPANSION ACTIVITIES

1. Correct the Statement! ★★

Make statements about the characters' vacation in Italy described in the exercises on text pages 18 and 19. Some statements should be true, and others false. Have students respond to your statements. If a statement is false, a student should correct it. For example:

> Teacher: They went to Italy.
> Student: That's right.
>
> Teacher: They went to Venice.
> Student: No, they didn't. They went to Rome.

Variation 1: ★★★ Have students make statements for others to react to.

Variation 2: ★★ Do the activity as a game with competing teams.

2. Tell a Story! ★★

a. Tell the following short story to the class:

> "Mr. and Mrs. Lane took a vacation last month. They went to Paris. They took the plane, but it was a terrible experience. The plane left three hours late, and they had very bad weather during the flight. When they arrived in Paris, it was raining. In fact, it rained for three days. They stayed in a small hotel and tried to eat in restaurants that weren't too expensive. They visited the Eiffel Tower and other famous places in Paris, they bought a few souvenirs, and they took a lot of photographs. They sent postcards to all their friends and told them about their trip. Mr. and Mrs. Lane didn't meet a lot of people because they didn't speak any French. But they didn't care. They had a very good time."

b. After you finish telling the story, make several statements about it. Some should be true, and others should be false.

c. Students listen to the statements and decide if they're true or false. If a statement is false, have students correct it. For example:

> Teacher: Mr. and Mrs. Lane went to Madrid.
> Student: False. They didn't go to Madrid. They went to Paris.

Variation: This activity can be done as a game with competing teams. The teams take turns deciding whether the statements are true or false.

3. Question Game ★★★

a. Write the following sentence on the board:

> Mrs. Watson went to Paris last week.

b. Underline different elements of the sentence, and have students create a question based on that portion of the sentence. For example:

> Mrs. Watson went to Paris last week.

Who went to Paris last week?

> Mrs. Watson went to Paris last week.

When did Mrs. Watson go to Paris?

> Mrs. Watson went to Paris last week.

Where did Mrs. Watson go last week?

> Mrs. Watson went to Paris last week.

What did Mrs. Watson do last week?

c. Continue with other sentences.

(continued)

CHAPTER 2   53

EXPANSION ACTIVITIES (Continued)

4. I'm Sorry I Can't Hear You! ★★★

In real-life conversations, people often miss some of what was said because of noise and distractions or a bad telephone connection. In this exercise, students practice asking for clarification about the part of the conversation they missed.

a. Give students cards with statements on them such as the following:

> I went to (Hawaii) last week.

> My (father) just got back from Spain.

> When my family went to Korea, our plane was (three) hours late.

> While we were visiting Rome, we ate in a lot of (expensive) restaurants.

> My friend and I went to Africa by (boat) last summer.

> I remember when I went to Chicago. The weather was (terrible).

> When I went to Germany, I spoke only (English).

> My family and I bought a lot of (clothing) when we went to France last year.

> I really enjoyed my trip to Greece. We (swam) every day.

> The best thing about my trip to New York was that I saw (the Statue of Liberty).

> I'll never forget my trip to Argentina because I lost my (suitcase).

> When I was in England, I traveled everywhere by (bicycle).

> I flew to (Tokyo) last summer, and I loved it.

> We wanted to go to (Portugal) two years ago, but we just weren't able to go.

b. Set the scene: "We're all at a party. We're talking about vacations and trips, but it's noisy and we can't always hear very well."

c. Have students who are holding cards choose another student to begin a conversation with. Have each student begin by reading the statement, but substituting the nonsense syllable *Bzzz* for the word in parentheses. For example:

   A. I went to *(Bzzz)* last week.

Student B must answer "I'm sorry" and ask a question about the part of the communication he or she didn't understand. For example:

   B. I'm sorry. WHERE did you go last week?

Student A repeats the statement, but this time he or she says the word in parentheses. The two students must then continue the dialog for two more lines, using any vocabulary they wish.

Example:

   A. My *(Bzzz)* just got back from Spain.
   B. I'm sorry. WHO just got back from Spain?

54   CHAPTER 2

A. My *father* just got back from Spain.
B. Oh. How long was he there?
A. He was there for a few weeks.

5. Grammar Chain: The Bakers' Bad Vacation ★★

a. Start the chain game by saying:

    Teacher: The Bakers went to Los Angeles last week. They had a terrible time!

    (to Student A): Did they *eat in good restaurants*?

b. Student A must answer the question negatively, then ask Student B another past tense question. For example:

    Student A: No, they didn't. They ate in very bad restaurants.

    (to Student B): Did they *meet any famous people*?

c. The chain continues. For example:

    Student B: No, they didn't. They didn't meet anyone.

    (to Student C): Did they *take many pictures*?

6. Group Story ★★★

a. Begin the following story: "The Jacksons went to Los Angeles last week. They had a wonderful time!"

b. Divide the class into small groups of 3 to 5 students.

c. Have each group continue the story with at least ten sentences about the Jacksons' vacation. Encourage students to use any vocabulary they wish and to draw from their own knowledge in describing the vacation.

d. Have one person from each group present that group's story to the class.

e. Have the class decide which group's story describes the best vacation of all.

7. Find the Right Person! ★★★

a. Collect information about the students' last vacation. Ask them:

    Where did you go on your last vacation?
    How did you get there?
    What interesting sights did you see?
    What did you do?

b. Put the information on a handout in the following form:

> Find someone who . . .
> 1. went to New York. _____
> 2. took a plane. _____
> 3. went to museums. _____
> 4. met famous people. _____
> 5. saw the Statue of Liberty. _____
> 6. ate in very good restaurants. _____

c. Have students circulate around the room, asking each other information questions to identify the above people.

d. The first student to find all the people, raise his or her hand, and identify the students is the winner of the game.

8. Telling About Our Travels ★★★

a. Have students tell the class about a tourist sight they visited. If possible, have students show the class photographs, postcards, and souvenirs.

b. As students listen, have them ask questions such as those in the lesson.

JOURNAL

Have students write their journal entries at home or in class. Encourage students to use a dictionary to look up words they would like to use. Students can share their written work with other students if appropriate. Have students discuss what they have written as a class, in pairs, or in small groups.

CHAPTER 2   55

Text Page 20

 PRONUNCIATION

Did you: The final /d/ sound of *did* combines with the initial /y/ sound of *you* to form a /j/ sound. This is very common in everyday conversational English.

Focus on Listening

Practice the sentences in the left column. Say each sentence or play the audio one or more times. Have students listen carefully and repeat.

Focus on Pronunciation

Practice the sentences in the right column. Have students say each sentence and then listen carefully as you say it or play the audio.

If you wish, have students continue practicing the sentences to improve their pronunciation.

 CHAPTER SUMMARY

GRAMMAR

1. Divide the class into pairs or small groups.
2. Have students take turns forming sentences from the words in the grammar boxes. Student A says a sentence, and Student B points to the words from each column that are in the sentence. Then have students switch: Student B says a sentence, and Student A points to the words.

KEY VOCABULARY

Have students ask you any questions about the meaning or pronunciation of the vocabulary. If students ask for the pronunciation, repeat after the student until the student is satisfied with his or her own pronunciation.

EXPANSION ACTIVITIES

1. **Do You Remember the Words?** ★

   Check students' retention of the vocabulary depicted on the opening page of Chapter 2 by doing the following activity:

   a. Have students open their books to page 11 and cover the list of verbs.
   b. Either call out a number and have students tell you the verb and its present and past form, or say a verb in the past and have students tell you the number.

   Variation: You can also do this activity as a game with competing teams.

2. **Student-Led Dictation** ★

   a. Tell each student to choose a word from the Key Vocabulary list on text page 20 and look at it very carefully.
   b. Have students take turns dictating their words to the class. Everybody writes down that student's word.
   c. When the dictation is completed, call on different students to write each word on the board to check the spelling.

3. **Beanbag Toss** ★

   a. Call out the topic: *Regular Verbs.*
   b. Have students toss a beanbag back and forth. The student to whom the beanbag is tossed must name a *regular verb* in its base form and past tense form. For example:

      Student 1: stay-stayed
      Student 2: shave-shaved
      Student 3: hike-hiked

   c. Continue until all the words in the category have been named.

   Variation: You can also do this activity as a game with competing teams.

4. **Letter Game** ★

   a. Divide the class into two teams.

56   CHAPTER 2

b. Say: "I'm thinking of an irregular past tense verb that begins with *d*."

c. The first person to raise his or her hand and guess correctly [*drank*] wins a point for his or her team.

d. Continue with other letters of the alphabet.

The team that gets the most correct answers wins the game.

5. Miming Verbs ★

   a. Write down on cards the verbs on text page 20.

   b. Have students take turns picking a card from the pile and pantomiming the action on the card.

   c. The class must guess the action verb and give its present and past tense forms.

   Variation: This can be done as a game with competing teams.

6. Tic Tac Verbs ★

   a. Have students draw a tic tac grid on a piece of paper and fill it in with the present tense form of any of the irregular verbs listed on text page 20.

   b. Call out the past tense form of any of these verbs. Tell students to cross out any present tense verb on their grid for which you have given a past tense form.

   c. The first person to cross out three verbs in a straight line—either vertically, horizontally, or diagonally—wins the game.

   d. Have the winner call out the words to check the accuracy.

CHAPTER 2 57

END-OF-CHAPTER ACTIVITIES

1. Board Game ★★★

   a. On poster boards or on manila file folders, make up game boards with a pathway consisting of separate spaces. You may use any theme or design you wish.

   b. Divide the class into groups of 2 to 4 students and give each group a game board and a die, and each student something to be used as a playing piece.

   c. Give each group a pile of cards face-down with sentences written on them. Some sentences should be correct and others incorrect. For example:

   > Did they study for the exam?
   > What did you delivered?
   > Why was he waving?
   > He cutted himself with a knife.
   > She didn't sang well at the concert today.
   > They didn't embarrassed.
   > They covered their eyes because they was scared.
   > I sprained my ankle while I was hiking in the woods.
   > He ripped his pants while he got on the bus.
   > How did they got there?
   > What did they see at the museum?
   > Were you watch a movie last night?
   > I poked myself in the eye at work.
   > The father teached his son how to ride a bicycle.

   d. Each student in turn rolls the die, moves the playing piece along the game path, and after landing on a space, picks a card, reads the sentence, and says if it is *correct* or *incorrect*. If the statement is incorrect, the student must correct it. If the response is correct, the student takes an additional turn.

   e. The first student to reach the end of the pathway is the winner.

2. Question Game ★★★

   a. Write the following sentence on the board:

   > Martin sprained his ankle while he was walking in the woods.

   b. Underline different elements of the sentence, and have students create a question based on that portion of the sentence. For example:

   > <u>Martin</u> sprained his ankle while he was walking in the woods.

   Who sprained his ankle while he was walking in the woods?

   > Martin sprained <u>his ankle</u> while he was walking in the woods.

   What did Martin sprain?

   > Martin sprained his ankle while <u>he was walking in the woods</u>.

   What was Martin doing when he sprained his ankle?

   or

   How did Martin sprain his ankle?

   > Martin sprained his ankle while he was walking <u>in the woods</u>.

   Where was Martin when he sprained his ankle?

   c. Continue with other sentences.

3. Expand the Sentence! ★★

   Tell students that the object of the activity is to build a long sentence on the board, one word at a time.

   a. Call on a student to write a pronoun or someone's name on the far left side of the board. For example:

58 CHAPTER 2

b. Have another student come to the board and add a word. For example:

c. Have a third student add a third word. For example:

> Matthew was walking

d. Continue until each student in the class has had one or more turns to add a word to expand the sentence into the longest one they can think of. For example:

> Matthew was walking home from work yesterday afternoon at five-thirty when he saw a very bad accident at the corner of Main Street and Central Boulevard.

e. Begin a new sentence about the accident and continue as above.

4. Dialog Builder! ★★★

a. Divide the class into pairs.

b. Write several lines such as the following on the board:

> No, he didn't.
> Yes, she did.
> What a shame!
> I'm sorry to hear that.
> He was too upset.
> Why?

c. Have each pair create a conversation incorporating those lines. Students can begin and end their conversations any way they wish, but they must include those lines in their dialogs.

d. Call on students to present their conversations to the class.

CHAPTER 2 59

WORKBOOK ANSWER KEY AND LISTENING SCRIPTS

WORKBOOK PAGE 12

A. HERBERT'S TERRIBLE DAY!

1. had
2. got up
3. ate
4. rushed
5. ran
6. missed
7. waited
8. decided
9. arrived
10. sat
11. began
12. called
13. typed
14. made
15. fixed
16. finished
17. put
18. spilled
19. went
20. ordered
21. felt
22. forgot
23. crashed
24. fell
25. broke
26. hurt
27. left
28. took
29. went

WORKBOOK PAGE 13

B. LISTENING

Listen and circle the correct answer.

1. They work.
2. They worked.
3. We study English.
4. I waited for the bus.
5. We visit our friends.
6. She met important people.
7. He taught Chinese.
8. She delivers the mail.
9. I wrote letters to my friends.
10. I ride my bicycle to work.
11. He sleeps very well.
12. I had a terrible headache.

Answers

1. every day
2. yesterday
3. every day
4. yesterday
5. every day
6. yesterday
7. yesterday
8. every day
9. yesterday
10. every day
11. every day
12. yesterday

C. WHAT'S THE WORD?

1. wanted
2. lifted
3. painted
4. roller-bladed
5. planted
6. needed
7. waited
8. decided

D. PUZZLE: *What Did They Do?*

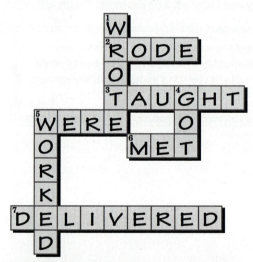

WORKBOOK PAGE 14

E. WHAT'S THE QUESTION?

1. Did you buy
2. Did they take
3. Did she see
4. Did he speak
5. Did you break
6. Did it begin
7. Did she fly
8. Did you have

60   CHAPTER 2

9. Did they go
10. Did I sing
11. Did he meet
12. Did you lose

F. WHAT'S THE ANSWER?

1. they were bored
2. I wasn't hungry
3. they were tired
4. she wasn't prepared
5. he was angry
6. I wasn't on time
7. she wasn't thirsty
8. I was scared
9. they were sad

WORKBOOK PAGE 15

G. SOMETHING DIFFERENT

1. didn't drive, drove
2. didn't come, came
3. didn't take, took
4. didn't go, went
5. didn't forget, forgot
6. didn't wear, wore
7. didn't teach, taught
8. didn't eat, ate
9. didn't give, gave
10. didn't sit, sat
11. didn't have, had
12. didn't sing, sang

WORKBOOK PAGES 16–17

H. WHAT ARE THEY SAYING?

1. Did you
   didn't, was
2. Did you
   didn't
   met
3. Did
   did
   wasn't
4. Did
   she didn't
   weren't
5. Did, fall
   he didn't
   fell
   was
6. Did
   I didn't, rode
   was
   was

7. Did you
   did, was
   didn't
   was
8. Was
   was, Were
   I wasn't, didn't
9. Did
   did
   didn't
   were
10. Did
    they didn't
    danced
    were
11. did
    I did, bought
    Did you
    didn't
    wasn't
12. were
    were
    I was, was
    was
    wasn't

WORKBOOK PAGE 18

I. HOW DID IT HAPPEN?

1. He sprained his ankle while he was playing tennis.
2. She ripped her pants while she was exercising.
3. I broke my arm while I was playing volleyball.
4. He poked himself in the eye while he was fixing his sink.
5. We hurt ourselves while we were skateboarding.
6. They tripped and fell while they were dancing.
7. He burned himself while he was cooking french fries.
8. She got a black eye while she was fighting with the kid across the street.
9. I cut myself while I was chopping carrots.
10. He lost his cell phone while he was jogging in the park.

WORKBOOK PAGE 20

L. WHAT'S THE QUESTION?

1. Who did you meet?
2. What did she lose?
3. Where did you do your exercises?
4. When did they leave?

CHAPTER 2

5. How did she get here?
6. Where did he sing?
7. How long did they stay?
8. What kind of movie did you see?
9. Why did he cry?
10. Who did she write a letter to?
11. What did they complain about?
12. How many grapes did you eat?
13. Where did he speak?
14. How long did they lift weights?
15. Who did she give a present to?
16. What kind of pie did you order?
17. How many videos did you rent?
18. Who did they send an e-mail to?
19. When did he fall asleep?
20. When did you lose your hat?

WORKBOOK PAGES 21–22

M. OUR VACATION

1. we didn't
   did you go
   We went
2. we didn't
   did you get there
   We got there by plane.
3. it didn't
   did it leave
   It left
4. we didn't
   weather did you have
   We had
5. we didn't
   hotel did you stay in
   We stayed in a small hotel.
6. we didn't
   food did you eat
   We ate Japanese food.
7. we didn't
   did you take (with you)
   We took

8. we didn't
   did you get around the city
   We got around the city by taxi.
9. we didn't
   did you meet
   We met
10. we didn't
    did you buy
    We bought
11. we didn't
    did you speak
    We spoke English.
12. we did
    money did you spend
    We spent . . .

WORKBOOK PAGE 23

N. SOUND IT OUT!

1. these
2. did
3. Rita
4. big
5. green
6. mittens
7. knit
8. Did Rita knit these big green mittens?
9. Greek
10. his
11. Richard
12. every
13. speaks
14. with
15. week
16. sister
17. Richard speaks Greek with his sister every week.

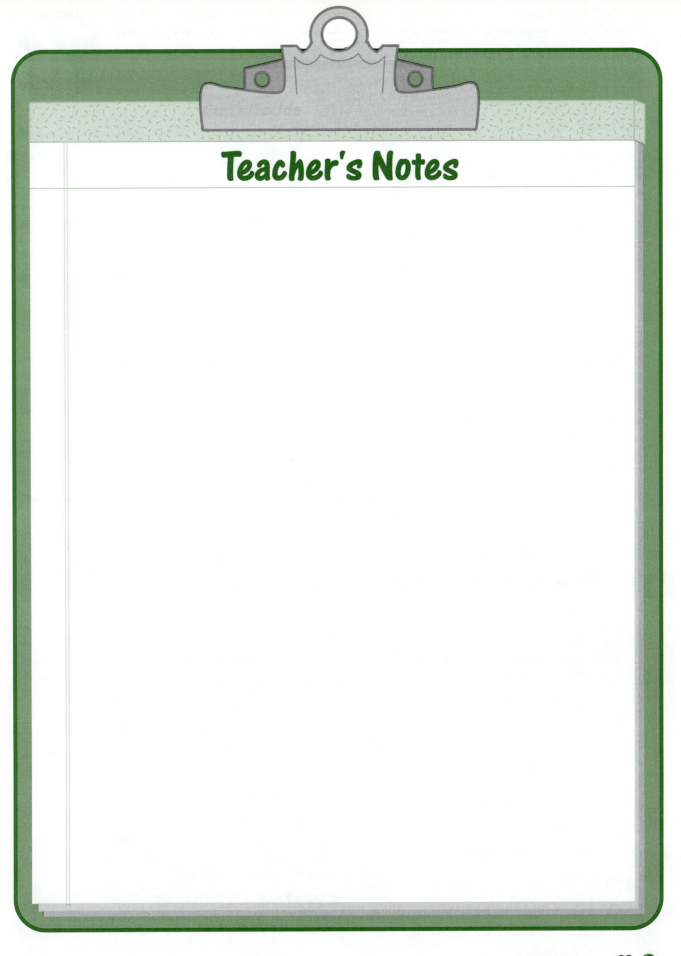

CHAPTER 3 OVERVIEW: Text Pages 21–32

GRAMMAR

FUTURE: GOING TO

What	am	I	going to do?
	is	he / she / it	
	are	we / you / they	

(I am)	I'm	going to read.
(He is)	He's	
(She is)	She's	
(It is)	It's	
(We are)	We're	
(You are)	You're	
(They are)	They're	

POSSESSIVE PRONOUNS

mine
his
hers
—
ours
yours
theirs

FUTURE: WILL

(I will)	I'll	work.
(He will)	He'll	
(She will)	She'll	
(It will)	It'll	
(We will)	We'll	
(You will)	You'll	
(They will)	They'll	

I / He / She / It / We / You / They	won't work.

FUTURE CONTINUOUS TENSE

(I will)	I'll	be working.
(He will)	He'll	
(She will)	She'll	
(It will)	It'll	
(We will)	We'll	
(You will)	You'll	
(They will)	They'll	

FUNCTIONS

ASKING FOR AND REPORTING INFORMATION

Will *Ms. Martinez return soon*?
 Yes, *she* will.
 No, *she* won't.

Will you *be home this evening*?
 Yes, I will. I'll be *watching videos*.
 No, I won't. I'll be *working overtime*.

Will *the play* begin soon?
Will *the train* arrive soon?

How much longer will you be *doing homework*?
 I'll probably be *doing homework* for another *30* minutes.

What are you looking forward to?

What's the weather forecast?

Do you know anybody who does?

Tell me, *Milton*, _____.

INQUIRING ABOUT INTENTION

What are you going to do?
What are you going to do *this weekend*?
What are you going to *buy*?

Are you going to *buy a donut this morning*?

EXPRESSING INTENTION

I'm going to *buy a muffin*.

I'll *call you in 30 minutes*.
I'll *call him* right away.

EXPRESSING PROBABILITY

I'll probably be *doing homework for another 30 minutes*.

REQUESTING

Could you do me a favor?
Could you possibly do me a favor?
Could you do a favor for me?
Could I ask you a favor?

Could I possibly *borrow yours*?

64 CHAPTER 3

RESPONDING TO REQUESTS

Sure. What is it?

GREETING PEOPLE

Hi, _____. This is _____.

Can you talk for a minute?
   I'm sorry. I can't talk right now. I'm *doing homework*. Can you call back a little later?

LEAVE-TAKING

Well, have a nice weekend.
   You, too.

Speak to you soon.
   Good-bye.

APOLOGIZING

I'm sorry.

EXPRESSING INABILITY

I'm sorry. I can't *talk right now*.

EXPRESSING OBLIGATION

I have to *fix a flat tire*.

ADMITTING

I'm afraid *I don't have one*.

OFFERING ADVICE

You should *call Joe*.

EXPRESSING CERTAINTY

I'm sure *he'll be happy to lend you his*.

EXPRESSING GRATITUDE

Thanks.

NEW VOCABULARY

Time Expressions

a little later
for a long time
last *January*
last *spring*
last *Sunday*
next *January*
next *spring*
next *Sunday*
this *Friday night*
this *January*
this *spring*
this *Sunday*

Free Time

day off
retirement
summer vacation

Verbs

adjust
browse the web
call back
come back
do research
give *the kids* a bath
go water-skiing
ice skate
relax
say good-bye
stay with
work out

Adverbs

perhaps
permanently
possibly

Adjectives

emotional
excited
lonely

Music

Broadway show tunes
folk songs

Foods

onion soup
pea soup

Subjects

astronomy
biology

Superheroes

Batman
Superman

Miscellaneous

Channel
composition
Europe
favor
flight
Halloween
income tax form
jack
jail
meeting
plan (n)
screwdriver
semester
tree house

EXPRESSIONS

as you can imagine
Fine.
have a good life
Have a nice weekend.
have a party for
look forward to
Speak to you soon.

CHAPTER 3   **65**

Text Page 21: Chapter Opening Page

VOCABULARY PREVIEW

You may want to introduce these time expressions before beginning the chapter, or you may choose to wait until they first occur in a specific lesson. If you choose to introduce them at this point, here are some suggestions:

1. Have students look at the illustrations on text page 21 and identify the time expressions they already know.

2. Present the vocabulary. Say each time expression and have the class repeat it chorally and individually. Check students' understanding and pronunciation.

3. Practice the vocabulary as a class, in pairs, or in small groups. Have students cover the word list and look at the pictures. Practice the time expressions in the following ways:

   To practice time expressions for *yesterday*, ask about 1, 4, 7, 10.
   To practice time expressions for *today*, ask about 2, 5, 8, 11.
   To practice time expressions for *tomorrow*, ask about 3, 6, 9, 12.

   To practice *morning* time expressions, ask about 1, 2, 3.
   To practice *afternoon* time expressions, ask about 4, 5, 6.
   To practice *evening* time expressions, ask about 7, 8, 9.
   To practice *night* time expressions, ask about 10, 11, 12.

   - Say a time expression and have students tell the number of the illustration.
   - Give the number of an illustration and have students say the time expression.

4. For further practice, ask about the situations that are depicted:

   Situations 1–3—morning:

   What did they do yesterday morning?
   Where are they this morning?
   Where are they going to be tomorrow morning?

   Situations 4–6—afternoon:

   What did he do yesterday afternoon?
   What's he doing this afternoon?
   What's going to happen tomorrow afternoon?

   Situations 7–9—evening:

   What did they do yesterday evening?
   What's happening this evening?
   What are they going to do tomorrow evening?

   Situations 10–12—night:

   What happened last night?
   What's happening tonight?
   Where are they going to be tomorrow night?

Text Pages 22–23: What Are They Going to Do?

FOCUS

- Review: Future: Going to
- Contrast: Future and Past Tenses
- Contrast: Future and Past Time Expressions

CLOSE UP

RULE: *Going to* + verb is used to express future plans or intentions.

EXAMPLES: I'm **going to buy** a muffin.
She's **going to sing** Broadway show tunes.
We're **going to go** to Hawaii.
They're **going to watch** the news program.

GETTING READY

Review time expressions and contracted forms with *going to*.

1. Have students look at the list of time expressions on text page 22 as you read the examples below.

   George couldn't go shopping yesterday.
   He's going to go shopping TODAY.

   Jane didn't study last night.
   She's going to study TONIGHT.

   It isn't going to rain this week.
   It's going to rain NEXT week.

2. Read the statements below and call on students to respond following the pattern above, using *going to* and a corresponding future time expression.

   Mr. and Mrs. Mason didn't come home from their vacation yesterday.
   Marylou didn't clean her apartment last week.
   David can't write to his girlfriend this week.
   Shirley couldn't take a trip last year.
   We didn't study very hard last month.
   Mr. Davis didn't visit his son last spring.
   Jim and Bob aren't going to study today.
   Bill didn't come to work last Monday.
   Gloria couldn't go skiing last January.
   Our neighbors didn't have a party yesterday.

INTRODUCING THE MODEL

1. Have students look at the model illustration.
2. Set the scene: "Two friends are talking."
3. Present the model.
4. Full-Class Repetition.

   Pronunciation Note

   The pronunciation focus of Chapter 3 is **Going to** (text page 32). Tell students that this is very common in informal speech. You may wish to model this pronunciation at this point and encourage students to incorporate it into their language practice.

   Are you "gonna" buy a donut this morning?
   I'm "gonna" buy a muffin.

5. Ask students if they have any questions. Check understanding of vocabulary.
6. Group Choral Repetition.
7. Choral Conversation.
8. Call on one or two pairs of students to present the dialog.

   (For additional practice, do Choral Conversation in small groups or by rows.)

CHAPTER 3 67

SIDE BY SIDE EXERCISES

Examples

> 1. A. Is Mr. Hopper going to have cake for dessert tonight?
>   B. No, he isn't. He had cake for dessert LAST night.
>   A. What's he going to have?
>   B. He's going to have ice cream.
> 2. A. Is Valerie going to sing folk songs this evening?
>   B. No, she isn't. She sang folk songs YESTERDAY evening.
>   A. What's she going to sing?
>   B. She's going to sing Broadway show tunes.

1. **Exercise 1:** Call on two students to present the dialog. Then do Choral Repetition and Choral Conversation practice.
2. **Exercise 2:** Introduce the expressions *folk songs, Broadway show tunes*. Same as above.

   ### Culture Notes

   Folk songs are traditional songs of ordinary country people. They are usually accompanied by instruments such as a guitar, banjo, or harmonica.

   Broadway show tunes are songs from musical productions that have been performed in theaters in the Broadway area of New York City.

3. **Exercises 3–10:** Either Full-Class Practice or Pair Practice.

New Vocabulary

3. Europe
4. Channel
   this Friday night
7. onion soup
   pea soup
8. biology
   semester
   astronomy
10. Superman
    Halloween
    Batman

Culture Notes

Exercise 10: *Superman* is a superhero who saves people in trouble. He can fly, see through objects, and hear sound from very far away. He wears a large *S* on his red, yellow, and blue costume.

Batman is a futuristic superhero who saves the world from bad people. A cave under his house is equipped with special technology. Batman has a special vehicle that can move very fast. His black and gray costume resembles a bat.

Halloween is a popular holiday in the United States. It takes place on October 31st. Children dress up as their favorite characters and go door to door asking for candy. If children don't receive candy, they play tricks on people.

WORKBOOK

Pages 24–26

EXPANSION ACTIVITIES

1. **Memory Chain** ★★

   a. Divide the class into groups of 5 or 6 students each.

   b. Have students answer the question *What are you going to do tomorrow?*

   c. One group at a time, have Student 1 begin. For example:

   > I'm going to have dinner at my favorite restaurant.

   d. Student 2 repeats what Student 1 said and adds a statement about himself or herself. For example:

   > Maria is going to have dinner at her favorite restaurant, and I'm going to go bowling.

   e. Student 3 continues in the same way. For example:

   > Maria is going to have dinner at her favorite restaurant, Edward is going to go bowling, and I'm going to visit my grandparents.

   f. Continue until everyone has had a chance to play the *memory chain*.

2. **Sense or Nonsense?** ★★

   a. Divide the class into four groups.

   b. Make four sets of split sentence cards with beginnings and endings of sentences. For example:

I'm not going to have cake for dessert, . . .	I'm going to have pie.
I'm not going to sing folk songs, . . .	I'm going to sing show tunes.
I'm not going to take biology this semester, . . .	I'm going to take astronomy.
I'm not going to play chess this afternoon, . . .	I'm going to play cards.
I'm not going to make soup today, . . .	I'm going to make stew.
I'm not going to wear a suit today, . . .	I'm going to wear jeans.
I'm not going to plant vegetables this year, . . .	I'm going to plant flowers.
I'm not going to go out with my friends, . . .	I'm going to go out with my cousins.
I'm not going to go to Europe this summer, . . .	I'm going to go to Canada.

   c. Mix up the cards and distribute sets of cards to each group, keeping the beginning and ending cards in different piles.

   d. Have students take turns picking up one card from each pile and reading the sentence to the group. For example:

I'm not going to take biology this semester, . . .	I'm going to sing show tunes.

   e. That group decides if the sentence makes *sense* or is *nonsense*.

   f. After all the cards have been picked, have the groups lay out all the cards and put together all the sentence combinations that make sense.

3. **Concentration** ★★

   a. Use the cards from the above activity. Place them face down in three rows of 6 each.

   b. Divide the class into two teams. The object of the game is for students to find the

   (continued)

CHAPTER 3 69

EXPANSION ACTIVITIES (Continued)

matching cards. Both teams should be able to see all the cards since *concentrating* on their location is an important part of playing the game.

c. A student from Team 1 turns over two cards. If they match, the student picks up the cards, that team gets a point, and the student takes another turn. If the cards don't match, the student turns them face down, and a member of Team 2 takes a turn.

d. The game continues until all the cards have been matched. The team with the most correct matches wins the game.

Variation: This game can also be played in groups or pairs.

4. Expand the Sentence ★★

Tell students that the object of the activity is to build a long sentence on the board, one word at a time.

a. Call on a student to write a pronoun or someone's name on the far left side of the board. For example:

> Jennifer

b. Have another student come to the board and add a word. For example:

> Jennifer isn't

c. Have a third student add a third word. For example:

> Jennifer isn't going

d. Continue until each student in the class has had one or more turns to add a word to expand the sentence into the longest one they can think of. For example:

> Jennifer isn't going to go to work today because she has a terrible sore throat, and she thinks she should go to the clinic to see her doctor instead.

5. You Just Did That! ★★

a. Put the following on the board:

> A. I'm going to _____ tomorrow.
> B. But you _____ last week!
> A. I know. But I'm going to _____ again.
> B. Why are you going to do that?
> A. _____.

b. Put the following cues on the board or on word cards that you can distribute to students:

> paint my ____
> fly to ____
> go to ____
> visit ____
> drive to ____
> go ____ing
> take a ____ to ____
> have ____ for dessert
> ride my bicycle to ____
> write a letter to ____
> complain about ____

c. Divide the class into pairs and have students create conversations based on the model on the board and the cues. Encourage students to expand their conversations any way they wish. For example:

> A. I'm going to paint my kitchen tomorrow.
> B. But you painted your kitchen last week!
> A. I know. But I'm going to paint my kitchen again.
> B. Why are you going to do that?
> A. Because I don't like the color.

A. I'm going to fly to Rio tomorrow.
B. But you flew to Rio last week!
A. I know. But I'm going to fly to Rio again.
B. Why are you going to do that?
A. I'm going to meet a friend and travel around Brazil.

6. Find the Right Person! ★★★

a. Write the following times on the board:

after class
tonight
this weekend

b. On a separate piece of paper, have students write three sentences about plans they have, using the time expressions on the board. For example:

> I'm going to have lunch after class.
> I'm going to watch TV tonight.
> I'm going to see a movie this weekend.

c. Collect the papers and distribute them randomly to different students in the class.

d. Have each student interview others (for example: "What are you going to do tonight?" "Are you going to see a movie this weekend?") in order to find out whose plans match those on his or her particular card.

e. Once everybody has identified the correct person, call on students to tell about the people on their cards. For example:

> Thomas is going to go home after class.
> He's going to study tonight.
> He's going to visit his cousins this weekend.

7. Class Story ★★★

a. Begin by saying "The Jones family is going to take a very exciting trip next summer. They're going to travel around the world."

b. Student 1 begins the story. For example: "First, they're going to go to Europe."

c. Student 2 continues. For example: "They're going to spend a week in London."

d. Continue around the room in this fashion, with each student telling more about the Jones family trip.

CHAPTER 3   71

Text Page 24

 READING *Plans for the Weekend*

FOCUS

- Future: Going to

NEW VOCABULARY

go water-skiing
plan (n)
tree house

READING THE STORY

Optional: Preview the story by having students talk about the story title and/or illustration. You may choose to introduce new vocabulary beforehand, or have students encounter the new vocabulary within the context of the reading.

1. Have students read silently or follow along silently as the story is read aloud by you, by one or more students, or on the audio program.

2. Ask students if they have any questions. Check understanding of vocabulary.

   Language Note

   To rain cats and dogs means to rain very hard.

3. Check students' comprehension, using some or all of the following questions:

   What's Milton going to do this weekend?
   What's Diane going to do?
   What are Carmen and Tom going to do?
   What's Jack going to do?
   What's Kate going to do?
   What are Ray and his family going to do?
   Why are they all going to be disappointed?

✓ READING *CHECK-UP*

Q & A

1. Call on a pair of students to present the model.

2. Ask students if they have any questions. Check understanding of the expression *Have a nice weekend*.

3. Have students work in pairs to create new dialogs.

4. Call on pairs to present their new dialogs to the class.

READING EXTENSION

Have students answer the following questions in groups and then share their ideas with the class:

   What are all the activities the employees at the Liberty Insurance Company want to do?
   What season of the year is it in the story?
   What are some popular outdoor activities for summer?
   What are some popular outdoor activities for fall?
   What are some popular outdoor activities for winter?
   What are some popular outdoor activities for spring?

How About You?

Have students answer the questions in pairs or as a class. If you do it as pair practice, call on students to report to the class about their conversation partner.

 **LISTENING**

Listen to the conversation and choose the answer that is true.

1. A. Are you going to wear your brown suit today?
   B. No, I don't think so. I wore my brown suit yesterday. I'm going to wear my gray suit.

2. A. Let's make beef stew for dinner!
   B. But we had that last week. Let's make spaghetti and meatballs instead.
   A. Okay.

3. A. Do you want to watch the game show on Channel 5 or the news program on Channel 9?
   B. Let's watch the news program.

4. A. What's the matter with it?
   B. The brakes don't work, and it doesn't start very well in the morning.

5. A. What are you going to do tomorrow?
   B. I'm going to plant carrots, tomatoes, and lettuce.

6. A. This computer is very powerful, but it's too expensive.
   B. You're right.

Answers

1. a
2. a
3. b
4. a
5. b
6. b

CHAPTER 3   73

Text Page 25: Will Ms. Martinez Return Soon?

FOCUS

- Review: Future Tense: Will

CLOSE UP

RULE:	The future tense with *will* expresses a predictable or expected future event.
EXAMPLES:	Will the play begin soon? Yes, **it will**. **It'll** begin at 7:30.
	Will Flight 216 arrive soon? No, **it won't**. **It won't** arrive for several hours.
RULE:	*Will* does not contract with subject pronouns in short answers.
EXAMPLES:	Will Ms. Martinez return soon? Yes, **she will**. (**She'll** return in a little while.)
	Will Ken and Kim see each other again soon? Yes, **they will**. (**They'll** see each other again this Saturday night.)

GETTING READY

Review *will* and *won't*.

1. Write the following on the board:

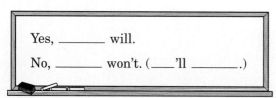

2. Ask Yes/No questions about some predictable future event in your students' lives. Have students respond, using any of the forms on the board. For example:

   Will we finish class at *(12 o'clock)*?
   Yes, we will.

   Will class start at *(9 o'clock)* tomorrow?
   No, it won't. It'll start at *(10 o'clock)*.

   Will you come to school *(next Sunday)*?
   No, I won't. I'll come to school *(next Monday)*.

INTRODUCING THE MODELS

There are two model conversations. Introduce and practice each separately. For each model:

1. Have students look at the model illustration.
2. Set the scene:

   1st model: "Someone is asking about Ms. Martinez."
   2nd model: "Two friends are talking."

3. Present the model.
4. Full-Class Repetition.
5. Ask students if they have any questions. Check understanding of new vocabulary:

   2nd model: *for a long time*

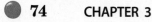

6. Group Choral Repetition.

7. Choral Conversation.

8. Call on one or two pairs of students to present the dialog.

   (For additional practice, do Choral Conversation in small groups or by rows.)

SIDE BY SIDE EXERCISES

Examples

1. A. Will the play begin soon?
   B. Yes, it will. It'll begin at 7:30.
2. A. Will the concert begin soon?
   B. No, it won't. It won't begin until 8:00.

1. **Exercise 1:** Call on two students to present the dialog. Then do Choral Repetition and Choral Conversation practice.
2. **Exercise 2:** Same as above.
3. **Exercises 3–8:** Either Full-Class Practice or Pair Practice.

New Vocabulary
6. flight
8. jail

WORKBOOK

Page 27

EXPANSION ACTIVITIES

1. **Can You Hear the Difference?** ★

   a. Write on the board:

Present	Future
They return at 7:00.	They'll return at 7:00.
I get out soon.	I'll get out soon.
You see each other every day.	You'll see each other every day.
We call each other.	We'll call each other.

   b. Choose a sentence randomly from one of the two columns and say it to the class. Have the class listen and identify whether the sentence is in the *present* or in the *future*.

   c. Have students continue the activity in pairs. One student says a sentence, and the other identifies the tense. Then have them reverse roles.

   d. Write other similar sentences on the board and continue the practice.

2. **Information Gap Handouts** ★★

   a. Tell students: "Ken and Kim plan to see each other this Saturday night." Write out their plans, but divide the information between two different charts. For example:

   Chart A:

6:00	
6:30	eat in a fancy restaurant
7:30	walk to the theater
8:00	
11:00	go out for dessert
12:00	

   Chart B:

6:00	take a taxi downtown
6:30	
7:30	
8:00	see a Broadway play
11:00	
12:00	make plans for their next date

   (continued)

CHAPTER 3

EXPANSION ACTIVITIES (Continued)

b. Divide the class into pairs. Give each member of the pair a different chart. Have students share their information and fill in their charts. For example:

Student A: What will they do at 6:00?
Student B: They'll take a taxi downtown.
Student A: [writes the information in Chart A]

c. The pairs continue until each has a complete chart.

d. Have students look at their partner's chart to make sure that they have written the information correctly.

3. At the Office ★★

a. Write the following on the board:

> A. Hello, _____. May I help you?
> B. Yes. Is _____ in?
> A. I'm sorry. _____ isn't in the office right now.
> B. When do you think _____'ll be back?
> A. _____'ll probably be back in _____.
> B. Thank you very much. I'll call back later.
> A. You're welcome. Good-bye.

b. Divide the class into pairs and have students role play the telephone conversation. Students can use any names and time expressions they wish.

c. Give Speaker A in each pair a card showing the name of a business, such as those below. Encourage students to make up other names of businesses if they wish.

Carlson Computers
Smith Tire Company
Gold Star Travel
Sure Technology Company
Wilson Trucking
Presto Furniture
Rock Village Apartments
Real Engineering Corporation
True Insurance Company
Big Boy Paper Company
Goodman's Department Store
Dr. Peterson's Office

d. Call on pairs to present their conversations to the class without referring to the model on the board. For example:

A. Hello, Carlson Computers. May I help you?
B. Yes. Is Ms. Blake in?
A. I'm sorry. She isn't in the office right now.
B. When do you think she'll be back?
A. She'll probably be back in a few hours.
B. Thank you very much. I'll call back later.
A. You're welcome. Good-bye.

4. Question the Answers! ★★

a. Dictate answers such as the following to the class:

Yes, he will. He'll get out in a week.
Yes, she will. She'll return in an hour.
No, it won't. It won't arrive for several hours.
Don't worry. They'll be back soon.
No, they won't. They won't see each other for several weeks.

b. Have students write questions for which these answers would be correct. For example:

Answer: Yes, he will. He'll get out in a week.
Question: Will your brother get out of the hospital soon?

Answer: Yes, she will. She'll return in an hour.
Question: Will Ms. Parker return to her office soon?

c. Have students compare their questions with each other.

Variation: Write the answers on cards. Divide the class into groups and give each group a set of cards.

5. Jigsaw Contest: When Will They Get Home? ★★★

a. Divide the class into groups of four. Give each member of the group one of these cards:

- Larry won't get home for four hours
- John won't get home until 4:00.

CHAPTER 3

- It's now 1:00.
- Ralph will get home an hour before John.

- Lisa will get home in an hour.
- Julie will get home at the same time as John.

- Valerie will arrive an hour after Larry gets home.
- David will get home at the same time as Lisa.

b. Have students share their information to create the correct schedule. Answer Key:

It's now 1:00.
Lisa and David will get home at 2:00.
Ralph will get home at 3:00.
John and Julie will get home at 4:00.
Larry will get home at 5:00.
Valerie will arrive at 6:00.

c. The first group to finish wins.

6. Mystery Conversations ★★★

a. Divide the class into pairs.

b. Write the following conversation framework on the board:

A. Will _____ soon?
B. No, ___ won't. ___ won't _____ until _____.

c. Write roles such as the following on word cards and give one to each pair of students:

| a parent and a child | a boss and an employee |

a teacher and a student	a mechanic and a car owner
a soccer coach and a player	a doctor and a patient
a wife and a husband	a ballet teacher and a dancer

d. Have each pair create a short dialog that begins "Will _____ soon?" The dialogs should be appropriate for the roles the students have on their cards.

e. Have each pair present their dialog to the class. Then have the other students guess who the people are: Are they married? Is a teacher talking to a student? For example:

[soccer coach–player]
A. Will I play in the game soon?
B. No, you won't. You won't play until the second half of the game.

7. Predictions for the Future ★★★

a. Divide the class into pairs or small groups.

b. Have students write predictions for the future and then discuss them with the class. For example:

We'll have a very hot summer this year.
(Maria) will be the president of her own company some day.
(George) will become a famous Hollywood movie star.
People will soon be able to fly in the air by themselves.
The world will be a safer place in the future.

CHAPTER 3   77

Text Page 26: Will You Be Home This Evening?

FOCUS

- Review: Future Continuous Tense

CLOSE UP

RULE: The future continuous tense emphasizes the ongoing nature or duration of an activity in the future.

EXAMPLES: Will you be home this evening?
Yes, I will. **I'll be watching** videos *(this evening)*.

Will Frank be home this evening?
Yes, he will. He**'ll be paying** bills *(this evening)*.

GETTING READY

Review the future continuous tense.

1. Write on the board:

Mr. Davis	Spanish
Mrs. Davis	Arabic
Betty and Fred Davis	Russian
Martha Davis	Chinese
Bob Davis	German

2. Set the scene: "Everyone in the Davis family loves languages. This year they'll all be studying new languages. For example, Mr. Davis will be studying Spanish."

3. Have students ask and answer about the others, using the future continuous tense. For example:

   A. What will Mrs. Davis be studying?
   B. She'll be studying Arabic.

   A. What will Bob Davis be studying?
   B. He'll be studying German.

   A. Martha, what will you be studying?
   B. I'll be studying Chinese.

INTRODUCING THE MODELS

There are two model conversations. Introduce and practice each separately. For each model:

1. Have students look at the model illustration in the book.

2. Set the scene:

   1st model: "Two friends are talking."
   2nd model: "Two people are talking about Nancy."

3. Present the model.

4. Full-Class Repetition.

5. Ask students if they have any questions. Check understanding of vocabulary.

   ### Culture Note

   Work overtime. Employees often have to work after their scheduled hours in order to finish a project or meet a deadline. This extra work time is called *overtime*. When employees are paid by the hour, they receive a higher rate for their overtime work.

6. Group Choral Repetition.

CHAPTER 3

7. Choral Conversation.

8. Call on one or two pairs of students to present the dialog.

   (For additional practice, do Choral Conversation in small groups or by rows.)

SIDE BY SIDE EXERCISES

Examples

1. A. Will you be home this evening?
   B. Yes, I will. I'll be paying bills.
2. A. Will Angela be home this evening?
   B. No, she won't. She'll be shopping at the mall.

1. **Exercise 1:** Call on two students to present the dialog. Then do Choral Repetition and Choral Conversation practice.
2. **Exercise 2:** Same as above.
3. **Exercises 3–9:** Either Full–Class Practice or Pair Practice.

New Vocabulary

4. meeting
5. ice skate
6. browse the web
7. do research
8. income tax form
9. work out

Culture Note

Exercise 8: Federal income taxes in the United States are due on April 15th of every year. Many people fill out the forms themselves, while others hire an accountant to fill out these forms for them.

WORKBOOK

Pages 28–29

EXPANSION ACTIVITIES

1. **What Will They Be Doing?** ★★
   a. Have the class listen as you tell about people who are getting new jobs or changing jobs.
   b. Then call on several students to tell what the person will be doing in his or her new job. Whenever possible, hold up a visual for the occupation as you talk about it. (You can use *Side by Side* Picture Cards 131–140.) For example:

      Jane will start her new job as an English teacher next week.

      Possible responses:

      She'll be going to school every day.
      She'll be teaching English.
      She'll be speaking English to students.

   Other possible introductions:

      (Larry) just got a new job as a (truck driver). He'll start his new job next month.
      A company just hired (Marie) as a (secretary). She'll start work next Monday.
      (John) studied (cooking) for several years. A very good (restaurant) just hired him to be the (chef).
      (Susan) is a (plumber). She'll start her first job soon.

2. **Writing Predictions: Five Years from Now** ★★
   a. Write on the board:

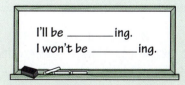

(continued)

CHAPTER 3   79

EXPANSION ACTIVITIES (Continued)

b. On a separate piece of paper, have each student use the patterns on the board to write a short prediction of what he or she will be doing five years from now. For example:

> Five years from now, I'll be living in Mexico City. I won't be studying English anymore. I'll be working for a large import-export company.

c. Collect the papers and read them aloud. Have the class guess which student wrote each prediction.

3. Find the Right Person ★★

a. Collect information about students' plans for a specific time later in the day (for example: *What will you be doing today at six o'clock?*).

b. Put this information in the following form:

> Find someone who . . .
> 1. will be doing research. _____
> 2. will be working out. _____
> 3. will be studying English. _____
> 4. will be driving home. _____
> 5. will be eating dinner. _____

c. Have students circulate around the room, asking each other information questions to identify the above people. For example:

> Student A: What will you be doing today at six o'clock?
> Student B: I'll be working out. How about you?

d. The first student to identify all the people wins.

4. Change the Sentence! ★★

a. Write a sentence on the board, underlining and numbering different portions of the sentence. For example:

> 1   2   3   4
> I'll be   watching   videos   this evening.

b. Have students sit in a circle.

c. Tell them that when you say a number, the first student in the circle makes a change in that part of the sentence. For example:

> Teacher: Two.
> Student 1: I'll be <u>buying</u> videos this evening.

d. The second student keeps the first student's sentence, but changes it based on the next number you say. For example:

> Teacher: Three.
> Student 2: I'll be buying <u>ice cream</u> this evening.

e. Continue this way with the rest of the students in the circle. For example:

> Teacher: Four.
> Student 3: I'll be buying ice cream <u>this afternoon</u>.

5. Memory Chain ★★

a. Divide the class into groups of 5 or 6 students each.

b. Tell each student to say what he or she will be doing tonight.

c. One group at a time, have Student 1 begin. For example:

> I'll be watching TV.

d. Student 2 repeats what Student 1 said and adds a statement about himself or herself. For example:

> Jane will be watching TV, and I'll be visiting my aunt in the hospital.

e. Student 3 continues in the same way. For example:

> Jane will be watching TV, Albert will be visiting his aunt in the hospital, and I'll be studying in the library.

f. Continue until everyone has had a chance to play the *memory chain*.

6. Likely or Unlikely? ★★★

a. Write the following on the board:

likely?
unlikely?

b. Make statements such as the following and have students tell you whether the statements are *likely* or *unlikely*:

> Fred will be watching TV at home tonight.
> Sally will be swimming in her office tomorrow morning.
> We'll be browsing the web at the bakery this afternoon.
> Mr. and Mrs. Chang will be planting flowers in their yard tomorrow.
> I'll be ice skating in my living room tonight.
> The president will be meeting several important people tomorrow.
> The electrician will be fixing our bathtub tomorrow morning.
> I'll be doing research at the library today.
> We'll be working at the office all day.
> Bob will be working out at the meeting this afternoon.

Variation: Divide the class into pairs or small groups and have students make up statements for others to react to.

Text Page 27: Can You Call Back a Little Later?

FOCUS

- Review: Future Continuous Tense

INTRODUCING THE MODEL

1. Have students look at the model illustration.
2. Set the scene: "Two friends are talking on the telephone."
3. Present the model, using any names, activity, and time expression you wish.
4. Full-Class Repetition.
5. Ask students if they have any questions. Check understanding of new vocabulary: *a little later, call back, Fine., Speak to you soon.*
6. Group Choral Repetition.
7. Choral Conversation.
8. Call on one or two pairs of students to present the dialog.

   (For additional practice, do Choral Conversation in small groups or by rows.)

SIDE BY SIDE EXERCISES

Examples

1. A. Hi, *(Karen)*. This is *(Bill)*. Can you talk for a minute?
   B. I'm sorry. I can't talk right now. I'm doing homework. Can you call back a little later?
   A. Sure. How much longer will you be doing homework?
   B. I'll probably be doing homework for another *(twenty)* minutes.
   A. Fine. I'll call you in *(twenty)* minutes.
   B. Speak to you soon.
   A. Good-bye.

2. A. Hi, *(Tim)*. This is *(Frank)*. Can you talk for a minute?
   B. I'm sorry. I can't talk right now. I'm ironing. Can you call back a little later?
   A. Sure. How much longer will you be ironing?
   B. I'll probably be ironing for another *(thirty)* minutes.
   A. Fine. I'll call you in *(thirty)* minutes.
   B. Speak to you soon.
   A. Good-bye.

1. **Exercise 1:** Call on two students to present the dialog. Then do Choral Repetition and Choral Conversation practice.
2. **Exercise 2:** Same as above.
3. **Exercises 3–5:** Either Full-Class Practice or Pair Practice.

New Vocabulary

5. give the kids a bath

4. **Exercise 6:** Have students use the model as a guide to create their own conversations, using vocabulary of their choice. Encourage students to use dictionaries to find new words they want to use. This exercise can be done orally in class or for written homework. If you assign it for homework, do one example in class to make sure students understand what's expected. Have students present their conversations in class the next day.

WORKBOOK

Page 30

EXPANSION ACTIVITIES

1. Disappearing Dialog ★

a. Write the model conversation on the board, using any names, time expression, and activity you wish.

b. Ask for two student volunteers to read the conversation.

c. Erase a few of the words from each line of the dialog. Have two different students read the conversation.

d. Erase more words and call on two more students to read the conversation.

e. Continue erasing words and calling on pairs of students to say the model until all the words have been erased and the dialog has *disappeared*.

2. Students' Plans ★★

a. Write the following on the board:

> What will you be doing next summer?
> What will you be studying next semester?

b. Divide the class into pairs or small groups.

c. Have students answer the questions on the board and then report to the class about each other's plans.

3. Information Gap Role Plays ★★★

a. Divide the class into pairs.

b. Write the following situations on index cards and give one of the situations to each pair. Give Role A to one member of the pair and Role B to the other.

c. Have students practice their role plays and then present them to the class. Compare different students' versions of the same situations.

Role A:

Your car is at the repair shop. Call the mechanic. You want to find out when your car will be ready. You need to have your car right away.

Role B:

You're a mechanic at a repair shop. Someone is going to call you about his or her car. You're still working on it. You found a lot of problems with the car.

Role A:

Call your friend. You really need to talk to her. It's very important. Someone else is going to answer the phone.

Role B:

Someone is calling your daughter, but she's busy now. She's fixing her bicycle. Then she has to study for a test.

Role A:

You're going to be late for work this morning. You have a flat tire, and you're fixing it right now. Call your boss from your cell phone.

Role B:

One of your employees is going to call you. This person is late for work, and you're very upset. This person needs to be at an important meeting.

Role A:

It's late. You made dinner for your wife and children, but your wife isn't home yet. Call her at the office.

Role B:

Your husband is going to call you. It's late, but you're very busy at your office. You still have to do a lot of things.

(continued)

CHAPTER 3   83

EXPANSION ACTIVITIES (Continued)

4. **Celebrity Travel Plans: Who Am I?** ★★★

   a. Divide the class into small groups.

   b. Give each person a card with the name of a famous person. For example:

   c. Write the following cues on the board:

   | I'll be _____ ing. |

   leave _____ for _____
   meet with _____
   go to _____
   visit _____
   talk to _____
   have lunch/dinner with _____
   return to _____

   d. Have each group work together, choosing expressions from the board, to write imaginary travel plans for the person on their card.

   e. When the groups have finished, call on one person to read each group's itinerary and have the other students in the class try to guess who the famous person is. For example:

   > Tonight I'll be leaving Washington for Miami. Tomorrow morning I'll be meeting with local politicians. In the afternoon, I'll be talking to the mayor about problems of the city. Then I'll be returning to Washington. Who am I?

Text Pages 28-29: Could You Do Me a Favor?

FOCUS

- Review: Possessive Pronouns
- Review: Should
- Review: Requests with *Could*

GETTING READY

Review possessive pronouns.

1. Write on the board:

2. Read statements such as those below and point to one of the three illustrations on the board. Have students make a similar statement about the person or people you are pointing to, using the possessive pronoun. For example:

   Teacher: I lost my wallet
   (point to Doris)
   Students: Doris lost hers, too.

   Teacher: I lost my book.
   (point to Steve)
   Students: Steve lost his, too.

Possible statements:

   I found my book.
   I lost my cat.
   I did well on the test.
   I like my job.
   I like my friends.
   I sold my bicycle.
   I called my boss.
   I want to sell my car.

INTRODUCING THE MODEL

1. Have students look at the model illustration.
2. Set the scene: "Two neighbors are talking. One of them is asking a favor."
3. Present the model.
4. Full-Class Repetition.
5. Ask students if they have any questions. Check understanding of new vocabulary and expressions: *Could you do me a favor? jack, possibly.*
6. Group Choral Repetition.
7. Choral Conversation.
8. Call on one or two pairs of students to present the dialog.

   (For additional practice, do Choral Conversation in small groups or by rows.)

SIDE BY SIDE EXERCISES

Examples

1. A. Could you do me a favor?
   B. Sure. What is it?
   A. I have to fix my front steps, and I don't have a hammer. Could I possibly borrow yours?
   B. I'm sorry. I'm afraid I don't have one.
   A. Oh. Do you know anyone who does?
   B. Yes. You should call Janet. I'm sure she'll be happy to lend you hers.
   A. Thanks. I'll call her right away.

2. A. Could you do me a favor?
   B. Sure. What is it?
   A. I have to assemble my new bookshelf, and I don't have a screwdriver. Could I possibly borrow yours?
   B. I'm sorry. I'm afraid I don't have one.
   A. Oh. Do you know anyone who does?
   B. Yes. You should call Bruce. I'm sure he'll be happy to lend you his.
   A. Thanks. I'll call him right away.

CHAPTER 3

1. **Exercise 1:** Call on two students to present the dialog. Then do Choral Repetition and Choral Conversation practice.
2. **Exercise 2:** Introduce the word *screwdriver*. Same as above.
3. **Exercises 3–5:** Either Full-Class Practice or Pair Practice.

> **New Vocabulary**
> 3. composition
> 4. adjust

4. **Exercise 6:** Have students use the model as a guide to create their own conversations, using vocabulary of their choice. Encourage students to use dictionaries to find new words they want to use. This exercise can be done orally in class or for written homework. If you assign it for homework, do one example in class to make sure students understand what's expected. Have students present their conversations in class the next day.

WORKBOOK

Pages 31–33

EXPANSION ACTIVITIES

1. **Different Emotions** ★★

   Have students practice reading the model conversation, using any combination of these different emotions:

   Speaker A is very worried.
   Speaker A isn't worried.
   Speaker B wants to help Speaker A.
   Speaker B isn't very friendly and doesn't want to help.

2. **Match the Conversations** ★★

   a. Make a set of matching cards. For example:

I have to assemble a desk.	I'll be happy to lend you my hammer and screwdriver.
I have to write a composition.	I'll be happy to lend you my dictionary.
I have to to a fancy party.	I'll be happy to lend you my tuxedo.
I have to adjust my TV antenna.	I'll be happy to lend you my ladder.
I have to change a flat tire.	I'll be happy to lend you my jack.
I have to move to my new apartment.	I'll be happy to lend you my truck.
I have to bake a cake for my friend's party.	I'll be happy to give you my recipe.

   b. Distribute a card to each student.

   c. Have students memorize the sentences on their cards, and then have students walk around the room saying their sentences until they find their match.

   d. Then have pairs of students say their matched sentences aloud to the class.

3. **Tic Tac Vocabulary** ★★

   a. Have students draw a tic tac grid and fill it in with any 9 of the following words:

camcorder	headphones
camera	jack
cell phone	ladder
cookbook	screwdriver
dictionary	tuxedo
fan	

   b. Say the beginnings of the following sentences, and tell students to cross out the word that finishes each sentence:

   It's very hot in my apartment. Could I possibly borrow your . . . ?

86 CHAPTER 3

I have to fix my satellite dish. Could I possibly borrow your . . . ?

I want to take photographs at our family reunion. Could I possibly borrow your . . . ?

My brother is going to a very fancy party. Could he possibly borrow your . . . ?

I've got to fix a flat tire on my car. Could I possibly borrow your . . . ?

I've got to write a composition for my English class. Could I possibly borrow your . . . ?

I'm looking for a good recipe for apple pie. Could I possibly borrow your . . . ?

I need to call my mother right away. Could I possibly borrow your . . . ?

I want to take videos at my daughter's wedding. Could I possibly borrow your . . . ?

I'm trying to assemble a new bookshelf. I have a hammer. Could I possibly borrow your . . . ?

I want to listen to some music on my CD player. Could I possibly borrow your . . . ?

c. The first student to cross out three words in a straight line—either horizontally, vertically, or diagonally—wins the game.

d. Have the winner call out the words to check for accuracy.

4. Information Gap Role Play: Could I Ask You a Favor? ★★★

a. Divide the class into pairs.

b. Write the following situations on index cards and give one situation to each pair. Give Role A to one member of the pair and Role B to the other.

c. Have students practice their role plays and then present them to the class. Compare different students' versions of the same situations.

Role A:
Your car is broken, and you need a ride to work today. Ask your friend.

Role B:
You aren't going to work today because you have a bad cold.

Role A:
Your car has a flat tire, and you can't find your jack. Ask your friend.

Role B:
Your sister borrowed your jack last week, and she forgot to return it.

Role A:
You're baking a cake, and you just realized you don't have any more flour! Your next-door neighbor is walking out of the building. Maybe your neighbor is going to the supermarket.

Role B:
You're walking out of your apartment building. First, you're going to the bank. Then you're going to the post office. After that, you're going to the drug store. And finally, you're going to the supermarket.

5. Category Dictation: Lending Practices ★★★

a. Have students draw two columns on a piece of paper. At the top of one column, have students write I'll be happy to lend you my . . . At the top of the other column, have them write I don't really like to lend my . . . .

b. Dictate items to the class. Tell the class to imagine lending each item to a close friend, and have students choose the appropriate column. For example:

I'll be happy to lend you my . . .	I don't really like to lend my . . .
bicycle	car
pen	cell phone
calculator	laptop computer

(continued)

CHAPTER 3

EXPANSION ACTIVITIES (Continued)

c. Have students compare their lists in small groups. Ask the class:

> What items are easy to lend?
> What items are difficult to lend?
> Why don't you like to lend these items to a friend?
> What do you do when a friend forgets to return an item?

b. Divide the class into small groups and have students discuss doing favors. Then call on students to tell about their discussions.

6. **Class Discussion** ★★★

a. Write the following questions on the board or on a handout for students:

> Do your friends or neighbors ever ask you to do a favor for them?
> How do you feel when someone asks you to do a favor?
> What was the biggest favor someone asked you to do? Tell about it.

How to Say It!

Asking for a Favor: There are many ways to request a favor. "Could you do me a favor?" "Could you possibly do me a favor?" "Could you do a favor for me?" "Could I ask you a favor?" are four common ways. The word *possibly* makes the request less direct and therefore more polite.

1. Set the scene: "The neighbors from text page 28 are talking."
2. Present the expressions.
3. Full-Class Repetition.
4. Ask students if they have any questions.
5. Group Choral Repetition.
6. Have student practice the conversations in this lesson again, asking for favors with any of these four expressions.
7. Call on pairs to present their conversations to the class.

Text Page 30

📖 READING *Saying Good-bye*

FOCUS

- Future Tense: Will
- Future Continuous Tense

NEW VOCABULARY

as you can imagine	lonely
Canada	perhaps
come back	permanently
emotional	say good-bye
excited	stay with
have a good life	Toronto

READING THE STORY

Optional: Preview the story by having students talk about the story title and/or illustrations. You may choose to introduce new vocabulary beforehand, or have students encounter the new vocabulary within the context of the reading.

1. Have students read silently or follow along silently as the story is read aloud by you, by one or more students, or on the audio program.

2. Ask students if they have any questions. Check understanding of vocabulary.

3. Check students' comprehension, using some or all of the following questions:

   Where are Mr. and Mrs. Karpov?
   What are they doing?
   What will Sasha and his family do in a few minutes?
   Why won't Mr. and Mrs. Karpov be seeing them for a long time?
   Where are Sasha and his family going to live?
   Who are they going to stay with?
   What will Sasha do?
   What will his wife, Marina, do?
   What will their children do?
   Why are Mr. and Mrs. Karpov happy?
   Why are Mr. and Mrs. Karpov sad?
   Why are they going to be lonely?
   What will Mr. and Mrs. Karpov do some day?

✓ READING *CHECK-UP*

TRUE OR FALSE?

1. False
2. True
3. False
4. True
5. False

READING EXTENSION

Class Discussion

1. Have students work in pairs to write several sentences in which they give advice to Sasha and Marina as they begin their new life in Canada. For example:

   They should try to learn English as quickly as possible.
   They should try to learn about their children's school.
   They should find a good doctor right away.

2. Have students share their sentences with the class and explain the rationale for their answers.

How About You?

Have students answer the questions in pairs or as a class. If you do it as pair practice, call on students to report to the class about their conversation partner.

CHAPTER 3   89

Text Page 31

 ON YOUR OWN *Looking Forward*

FOCUS

- Review: Going to

For each situation:

1. Have students look at the illustrations and cover the text as you read or play the audio.

2. Then have students look at the text and follow along as you read or play the audio again.

3. Ask students if they have any questions. Check understanding of new vocabulary: *have a party for, look forward to, relax, retirement, summer vacation.*

4. Ask questions about the situations and/or have students ask each other questions. For example:

    What's Jerry looking forward to?
    Is he going to think about work this weekend?
    What's he going to do?

    What's Amanda looking forward to?
    Why?
    Who's going to be at the party?

    What are Mr. and Mrs. Cook looking forward to?
    Where are they going to go?
    What are they going to do there?

    What are Mr. and Mrs. Lee looking forward to?
    Why?

5. Have students talk about what *they* are looking forward to.

    a. Check understanding of the expression *day off*.

    b. Divide the class into pairs. Have each student find out something the other is looking forward to and then report back to the class. For example:

        Barbara is looking forward to this weekend because she's going to go to her sister's wedding. She's looking forward to it because everybody in her family is going to be there.

        Richard is looking forward to his winter vacation because he's going to go skiing during the day and sit in front of a warm fireplace every evening.

 JOURNAL

Have students write their journal entries at home or in class. Encourage students to use a dictionary to look up words they would like to use. Students can share their written work with other students if appropriate. Have students discuss what they have written as a class, in pairs, or in small groups.

90 CHAPTER 3

Text Page 32

 PRONUNCIATION

Going to: In daily English usage, the pronunciation of the verb phrase *going to* is reduced to *gonna*.

Focus on Listening

Practice the sentences in the left column. Say each sentence or play the audio one or more times. Have students listen carefully and repeat.

Focus on Pronunciation

Practice the sentences in the right column. Have students say each sentence and then listen carefully as you say it or play the audio.

If you wish, have students continue practicing the sentences to improve their pronunciation.

WORKBOOK

Check-Up Test: Pages 34–35

 CHAPTER SUMMARY

GRAMMAR

1. Divide the class into pairs or small groups.
2. Have students take turns forming sentences from the words in the grammar boxes. Student A says a sentence, and Student B points to the words from each column that are in the sentence. Then have students switch: Student B says a sentence, and Student A points to the words.

KEY VOCABULARY

Have students ask you any questions about the meaning or pronunciation of the vocabulary. If students ask for the pronunciation, repeat after the student until the student is satisfied with his or her own pronunciation.

EXPANSION ACTIVITIES

1. Do You Remember the Words? ★

   Check students' retention of the vocabulary depicted on the opening page of Chapter 3 by doing the following activity:

   a. Have students open their books to page 21 and cover the list of time expressions.
   b. Either call out a number and have students tell you the time expression, or say a time expression and have students tell you the number.

   Variation: You can also do this activity as a game with competing teams.

2. Student-Led Dictation ★

   a. Tell each student to choose a word or phrase from the Key Vocabulary list on text page 32 and look at it very carefully.
   b. Have students take turns dictating their words to the class. Everybody writes down that student's word.
   c. When the dictation is completed, call on different students to write each word on the board to check the spelling.

3. Letter Game ★

   a. Divide the class into two teams.
   b. Say, "I'm thinking of a verb that starts with g."
   c. The first person to raise his or her hand and guess correctly [*give*] wins a point for his or her team.
   d. Continue with other letters of the alphabet and other verbs.

   The team that gets the most correct answers wins the game.

4. Miming ★

   a. Write on cards some of the actions and activities listed on text page 32.

   (continued)

CHAPTER 3   91

EXPANSION ACTIVITIES (Continued)

    b. Have students take turns picking a card from the pile and pantomiming the action on the card.

    c. The class must guess what the person is doing.

Variation: This can be done as a game with competing teams.

5. Finish the Sentence! ★★

Begin a sentence using the verbs listed on text page 32 and have students repeat what you said and add appropriate endings to the sentence. For example:

Teacher	Students
I'll assemble . . .	I'll assemble the furniture.
	I'll assemble the toy.
He'll browse . . .	He'll browse the web.
	He'll browse the Internet.
We'll paint . . .	We'll paint a picture.
	We'll paint the walls.
	We'll paint the house.

Variation: This activity may be done as a class, in pairs or small groups, or as a game with competing teams.

END-OF-CHAPTER ACTIVITIES

1. **Board Game** ★★★

    a. On poster boards or on manila file folders, make up game boards with a pathway consisting of separate spaces. You may use any theme or design you wish.

    b. Divide the class into groups of 2 to 4 students and give each group a game board and a die, and each student something to be used as a playing piece.

    c. Give each group a pile of cards face-down with statements written on them. Some sentences should be correct, and others incorrect. For example:

    > What will he going to do?
    > What will they doing tonight?
    > She's going to read.
    > That book is their.
    > Those tools are his.
    > They'll work tomorrow night.
    > She's going to go water-skiing.
    > That's our car. That's ours.
    > I'll be home. I'll be fix our TV.
    > Could you give me a favor?
    > I'm sure he'll be happy to borrow you his.
    > They're be seeing each other soon.
    > What's he will wear?
    > This is my screwdriver. This is mine.
    > Theirs going to be a retirement party for Mr. and Mrs. Lee.

    d. Each student in turn rolls the die, moves the playing piece along the game path, and after landing on a space, picks a card, reads the sentence, and says if it is *correct* or *incorrect*. If the statement is incorrect, the student must correct it. If the response is correct, the student takes an additional turn.

    e. The first student to reach the end of the pathway is the winner.

2. **Question Game** ★★★

    a. Write the following sentences on the board:

    > Nancy will be home this evening.
    > She'll be paying bills.

    b. Underline different elements of one of the sentences, and have students create a question based on that portion of the sentence. For example:

    > Nancy will be home <u>this evening</u>.
    > She'll be paying bills.

    When will Nancy be home?

    > Nancy will be <u>home</u> this evening.
    > She'll be paying bills.

    Where will Nancy be this evening?

    > Nancy will be home this evening.
    > She'll be <u>paying bills</u>.

    What will Nancy be doing this evening?

    c. Continue with other sentences.

3. **Dialog Builder** ★★★

    a. Divide the class into pairs.

    b. Write several lines on the board from several conversations such as the following:

    > Could you do a favor for me?
    > I'm sorry. I'm afraid I don't have one.
    > Thank you.
    > Speak to you soon.
    > Oh.
    > I'll call him right away.

    c. Have each pair create a conversation incorporating those lines. Students can begin and end their conversations any way they wish, but they must include those lines in their dialogs.

    d. Call on students to present their conversations to the class.

CHAPTER 3

WORKBOOK ANSWER KEY AND LISTENING SCRIPTS

WORKBOOK PAGE 24

A. WHAT ARE THEY SAYING?

1. No, I didn't.
   rode
   I'm going to ride
2. No, he didn't.
   wore
   He's going to wear
3. No, she didn't.
   gave
   She's going to give
4. No, they didn't.
   drove
   They're going to drive
5. No, we didn't.
   had
   We're going to have
6. No, I didn't.
   went
   I'm going to go
7. No, he didn't.
   wrote
   He's going to write
8. No, she didn't.
   left
   She's going to leave

WORKBOOK PAGES 25–26

B. BAD CONNECTIONS!

1. your dentist going to do
2. are you going to go
3. is she going to move to Alaska
4. What are they going to give you?
5. What are you going to do?
6. When are you going to get married?
7. Who are you going to meet?
8. What are you going to name your new puppy?
9. Why are they going to sell your house?
10. Where are you going to go?
11. Who do you have to call?
12. Why are you going to fire me?

C. LISTENING

Listen and choose the time of the action.

1. My daughter is going to sing Broadway show tunes in her high school show.
2. Janet bought a new dress for her friend's party.
3. Are you going to go out with George?
4. I went shopping at the new mall.
5. How did you poke yourself in the eye?
6. Who's going to prepare dinner?
7. Did the baby sleep well?
8. I'm really looking forward to Saturday night.
9. Is your son going to play games on his computer?
10. We're going to complain to the landlord about the heat in our apartment.
11. We bought a dozen donuts.
12. I'm going to take astronomy.

Answers

1. b   7. b
2. a   8. a
3. a   9. a
4. b   10. b
5. a   11. b
6. b   12. a

WORKBOOK PAGE 27

D. THE PESSIMIST AND THE OPTIMISTS

1. won't have   you will, You'll
2. will hurt   he won't, He won't
3. won't   she will, She'll
4. will be   she won't, She won't
5. won't lose   you will, You'll
6. will forget   they won't, They won't
7. won't fix   he will, He'll
8. won't   they will, They'll like
9. I'll   you won't, You won't

WORKBOOK PAGE 28

E. WHAT WILL BE HAPPENING?

1. she will, She'll be doing
2. I will, I'll be filling out
3. he won't, He'll be working out
4. they will, They'll be cleaning
5. he will, He'll be browsing
6. we will, We'll be watching
7. she won't, She'll be attending
8. it won't, It'll be raining

WORKBOOK PAGE 29

G. WHAT ARE THEY SAYING?

1. giving, will you be giving
2. will you be doing, be doing
3. talk, talk, studying
4. having/eating, will you be having/eating

94   CHAPTER 3

WORKBOOK PAGE 31

I. WHOSE IS IT?

1. yours
2. mine
3. his
4. hers
5. theirs
6. ours
7. hers
8. hers

WORKBOOK PAGES 32–33

K. WHAT DOES IT MEAN?

1. b	13. a
2. c	14. b
3. b	15. a
4. b	16. b
5. a	17. a
6. a	18. b
7. c	19. c
8. b	20. a
9. a	21. c
10. c	22. a
11. a	23. b
12. c	24. c

L. LISTENING: *Looking Forward*

Listen to each story. Then answer the questions.

What Are Mr. and Mrs. Miller Looking Forward to?

Mr. and Mrs. Miller moved into their new house in Los Angeles last week. They're happy because the house has a large, bright living room and a big, beautiful yard. They're looking forward to life in their new home. Every weekend they'll be able to relax in their living room and enjoy the beautiful California weather in their big, beautiful yard. But this weekend Mr. and Mrs. Miller won't be relaxing. They're going to be very busy. First, they're going to repaint the living room. Then, they're going to assemble their new computer and VCR. And finally, they're going to plant some flowers in their yard. They'll finally be able to relax NEXT weekend.

Answers

1. a
2. c
3. b

What's Jonathan Looking Forward to?

I'm so excited! I'm sitting at my computer in my office, but I'm not thinking about my work today. I'm thinking about next weekend because next Saturday is the day I'll be getting married. After the wedding, my wife and I will be going to Hawaii for a week. I can't wait! For one week, we won't be working, we won't be cooking, we won't be cleaning, and we won't be paying bills. We'll be swimming in the ocean, relaxing on the beach, and eating in fantastic restaurants.

Answers

4. b
5. c
6. b

What's Mrs. Grant Looking Forward to?

Mrs. Grant is going to retire this year, and she's really looking forward to her new life. She won't be getting up early every morning and taking the bus to work. She'll be able to sleep late every day of the week. She'll read books, she'll work in her garden, and she'll go to museums with her friends And she's very happy that she'll be able to spend more time with her grandchildren. She'll take them to the park to feed the birds, she'll take them to the zoo to see the animals, and she'll baby-sit when her son and daughter-in-law go out on Saturday nights.

Answers

7. b
8. a
9. c

WORKBOOK PAGES 34–35

CHECK-UP TEST: Chapters 1–3

A.

1. are
   dance
2. drives
3. you're
   swimmers
4. I'm
   typist
5. aren't, skiers

B.

1. didn't, was
   spoke
2. didn't
   bought
3. Did
   didn't, got
4. didn't, taught
   was

CHAPTER 3 95

5. Did
didn't, talked
wasn't

C.
1. What are you writing about?
2. What are they going to fix?
3. Where did he hike?
4. When will she be ready?
5. How did they arrive?
6. How long will you be staying?
7. How many people is she going to hire?

D.
1. She's adjusting her satellite dish.
2. He chats online.
3. I'm going to visit my mother-in-law.
4. They delivered groceries.
5. He was baking a cake.
6. I'll take the bus.
7. We'll be watching TV.
8. I was chopping carrots.

E.
Listen to each question and then complete the answer.

Ex. Does your brother like to swim?
1. Are you going to buy donuts tomorrow?
2. Will Jennifer and John see each other again soon?
3. Doctor, did I sprain my ankle?
4. Does Tommy have a black eye?
5. Is your daughter practicing the violin?
6. Do you and your husband go to the movies very often?
7. Does Diane go out with her boyfriend every Saturday evening?
8. Will you and your wife be visiting us tonight?

Answers
1. I am
2. they won't
3. you did
4. he does
5. she isn't
6. we do
7. she doesn't
8. we will

Text Pages 33–36: *Side by Side Gazette*

FEATURE ARTICLE
Immigration Around the World

PREVIEWING THE ARTICLE

1. Have students talk about the title of the article and the accompanying photograph.

2. You may choose to introduce the following new vocabulary beforehand, or have students encounter it within the context of the article:

> earthquake
> economic
> flood
> flow (n)
> for example
> foreign
> foreign born
> historic
> immigrant
> immigration
> living conditions
> marry
> native
> natural disaster
> political
> public school
> reason
> republic
> total
> war

> *Places Around the World*
> Africa
> Albania
> Asia
> Bulgaria
> Eastern Europe
> former Soviet republics
> Latin America
> Middle East
> Moldova
> North Africa
> Saudi Arabia
> Ukraine
> Western Europe

READING THE ARTICLE

1. Have students read silently, or follow along silently as the article is read aloud by you, by one or more students, or on the audio program.

2. Ask students if they have any questions and check understanding of new vocabulary. Show the class a world map and have students identify the locations of all the place names mentioned in the article.

3. Check students' comprehension by asking the following questions:

> Why do people move to other countries?
> What are examples of natural disasters?
> Name three different flows of immigrants.
> Where do immigrants often live in their new countries?
> What changes do immigrants bring to their new neighborhoods?
> In the Los Angeles public schools, how many different languages do children speak?
> How many people in New York are foreign born?

EXPANSION ACTIVITIES

1. World Map ★★

   Cut out seven large arrows that can be taped to a large world map. Have students tape the arrows on the world map to indicate the flows of immigrants according to the feature article.

2. Class Discussion ★★★

   a. In small groups, have students discuss the following questions:

   > Are there immigrants in your city, your town, or your neighborhood?
   > Where do these immigrants come from?
   > Why did they come to your country?
   > What changes have they brought to your community?

   b. Have the groups report back to the class.

SIDE BY SIDE GAZETTE 97

2nd ARTICLE
Ellis Island

PREVIEWING THE ARTICLE

1. Have students talk about the title of the article and the accompanying photograph.

2. You may choose to introduce the following new vocabulary beforehand, or have students encounter it within the context of the article:

   > check
   > come through
   > document
   > former
   > harbor
   > immigration official
   > island
   > medical examination
   > official
   > pass through
   > reception hall

   > *Places Around the World*
   > Austria
   > Austria-Hungary
   > England
   > Germany
   > Hungary
   > Ireland
   > Italy
   > Russia

READING THE ARTICLE

1. Have students read silently, or follow along silently as the article is read aloud by you, by one or more students, or on the audio program.

2. Ask students if they have any questions and check understanding of new vocabulary. Show the class a world map and have students identify the locations of all the place names.

3. Check students' comprehension by having them decide if the following statements are true or false:

   Ellis Island was an immigration center in the United States. *(True)*
   Ellis Island was an immigration center for 75 years. *(False)*
   At Ellis Island, officials checked immigrants' health and their documents. *(True)*
   Some immigrants couldn't stay in the United States. *(True)*
   Most immigrants who came through Ellis Island were from the Soviet Republics. *(False)*
   Forty percent of the present U.S. population came through Ellis Island. *(False)*

EXPANSION ACTIVITY

Class Discussion ★★★

1. In small groups, have students discuss the following questions:

   How do you think immigrants traveled to Ellis Island?
   What do you think they brought with them?
   How do you think they felt when immigration officials checked their documents and gave them medical exams?
   Which immigrants probably had to return to their countries?

2. Have the groups report back to the class.

 FACT FILE *Countries with Large Number of Immigrants*

1. Before reading the Fact File, show the class a world map. Have students identify the locations of the following place names:

   > Australia
   > Canada
   > France
   > Germany
   > Saudi Arabia
   > the United States

2. Have students rank the countries according to which they believe would have the largest immigrant populations. Write students' ideas on the board. Then have students read the table on text page 33 to check their predictions.

98 SIDE BY SIDE GAZETTE

3. Read the table aloud as the class follows along. Ask students: "Is this list different from your list? How is your list different?"

4. For a comprehension activity, have students read the Feature Article again and identify where the immigrants in the listed countries probably came from. For example:

> United States: *Latin America and Asia*
> Germany: *Eastern Europe, the former Soviet republics, and North Africa*
> France: *Eastern Europe, the former Soviet republics, and North Africa*
> Saudi Arabia: *Africa and Asia*

AROUND THE WORLD
Immigrant Neighborhoods

1. Have students read silently or follow along silently as the text is read aloud by you, by one or more students, or on the audio program.

2. Bring a world map to class and point out the locations of the places depicted in the photographs. Introduce the words *Chinatown, Cuban, Sydney, Turkish*.

3. Have students first work in pairs or small groups, responding to the question. Then have students tell the class what they talked about. Write any new vocabulary on the board.

EXPANSION ACTIVITY

Investigating Interesting Immigrant Neighborhoods ★★★

1. Brainstorm with the class interesting immigrant neighborhoods in your area.

2. Have students think of information they would like to learn about each neighborhood. For example:

> What are the directions to the neighborhood?
> What are some interesting things to do there?
> Is there a special festival that is interesting to visit?
> What are the best restaurants?

3. Have each student chose a neighborhood to investigate. Have students begin their investigations by circulating around the room to see if other classmates know the answers to the questions. Students may also want to interview people outside the classroom. Students can also visit the neighborhood to get the information firsthand.

4. For homework, have students write up the information they learned and present it in class.

Option: The class can publish their information as a *Neighborhood Guide to Our City*.

INTERVIEW

1. Have students read silently, or follow along silently as the interview is read aloud by you, by one or more students, or on the audio program.

2. Ask students if they have any questions. Check understanding of the words *immigrate, Melbourne, opportunity, recently*, and the expression *seven days a week*.

3. Check students' comprehension by having them decide if the following statements are true or false:

> Mr. Nguyen came from Vietnam with his brother. *(False)*
> Mr. Nguyen never takes a day off from work. *(True)*
> Mr. Nguyen wants his children to work in the restaurant when they grow up. *(False)*
> Mr. Nguyen likes to teach mathematics. *(True)*
> Mr. Nguyen works in the restaurant so he can send his children to college. *(True)*
> Mr. Nguyen likes the way Australians spend their time. *(False)*
> Mr. Nguyen likes the opportunities in Australia. *(True)*

SIDE BY SIDE GAZETTE

EXPANSION ACTIVITIES

1. Before and After Immigrating ★★

a. Write the following on the board:

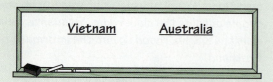

b. Have students read the article again and compare Mr. Nguyen's life in Vietnam to his life in Australia by completing the chart. For example:

> Vietnam
> He lived with his wife and children.
> He was a mathematics teacher.
> People took care of each other.
> There wasn't a very good future.
>
> Australia
> He lives with his wife and children.
> He works in a restaurant.
> People don't have much time to be with friends.
> There are many opportunities.

c. Have students share their ideas.

d. Discuss with the class:

> How did Tran Nguyen's life change when he moved to Australia?
> Is he happy he moved?
> What is the most important opportunity for Tran Nguyen and his family in Australia?

2. Student Interviews ★★★

a. If possible, have students ask the same interview questions of an immigrant they know.

b. Have students report their findings to the class.

WE'VE GOT MAIL!

THE LETTER TO *SIDE BY SIDE*

1. Have students read silently, or follow along silently as the letter is read aloud by you, by one or more students, or on the audio program.

2. Ask students if they have any questions. Check understanding of the words *future tense, present tense, sincerely, tense (adj), tense (n), TV program*.

3. Check students' comprehension by having them decide whether these statements are true or false:

> The writer is confused about why English speakers use the present tense to talk about the past. (*False*)
> "I'm flying to London" is in the present continuous tense. (*True*)
> "My plane leaves at 9:30" is in the simple future tense. (*False*)
> The writer thinks it isn't correct to say "I'm flying to London tomorrow" because it's in the present tense, and tomorrow is in the future. (*True*)

4. Ask students:

> Did you ever have this question?
> Can you think of another example in English where someone uses the present tense to talk about the future?

THE RESPONSE FROM *SIDE BY SIDE*

1. Have students read silently, or follow along silently as the letter is read aloud by you, by one or more students, or on the audio program.

2. Ask students if they have any questions. Check understanding of the words *definite, event, regular, schedule*.

3. Check students' comprehension by having them decide whether these statements are true or false:

> The man made a mistake when he said "I'm flying to London tomorrow." (*False*)
> People use the present continuous tense to

100   SIDE BY SIDE GAZETTE

talk about definite plans in the future. *(True)*

People use the simple present tense to talk about special schedules and unusual events. *(False)*

"My planes leaves at 9:30" means the same as "My plane will leave at 9:30." *(True)*

4. Ask students:

Can you use the present tense for the future in your language?

GLOBAL EXCHANGE

1. Set the scene: "Two keypals are writing to each other."

2. Have students read silently or follow along silently as the messages are read aloud by you, by one or more students, or on the audio program.

3. Ask students if they have any questions. Check understanding of the following new words and expressions: *after midnight, campfire, computer lab, family reunion, final exam, lake, turn off.*

4. Options for additional practice:

   • Have students write about their activities last weekend and their plans for next weekend and share their writing in pairs.

   • Have students correspond with a keypal on the Internet and then share their experience with the class.

LISTENING You Have Five Messages!

Set the scene: "Dave invited his friends to a party. These are phone messages that his friends left for him."

LISTENING SCRIPT

Listen to the messages on Dave's machine. Match the messages

You have five messages.

Message Number One: "Hi, Dave. It's Sarah. Thanks for the invitation, but I can't come to your party tomorrow. I'll be taking my uncle to the hospital. Maybe next time." *[beep]*

Message Number Two: "Hello, Dave. It's Bob. I'm sorry that my wife and I won't be able to come to your party tomorrow. We'll be attending a wedding out of town. I hope it's a great party. Have fun!" *[beep]*

Message Number Three: "Dave? It's Paula. How's it going? I got your message about the party tomorrow. Unfortunately, I won't be able to go. I'll be studying all weekend. Talk to you soon." *[beep]*

Message Number Four: "Hi, Dave. It's Joe. Thanks for the invitation to your party. I'll be visiting my parents in New York City, so I'm afraid I won't be around. I'll call you when I get back." *[beep]*

Message Number Five: "Hello, Dave? It's Carla. Thanks for the invitation to your party. I don't have anything to do tomorrow night, so I'll definitely be there. I'm really looking forward to it. See you tomorrow. " *[beep]*

Answers

1. e
2. c
3. b
4. a
5. d

FUN WITH IDIOMS

> a piece of cake
> give someone a ring
> no picnic
> raining cats and dogs
> tied up
> What's cooking?

INTRODUCTION AND PRACTICE

For each idiom, do the following:

1. Have students look at the illustration.

SIDE BY SIDE GAZETTE   101

2. Present the idiom. Say the expression and have the class repeat it chorally and individually. Check students' pronunciation of the words.

DO YOU KNOW THESE EXPRESSIONS?

Have students match the expressions with their meanings.

Answers

1. e
2. d
3. f
4. a
5. c
6. b

EXPANSION ACTIVITIES

1. Line Prompts ★★

    Call out one of the following line prompts and have students respond appropriately with one of the idioms:

    You look terrible. How was your English test?
    (It was no picnic!)

    You look very happy. How was your English test?
    (It was a piece of cake!)

    Do you have a minute to talk?
    (I'm tied up right now.)

    Let's talk soon.
    (I'll give you a ring tomorrow.)

    How's the weather?
    (It's raining cats and dogs!)

    Hi!
    (What's cooking?)

2. Idiom Challenge! ★★★

    a. Divide the class into pairs.

    b. Have each pair create a conversation in which they use as many of the idioms from text page 36 as they can.

    c. Have the pairs present their conversations to the class. Which pair used the most idioms?

 WHAT ARE THEY SAYING?

FOCUS

- Saying Good-bye, Giving Personal Information

Have students talk about the characters and the situations, and then create role plays based on the scenes. Students may refer back to previous lessons as a resource, but they should not simply reuse specific conversations.

Note: You may want to assign this exercise as written homework, having students prepare their role plays, practice them the next day with other students, and then present them to the class.

102 SIDE BY SIDE GAZETTE

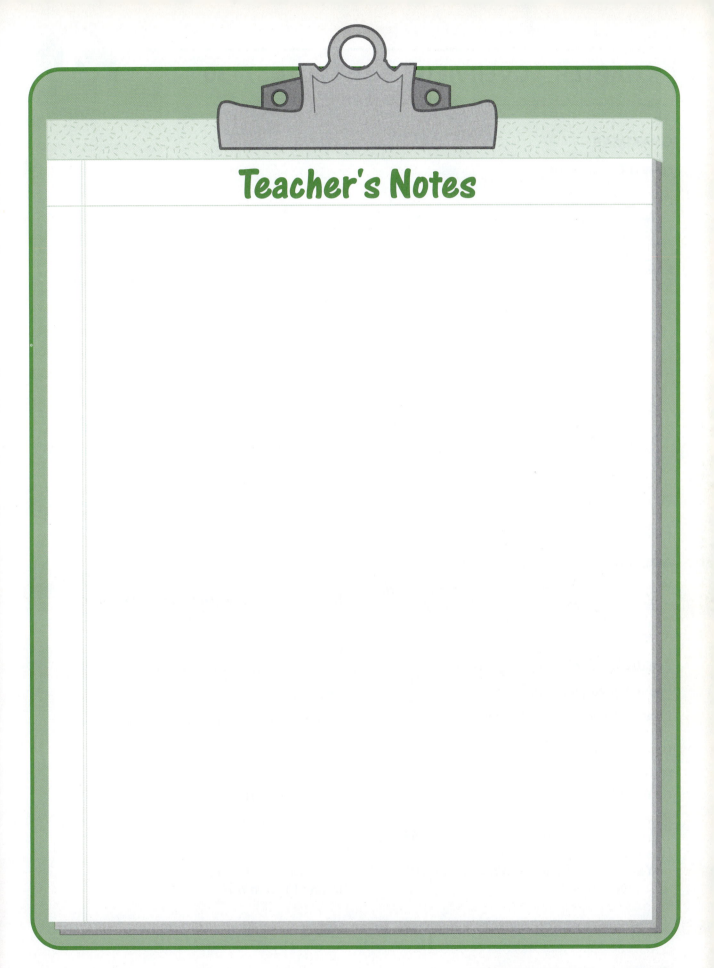

CHAPTER 4 OVERVIEW: Text Pages 37–50

GRAMMAR

Present Perfect Tense

(I have)	I've
(We have)	We've
(You have)	You've
(They have)	They've

eaten.

(He has)	He's
(She has)	She's
(It has)	It's

I	
We	haven't
You	
They	

eaten.

He	
She	hasn't
It	

| Have | I / we / you / they | eaten? |
| Has | he / she / it | |

| Yes, | I / we / you / they | have. |
| | he / she / it | has. |

| No, | I / we / you / they | haven't. |
| | he / she / it | hasn't. |

FUNCTIONS

Asking for and Reporting Information

Why isn't *Charlie going to go bowling tonight*?
　He's already *gone bowling this week.*
Really? When?
　He went bowling yesterday.

I've *driven trucks* for many years.

I've never *eaten lunch with the boss*.

I haven't *swum* in a long time.
　Why not?
I haven't had the time.

Have you ever *seen a rainbow*?
　Yes, I have. I *saw a rainbow last year*.

Have you *written the report* yet?
　Yes, I have. I *wrote it a little while ago*.
Has *David gone to the bank* yet?
　Yes, *he* has. *He went to the bank a little while ago.*

Has *Timmy gone to bed* yet?
　No, *he* hasn't.

I still haven't *typed two important letters*.

Have you *seen any good movies* recently?
　Yes, I have. I *saw a very good movie last week.*
What *movie* did you *see*?
　I *saw The Wedding Dancer*.

Intention

I'm going to *eat lunch with the boss tomorrow*.

Inquiring About Ability

Do you know how to *drive trucks*?

Inquiring About Likes/Dislikes

Do you like to *swim*?

Expressing Obligation

I have to *take it now*.
He has to *go to bed now*.

104　CHAPTER 4

Expressing an Opinion

It's one of the best *movies* I've ever *seen*.

Expressing Satisfaction

How was it?
  It was excellent/very good/wonderful/great/
  fantastic/terrific/phenomenal/
  awesome.

Initiating a Conversation

I see *you haven't gone home yet*.

Expressing Agreement

That's right.

Leave-Taking

Have a good weekend.
  You, too.

NEW VOCABULARY

At Work

bookkeeper
inventory
mail room
office clerk
paycheck
presentation
report

Free Time

Bingo
Broadway show
cruise
hot-air balloon
Monopoly

Tourist Attractions

Alcatraz Prison
Chinatown
Empire State Building
Fisherman's Wharf
Golden Gate Park
Statue of Liberty
Times Square
United Nations

Time Expressions

already
at the beginning
at this point
ever
for many years
in a long time
recently
yet

Transportation

cable car
helicopter
limousine

Medical Words

aspirin
blood
first-aid course
injection
medicine

Verbs

draw
explain
get a raise
get rid of
get stuck
give blood
go kayaking
go scuba diving
go to bed
have the time
leave for *school*
take a cruise
take a ride
take a tour
take *your* medicine

Adjectives

jealous
surprised

Miscellaneous

beginning (n)
best friend
chopsticks
cotton candy
dance lesson
electric bill
extremely
horse
kimono
present perfect tense
rainbow
speech
Swahili
term paper
top

EXPRESSIONS

as for me
Have a good weekend.
Look!

Text Page 37: Chapter Opening Page

VOCABULARY PREVIEW

These are the irregular past participles that are introduced in Chapter 4. You may want to introduce these forms before beginning the chapter, or you may choose to wait until they first occur in a specific lesson. If you choose to introduce them at this point, here are some suggestions:

1. Write the phrases with their base forms on the board:

   1. go to the bank
   2. do the laundry
   3. get a haircut
   4. write to Grandma
   5. take the dog for a walk
   6. give the dog a bath
   7. speak to the landlord
   8. drive the kids to their dance lesson
   9. eat lunch
   10. ride my exercise bike
   11. swim
   12. see a movie

2. Have students look at the illustrations on text page 37. Tell the class that these are all the things this person has to do today. Say each phrase and have the class repeat after you. Check students' understanding and pronunciation of the words.

3. One phrase at a time, erase the base form of the verb and replace it with the past participle form. Tell students that this person *has done* all these things. Say each phrase in the present perfect (for example: "I've gone to the bank, I've done the laundry") and have students repeat it chorally and individually. Check students' understanding and pronunciation of the verb forms.

4. After students have practiced saying the present perfect forms, erase the phrases on the board and have students look again at the illustrations on text page 37.

5. Practice the vocabulary as a class, in pairs, or in small groups. Have students cover the word list and look at the pictures. Practice the words in the following way:

   • Give the number of an illustration and have students say the phrase in the present perfect.

Text Page 38: I've Driven Trucks for Many Years

FOCUS

- Introduction of the Present Perfect Tense: 1st Person Positive Statements

CLOSE UP

RULE:	The present perfect tense is formed with the auxiliary verb *have* + the past participle. The auxiliary verb can contract with the subject pronoun unlike the verb *have*, which cannot contract with the subject pronoun.
EXAMPLES:	I **have driven**. I**'ve driven**. You **have driven**. You**'ve driven**. He **has driven**. He**'s driven**. We **have driven**. We**'ve driven**. They **have driven**. They**'ve driven**.
RULE:	The past participle of all regular verbs and some irregular verbs is the same as the past tense form.
EXAMPLES:	Yesterday I **washed** the dishes. I**'ve washed** dishes for many years. Yesterday I **played** the piano. I**'ve played** the piano for many years. Yesterday I **bought** oranges from Florida. I**'ve bought** oranges from Florida for many years.
RULE:	Most irregular verbs have a different past participle form.
EXAMPLES:	Present Past Past Participle be was/were been do did done draw drew drawn drive drove driven eat ate eaten fall fell fallen fly flew flown get got gotten go went gone give gave given ride rode ridden see saw seen sing sang sung speak spoke spoken swim swam swum

(continued)

Present	Past	Past Participle
take	took	taken
wear	wore	worn
write	wrote	written

RULE: When the present perfect tense is used with *for*, it describes a situation that began in the past and continues until the present. *For* is followed by a length of time.

EXAMPLES: I've **driven** trucks **for** many years.
(I continue to drive trucks.)

I've **written** reports **for** many years.
(I continue to write reports.)

GETTING READY

Review the language of ability.

1. Write on the board:

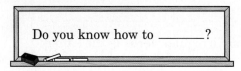

2. Ask students the above question with the following:

> ride a motorcycle
> drive a car
> eat with chopsticks
> speak Spanish
> do karate
> write in Chinese

For example:

> Teacher: Do you know how to ride a motorcycle?
> Student: Yes, I do.
>
> Teacher: Do you know how to write in Chinese?
> Student: No, I don't.

INTRODUCING THE MODEL

1. Have students look at the model illustration.
2. Set the scene: "Someone is at a job interview."

3. Present the model.
4. Full-Class Repetition.
5. Ask students if they have any questions. Check understanding of vocabulary.
6. Group Choral Repetition.
7. Choral Conversation.
8. Call on one or two pairs of students to present the dialog.

   (For additional practice, do Choral Conversation in small groups or by rows.)

SIDE BY SIDE EXERCISES

Examples

1. A. Do you know how to write reports?
   B. Yes. I've written reports for many years.

2. A. Do you know how to fly airplanes?
   B. Yes. I've flown airplanes for many years.

1. **Exercise 1:** Introduce the word *report*. Call on two students to present the dialog. Then do Choral Repetition and Choral Conversation practice.

2. **Exercise 2:** Same as above.

3. **Exercises 3–9:** Either Full-Class Practice or Pair Practice.

> **New Vocabulary**
> 4. Swahili
> 5. chopsticks
> 6. injection
> 7. draw
> 9. horse

WORKBOOK

Page 36

EXPANSION ACTIVITIES

1. **Tic Tac Grammar** ★

   a. Have students draw a tic tac grid on a piece of paper and fill it in with any nine of the following verbs:

drive	write
fly	take
speak	eat
give	draw
do	ride

   b. Call out the past participle of any of these verbs. Tell students to cross out any present tense verb on their grid for which you have given a past participle form.

   c. The first person to cross out three verbs in a straight line—either vertically, horizontally, or diagonally—wins the game.

   d. Have the winner call out the words to check the accuracy.

2. **Concentration** ★

   a. Write the following verbs on separate cards:

drive	drove
ride	rode
write	wrote
give	given

fly	flown
take	taken
speak	spoken
eat	eaten
draw	drawn
do	done

   b. Shuffle the cards and place them face down in five rows of 4 each.

   c. Divide the class into two teams. The object of the game is for students to find the matching cards. Both teams should be able to see all the cards, since *concentrating* on their location is an important part of playing the game.

   d. A student from Team 1 turns over two cards. If they match, the student picks up the cards, that team gets a point, and the student takes another turn. If the cards don't match, the student turns them face down, and a member of Team 2 takes a turn.

   e. The game continues until all the cards have been matched. The team with the most correct matches wins the game.

   (continued)

CHAPTER 4

EXPANSION ACTIVITIES (Continued)

Variation: This game can also be played in groups and pairs.

3. Grammar Chain ★★

a. Write the following conversation model and verbs on the board:

```
A. Do you know how to _____?
B. Yes. I've _____ for many years.
   Do you know how to _____?
```

do   give
drive   ride
draw   speak
eat   take
fly   write

b. Start the chain game by saying:

   Teacher (to Student A): Do you know how to speak Spanish?

c. Student A answers "Yes." and makes a statement using the present perfect: "I've spoken Spanish for many years." Then Student A asks Student B another ability question, using another verb on the board, and the chain continues. For example:

   Student A: Yes. I've spoken Spanish for many years.
   (to Student B): Do you know how to *ride a bicycle?*

   Student B: Yes. I've ridden a bicycle for many years.
   (to Student C): Do you know how to *fly an airplane?*

d. Continue until everyone has had a chance to answer and ask a question.

4. Match the Conversations ★★

a. Make a set of matching cards based on the model and exercises on text page 38.

Do you know how to drive trucks?	Yes. I've driven trucks for many years.
Do you know how to write reports?	Yes. I've written reports for many years.
Do you know how to fly airplanes?	Yes. I've flown airplanes for many years.
Do you know how to take X-rays?	Yes. I've taken X-rays for many years.
Do you know how to speak Swahili?	Yes. I've spoken Swahili for many years.
Do you know how to eat with chopsticks?	Yes. I've eaten with chopsticks for many years.
Do you know how to draw cartoons?	Yes. I've drawn cartoons for many years.
Do you know how to do yoga?	Yes. I've done yoga for many years.
Do you know how to ride horses?	Yes. I've ridden horses for many years.

b. Distribute a card to each student.

c. Have students memorize the sentences on their cards, and then have students walk around the room saying their sentences until they find their match.

d. Then have pairs of students say their matched sentences aloud to the class.

5. **Which One Isn't True?** ★★★

   a. Put the following verb list on the board:

   do give
   draw ride
   drive speak
   eat take
   fly write

   b. Tell students to write two true statements and one false statement about themselves using any of the verbs on the board and the phrase "for many years." For example:

   I've driven a car for many years.
   I've done yoga for many years.
   I've ridden a motorcycle for many years.

   c. Have students take turns reading their statements to the class. Have the class determine which statement isn't true.

Text Page 39: I've Never Eaten Lunch with the Boss

FOCUS

- Present Perfect Tense: 1st Person Negative Statements with *never*

CLOSE UP

RULE: When the present perfect tense is used with *never*, it describes a situation that began in the past and continues until the present.

EXAMPLES: **I've never eaten** lunch with the boss.
I've never flown in a helicopter.

INTRODUCING THE MODEL

1. Have students look at the model illustration.
2. Set the scene: "Two co-workers are talking."
3. Present the model.
4. Full-Class Repetition.
5. Ask students if they have any questions. Check understanding of the word *jealous*.
6. Group Choral Repetition.
7. Choral Conversation.
8. Call on one or two pairs of students to present the dialog.

   (For additional practice, do Choral Conversation in small groups or by rows.)

1. **Exercise 1:** Introduce the word *helicopter*. Call on two students to present the dialog. Then do Choral Repetition and Choral Conversation practice.
2. **Exercise 2:** Introduce the expression *Broadway show*. Same as above.
3. **Exercises 3–9:** Either Full-Class Practice or Pair Practice.

New Vocabulary

3. cruise
6. get a raise
8. take a ride
   hot-air balloon
9. limousine

SIDE BY SIDE EXERCISES

Examples

1. A. I'm going to fly in a helicopter tomorrow.
   B. I'm jealous. I've never flown in a helicopter.
2. A. I'm going to see a Broadway show tomorrow.
   B. I'm jealous. I've never seen a Broadway show.

WORKBOOK

Page 37

EXPANSION ACTIVITIES

1. Tic Tac Grammar ★

a. Have students draw a tic tac grid on a piece of paper and fill it in with any nine of the following verbs:

see	go
sing	swim
get	be
drive	write
fly	take
speak	eat
give	draw
do	ride

b. Call out the past participle of any of these verbs. Tell students to cross out any present tense verb on their grid for which you have given a past participle form.

c. The first person to cross out three verbs in a straight line—either vertically, horizontally, or diagonally—wins the game.

d. Have the winner call out the words to check the accuracy.

2. Grammar Chain: Tall Tales ★★

a. Write on the board:

> A. Tomorrow I'm going to _____.
> B. I've never _____, but tomorrow I'M going to _____.

b. Start the chain game by saying:

Teacher (to Student A): Tomorrow I'm going to fly in a hot-air balloon.

c. Student A responds to Student B according to the model on the board. For example:

Student A: I've never flown in a hot-air
(to Student B) balloon, but tomorrow I'M going to swim in the Mediterranean.

Student B continues the chain. For example:

Student B: I've never swum in the
(to Student C) Mediterranean, but tomorrow I'M going to be on TV.

3. Which One Isn't True? ★★★

a. Tell students to write two true statements and one false statement about themselves in the present perfect with never. For example:

> I've never ridden a motorcycle.
> I've never eaten with chopsticks.
> I've never gone to the White House.

b. Have students take turns reading their statements to the class, and have the class guess which statement isn't true.

4. Category Dictation ★★

a. Have students draw two columns on a piece of paper. At the top of one column, have students write I've never. At the top of the other column, have them write I've.

b. Dictate phrases such as the following to the class:

> go out all night
> speak Greek
> take guitar lessons
> get a raise
> be in a boat
> swim in a lake
> draw a picture of our teacher
> meet a famous person
> give a ring to someone
> be on the radio
> see a Broadway show
> be on TV
> go on a cruise
> take a ride on the back of a bicycle
> write a love letter
> sing with an orchestra

c. Have students choose the appropriate column according to their own experience and write the verb with its past participle. For example:

I've never	I've
met a famous person	gone out all night
been on the radio	seen a Broadway show

d. In pairs, have students compare their lists.

(continued)

CHAPTER 4   113

EXPANSION ACTIVITIES (Continued)

5. Class Discussion: Our Greatest Wishes ★★★

   a. Divide the class into groups of three. Have students answer the following question:

   What is something you have always wanted to do but have never done?

   b. Have the groups share their greatest wishes with the class.

Text Page 40: Have You Ever Seen a Rainbow?

FOCUS

- Present Perfect Tense:
    Yes/No Questions with *You*
    Affirmative Short Answers
- Contrast: Present Perfect and Simple Past

CLOSE UP

RULE:	The present perfect describes an activity that occurred at an unspecified time in the past.
EXAMPLE:	**Have** you ever **seen** a rainbow? *(In your general past, have you seen a rainbow?)*
RULE:	The simple past describes an activity that occurred at a specific time in the past.
EXAMPLE:	I **saw** a rainbow last year. *(I saw a rainbow at a specific time in the past.)*
RULE:	*Ever* is placed between the subject and the past participle.
EXAMPLES:	Have you **ever** given a speech? Have you **ever** been in the hospital?
RULE:	The short answer response in the present perfect is formed with the auxiliary verb *have*.

EXAMPLES:	**Have** you ever **eaten** cotton candy?
	    Yes, I **have**.
	Have you ever **fallen** asleep in class?
	    Yes, I **have**.

INTRODUCING THE MODEL

1. Have students look at the model illustration.
2. Set the scene: "Two people on a date are talking."
3. Present the model.
4. Full-Class Repetition.
5. Ask students if they have any questions. Check understanding of the word *rainbow*.
6. Group Choral Repetition.
7. Choral Conversation.
8. Call on one or two pairs of students to present the dialog.

    (For additional practice, do Choral Conversation in small groups or by rows.)

CHAPTER 4   115

SIDE BY SIDE EXERCISES

Examples

1. A. Have you ever gone scuba diving?
   B. Yes, I have. I went scuba diving last year.
2. A. Have you ever given a speech?
   B. Yes, I have. I gave a speech last year.

1. **Exercise 1:** Introduce the expression *go scuba diving*. Call on two students to present the dialog. Then do Choral Repetition and Choral Conversation practice.

2. **Exercise 2:** Introduce the word *speech*. Same as above.

3. **Exercises 3–9:** Either Full-Class Practice or Pair Practice.

New Vocabulary

3. kimono
4. cotton candy
5. first-aid course
8. get stuck

Culture Notes

Exercise 3: A *kimono* is a long Japanese dress for women. In modern times it is used for very formal occasions such as weddings.

Exercise 4: *Cotton candy* is a sweet treat of spun sugar wrapped around a stick. It is usually served at carnivals and amusements parks.

Exercise 5: A *first-aid course* teaches people how to treat minor medical emergencies.

WORKBOOK

Page 38

EXPANSION ACTIVITIES

1. **Match the Conversations ★**

   a. Make the following set of matching cards:

Have you ever seen one?	Yes, I have. I saw one last year.
Have you ever gotten one?	Yes, I have. I got one last year.
Have you ever written one?	Yes, I have. I wrote one last year.
Have you ever worn one?	Yes, I have. I wore one last year.

Have you ever taken one?	Yes, I have. I took one last year.
Have you ever given one?	Yes, I have. I gave one last year.
Have you ever driven one?	Yes, I have. I drove one last year.
Have you ever ridden one?	Yes, I have. I rode one last year.
Have you ever drawn one?	Yes, I have. I drew one last year.

Have you ever eaten one?	Yes, I have. I ate one last year.
Have you ever flown there?	Yes, I have. I flew there last year.
Have you ever gone there?	Yes, I have. I went there last year.
Have you ever swum there?	Yes, I have. I swam there last year.
Have you ever sung there?	Yes, I have. I sang there last year.
Have you ever been there?	Yes, I have. I was there last year.

b. Distribute a card to each student.

c. Have students memorize the sentences on their cards, and then have students walk around the room saying their sentences until they find their match.

d. Then have pairs of students say their matched sentences aloud to the class.

2. Clap in Rhythm ★★

a. Write the following verbs on the board:

```
be      fly     sing
do      get     speak
draw    give    swim
drive   go      take
eat     ride    wear
fall    see     write
```

b. Have students sit in a circle.

c. Establish a steady, even beat—one-two-three-four, one-two-three-four—by having students clap their hands to their laps twice and then clap their hands together twice. Repeat throughout the game, maintaining the same rhythm.

d. In this activity, Student 1 says a verb (for example: *see*). Student 2 gives the past of that verb (for example: *saw*), and Student 3 gives the past participle of that verb (for example: *seen*). Student 4 says a new verb (for example: *go*), and the activity continues until all the verbs on the board have been practiced.

The object is for each student in turn to give a verb form each time the hands are clapped together twice. Nothing is said when students clap their hands on their laps.

Note: The beat never stops! If a student misses a beat, he or she can either wait for the next beat or pass to the next student.

3. Grammar Chain ★★

a. Write the following verb phrases on the board:

```
go to a ballgame
swim in the ocean
eat a pizza
give advice to a friend
wear a tuxedo
take the subway
fall asleep on your couch
get stuck in traffic
go on a merry-go-round
be late for class
draw a picture of a friend
write a letter to a famous person
fly to Rio
see the president
```

b. Start the chain game by saying:

Teacher (to Student A): Have you ever *gone to a ballgame*?

c. Student A answers: "Yes, I have. I went to a ballgame last week." Then Student A asks Student B another question using another phrase on the board, and the chain continues. For example:

(continued)

CHAPTER 4   117

EXPANSION ACTIVITIES (Continued)

　　　Student A:　　Yes, I have. I went to a ballgame last week.
　(to Student B):　Have you ever *eaten a pizza*?
　　　Student B:　　Yes, I have. I ate a pizza last week.
　(to Student C):　Have you ever *gotten stuck in traffic*?

d. Continue until everyone has had a chance to answer and ask a question.

4. Question the Answers! ★★

a. Dictate answers such as the following to the class:

   Yes, I have. I went to Japan last summer.
   Yes, I have. I took a French course last semester.
   Yes, I have. I saw a famous person last week.

b. Have students write questions for which these answers would be correct.

   For example:

   　Answer:　　Yes, I have. I went to Japan last summer.
   　Question:　Have you ever gone to Japan?

   　Answer:　　Yes, I have. I took a French course last summer.
   　Question:　Have you ever taken a French course?

c. Have students compare their questions with each other.

Variation: Write the answers on cards. Divide the class into groups and give each group a set of cards.

5. Question Game: How Many Questions? ★★

a. Divide the class into pairs.

b. Dictate the following answers to the class:

   Yes, I have.
   Yes, I did.

c. Tell students that in five minutes, they should write as many questions as they can think of for which these answers would be correct. For example:

   Yes, I have.　Have you ever driven a truck?
   　　　　　　Have you ever gone fishing?
   　　　　　　Have you ever worn jeans to work?

   Yes, I did.　 Did you write your report last night?
   　　　　　　Did you see a movie last weekend?
   　　　　　　Did you go to a ballgame yesterday?

d. Have students read their questions to the class. The pair with the most correct questions wins the *question game*.

6. Class Survey: Have You Ever? ★★

a. Make up the following handout based on the lesson on student text page 40, and give each student a copy:

Have you ever . . .	Yes	No
seen a rainbow?	____	____
gone scuba diving?	____	____
given a speech?	____	____
worn a kimono?	____	____
eaten cotton candy?	____	____
taken a first-aid course?	____	____
fallen asleep in class?	____	____
been in the hospital?	____	____
gotten stuck in an elevator?	____	____

b. Have students go around the room interviewing each other.

c. Have students report their findings to the class.

Variation: Have students do the same activity with questions based on the situations on text pages 38 and 39.

7. Find the Right Person! ★★

a. Write the following on the board:

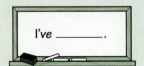

118　CHAPTER 4

b. Have each student write one special thing that he or she has done.

c. Collect the information and put it on a handout in the following form:

> Find someone who . . .
> 1. has gone scuba diving. _____
> 2. has given a speech in front _____
>   of a hundred people.
> 3. has eaten octopus. _____
> 4. has ridden in a limousine. _____
> 5. has flown in a helicopter. _____

d. Have students circulate around the room, asking each other questions to identify the above people. For example:

    Student A: Have you ever gone scuba diving?
    Student B: Yes, I have. I went scuba diving last summer.

e. The first student to find all the people, raise his or her hand, and identify the students is the winner of the game.

Text Page 41: Have You Written the Report Yet?

FOCUS

- Present Perfect Tense:
    Yes/No Questions
    Affirmative Short Answers
- Questions with *Yet*

CLOSE UP

RULE: Yes/No questions with *yet* express the expectation that something has happened before now. The word *yet* is always at the end of the question.

EXAMPLES: Have you driven the new van **yet**?
Has Nancy given her presentation **yet**?

INTRODUCING THE MODELS

There are two model conversations. Introduce and practice each separately. For each model:

1. Have students look at the model illustration.
2. Set the scene.

    1st model: "A supervisor is talking to an employee."
    2nd model: "Two co-workers are talking about David."

3. Present the model.
4. Full-Class Repetition.
5. Ask students if they have any questions.
6. Group Choral Repetition.
7. Choral Conversation.
8. Call on one or two pairs of students to present the dialog.

    (For additional practice, do Choral Conversation in small groups or by rows.)

SIDE BY SIDE EXERCISES

Examples

1. A. Have you driven the new van yet?
   B. Yes, I have. I drove the new van a little while ago.
2. A. Has Nancy given her presentation yet?
   B. Yes, she has. She gave her presentation a little while ago.

1. **Exercise 1:** Call on two students to present the dialog. Then do Choral Repetition and Choral Conversation practice.
2. **Exercise 2:** Introduce the word *presentation*. Same as above.
3. **Exercises 3–6:** Either Full-Class Practice or Pair Practice.

New Vocabulary

3. paycheck
4. take inventory
6. explain
   present perfect tense

WORKBOOK

Page 39

EXPANSION ACTIVITIES

1. Tic Tac Grammar ★

a. Have students draw a tic tac grid on a piece of paper and fill it in with any nine of the following verbs:

be	fly	sing
do	get	speak
draw	give	swim
drive	go	take
eat	ride	wear
fall	see	write

b. Call out the past participle of any of these verbs. Tell students to cross out any present tense verb on their grid for which you have given a past participle form.

c. The first person to cross out three verbs in a straight line—either vertically, horizontally, or diagonally—wins the game.

d. Have the winner call out the words to check the accuracy.

2. Match the Conversations ★

a. Make the following set of matching cards:

Has he seen them?	Yes, he has. He saw them a little while ago.
Has she seen them?	Yes, she has. She saw them a little while ago.
Have you seen them?	Yes, I have. I saw them a little while ago.
Have they seen you?	Yes, they have. They saw me a little while ago.
Have you seen him?	Yes, we have. We saw him a little while ago.
Have I seen them?	Yes, you have. You saw them a little while ago.

b. Distribute a card to each student.

c. Have students memorize the sentences on their cards, and then have students walk around the room saying their sentences until they find their match.

d. Then have pairs of students say their matched sentences aloud to the class.

3. Concentration ★

a. Write the following sentences on separate cards:

Have you gone there?	Yes, I have.
Have they gone there?	Yes, they have.
Have I gone there?	Yes, you have.
Has she gone there?	Yes, she has.

(continued)

CHAPTER 4

EXPANSION ACTIVITIES (Continued)

| Has he gone there? | Yes, he has. |
| Has it gone there? | Yes, it has. |

b. Shuffle the cards and place them face down in three rows of four each.

c. Divide the class into two teams. The object of the game is for students to find the matching cards. Both teams should be able to see all the cards, since *concentrating* on their location is an important part of playing the game.

d. A student from Team 1 turns over two cards. If they match, the student picks up the cards, that team gets a point, and the student takes another turn. If the cards don't match, the student turns them face down, and a member of Team 2 takes a turn.

e. The game continues until all the cards have been matched. The team with the most correct matches wins the game.

Variation: This game can also be played in groups and pairs.

4. Question the Answers! ★★

a. Dictate answers such as the following to the class:

> Yes, he has. He wore his new suit yesterday.
> Yes, she has. She went to the post office a few minutes ago.
> Yes, they have. They ate there yesterday.

b. Have students write questions for which these answers would be correct. For example:

> Answer: Yes, he has. He wore his new suit yesterday.
> Question: Has Tom worn his new suit yet?
>
> Answer: Yes, she has. She went to the post office a few minutes ago.
> Question: Has Nancy gone to the post office yet?
>
> Answer: Yes, they have. They ate there yesterday.
> Question: Have your friends eaten there yet?

c. Have students compare their questions with each other.

Variation: Write the answers on cards. Divide the class into groups and give each group a set of cards.

Text Pages 42–43: He's Already Gone Bowling This Week

FOCUS

- Present Perfect Tense
- Contrast: Present Perfect, Simple Past, Future: Going to

CLOSE UP

RULE: *Already* is placed between the auxiliary and the past participle.

EXAMPLES: He's **already** gone bowling this week.
She's **already** seen a movie this week.
They've **already** eaten at a restaurant this week.

INTRODUCING THE MODEL

1. Have students look at the model illustration.
2. Set the scene: "Charlie's wife and a friend are talking about Charlie."
3. Present the model.
4. Full-Class Repetition.
5. Ask students if they have any questions. Check understanding of the word *already*.
6. Group Choral Repetition.
7. Choral Conversation.
8. Call on one or two pairs of students to present the dialog.

    (For additional practice, do Choral Conversation in small groups or by rows.)

9. Use the sentence *He's already gone bowling this week* to practice the other forms of the present perfect tense.

    a. Point to yourself and say: "I've already gone bowling this week." Have students repeat chorally and individually.

    b. Continue in the same way with the other pronouns. For example:

    We've already gone bowling this week.
    She's already gone bowling this week.
    They've already gone bowling this week.

Have students refer to the grammar box at the top of text page 42. Check pronunciation of contractions with *have* and provide additional practice if necessary.

SIDE BY SIDE EXERCISES

Examples

1. A. Why isn't Vicky going to see a movie this evening?
   B. She's already seen a movie this week.
   A. Really? When?
   B. She saw a movie yesterday.
2. A. Why aren't Mr. and Mrs. Kendall going to eat at a restaurant tonight?
   B. They've already eaten at a restaurant this week.
   A. Really? When?
   B. They ate at a restaurant yesterday.

1. **Exercise 1:** Call on two students to present the dialog. Then do Choral Repetition and Choral Conversation practice.
2. **Exercise 2:** Call on two students to present the dialog.

CHAPTER 4   123

3. **Exercises 3–14:** Either Full-Class Practice or Pair Practice.

> **New Vocabulary**
> 4. give blood
> 8. best friend
> 14. Bingo

Culture Note

Exercise 14: *Bingo* is a popular game. Numbers are called out, and players listen to match the numbers they hear with those on their game cards.

WORKBOOK

Pages 40–43

EXPANSION ACTIVITIES

1. Practice Makes It Perfect! ★

a. Write the following on the board:

> No. ___'ve already ___ .
> No. ___'s already ___ .

b. Ask students each of the following questions. Have students respond, using the present perfect model on the board. For example:

> Teacher: Are you going to write your English composition tonight?
> Student: No. I've already written it.
>
> Teacher: Is Maria going to go to the dentist today?
> Student: No. She's already gone to the dentist.

Questions:

Are you going to write your English composition tonight?
Is (Maria) going to go to the dentist today?
Are your friends going to do their homework this afternoon?
It's late. Is your brother going to get dressed for the party?
Tomorrow is your sister's birthday. Are you going to give her a birthday gift?
Are you and your (husband) going to do your laundry this morning?
Sally's dog is sick. Is she going to take him to the vet today?
Are you going to write to your uncle in (Chicago) this weekend?
Are you going to go jogging after class today?
Are you going to see the new movie at the (Regency) Theater?
Are your friends (Barbara) and (Bill) going to get married this weekend?
Are you going to do your exercises tonight before you go to bed?
Is (Peter) going to eat lunch with us today?
Are you going to ride your new exercise bike today?
Are you going to take your daughter to her piano lessons this afternoon?
(Tom) isn't feeling very well. Is he going to see the doctor this afternoon?
Is Professor (Jones) going to give his famous lecture on American birds tonight?

2. Grammar Chain ★★

a. Write on the board:

> A. Why aren't you going to ___ ?
> B. Because I've already ___ this week. I ___ yesterday. Why aren't you ___ ?

b. Start the chain game by saying:

> Teacher (to Student A): Why aren't you going to see a movie tonight?

c. Student A answers according to the model on the board and then asks Student B another present perfect question. For example:

> Student A: Because I've already seen a movie this week. I saw a movie yesterday.
>
> (to Student B): Why aren't you going to go skating tomorrow?

124   CHAPTER 4

Student B: Because I've already gone skating this week. I went skating yesterday.

(to Student C): Why aren't you going to write your report today?

d. Continue until everyone has had a chance to answer and ask a question.

3. Can You Hear the Difference? ★

a. Write the following sentences on the board:

A
He's eating here.
We drive there.
She had time.
I wore it.
We bought them.
He sees her.
I go there.

B
He's eaten here.
We've driven there.
She's had time.
I've worn it.
We've bought them.
He's seen her.
I've gone there.

b. Choose a sentence randomly from one of the two columns and say it to the class. Have the class listen and identify whether the sentence is from Column A or Column B.

c. Have students continue the activity in pairs. One student pronounces a sentence, and the other identifies whether it's from Column A or Column B. Then have them reverse roles.

d. Write other similar sentences on the board and continue the practice.

4. Sentence Cues ★★

a. On separate cards, write key words that can be put together to form sentences or questions. Clip together the cards for each sentence. For example:

you	speak	to	grandparents	yet	?
she	speak	boyfriend	last night	.
they	ever	go bowling	with you	?

she	wear	kimono	last year	.
he	ever	fall asleep	in the library	?
they	already	get	their paychecks	?

b. Divide the class into small groups and give a clipped set of cards to each group.

c. Have each group write a sentence based on their set of cards.

d. Have one member of each group write that group's sentence on the board. Then compare everybody's sentences. Did they choose the correct tense? What words helped them choose the correct tense?

5. What's Wrong? ★★★

a. Divide the class into pairs or small groups.

b. Write several sentences such as the following on the board or on a handout. Some of the sentences should be correct, and others incorrect. For example:

I flew there last month.
I've never went there.
She's already written the letter.
I've never saw them.
We've already done that.
I drive trucks for many years.
I've never saw her.
They've never swum there.
Have you ever be to Chicago?
I've gotten a very short haircut last week.

c. The object of the activity is for students to identify which sentences are incorrect and then correct them.

d. Have students compare their answers.

Variation: Do the activity as a game with competing teams. The team that successfully completes the task in the shortest time is the winner.

(continued)

CHAPTER 4 125

EXPANSION ACTIVITIES (Continued)

6. Don't You Remember? ★★★

a. Write the following on the board:

> A. You know, _____.
> B. But { ___'s / ___'ve } already _____.
> A. Really? When?
> B. Don't you remember? _____ a few days ago.
> A. Oh. That's right. I forgot.

b. Call on pairs of students to create conversations based on the model on the board. Give one member of the pair one of these cards as a cue for the conversation.

You know, we should see the new science fiction movie at the Regency Theater.	You know, Timmy should get a haircut.
You know, we really should do the laundry.	You know, we should write to Uncle Charlie.
You know, you should wear the wool sweater your grandmother gave you for your birthday.	You know, you should take the car to the mechanic.
You know, your sister should really invite us for dinner.	You know, our friends should visit us in our new apartment.

126 CHAPTER 4

Text Page 44

 READING *We Can't Decide*

FOCUS

- Present Perfect Tense

READING THE STORY

Optional: *Preview the story by having students talk about the story title and/or illustration. You may choose to introduce new vocabulary beforehand, or have students encounter the new vocabulary within the context of the reading.*

1. Have students read silently or follow along silently as the story is read aloud by you, by one or more students, or on the audio program.

2. Ask students if they have any questions. Check understanding of vocabulary.

3. Check students' comprehension, using some or all of the following questions:

   What don't I want to do tonight?
   Why not?
   What doesn't Maggie want to do tonight?
   Why not?
   What doesn't Mark want to do tonight?
   Why not?
   What don't Betty and Mike want to do tonight?
   Why not?
   Who wants to go dancing?
   Why not?

 ROLE PLAY

1. Make sure students understand the instructions. Check understanding of the expression *Look!*

2. Have students work in groups to create a role play based on the model. Encourage them to continue the conversation any way they wish.

3. Call on groups to present their role plays to the class.

READING EXTENSION

Have students answer these questions in groups and then share their ideas with the class.

   What have you done in your free time this week?

   What are you going to do in your free time next weekend?

 COMPLETE THE STORY

Before doing the activity, introduce the following new vocabulary:

> aspirin
> at the beginning
> at this point
> extremely
> get rid of

Answers

1. gone
2. seen
3. stayed
4. taken
5. drunk
6. eaten
7. rested
8. done

CHAPTER 4   127

Text Page 45: They Haven't Had the Time

FOCUS

- Present Perfect Tense: Negative Statements

CLOSE UP

RULE: In spoken and informal written English, the auxiliary verb *have/has* contracts with *not*.

EXAMPLES: I **haven't** (have not) had the time.
She **hasn't** (has not) drawn in a long time.

INTRODUCING THE MODELS

There are two model conversations. Introduce and practice each separately. For each model:

1. Have students look at the model illustration.
2. Set the scene.
    - 1st model: "Two co-workers are talking after work."
    - 2nd model: "A friend is asking Rita's mother a question."
3. Present the model.
4. Full-Class Repetition.
5. Ask students if they have any questions. Check understanding of the expressions *in a long time, have the time*.
6. Group Choral Repetition.
7. Choral Conversation.
8. Call on one or two pairs of students to present the dialog.

    (For additional practice, do Choral Conversation in small groups or by rows.)

SIDE BY SIDE EXERCISES

Examples

1. A. Do you like to ride your bicycle?
   B. Yes, but I haven't ridden my bicycle in a long time.
   A. Why not?
   B. I haven't had the time.
2. A. Does Arthur like to write poetry?
   B. Yes, but he hasn't written poetry in a long time.
   A. Why not?
   B. He hasn't had the time.

1. **Exercise 1:** Call on two students to present the dialog. Then do Choral Repetition and Choral Conversation practice.
2. **Exercise 2:** Same as above.
3. **Exercises 3–8:** Either Full-Class Practice or Pair Practice.

128   CHAPTER 4

New Vocabulary

3. go kayaking
4. Monopoly
7. dance lesson

Culture Note:

Exercise 4: *Monopoly* is a popular board game.

4. **Exercise 9:** Have students use the model as a guide to create their own conversations, using vocabulary of their choice. Encourage students to use dictionaries to find new words they want to use. This exercise can be done orally in class or for written homework. If you assign it for homework, do one example in class to make sure students understand what's expected. Have students present their conversations in class the next day.

WORKBOOK

Pages 44–45

EXPANSION ACTIVITIES

1. **Can You Hear the Difference?** ★

    a. Write on the board:

Positive	Negative
I have seen that play.	I haven't seen that play.
You have met them before.	You haven't met them before.
She has written many letters.	She hasn't written many letters.
It has been a long time.	It hasn't been a long time.
We have eaten all the pie.	We haven't eaten all the pie.
They have bought the milk.	They haven't bought the milk.

    b. Choose a sentence randomly from one of the two columns and say it to the class. Have the class listen and identify whether the sentence is *positive* or *negative*.

    c. Have students continue the activity in pairs. One student says a sentence, and the other tells whether it's positive or negative. Then have them reverse roles.

    d. Write other similar sentences on the board and continue the practice.

2. **Telephone** ★

    a. Divide the class into large groups. Have each group sit in a circle.

    b. Whisper the following sentence to a student:

    "He's gotten up, he's taken a shower, he's done his exercises, and he's eaten breakfast, but he hasn't gone to work yet."

    c. The first student whispers the message to the second student, and so forth around the circle. The student listening may ask for clarification by saying "I'm sorry. Could you repeat that?"

    d. When the message gets to the last student, that person says it aloud. Is it the same message you started with? The group with the most accurate message wins.

3. **Match the Sentences** ★★

    a. Make the following set of split sentence cards:

I like to swim, . . .	but I haven't swum in a long time.
I like to sing, . . .	but I haven't sung in a long time.
I like to draw, . . .	but I haven't drawn in a long time.
I like to write music, . . .	but I haven't written music in a long time.

    (continued)

CHAPTER 4   129

EXPANSION ACTIVITIES (Continued)

I like to ride my bicycle, …	but I haven't ridden my bicycle in a long time.
I like to see movies, …	but I haven't seen a movie in a long time.
I like to eat pizza, …	but I haven't eaten pizza in a long time.
I like to go dancing, …	but I haven't gone dancing in a long time.
I like to speak French, …	but I haven't spoken French in a long time.

b. Distribute a card to each student.

c. Have students memorize the phrases on their cards, and then have students walk around the room saying their phrases until they find their match.

d. Then have pairs of students say their matched sentences aloud to the class.

4. Change the Sentence! ★★

a. Write a sentence on the board, underlining and numbering different portions of the sentence. For example:

```
   1          2        3              4
I haven't   seen   my friends   in a long time.
```

b. Have students sit in a circle.

c. Tell them that when you say a number, the first student in the circle makes a change in that part of the sentence. For example:

    Teacher: Two.
    Student 1: I haven't <u>spoken to</u> my friends in a long time.

d. The second student keeps the first student's sentence, but changes it based on the next number you say. For example:

    Teacher: Three.
    Student 2: I haven't spoken to <u>my neighbors</u> in a long time.

e. Continue this way with the rest of the students in the circle. For example:

    Teacher: Four.
    Student 3: I haven't spoken to my neighbors <u>this week</u>.

5. Not This Week! ★★

a. Write the following on the board:

b. Read each of the following sentences, and have students complete the follow-up sentence on the board. For example:

    Teacher: Rita usually draws cartoons.
    Student: I know. But this week she hasn't drawn cartoons at all.

Possible sentences:

    Rita usually draws cartoons.
    David usually does yoga in the morning.
    We usually see our friends after class.
    Bob usually rides his bicycle to work.
    Susan usually takes the bus to work.
    Arthur usually writes in his journal every day.
    My father usually drives his car to work.
    My friends and I usually meet at a cafe.
    Vicky usually eats lunch in a restaurant.
    Nancy usually goes to the health club every evening.

6. Plans for the Weekend ★★

a. Write the following on the board:

> A. What are you going to do this weekend?
> B. I'm not sure. I think I'll _____.
>   I haven't _____ in a long time.

b. Have pairs of students create conversations about their weekend plans, using the model on the board.

c. Call on pairs to present their conversations to the class.

Example:

> A. What are you going to do this weekend?
> B. I'm not sure. I think I'll drive to the beach.
>   I haven't driven to the beach in a long time.

7. Category Dictation ★★

a. Have students draw two columns on a piece of paper. At the top of one column, have students write Things I've Done This Week. At the top of the other column, have them write Things I Haven't Done This Week.

b. Dictate activities such as the following:

do my laundry   ride my bicycle
write to a friend   swim
go to the bank   see a movie
get a haircut   fly in an airplane
take the bus   draw a picture
drive my car

c. Have students write sentences about these activities in the appropriate column. For example:

Things I've Done This Week	Things I Haven't Done This Week
I've gone to the bank.	I haven't done my laundry.
I've gotten a haircut.	I haven't written to a friend.
I've taken the bus.	I haven't ridden my bicycle.

8. Which One Isn't True? ★★

a. Tell students to write three true present perfect statements and one false statement about themselves. For example:

> I've never gone kayaking.
> I've done yoga for many years.
> I've seen ten Broadway shows.
> I've had a bad headache all day.

b. Have students take turns reading their statements to the class, and have the class guess which statement isn't true.

9. New in Town! ★★★

a. Put the following on the board:

The Henderson Family
Joan   Mark   Bob   Sally

A. {Has / Have} _____ yet?
B. Yes, _____.
   or
   No. They haven't had the time.

b. Set the scene: "Mr. and Mrs. Henderson and their children are new in town. They've just moved here, and they've been very busy. I think they're going to like (name of your city) very much."

c. Have students create conversations in which they ask about all the experiences the Hendersons have had in their new city. For example, students can ask about getting an apartment, finding work, starting school, and going to local tourist sights and landmarks.

Examples:

> A. Have the Hendersons found an apartment yet?
> B. Yes, they have. They found an apartment on Maple Street.

> A. Have the children started school yet?
> B. Yes, they have. They started school last month, and they like it very much.

> A. Have they visited the museum yet?
> B. No. They haven't had the time.

Text Page 46: Has Timmy Gone to Bed Yet?

FOCUS

- Present Perfect Tense:
  Negative Short Answers
  Questions with *Yet*

INTRODUCING THE MODEL

1. Have students look at the model illustration.
2. Set the scene: "Timmy's parents are talking about Timmy."
3. Present the model.
4. Full-Class Choral Repetition.
5. Ask students if they have any questions. Check understanding of the expression *go to bed*.
6. Group Choral Repetition.
7. Choral Conversation.
8. Call on one or two pairs of students to present the dialog.

    (For additional practice, do Choral Conversation in small groups or by rows.)

SIDE BY SIDE EXERCISES

Examples

1. A. Has Amanda done her homework yet?
   B. No, she hasn't. She has to do her homework now.
2. A. Have you taken your medicine yet?
   B. No, I haven't. I have to take my medicine now.

1. **Exercise 1:** Call on two students to present the dialog. Then do Choral Repetition and Choral Conversation practice.
2. **Exercise 2:** Introduce the word *medicine*. Same as above.
3. **Exercises 3–9:** Either Full-Class Practice or Pair Practice.

New Vocabulary

4. leave for school
6. term paper
9. electric bill

WORKBOOK

Pages 46–47

132   CHAPTER 4

EXPANSION ACTIVITIES

1. **Grammar Chain** ★★

   a. Write on the board:

   > A. Have you _____ yet?
   > B. No, I haven't. I have to _____ now.
   >   Have you _____ yet?

   b. Start the chain game by saying:

   > Teacher (to Student A): Have you *done your homework* yet?

   c. Student A answers according to the model, then asks Student B another present perfect question, and the chain continues. For example:

   > Student A: No, I haven't. I have to do my homework now.
   > (to Student B): Have you *written your paper* yet?
   > Student B: No, I haven't. I have to write my paper now.
   > (to Student C): Have you *eaten lunch* yet?

   d. Continue until everyone gets a chance to answer and ask a question.

2. **Tic Tac Question the Answer** ★★

   a. Draw a tic tac grid on the board and fill it in with the following short answers to questions:

Yes, we have.	No, she hasn't.	Yes, he did.
No, I didn't.	Yes, I have.	No, it hasn't.
No, they haven't.	Yes, he has.	No, we didn't.

   b. Divide the class into teams. Give each team a mark: X or O.

   c. Have each team ask a question for an answer in the grid. For example:

   > X Team: Have you done your homework yet?
   >   Yes, I have.

   d. If the question is appropriate and is stated correctly, that team may replace the answer with its team mark. For example:

Yes, we have.	No, she hasn't.	Yes, he did.
No, I didn't.	X	No, it hasn't.
No, they haven't.	Yes, he has.	No, we didn't.

   e. The first team to mark out three boxes in a straight line—either vertically, horizontally, or diagonally—wins.

3. **Mystery Conversations** ★★★

   a. Divide the class into pairs.

   b. Write the following conversation framework on the board:

   c. Write roles such as the following on word cards and give one to each pair of students:

a parent and a child	a boss and an employee
a teacher and a student	two friends
two neighbors	a nurse and a patient
a wife and a husband	a brother and a sister

   (continued)

   CHAPTER 4   133

EXPANSION ACTIVITIES (Continued)

d. Have each pair create a short dialog that begins "Have you _____ yet?" The dialogs should be appropriate for the roles the students have on their cards.

e. Have each pair present their dialog to the class. Then have the other students guess who the people are: Are they friends? Is a teacher talking to a student? For example:

[parent–child]
A. Have you cleaned your room yet?
B. No, I haven't. But I'm going to clean it tonight.
A. Well, please don't forget. I've already asked you two times.
B. Don't worry. I won't forget.

[boss–employee]
A. Have you typed those letters yet?
B. Yes, I have. I just finished them a few minutes ago.
A. Can I see them, please?
B. Certainly. Here they are.

4. Asking Questions ★★★

a. Write the following on the board:

```
          Have/Has _____?

take his medicine       finish her homework
get up                  say good-bye
feed him                call her boss
go to bed               speak to your
pay his electric bill     landlord
```

b. Read the situations below and call on students to respond, using the present perfect and an appropriate phrase from the list on the board. For example:

Teacher: I don't have any heat in my apartment!
Student: Have you spoken to your landlord?

Situations:

I don't have any heat in my apartment!
(Have you spoken to your landlord?)

The lights in Henry's house won't go on.
(Has he paid his electric bill?)

Walter is feeling very sick.
(Has he taken his medicine?)

The dog is very hungry, and he's barking loudly.
(Have you fed him?)

My daughter wants to watch TV.
(Has she finished her homework?)

Mary's alarm clock is ringing.
(Has she gotten up?)

Alice has decided to stay home from work today.
(Has she called her boss?)

My son is very tired.
(Has he gone to bed?)

Margaret and Michael are leaving for the airport.
(Have they said good-bye?)

5. Going Abroad ★★★

a. Write the following on the board:

```
Have you _____ yet?

get your passport
apply for your visa
buy _____ for the trip
make hotel reservations
pack
buy your plane ticket
_____
```

b. Divide the class into pairs and set the scene: "One of you is going on a trip and you have a lot of things to do before you go. Your friend is trying to help you remember everything you have to do."

c. Using cues on the board, have pairs create conversations about the trip one of them is going to take.

d. After the students have *rehearsed* their conversations, call on several pairs to present their conversations to the class. For example:

134   CHAPTER 4

A. Where are you going?
B. To China.
A. When are you leaving?
B. Next month.
A. Have you gotten your passport yet?
B. Yes, I have. I got it yesterday.
A. Have you bought clothes for the trip yet?
B. Yes. I've already bought everything I need.
A. Have you packed yet?
B. No, I haven't. I'll pack the night before I leave.
A. Have you learned any Chinese phrases yet?
B. Yes. I've learned how to say "Hello" and "Good-bye."

Text Page 47

READING Working Overtime

FOCUS

- Present Perfect Tense
- Expressions with *Still*

NEW VOCABULARY

as for me   office clerk
bookkeeper   surprised

READING THE STORY

Optional: Preview the story by having students talk about the story title and/or illustration. You may choose to introduce new vocabulary beforehand, or have students encounter the new vocabulary within the context of the reading.

1. Have students read silently or follow along silently as the story is read aloud by you, by one or more students, or on the audio program.

2. Ask students if they have any questions. Check understanding of vocabulary.

   Culture Note

   Overtime is any work done over the 40-hour work week. Workers are usually paid more per hour than their normal salary, usually one and a half times their hourly wage.

3. Check students' comprehension, using some or all of the following questions:

   Have the employees of the Goodwell Computer Company gone home yet?
   Why not?
   Why hasn't the secretary gone home yet?
   Why hasn't the bookkeeper gone home yet?
   Why haven't the office clerks gone home yet?
   Why hasn't the boss gone home yet?
   Why hasn't the custodian gone home yet?
   Why hasn't he cleaned all the offices?
   Why isn't he surprised?

✓ READING CHECK-UP

Q & A

1. Call on a pair of students to present the model. Check understanding of the expression *Have a good weekend*.

2. Have students work in pairs to create new dialogs.

3. Call on pairs to present their new dialogs to the class.

READING EXTENSION

Tic Tac Question Formation

1. Draw a tic tac grid on the board and fill it with question words. For example:

Have?	Who?	What?
Has?	How many?	What day?
Is?	Are?	Where?

2. Divide the class into two teams. Give each team a mark: *X* or *O*.

3. Have each team ask a question that begins with one of the question words and then provide the answer to the question. If the question and answer are correct, the team gets to put its mark in that space. For example:

   X Team: Have the office clerks delivered all the mail?
   No, they haven't.

136   CHAPTER 4

X	Who?	What?
Has?	How many?	What day?
Is?	Are?	Where?

4. The first team to mark out three boxes in a straight line—vertically, horizontally, or diagonally—wins.

WHAT'S THE WORD?

Before doing the exercise, check understanding of the expression *mail room* in Exercise 7.

1. seen
   saw

2. eaten
   ate

3. gone
   has, went

4. spoken
   have, spoke

5. made
   made

6. read
   read

7. taken
   hasn't, took
   he hasn't taken

8. finished
   has, gone

CHAPTER 4   137

Text Page 48: Have You Seen Any Good Movies Recently?

FOCUS

- Present Perfect Tense
- Expressions with *Recently* and *Ever*

INTRODUCING THE MODEL

1. Have students look at the model illustration.
2. Set the scene: "Two co-workers are talking during a break on the job."
3. Present the model.
4. Full-Class Repetition.
5. Ask students if they have any questions. Check understanding of the word *recently*.
6. Group Choral Repetition.
7. Choral Conversation.
8. Call on one or two pairs of students to present the dialog.

   (For additional practice, do Choral Conversation in small groups or by rows.)

SIDE BY SIDE EXERCISES

Example

1. A. Have you read any good books recently?
   B. Yes, I have. I read a very good book last week.
   A. Really? What book did you read?
   B. I read *(War and Peace)*.
   A. Oh. How was it?
   B. It was excellent. It's one of the best books I've ever read.

1. **Exercise 1:** Call on two students to present the dialog. Then do Choral Repetition and Choral Conversation practice.
2. **Exercises 2–3:** Either Full-Class Practice or Pair Practice.

How to Say It!

Expressing Satisfaction: In informal and spoken English, there are many ways to express satisfaction, such as the ones listed on text page 48. "Awesome" and "phenomenal" are popular expressions among younger speakers.

1. Set the scene: "The co-workers from the conversation above are talking."
2. Present the expressions.
3. Full-Class Repetition.
4. Ask students if they have any questions.
5. Group Choral Repetition.
6. Have students practice the conversations in this lesson again, using any of these new expressions.
7. Call on pairs to present their conversations to the class.

WORKBOOK

Pages 48–50

138   CHAPTER 4

EXPANSION ACTIVITIES

1. **Disappearing Dialog** ★
   a. Write the model conversation on the board.
   b. Ask for two student volunteers to read the conversation.
   c. Erase a few of the words from each line of the dialog. Have two different students read the conversation.
   d. Erase more words and call on two more students to read the conversation.
   e. Continue erasing words and calling on pairs of students to say the model until all the words have been erased and the dialog has disappeared.

2. **Role Play: Meeting a Famous Person** ★★
   a. Ask students to name a few of their favorite writers, actors/actresses, dancers, singers, or other artists.
   b. Write on the board:

   > A. Excuse me. Aren't you _____?
   > B. Yes, I am.
   > A. (Mr./Mrs./Miss/Ms.) _____, I've always wanted to meet you! I've _____ all your _____s, and I think they're the _____ _____s I've ever _____.
   > B. Thank you very much.

   (Have students expand the dialog.)

   c. Set the scene: "Imagine that you're walking down the street and you see a famous person you have always wanted to meet."
   d. Call on pairs of students to role play this chance encounter. Student A can pretend to meet the writer/actor/etc, he or she really admires. For example:

   > A. Excuse me. Aren't you Sophia Loren?
   > B. Yes, I am.
   > A. Ms. Loren, I've always wanted to meet you! I've seen all your movies, and I think they're the best movies I've ever seen.
   > B. Thank you very much.

   (Possible expansion)
   > A. Ms. Loren. Could you possibly do me a favor?
   > B. Of course. What is it?
   > A. Could you please give me your autograph?
   > B. I'll be happy to.

3. **Our Recommendations** ★★
   a. Write the following conversation model on the board:

   > A. Can you recommend a good { book / movie / restaurant / hotel / TV program / _____ }?
   > B. Yes. _____ is a good _____. As a matter of fact, I think it's one of the best _____s I've ever _____.
   > A. _____.
   > B. _____.
   > A. That's great! Thanks for the recommendation.

   b. Call on pairs of students to create conversations based on the model, using names of real books, movies, restaurants, hotels, etc. For example:

   > A. Can you recommend a good restaurant?
   > B. Yes. Luigi's is a good restaurant. As a matter of fact, I think it's one of the best restaurants I've ever eaten at.
   > A. Is it very expensive?
   > B. No, not at all.
   > A. That's great! Thanks for the recommendation.
   >
   > A. Can you recommend a good hotel?
   > B. Yes. The Windsor is a good hotel. As a matter of fact, I think it's one of the best hotels I've ever stayed at.
   > A. Where is it located?
   > B. It's on Jackson Boulevard, near the park.
   > A. That's great! Thanks for the recommendation.

   (continued)

EXPANSION ACTIVITIES (Continued)

4. Write a Review ★★★

   a. Have students pretend they work for a newspaper and write a review of one of the following:

   a movie they've seen
   a play they've seen
   a book they've read
   a restaurant where they've eaten

   b. Have students read their reviews to the class, and have others react to the reviews by agreeing or disagreeing, or perhaps by asking for more information about the movie, play, book, or restaurant.

5. The Best! ★★

   a. Divide the class into small groups. Have students develop a listing of their recommendations for the following:

   the best restaurant
   the best fast-food restaurant
   the best newspaper
   the best magazine
   the best new movie
   the best TV program
   the best CD

   b. Have the groups share their ideas with the class and compile the top three picks for each category, if necessary through voting.

   Option: ★★★ Have students "publish" their listing and distribute it to other classes in your school.

140   CHAPTER 4

Text Page 49

 **READING** *Linda Likes New York*

FOCUS

- Present Perfect Tense

NEW VOCABULARY

Empire State Building
Statue of Liberty
take a tour
Times Square
top
United Nations

READING THE STORY

Optional: Preview the story by having students talk about the story title and/or illustration. You may choose to introduce new vocabulary beforehand, or have students encounter the new vocabulary within the context of the reading.

1. Have students read silently or follow along silently as the story is read aloud by you, by one or more students, or on the audio program.
2. Ask students if they have any questions. Check understanding of vocabulary.
3. Check students' comprehension, using the following questions:

   What has Linda done in New York?
   What hasn't she done yet?

   Culture Note

   Times Square on New Year's Eve: Thousands of people gather in Times Square in New York City to count down the last minute of the old year as a giant ball descends. Everyone cheers when the ball touches down and marks the new year.

READING EXTENSION

Have students answer these questions in pairs or small groups and then share their ideas.

1. *Places We Have Visited*

   Have students tell about interesting places they have visited.

   Where did they go?
   What interesting things did they see?
   What did they do there?

2. *Places We Want to Visit*

   Have students tell about interesting places they *want to* visit.

   What places around the world do you want to visit?
   What do you want to do and see in those places?
   What are some places you want to visit in your own city or region?

 LISTENING

Before doing the listening, introduce the new words *cable car, Golden Gate Bridge, Golden Gate Park, Alcatraz Prison, Chinatown, Fisherman's Wharf.*

1. **Linda is on vacation in San Francisco. This is her list of things to do. Check the things on the list Linda has already done.**

   Linda has already seen the Golden Gate Bridge. She hasn't visited Golden Gate Park yet. She took a tour of Alcatraz Prison yesterday. She's going to go to Chinatown tomorrow. She hasn't ridden a cable car yet. She's eaten at Fisherman's Wharf, but she hasn't had time to buy souvenirs.

2. **Alan is a secretary in a very busy office. This is his list of things to do before 5 P.M. on Friday. Check the things on the list Alan has already done.**

CHAPTER 4   141

Alan has already called Mrs. Porter. He has to type the letter to the Mervis Company. He hasn't taken the mail to the post office yet. He's gone to the bank. He hasn't sent an e-mail to the company's office in Denver, and he's going to speak to the boss about his salary next week.

3. **It's Saturday, and Judy and Paul Johnson are doing lots of things around the house. This is the list of things they have to do today. Check the things on the list they've already done.**

Judy and Paul haven't done the laundry. They have to wash the kitchen windows. They've paid the bills. They haven't given the dog a bath. They'll clean the garage later. They couldn't fix the bathroom sink or repair the fence, but they vacuumed the living room rug.

Answers

- ✓ see the Golden Gate Bridge
- ___ visit Golden Gate Park
- ✓ take a tour of Alcatraz Prison
- ___ go to Chinatown
- ___ ride a cable car
- ✓ eat at Fisherman's Wharf
- ___ buy souvenirs

- ✓ call Mrs. Porter
- ___ type the letter to the Mervis Company
- ___ take the mail to the post office
- ✓ go to the bank
- ___ send an e-mail to the company's office in Denver
- ___ speak to the boss about my salary

- ___ do the laundry
- ___ wash the kitchen windows
- ✓ pay the bills
- ___ give the dog a bath
- ___ clean the garage
- ___ the bathroom sink
- ___ repair the fence
- ✓ vacuum the living room rug

 Make a List!

Have students share their lists of *things they have and haven't done this week* with each other in pairs or small groups.

142 CHAPTER 4

Text Page 50

 PRONUNCIATION
Contractions with *is* & *has*

 JOURNAL

> **Contractions with *is* & *has*:** When the auxiliary verbs *is* and *has* are contracted, they are indistinguishable. *He's (he is)* is pronounced and written the same way as *he's (he has)*.

Have students write their journal entries at home or in class. Encourage students to use a dictionary to look up words they would like to use. Students can share their written work with other students if appropriate. Have students discuss what they have written as a class, in pairs, or in small groups.

Focus on Listening

Practice the sentences in the left column. Say each sentence or play the audio one or more times. Have students listen carefully and repeat.

 CHAPTER SUMMARY

Focus on Pronunciation

Practice the sentences in the right column. Have students say each sentence and then listen carefully as you say it or play the audio.

If you wish, have students continue practicing the sentences to improve their pronunciation.

GRAMMAR

1. Divide the class into pairs or small groups.
2. Have students take turns forming sentences from the words in the grammar boxes. Student A says a sentence, and Student B points to the words from each column that are in the sentence. Then have students switch: Student B says a sentence, and Student A points to the words.

WORKBOOK

Page 51

EXPANSION ACTIVITY

Category Dictation ★★

1. Have students draw two columns on a piece of paper. At the top of one column, have students write *is*. At the top of the other column, have them write *has*.
2. Dictate various sentences with *is* and *has* (as an auxiliary), and have students write them in the appropriate columns. For example:

is	*has*
He's going to see a movie.	He's seen a movie.
She's very tired.	She's been very tired.
It's working well.	It's worked well.

EXPANSION ACTIVITY

Tic Tac Grammar ★

1. Have students draw a tic tac grid on a piece of paper and fill it in with the present form of any of the verbs on text page 50.
2. Call out the past participle of any of these verbs. Tell students to cross out any present tense verb on their grid for which you have given a past participle form.
3. The first person to cross out three verbs in a straight line—either vertically, horizontally, or diagonally—wins the game.
4. Have the winner call out the words to check the accuracy.

CHAPTER 4   143

KEY VOCABULARY

Have students ask you any questions about the meaning or pronunciation of the vocabulary. If students ask for the pronunciation, repeat after the student until the student is satisfied with his or her own pronunciation.

EXPANSION ACTIVITIES

1. **Do You Remember the Verbs?** ★

   Check students' retention of the vocabulary depicted on the opening page of Chapter 4 by doing the following activity:

   a. Have students open their books to text page 37 and cover the list of verb phrases.

   b. Call out a number and have students tell you the phrase in the present perfect.

   Variation: You can also do this activity as a game with competing teams.

2. **Student-Led Dictation** ★

   a. Tell each student to choose a verb in its three forms from the Key Vocabulary list on text page 50 and look at it very carefully.

   b. Have students take turns dictating their words to the class. Everybody writes down that student's words.

   c. When the dictation is completed, call on different students to write each word on the board to check the spelling.

3. **Letter Game** ★

   a. Divide the class into two teams.

   b. Say: "I'm thinking of a verb that starts with *g.*"

   c. The first person to raise his or her hand and guess correctly and say its present, simple past, and past participle forms [*give-gave-given*] wins a point for his or her team.

   d. Continue with other letters of the alphabet and verbs.

   The team that gets the most correct answers wins the game.

4. **Miming** ★

   a. Write down on cards some of the actions and activities listed on text page 50.

   b. Have students take turns picking a card from the pile and pantomiming the action on the card.

   c. The class must guess what the person is doing and say the present, simple past, and past participle forms.

   Variation: This can be done as a game with competing teams.

5. **Finish the Sentence!** ★★

   Begin a sentence using the verbs listed on text page 50, and have students repeat what you said and add appropriate endings to the sentence. For example:

Teacher	Students
I've drawn . . .	I've drawn cartoons.
	I've drawn pictures.
He's written . . .	He's written reports.
	He's written term papers.
	He's written letters.
We've ridden . . .	We've ridden horses.
	We've ridden motorcycles
	We've ridden bicycles.

   Variation: This activity may be done as a class, in pairs or small groups, or as a game with competing teams.

END-OF-CHAPTER ACTIVITIES

1. Board Game ★★★

    a. On poster boards or on manila file folders, make up game boards with a pathway consisting of separate spaces. You may use any theme or design you wish.

    b. Divide the class into groups of 2 to 4 students and give each group a game board and a die, and each student something to be used as a playing piece.

    c. Give each group a pile of cards face-down with statements written on them. Some sentences should be correct, and others incorrect. For example:

    > I have flew airplanes.
    > Do you know how to speak Spanish?
    > I've sung on Broadway.
    > Have you gone to the zoo ever?
    > Never I've eaten lunch with the president.
    > Have you ever fallen asleep in class?
    > Is the teacher explained it yet?
    > She's given a speech last year.
    > She's gone already to the mall.
    > We have done yoga yesterday.
    > He hasn't gotten a haircut yet.
    > I've already went to the bank.
    > We have to pay the bills now.
    > That is one of the best videos I ever saw.

    d. Each student in turn rolls the die, moves the playing piece along the game path, and after landing on a space, picks a card, reads the sentence, and says if it is *correct* or *incorrect*. If the statement is incorrect, the student must correct it. If the response is correct, the student takes an additional turn.

    e. The first student to reach the end of the pathway is the winner.

2. Question Game ★★

    a. Write the following sentence on the board:

    > Laura likes to go to the museum, but hasn't gone in a long time because she hasn't had the time.

    b. Underline different elements of the sentence, and have students create a question based on that portion of the sentence. For example:

    > Laura likes to go <u>to the museum</u>, but hasn't gone in a long time because she hasn't had the time.

    Where does Laura like to go?

    > Laura likes to go to the museum, but hasn't gone in a long time <u>because she hasn't had the time</u>.

    Why hasn't Laura gone to the museum in a long time?

    c. Continue with other sentences.

3. Dialog Builder! ★★★

    a. Divide the class into pairs.

    b. Write several lines on the board from conversations in Chapter 4 such as the following:

    > I'm jealous.
    > Yes, I have.
    > A little while ago.
    > Really?
    > When?
    > Why not?
    > It was phenomenal.

    c. Have each pair create a conversation incorporating those lines. Students can begin and end their conversations any way they wish, but they must include those lines in their dialogs.

    d. Call on students to present their conversations to the class.

CHAPTER 4

WORKBOOK ANSWER KEY AND LISTENING SCRIPTS

WORKBOOK PAGE 36

A. FOR MANY YEARS

1. I've given
2. I've flown
3. I've ridden
4. I've spoken
5. I've taken
6. I've done
7. I've drawn
8. I've written
9. I've driven

B. LISTENING

Listen and choose the word you hear.

1. I've ridden them for many years.
2. Yes. I've taken French.
3. I'm giving injections.
4. I've driven one for many years.
5. Yes. I've written it.
6. I'm drawing it right now.
7. I've spoken it for many years.
8. Yes. I've drawn that.

Answers

1. a
2. b
3. a
4. b
5. b
6. a
7. a
8. b

WORKBOOK PAGE 37

C. I'VE NEVER

1. I've never flown
2. I've never gotten
3. I've never ridden
4. I've never drawn
5. I've never written
6. I've never taken
7. I've never sung
8. I've never swum
9. I've never been
10. I've never gone
11. I've never given
12. I've never seen

D. LISTENING

Is Speaker B answering *Yes* or *No*? Listen to each conversation and circle the correct answer.

1. A. Do you know how to drive a bus?
   B. I've driven a bus for many years.
2. A. I usually take the train to work. Do you also take the train?
   B. Actually, I've never taken the train to work.
3. A. Are you a good swimmer?
   B. To tell the truth, I've never swum very well.
4. A. Did you get up early this morning?
   B. I've gotten up early every morning this week.
5. A. I'm going to give my dog a bath today. Do you have any advice?
   B. Sorry. I don't. I've never given my dog a bath.
6. A. Do you like to eat sushi?
   B. Of course! I've eaten sushi for many years.
7. A. I just got a big raise! Did you also get one?
   B. Actually, I've never gotten a raise.
8. A. I did very well on the math exam. How about you?
   B. I've never done well on a math exam.

Answers

1. Yes
2. No
3. No
4. Yes
5. No
6. Yes
7. No
8. No

WORKBOOK PAGE 38

E. WHAT ARE THEY SAYING?

1. Have you ever gotten
   I got
2. Have you ever ridden
   I rode
3. Have you ever worn
   I wore
4. Have you ever gone
   I went
5. Have you ever given
   I gave
6. Have you ever fallen
   I fell

WORKBOOK PAGE 39

G. WHAT ARE THEY SAYING?

1. Have, eaten
   they have, They ate
2. Has, driven
   he has, He drove

146   CHAPTER 4

3. Has, gone
   she has, She went
4. Have, seen
   we have, We saw
5. Have, taken
   they have, They took
6. Have, spoken
   I have, I spoke
7. Have, written
   you have, You wrote
8. Have, met
   we have, We met

WORKBOOK PAGE 40

H. NOT TODAY

1. They've, eaten
   They ate
2. She's, gone
   She went
3. He's, worn
   He wore
4. We've, done
   We did
5. He's, given
   He gave
6. I've, seen
   I saw
7. We've, bought
   We bought
8. She's, visited
   She visited
9. He's, taken
   He took

WORKBOOK PAGE 41

I. WHAT'S THE WORD?

1. go
2. went
3. gone
4. seen
5. saw
6. see
7. ate
8. eaten
9. eat
10. write
11. written
12. wrote
13. wear
14. worn
15. wore
16. spoke
17. speak
18. spoken
19. driven
20. drive
21. drove
22. do
23. did
24. done

WORKBOOK PAGES 42–43

J. WHAT ARE THEY SAYING?

1. I've, done
   I did
   have, written
   I have
2. I've, swum
   I swam
3. I've, taken
   I took
   Have, taken
   I have, took
4. He's, gotten
   He got
5. We've, eaten
   We ate
   eaten
6. I've, spoken
   I spoke

WORKBOOK PAGES 44–45

L. IN A LONG TIME

1. I haven't ridden
2. haven't bought
3. I haven't flown
4. I haven't taken
5. I haven't swum
6. hasn't eaten
7. hasn't cleaned
8. He hasn't read
9. I haven't studied
10. haven't seen
11. I haven't given
12. He hasn't made
13. haven't gone
14. I haven't danced

M. PUZZLE: What Have They Already Done?

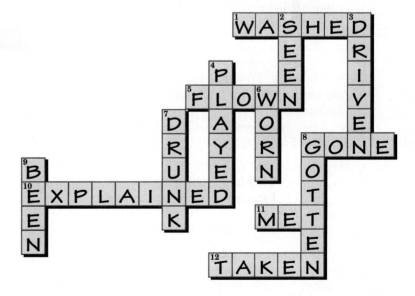

CHAPTER 4   147

WORKBOOK PAGES 46–47

N. A LOT OF THINGS TO DO

1. He's already gone to the supermarket.
2. He hasn't cleaned his apartment yet.
3. He's already gotten a haircut.
4. He hasn't baked a cake yet.
5. He's already fixed his CD player.
6. She's already taken a shower.
7. She hasn't done her exercises yet.
8. She hasn't fed the cat yet.
9. She's already walked the dog.
10. She hasn't eaten breakfast yet.
11. They haven't done their laundry yet.
12. They've already gotten their paychecks.
13. They've already paid their bills.
14. They haven't packed their suitcases yet.
15. They haven't said good-bye to their friends yet.
16. She's already written to Mrs. Lane.
17. She's already called Mr. Sanchez.
18. She hasn't met with Ms. Wong yet.
19. She hasn't read her e-mail yet.
20. She's already sent a fax to the Ace Company.

O. LISTENING

What things have these people done? What haven't they done? Listen and check *Yes* or *No*.

1. A. Carla, have you done your homework yet?
   B. Yes, I have. I did my homework this morning.
   A. And have you practiced the violin?
   B. No, I haven't practiced yet. I promise I'll practice this afternoon.

2. A. Kevin?
   B. Yes, Mrs. Blackwell?
   A. Have you written your report yet?
   B. No, I haven't. I'll write it immediately.
   A. And have you sent a fax to the Crane Company?
   B. No, I haven't. I promise I'll send them a fax after I write the report.

3. A. Have you fed the dog yet?
   B. Yes, I have. I fed him a few minutes ago.
   A. Good. Well, I guess we can leave for work now.
   B. But we haven't eaten breakfast yet!

4. A. I'm leaving now, Mr. Green.
   B. Have you fixed the pipes in the basement, Charlie?
   A. Yes, I have.
   B. And have you repaired the washing machine?
   A. Yes, I have. It's working again.
   B. That's great! Thank you, Charlie.
   A. I'll send you a bill, Mr. Green.

5. A. You know, we haven't done the laundry all week.
   B. I know. We should do it today.
   A. We also haven't vacuumed the rugs!
   B. We haven't?
   A. No, we haven't.
   B. Oh. I guess we should vacuum them today.

6. A. Are we ready for the party?
   B. I think so. We've gotten all the food at the supermarket, and we've cleaned the house from top to bottom!
   A. Well, I guess we're ready for the party!

7. A. Have you spoken to the landlord about our broken light?
   B. Yes, I have. I spoke to him this morning.
   A. What did he say?
   B. He said we should call an electrician.
   A. Okay. Let's call Ajax Electric.
   B. Don't worry. I've already called them, and they're coming this afternoon.

8. A. Have you hooked up the new VCR yet?
   B. I can't do it. It's really difficult.
   A. Have you read the instructions?
   B. Yes, I have. I've read them ten times, and I still can't understand them!

Answers

	Yes	No
1.	✔	
		✔
2.		✔
		✔
3.	✔	
		✔
4.	✔	
	✔	
5.		✔
		✔
6.	✔	
	✔	
7.	✔	
	✔	
8.		✔
	✔	

WORKBOOK PAGES 48–49

P. WHAT ARE THEY SAYING?

1. have, spoke
   did
   flown
2. Have
   haven't, saw
   see
   seen
3. taken
   took
   Have, sent
   sent
   Have, given
4. Have
   have, went
   Have, gone/been
   have, I went/was
5. did
   gave
   are you going to buy
   spent
   did you
   bought
   listen
6. I'm not, taken
   got
   Have
   I have, ate
   washed/done

WORKBOOK PAGE 50

R.   _J_ ULIA'S BROKEN KEYBOARD

1.

> _J_udy,
>
> Have you seen my blue and _y_ellow _j_acket at _y_our house? I think I left it there _y_esterday after the _j_azz concert. I've looked everywhere, and I _j_ust can't find it anywhere.
>
>   _J_ulia

2.

> Dear _J_ennifer,
>
> We're sorry _y_ou haven't been able to visit us this _y_ear. Do _y_ou think _y_ou could come in _J_une or _J_uly? We really en_j_oyed _y_our visit last _y_ear. We really want to see _y_ou again.
>
>   _J_ulia

3.

> _J_eff,
>
> _J_ack and I have gone out _j_ogging, but we'll be back in _j_ust a few minutes. Make _y_ourself comfortable. _Y_ou can wait for us in the _y_ard. We haven't eaten lunch _y_et. We'll have some _y_ogurt and orange _j_uice when we get back.
>
>   _J_ulia

4.

> Dear _J_ane,
>
> We _j_ust received the beautiful pa_j_amas _y_ou sent to _J_immy. Thank _y_ou very much. _J_immy is too _y_oung to write to _y_ou himself, but he says "Thank _y_ou." He's already worn the pa_j_amas, and he's en_j_oying them a lot.
>
>   _J_ulia

5.

> Dear _J_anet,
>
> _J_ack and I are coming to visit _y_ou and _J_ohn in New _Y_ork. We've been to New _Y_ork before, but we haven't visited the Statue of Liberty or the Empire State Building _y_et. See _y_ou in _J_anuary or maybe in _J_une.
>
>   _J_ulia

6.

> Dear _J_oe,
>
> We got a letter from _J_ames last week. He has en_j_oyed college a lot this _y_ear. His favorite sub_j_ects are German and _J_apanese. He's looking for a _j_ob as a _j_ournalist in _J_apan, but he hasn't found one _y_et.
>
>   _J_ulia

WORKBOOK PAGE 51

S. *IS* OR *HAS*?

1. has		11. is
2. is		12. has
3. is		13. is
4. has		14. has
5. is		15. has
6. is		16. is
7. has		17. has
8. is		18. is
9. is		19. is
10. has		20. has

CHAPTER 5 OVERVIEW: Text Pages 51–64

GRAMMAR

Since/For

We've known each other	since	three o'clock. yesterday afternoon. last week. 2000. we were in high school.
	for	three hours. two days. a week. a long time.

Present Perfect vs. Present Tense

I **know** how to ski.

I'**ve known** how to ski since I was a little girl.

Present Perfect vs. Past Tense

Victor **was** an engineer.

He'**s been** a taxi driver since he immigrated.

FUNCTIONS

Asking for and Reporting Information

How long *has your neck been stiff*?
  For *more than a week*.

Do you know *how to ski*?
  Yes, I do. I've known *how to ski* since *I was a little girl*.

How long have you *known each other*?
  We've known *each other* for *three years*.
  We've known *each other* since *1998*.

Has *Victor* always been *a taxi driver*?
  No. *He's* been *a taxi driver* since *he immigrated*.
  Before that, *he* was *an engineer*.

Have you always *taught history*?
  No. I've *taught history* for *the past three years*.
  Before that, I *taught geography*.

Do you still *live on Main Street*?
  No. I haven't *lived on Main Street* for *several years*.

Are you still *a barber*?
  No. I haven't been *a barber* for *several years*.

So how are you feeling today, *George*?
  Not very well, *Dr. Fernando*.
What seems to be the problem?
  My neck is stiff.

What is your present address?
How long have you lived there?
What was your last address?
How long did you live there?
Tell me, _____.
Tell me, *Tony*, _____.
And how about YOU?

Reacting to Information

Oh. I didn't know that.
Oh. I didn't realize that.
Oh. I wasn't aware of that.

Indicating Understanding

I see.

Greeting People

George!
  Tony!

How have you been?
  Fine. And how about YOU?
Everything's fine with me, too.

Expressing Surprise-Disbelief

I can't believe it's you!

Expressing Agreement

That's right, *George*.

Leave-Taking

Well, *George*, I'm afraid I have to go now. We should get together soon.
Good idea, *Tony*.

150 CHAPTER 5

NEW VOCABULARY

Occupations
assistant manager
astronaut
barber
clerk
computer programmer
engineer
guidance counselor
guitarist
manager
musician
physician
store manager
taxi driver
vice president

Medical Care
black and blue
body
dizzy
feel dizzy
have *the measles*
high fever
neck
pain
patient
stiff
swollen
waiting room

The Arts
art
modern art
photography
Picasso

Time Expressions
early this morning
more than *a week*
the past *three years*

Verbs
count
graduate
immigrate
own
take time

Adjectives
dedicated
engaged
fortunate
interested (in)
present
successful

School
medical school
music school

Musical Instruments
cello
saxophone

Places Around the World
Dallas
Georgia
Singapore
Texas

Miscellaneous
accent
   New York accent
   southern accent
bachelor
bottom
department
leader
lottery
personal computer
satellite
space
termites
whole milk

EXPRESSIONS

Good idea.
happily married
in love
It's been a long time.
start at the bottom
"the birds and the bees"
the facts of life
work *his* way up to the top

Text Page 51: Chapter Opening Page

VOCABULARY PREVIEW

You may want to introduce these words before beginning the chapter, or you may choose to wait until they first occur in a specific lesson. If you choose to introduce them at this point, here are some suggestions:

1. Have students look at the illustrations on text page 51 and identify the words they already know.

2. Present the vocabulary. Say each word and have the class repeat it chorally and individually. Check students' understanding and pronunciation of the words.

3. Practice the vocabulary as a class, in pairs, or in small groups. Have students cover the word list and look at the pictures. Practice the words in the following ways:
   - Say a word and have students tell the number of the illustration.
   - Give the number of an illustration and have students say the word.

Text Pages 52-53: How Long?

FOCUS

- Present Perfect Tense:
    Questions with *How Long*
    Expressions with *For* and *Since*

CLOSE UP

Time expressions with *for* and *since* are commonly used with the present perfect tense to describe something that began in the past and continues in the present.

RULE: *For* is used with expressions describing a period of time.

EXAMPLES: We've known each other **for three years**.
She's had the measles **for five days**.

RULE: *Since* is used with expressions referring to a definite point in time.

EXAMPLES: I've been sick **since last Friday**.
They've been married **since 1985**.

INTRODUCING THE MODELS

There are two model conversations. Introduce and practice each separately. For each model:

1. Have students look at the model illustration.
2. Set the scene:
    1st model: "A salesperson in a jewelry store is talking to a couple who are looking for a wedding ring."
    2nd model: "One friend is visiting another friend who is sick."
3. Present the model.
4. Full-Class Repetition.

   Pronunciation Note

   The pronunciation focus of Chapter 5 is **Reduced *have* & *has*** (text page 64). You may wish to model this pronunciation at this point *(How long have you been sick? How long have you known each other?)* and encourage students to incorporate it into their language practice.

5. Ask students if they have any questions. Check understanding of the word *known* in the 1st model.
6. Group Choral Repetition.
7. Choral Conversation.
8. Call on one or two pairs of students to present the dialog.

   (For additional practice, do Choral Conversation in small groups or by rows.)

9. Further practice with *for* and *since*:

    a. After the 1st model, call on pairs of students to present the model again, using some of the other expressions under *for* in the box at the top of text page 52. For example:

      a long time

      A. How long have you known each other?
      B. We've known each other for a long time.

    b. After the 2nd model, same as above, using some of the expressions under *since* in the box at the top of text page 52. For example:

CHAPTER 5   153

last week
- A. How long have you been sick?
- B. I've been sick since last week.

SIDE BY SIDE EXERCISES

New Vocabulary

5. guidance counselor
6. satellite
7. space
8. own (v)
9. interested in
10. photography

Examples

1. A. How long have Tom and Janet known each other?
   B. They've known each other for two years.
2. A. How long have Mr. and Mrs. Garcia been married?
   B. They've been married since 1995.

Culture Note

Exercise 5: A *guidance counselor* is a person who helps high school students select classes according to their interests and career plans.

1. **Exercise 1:** Call on two students to present the dialog. Then do Choral Repetition and Choral Conversation practice.
2. **Exercise 2:** Same as above.
3. **Exercises 3–12:** Either Full-Class Practice or Pair Practice.

WORKBOOK

Pages 52–54

EXPANSION ACTIVITIES

1. *For or Since?* ★

    a. Write on the board:

    for _____
    since _____

    b. Say time expressions such as those below and have students rephrase them with *for* or *since*. For example:

    Teacher: a long time
    Student: for a long time

    Teacher: last week
    Student: since last week

    Time expressions:

    yesterday   (since)
    two hours   (for)
    a few minutes   (for)
    this morning   (since)
    2000   (since)
    several weeks   (for)
    a long time   (for)
    a quarter to three (since)
    ten years   (for)
    Wednesday   (since)
    last month   (since)
    three days   (for)
    1999   (since)
    three and a half weeks (for)
    eleven o'clock last night (since)

    Variation: Do the activity as a game with competing teams.

2. *Rephrase the Sentences!* ★★

    a. Have students open their books to text pages 52 and 53.

154   CHAPTER 5

b. Write the current year on the board. For example:

This year is (2004).

c. Based on what the year is, have students rephrase the sentences about the characters in Exercises 1, 2, 5, 6, 7, 8, and 11 on text pages 52 and 53. Have students either say or write their new sentences. For example:

Exercise 1: Tom and Janet have known each other for two years.
rephrased: They've known each other since (2002).

Exercise 2: Mr. and Mrs. Garcia have been married since 1985.
rephrased: They've been married for (19) years.

Exercise 5: Ms. Bennett has been a guidance counselor for 19 years.
rephrased: She's been a guidance counselor since (1985).

Exercise 6: There have been satellites in space since 1957.
rephrased: There have been satellites in space for (47) years.

Exercise 7: I've owned this car for three and a half years.
rephrased: I've owned this car since (2001).

Exercise 8: Bob has owned his own house since 1991.
rephrased: Bob has owned his own house for (13) years.

Exercise 11: I've been here since 1979.
rephrased: I've been here for (25) years.

d. Call on individual students to give their answers.

Variation: Do the activity as a game with competing teams. The team that writes the sentences in the shortest time is the winner.

3. **Grammar Chain: How Long Have You Lived Here?** ★★

a. Write the following conversation model on the board:

A. How long have you lived here?
B. I've lived here since _____.
A. Since _____? You've lived here for _____ years!
B. That's right. How long have YOU lived here?

b. Start the chain game by modeling the conversation with a student. Then have students continue the chain. For example:

Teacher: How long have you lived here?
Student A: I've lived here since (1991).
Teacher: Since (1991)? You've lived here for (13) years!
Student A: That's right. [to Student B:] How long have YOU lived here?
Student B: I've lived here since (2001).

Tell students they can use any date they wish to answer the first question.

4. **Get to Know Your Classmates** ★★★

a. Write the following on the board:

study
live in
be interested in
own
have
be
know

b. Divide the class into pairs and have students ask each other questions with *how long*, using the verbs on the board. For example:

A. How long have you studied English?
B. I've studied English for two years.

A. How long have you owned a bicycle?
B. I've owned a bicycle since 2000.

c. Have students tell the class about the person they interviewed.

(continued)

CHAPTER 5   155

EXPANSION ACTIVITIES (Continued)

5. Find the Right Person! ★★★

a. From the prior activity, write down information about the students.

b. Put the information on a handout in the following form:

> Find someone who . . .
> 1. has lived here since 1986. _____
> 2. has studied English for _____
>   five years.
> 3. has owned a bicycle for _____
>   ten years.
> 4. has been interested in jazz _____
>   since he was a teenager.

c. Have students circulate around the room, asking each other questions to identify the above people.

d. The first student to find all the people, raise his or her hand, and correctly identify the people is the winner of the game.

6. Which One Isn't True? ★★★

a. Tell students to write two true statements and one false statement about themselves. For example:

> I've owned a car since 2001.
> I've been interested in ballet since I was ten.
> I've had a bad headache since last night.

b. Have students take turns reading their statements to the class, and have the class guess which statement isn't true.

Text Pages 54–55

READING *A Very Dedicated Doctor*

FOCUS

- Present Perfect Tense
- Since/For

NEW VOCABULARY

black and blue	more than *a week*
body	neck
dedicated	pain
dizzy	patient (n)
early this morning	stiff
feel dizzy	swollen
for the past *24 hours*	take time
high fever	waiting room

READING THE STORY

Optional: *Preview the story by having students talk about the story title and/or illustrations. You may choose to introduce new vocabulary beforehand, or have students encounter the new vocabulary within the context of the reading.*

1. Have students read silently, or follow along silently as the story is read aloud by you, by one or more students, or on the audio program.
2. Ask students if they have any questions. Check understanding of vocabulary.
3. Check students' comprehension, using some or all of the following questions:

   What's the matter with George?
   What's the matter with Martha?
   What's the matter with Lenny?
   What's the matter with Carol?
   What's the matter with Bob?
   What's the matter with Bill?

What's the matter with Tommy and Julie?
How long has Dr. Fernando been in his office?
What don't his patients know?
What's the matter with him?
Why hasn't he taken time to stay at home and rest?

✓ READING CHECK-UP

Q & A

1. Call on a pair of students to present the model.
2. Have students work in pairs to create new dialogs.
3. Call on pairs to present their new dialogs to the class.

CHOOSE

1. a	5. a
2. b	6. b
3. b	7. a
4. a	8. a

CHOOSE

1. b	4. a
2. a	5. b
3. b	6. b

READING EXTENSION

1. ***Miming***

   a. Write on cards the symptoms from the reading. For example:

dizzy	fever	red spots	headache
black and blue arm	pain in the back	stiff neck	swollen knee

CHAPTER 5   157

b. Have students take turns picking a card from the pile and pantomiming the symptom on the card.

c. The class must guess what symptom the person is miming and which character in the story has that symptom.

Variation: Do the activity as a game with competing teams.

2. ***Class Discussion: A Good Doctor***

   a. Write the following on the board:

   > A good doctor is dedicated.
   > A good doctor is _____ and _____.
   > A good doctor doesn't think about _____.
   > A good doctor always _____.
   > A good doctor never _____.

   b. Have students complete the sentences and then compare their answers.

   c. Follow up with a class discussion about what qualities make a good doctor.

158   CHAPTER 5

Text Pages 56–57: Since I Was a Little Girl

FOCUS

- Present Perfect Tense:
  Contrast with the Present Tense
  Since Expressions

CLOSE UP

RULE: *Since* is used with past time phrases that describe a point in time in the past.

EXAMPLES: I've known how to ski **since I was a little girl**.
We've been engaged **since we finished college**.

GETTING READY

Contrast the simple present tense and the present perfect tense.

1. Put these cues on the board:

speak English
interested/astronomy
married
own/house
work/restaurant

Lucy

2. Make two statements about each cue: one in the present tense and one in the present perfect tense. For example:

   Lucy speaks English.
   She's spoken English since she was young.

   Lucy is interested in astronomy.
   She's been interested in astronomy for a long time.

3. Point to each cue and call on one or more students to tell about Lucy in the same way.

INTRODUCING THE MODELS

There are two model conversations. Introduce and practice each separately. For each model:

1. Have students look at the model illustration.
2. Set the scene:

   1st model: "Two friends are talking."
   2nd model: "A woman is talking to a young couple at a party."

3. Present the model.
4. Full-Class Repetition.
5. Ask students if they have any questions. Check understanding of the word *engaged* in the 2nd model.

   Culture Note

   In traditional U.S. culture, a couple who are planning to get married may announce their intentions by becoming *engaged* to be married. The man may also give the woman an engagement ring.

6. Group Choral Repetition.
7. Choral Conversation.
8. Call on one or two pairs of students to present the dialog.

   (For additional practice, do Choral Conversation in small groups or by rows.)

CHAPTER 5   159

SIDE BY SIDE EXERCISES

Examples

1. A. Does your sister Jennifer play the cello?
   B. Yes. She's played the cello since she was eight years old.
2. A. Is your friend Michael a professional musician?
   B. Yes. He's been a professional musician since he graduated from music school.

1. **Exercise 1:** Introduce the word *cello*. Call on two students to present the dialog. Then do Choral Repetition and Choral Conversation practice.

2. **Exercise 2:** Introduce the words *musician, graduate* (v), *music school*. Same as above.

3. **Exercises 3–12:** Either Full-Class Practice or Pair Practice.

New Vocabulary

3. personal computer
4. modern art
   Picasso
6. count (v)
10. termites
12. the birds and the bees
    the facts of life

Culture Notes

Exercise 4: Pablo Picasso is a famous 20th-century artist.

Exercise 11: *Titanic* is the true story of a large ship that sank in the North Atlantic. Most of the ship's passengers died in the disaster.

Exercise 12: The euphemistic expression "the birds and the bees" is used in polite conversation to refer to the *facts of life* or *where babies come from*.

WORKBOOK

Pages 55–57

EXPANSION ACTIVITIES

1. **Sense or Nonsense?** ★★

   a. Divide the class into four groups.

   b. Make many sets of split sentence cards with beginnings and endings of sentences. For example:

   | She's had a stomachache since . . . | she ate a donut this morning. |

He's liked classical music since . . .	he heard his first concert.
She's been interested in astronomy since . . .	she first saw the stars at night.
He's studied Spanish since . . .	he went to Mexico on vacation.

160 CHAPTER 5

She's owned her own business since . . .	she graduated from business school.
They've had blue hair since . . .	they became rock stars.
She's been interested in photography since . . .	she bought a new camera.
He's had pain in his back since . . .	he worked in his garden yesterday.
My children have stayed in bed since . . .	they got the measles.
Her neck has been stiff since . . .	she was in a car accident.

c. Mix up the cards and distribute sets of cards to each group, keeping the beginning and ending cards in different piles.

d. Have students take turns picking up one card from each pile and reading the sentence to the group. For example:

She's been interested in photography since . . .	they got the measles.

e. That group decides if the sentence makes *sense* or is *nonsense*.

f. After all the cards have been picked, have the groups lay out all the cards and put together all the sentence combinations that make sense.

2. Change the Sentence! ★★

a. Write a sentence on the board, underlining and numbering different portions of the sentence. For example:

```
    1              2
   Paul    has been interested in
    3                    4
Russian history   since he visited Moscow.
```

b. Have students sit in a circle.

c. Tell them that when you say a number, the first student in the circle makes a change in that part of the sentence. For example:

    Teacher: Two.
    Student 1: Paul <u>has wanted to study</u> Russian history since he visited Moscow.

d. The second student keeps the first student's sentence, but changes it based on the next number you say. For example:

    Teacher: Three.
    Student 2: Paul has wanted to study <u>Russian poetry</u> since he visited Moscow.

e. Continue this way with the rest of the students in the circle. For example:

    Teacher: Four.
    Student 3: Paul has wanted to study Russian poetry <u>since he met Anna</u>.

3. Expand the Sentence! ★★

Tell students that the object of the activity is to build a long sentence on the board, one word at a time.

a. Call on a student to write a pronoun or someone's name on the far left side of the board. For example:

```
Barbara
```

b. Have another student come to the board and add a word. For example:

```
Barbara has
```

(continued)

CHAPTER 5   161

EXPANSION ACTIVITIES (Continued)

c. Have a third student add a third word. For example:

> Barbara has been

d. Continue until each student in the class has had one or more turns to add a word to expand the sentence into the longest one they can think of. For example:

> Barbara has been interested in modern art since she found a wonderful book about Picasso in the library in the center of her city.

4. Class Discussion: Complete the Sentences ★★

a. Write on the board the following sentence beginnings:

> Since I was a child, I've known how to _____.
> Since I was a child, I've liked _____.
> Since I started English classes, I've _____.
> Since I read about _____, I've wanted to _____.

b. Have students complete the sentences individually and then share their sentences in small groups or as a class.

5. Sentence Cues ★★

a. On separate cards, write key words that can be put together to form sentences or questions. Clip together the cards for each sentence. For example:

| you | speak | Spanish | since | go to Caracas |

b. Divide the class into small groups and give a clipped set of cards to each group.

c. Have each group write a sentence based on their set of cards.

d. Have one member of each group write that group's sentence on the board and compare everybody's sentences.

6. Guess Who! ★★★

a. Write on the board:

> I like _____.
> I'm interested in _____.
> I know how to _____
> I play _____.
> I'm a _____.
> I want to be a _____.
> I have _____.

b. Have each student write three sentences about himself or herself, using some of the cues on the board. For example:

> I'm interested in computers.
> I play the guitar.
> I have a pet bird.

c. Have students fold their papers and give them to you. Mix them up and give each student someone else's paper.

d. Call on students to read the sentences. Then have the class guess who wrote them.

e. After the class has identified the person who wrote the statements, have students ask that person any questions they wish, using how long.

7. **Key Word Role Play: At a Party** ★★★

   a. Write the following on the board:

   interested in?
   live?
   work?
   how long?

   b. Divide the class into pairs.

   c. Tell each pair that they've just met at a party. Have them create a role play, using the key expressions on the board.

   d. Call on pairs to present their role plays to the class.

8. **What's Wrong?** ★★★

   a. Divide the class into pairs or small groups.

   b. Write several sentences such as the following on the board or on a handout. Some of the sentences should be correct, and others incorrect. For example:

   > I know them for a long time.
   > He's been interested in computers since many years.
   > She's played the piano since she was a child.
   > They been married for fifty years.
   > How long you own that car?
   > I been sick since last Monday.
   > You've had a backache for a week.
   > How long there be problems at your company?

   c. The object of the activity is for students to identify which sentences are incorrect and then correct them.

   d. Have students compare their answers.

   Variation: Do the activity as a game with competing teams. The team that successfully completes the task in the shortest time is the winner.

CHAPTER 5   163

Text Pages 58–59: Have You Always Taught History?

FOCUS

- Present Perfect Tense:
    Contrast with the Past Tense
    Review of Yes/No Questions

CLOSE UP

RULE: The present perfect describes an activity that began in the past and continues up to the present. The simple past describes an activity that began and ended in the past.

EXAMPLES: I've **taught** history for the past three years. *(I continue to teach history.)*
Before that, I **taught** geography. *(I don't teach geography now.)*

INTRODUCING THE MODELS

There are two model conversations. Introduce and practice each separately. For each model:

1. Have students look at the model illustration.
2. Set the scene.
    1st model: "A student is talking to his history professor."
    2nd model: "Two people are talking about Victor."
3. Present the model.
4. Full-Class Repetition.
5. Ask students if they have any questions. Check understanding of new vocabulary:
    1st model: *geography*
    2nd model: *immigrate, engineer*
6. Group Choral Repetition.
7. Choral Conversation.
8. Call on one or two pairs of students to present the dialog.

    (For additional practice, do Choral Conversation in small groups or by rows.)

SIDE BY SIDE EXERCISES

Examples

1. A. Have you always liked classical music?
   B. No. I've liked classical music for the past five years. Before that, I liked jazz.
2. A. Has Carlos always been the store manager?
   B. No. He's been the store manager since last January. Before that, he was a cashier.

1. **Exercise 1:** Call on two students to present the dialog. Then do Choral Repetition and Choral Conversation practice.
2. **Exercise 2:** Introduce the expression *store manager*. Same as above.
3. **Exercises 3–8:** Either Full-Class Practice or Pair Practice.

New Vocabulary

4. astronaut
5. southern accent
   New York accent
   Georgia
7. whole milk
8. lottery

How to Say It!

Reacting to Information: In spoken English, it is common to react to new information with any of these three phrases: "Oh. I didn't know that." "Oh. I didn't realize that." "Oh. I wasn't aware of that."

1. Present the expressions.
2. Full-Class Repetition.
3. Ask students if they have any questions.
4. Group Choral Repetition.
5. Have students practice the conversations in this lesson again, using any of these new expressions.
5. Call pairs of students to present their conversations to the class.

How About You?

1. Go over the questions before students do the activity.
2. Call on a few pairs of students to ask and answer the questions.
3. Divide the class into pairs, and have students ask and answer the questions. Remind students to use the expressions for *Reacting to Information* from the *How to Say It!* section above.

WORKBOOK

Pages 58–59

EXPANSION ACTIVITIES

1. Summarizing with the Present Perfect ★★

Have students listen as you read each of the situations below. Then call on a student to summarize what happened, using the present perfect. (There may be more than one way to summarize what happened.) For example:

Situation: Bill saw Jim this morning. He saw him again at lunch. Then he saw him again in the parking lot.
Summary: Bill has seen Jim three times today.
   or
   Bill has seen Jim several times/ a lot today.

Situations:
   Gloria called her cousin this morning, and she called him again this afternoon.
   Robert wrote two letters to the Kendall Company last week, and he wrote them another one this morning.
   We saw Mr. and Mrs. Chen at a basketball game on Tuesday night and at a concert on Thursday night.
   Alan studied French in high school. He studied Spanish in college. And last year he studied Japanese.
   Mrs. Phillips went to Europe in 1995. She went to Europe again in 2000.
   Larry is reading a lot this year in school. He read four books last semester. And he read two more books last month.
   Joe came to class late yesterday. He came to class late again today.
   Julie's aunt sent her a birthday gift this week. Her friend Eileen sent her one, too.
   Veronica had a baby girl in 1998. In 2001 she had a baby boy.
   Mrs. Garcia's students did well on their history tests last semester. They did well on their tests this semester, too.

(continued)

CHAPTER 5   165

EXPANSION ACTIVITIES (Continued)

2. **Find the Right Person!** ★★

   a. Write the following on the board:

   > For the past six months I have _____.
   > For the past few years I have _____.
   > I have always _____.

   b. Have students complete these sentences any way they wish and hand them in to you.

   c. Put the information on a handout in the following form:

   > Find someone who . . .
   > 1. has been school president _____ for the past six months.
   > 2. has studied piano for the _____ past few years.
   > 3. has always wanted to fly _____ an airplane.

   d. Have students circulate around the room, asking each other questions to identify the above people. For example:

   > Student A: Have you ever been school president?
   > Student B: Yes, I have. I've been school president for the past six months.

   e. The first student to find all the people, raise his or her hand, and identify the people is the winner of the game.

3. **Same and Different: Musical Tastes** ★★★

   a. Put the following on the board:

   > I have _____.
   > My partner has _____.
   > We both have _____.

   b. Write a list of questions about students' musical tastes such as the following on the board or on a handout for students:

   > What kind of music do you like?
   > How long have you liked/listened to _____?
   > Do you play any musical instruments?
   > How long have you studied _____?

   c. Divide the class into pairs.

   d. Have students interview each other and then report to the class about the ways in which they're *the same* and the ways in which they're *different*. For example:

   > I have listened to jazz since I was young.
   > My partner has studied the piano for ten years.
   > We both have always liked classical music.

4. **Sharing Histories** ★★★

   a. Write on the board:

   > I've _____ since/for _____.
   > Before that I _____.

   b. Have students complete the sentences, using the model on the board. Have them write about their work histories, where they have lived, where they have gone to school, sports they have played, or general facts about themselves.

   c. Divide the class into groups. Have students share their information with the class. Remind students that they can react using the expressions in the *How to Say It!* section on student text page 59.

Text Page 60

 READING *A Wonderful Family*

FOCUS

- Present Perfect vs. Present Tense

NEW VOCABULARY

bachelor	medical school
computer programmer	physician
fortunate	Singapore
guitarist	successful
happily married	

READING THE STORY

Optional: Preview the story by having students talk about the story title and/or illustration. You may choose to introduce new vocabulary beforehand, or have students encounter the new vocabulary within the context of the reading.

1. Have students read silently or follow along silently as the story is read aloud by you, by one or more students, or on the audio program.

2. Ask students if they have any questions. Check understanding of vocabulary.

3. Check students' comprehension, using some or all of the following questions:

   What does Ruth do?
   How long has she been an engineer?
   How long have Ruth and Pablo been married?
   What does Pablo do?
   How long has he known how to play the guitar?
   What does David do?
   How long has he been interested in computers?
   What does Rita do?
   How long has she been a physician?
   Is Herbert married?
   What does Herbert do?
   Have Mr. and Mrs. Patterson seen him recently?

✓ READING CHECK-UP

1. True
2. False
3. False
4. True
5. False
6. True
7. False

READING EXTENSION

Family Trees

1. Have students draw a family tree for the Patterson family in the reading. Have pairs of students compare their drawings.

2. Have students then draw their own family trees. Have students share their family trees in small groups. Have students ask and answer questions about each other's family. For example:

   Where does he/she live?
   How long has he/she lived there?
   What does he/she do?
   How long has he/she been a _____?

 LISTENING

Listen to the conversation and choose the answer that is true.

1. A. How long have you had a backache?
   B. For three days.

2. A. Has your father always been an engineer?
   B. No, he hasn't.

CHAPTER 5   167

3. A. How long has your knee been swollen?
   B. For a week.

4. A. How long have you known how to ski?
   B. Since I was a teenager.

5. A. Did you live in Tokyo for a long time?
   B. Yes. Five years.

6. A. How long has Roger been interested in Egyptian history?
   B. Since he lived in Cairo.

7. A. Is Amy still in the hospital?
   B. Oh. I forgot to tell you. She's been home for two days.

8. A. Have you played hockey for a long time?
   B. Yes. I've played hockey since I moved to Toronto three years ago.

Answers

1. b
2. a
3. b
4. a
5. b
6. b
7. a
8. a

Text Page 61

READING Working Their Way to the Top

FOCUS

- Present Perfect vs. Past Tense

NEW VOCABULARY

assistant manager
bottom
Dallas
department
start at the bottom
Texas
vice president
work *his* way up to the top

READING THE STORY

Optional: Preview the story by having students talk about the story title and/or illustrations. You may choose to introduce new vocabulary beforehand, or have students encounter the new vocabulary within the context of the reading.

1. Have students read silently or follow along silently as the story is read aloud by you, by one or more students, or on the audio program.

2. Ask students if they have any questions. Check understanding of vocabulary.

3. Check students' comprehension, using some or all of the following questions:

    How long has Louis been the store manager?
    How long was he a clerk?
    How long was he a cashier?
    How long was he an assistant manager?
    When did he become the manager?
    Why is everybody at the Big Value Supermarket proud of Louis?

    How long has Kate been the president?
    How long was she a salesperson?
    How long was she the manager of the Women's Clothing Department?
    How long was she the store manager?
    What happened after that?
    When did she become the president?
    Why is everybody at the Marcy Department Store in Dallas proud of Kate?

✓ READING *CHECK-UP*

1. False
2. True
3. Maybe
4. False
5. Maybe
6. True

READING EXTENSION

1. **Tic Tac Question the Answer**

    a. Draw a tic tac grid on the board and fill it in with short answers to questions:

For six years.	Two years ago.	Yes, he did.
For three years.	Yes, they have.	No, he didn't.
Yes, she has.	Yes, he has.	Yes, she did.

    b. Divide the class into teams. Give each team a mark: *X* or *O*.

    c. Have each team ask a question about the story on text page 61 for an answer in the grid. For example:

        X Team: Has Kate worked very hard to get where she is today?
        Yes, she has.

    d. If an answer is appropriate and is stated correctly, that team may replace the answer with its team mark. For example:

CHAPTER 5   169

For six years.	Two years ago.	Yes, he did.
For three years.	Yes, they have.	No, he didn't.
X	Yes, he has.	Yes, she did.

    e. The first team to mark out three boxes in a straight line—either vertically, horizontally, or diagonally—wins.

2. ***Time Lines***

    a. Have students draw a time line for the two characters in the reading. Have pairs of students compare their time lines.

    b. Have students then draw a time line of someone they know. Have students share their time lines with a partner. Have students ask and answer questions about each other's time line. For example:

        When did he/she begin that job?
        Where did he/she live?
        How long did he/she work there?
        What does he/she do now?

Writing

1. Make sure students understand the questions.
2. Have students ask you the questions and take notes based on your answers.
3. Have students write their stories about you at home, using a dictionary for any new words they wish to use.
4. Have students present and discuss what they have written in pairs, small groups, or as a class.

Text Pages 62–63

 ROLE PLAY *It's Been a Long Time*

FOCUS

- Review: Present Perfect Tense

INTRODUCING THE MODEL

1. Have students look at the model illustration.
2. Set the scene: "Two old friends have just met on the street. They haven't seen each other in a long time."
3. Have students listen as you present the dialog or play the audio one or more times.
4. Ask students if they have any questions. Check understanding of new vocabulary: *barber, taxi driver, saxophone, Good idea, It's been a long time.*

   Language Note

   Good idea is a reduced form of the expression *That's a good idea.*

5. Divide the class into pairs. Have students practice the dialog.
6. Call on one or two pairs of students to present the dialog.

ROLE PLAY

1. Divide the class into pairs. Have students role play the dialog using the guide on text page 63 and any vocabulary they wish.
2. Call on pairs of students to present their role plays to the class without referring to the text.

EXPANSION ACTIVITY

Scrambled Dialog Game ★★

1. Divide the class into five teams.
2. Make five sets of the conversation from student text page 62, writing each line on a separate card.
3. Give each group one set of the cards, and have the group members reorder the conversations.
4. The first team to put the conversation in the correct order is the winner.

WORKBOOK

Pages 60–61

CHAPTER 5   171

Text Page 64

 PRONUNCIATION Reduced *have & has*

Reduced *have* & *has*: In spoken English, the pronunciation of the *h* in the auxiliaries *have* and *has* is often omitted. The reduced pronunciation of *have* is [əv] and of *has* is [əz].

Focus on Listening

Practice the sentences in the left column. Say each sentence or play the audio one or more times. Have students listen carefully and repeat.

Focus on Pronunciation

Practice the sentences in the right column. Have students say each sentence and then listen carefully as you say it or play the audio.

If you wish, have students continue practicing the sentences to improve their pronunciation.

 JOURNAL

Have students write their journal entries at home or in class. Encourage students to use a dictionary to look up words they would like to use. Students can share their written work with other students if appropriate. Have students discuss what they have written as a class, in pairs, or in small groups

 CHAPTER SUMMARY

GRAMMAR

1. Divide the class into pairs or small groups.
2. Have students take turns forming sentences from the words in the grammar boxes. Student A says a sentence, and Student B points to the words from each column that are in the sentence. Then have students switch: Student B says a sentence, and Student A points to the words.

EXPANSION ACTIVITY

Category Dictation ★★

1. Have students draw two columns on a piece of paper. At the top of one column, have students write <u>since</u>. At the top of the other column, have them write <u>for</u>.
2. Dictate various time expressions and have students write them in the appropriate column. For example:

since	for
she was born	three years
last night	the past ten minutes
he saw her	a long time

KEY VOCABULARY

Have students ask you any questions about the meaning or pronunciation of the vocabulary. If students ask for the pronunciation, repeat after the student until the student is satisfied with his or her own pronunciation.

EXPANSION ACTIVITIES

1. **Do You Remember the Words?** ★

   Check students' retention of the vocabulary depicted on the opening page of Chapter 5 by doing the following activity:

   a. Have students open their books to text page 51 and cover the list of vocabulary words and phrases.

   b. Either call out a number and have students tell you the word or phrase, or say a word or phrase and have students tell you the number.

   Variation: You can also do this activity as a game with competing teams.

2. **Student-Led Dictation** ★

   a. Tell each student to choose a word or phrase from the Key Vocabulary list on text page 64 and look at it very carefully.

   b. Have students take turns dictating their words to the class. Everybody writes down that student's word.

   c. When the dictation is completed, call on different students to write each word on the board to check the spelling.

3. **Letter Game** ★

   a. Divide the class into two teams.

   b. Say: "I'm thinking of a *medical care* word that starts with *h*."

   c. The first person to raise his or her hand and guess correctly *[headache]* wins a point for his or her team.

   d. Continue with other letters of the alphabet and words.

   The team that gets the most correct answers wins the game.

4. **Tic Tac Occupation** ★★

   a. Have students draw a tic tac grid on their papers and fill in the grid with any nine of the occupations listed on text page 64.

   b. Give definitions of the occupations, and tell students to cross out any word on their grids for which you have given the definition.

   c. The first person to cross out three words in a straight line—either vertically, horizontally, or diagonally—wins the game.

   d. Have the winner call out the words to check the accuracy.

END-OF-CHAPTER ACTIVITIES

1. Board Game ★★★

   a. On poster boards or on manila file folders, make up game boards with a pathway consisting of separate spaces. You may use any theme or design you wish.

   b. Divide the class into groups of 2 to 4 students and give each group a game board and a die, and each student something to be used as a playing piece.

   c. Give each group a pile of cards face-down with statements written on them. Some sentences should be correct, and others incorrect. For example:

   > I have known him for twenty years.
   > She's owned her own house since two years.
   > They've been interested in modern art for last year.
   > He's played the guitar since he was five years old.
   > I have known how to ride a bicycle since five years ago.
   > We have been tired when the baby was born.
   > He's been president since the past three months.
   > Before that, he has been vice-president.
   > She has always wanted to be an astronaut.
   > He hasn't always spoken with a New York accent.
   > They have been on vacation since they won the lottery.
   > We have had a cat for last year.

   d. Each student in turn rolls the die, moves the playing piece along the game path, and after landing on a space, picks a card, reads the sentence, and says if it is *correct* or *incorrect*. If the statement is incorrect, the student must correct it. If the response is correct, the student takes an additional turn.

   e. The first student to reach the end of the pathway is the winner.

2. Question Game ★★

   a. Write the following sentence on the board:

   > Michael has been interested in Japanese art since he went to Japan last year.

   b. Underline different elements of the sentence, and have students create a question based on that portion of the sentence. For example:

   > Michael has been interested in Japanese art <u>since he went to Japan last year</u>.

   How long has Michael been interested in Japanese art?

   > Michael has been interested <u>in Japanese art</u> since he went to Japan last year.

   What has Michael been interested in since he went to Japan last year?

   c. Continue with other sentences.

3. Scrambled Sentences ★★

   a. Divide the class into two teams.

   b. Write individual sentences out of order on the board. Use sentences similar to the ones in the lesson on text pages 56 and 57. For example:

   > she   musician   finished   she
   > 2000   in   has   music school   a
   > since   professional   been

   c. The first person to raise his or her hand, come to the board, and write the sentence in the correct order earns a point for that team. (She has been a professional musician since she finished music school in 2000.)

CHAPTER 5

d. The team with the most points wins the scrambled sentence game.

Variation: Write the words to several sentences on separate cards. Divide the class into small groups, and have students work together to put the sentences into correct order.

4. **Mystery Conversations** ★★★

   a. Divide the class into pairs.
   b. Write the following on the board:

   c. Write roles such as the following on word cards and give one to each pair of students:

a parent and a child	a boss and an employee
a teacher and a student	two friends
two neighbors	a nurse and a patient
a wife and a husband	a brother and a sister

   d. Have each pair create a short dialog that begins "Are you still _____?" The dialogs should be appropriate for the roles the students have on their cards.
   e. Have each pair present their dialog to the class. Then have the other students guess who the people are: Are they friends? Is a teacher talking to a student? For example:

   [parent–child]
   A. Are you still on the phone?
   B. No, I'm not. I haven't been on the phone for ten minutes!

   [boss–employee]
   A. Are you still working on the report?
   B. No. I've already finished it.

CHAPTER 5   175

WORKBOOK ANSWER KEY AND LISTENING SCRIPTS

WORKBOOK PAGE 52

A. HOW LONG?

1. I've had a headache since
2. They've been married for
3. He's owned a motorcycle since
4. She's been interested in astronomy for
5. I've had a cell phone since
6. We've known each other since
7. They've had a dog for
8. I've had problems with my upstairs neighbor for
9. She's been a computer programmer since
10. He's played in the school orchestra since
11. There have been mice in our attic for

WORKBOOK PAGE 53

B. WHAT'S THE QUESTION?

1. How long has, wanted to be an engineer
2. How long has, owned his own house
3. How long have, been married
4. How long have, been interested in photography
5. How long has, worn glasses
6. How long have, known how to snowboard
7. How long has, had a girlfriend
8. How long has, been a pizza shop in town

WORKBOOK PAGE 55

D. SINCE WHEN?

1. I'm
   I've been sick
2. has
   She's had
3. knows
   He's known
4. They're
   They've been
5. We're
   We've been
6. have
   I've had
7. It's
   It's been
8. plays
   She's
9. is
   He's been
10. I'm
    I've been

WORKBOOK PAGE 56

E. LISTENING

Listen and choose the correct answer.

1. Bob has been engaged since he got out of the army.
2. My sister Carol has been a professional musician since she finished music school.
3. Michael has been home since he fell and hurt himself last week.
4. My wife has gotten up early every morning since she started her new job.
5. Richard has eaten breakfast in the school cafeteria every morning since he started college.
6. Nancy and Tom have known each other for five and a half years.
7. My friend Charlie and I have played soccer every weekend since we were eight years old.
8. Patty has had short hair since she was a teenager.
9. Ron has owned his own business since he moved to Chicago nine years ago.
10. I've been interested in astronomy for the past eleven years.
11. I use my personal computer all the time. I've had it since I was in high school.
12. Alan has had problems with his house since he bought it fifteen years ago.

Answers

1. b   7. a
2. b   8. b
3. a   9. b
4. b   10. a
5. a   11. b
6. a   12. a

F. CROSSWORD

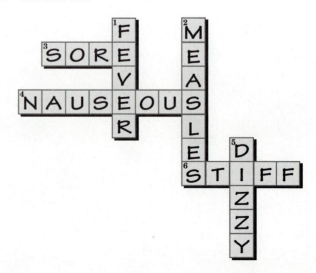

176   CHAPTER 5

WORKBOOK PAGE 57

G. SCRAMBLED SENTENCES

1. Julie has liked jazz since she was a teenager.
2. He's known how to play the piano since he was a little boy.
3. I've been interested in astronomy since I was young.
4. They've been engaged since they finished college.
5. He's been a chef since he graduated from cooking school.
6. She's wanted to be a teacher since she was eighteen years old.
7. They've owned their own business since they moved here a year ago.

WORKBOOK PAGE 58

I. THEN AND NOW

1. walk
   They've walked
   they
   walked
2. speaks
   He's spoken
   he spoke
3. is
   She's been
   she was
4. taught
   he teaches
   He's taught
5. has
   visited
   visited
   visit
6. has
   She's had
   had

WORKBOOK PAGE 59

J. LOOKING BACK

1. has Victor been
   He's been a musician, 1990
2. was he
   He was a photographer, 7 years
3. has Mrs. Sanchez taught
   She's taught science, 1995
4. did she teach
   She taught math, 9 years
5. did your grandparents have
   They had a cat, 11 years
6. have they had
   They've had a dog, 1998
7. has Betty worked
   She's worked at the bank, 2000
8. did she work
   She worked at the mall, 2 years
9. did your parents live
   They lived in New York, 20 years
10. have they lived
    They've lived in Miami, 2001

WORKBOOK PAGE 61

L. LISTENING

Listen and choose the correct answer.

1. A. Have you always been a salesperson?
   B. No. I've been a salesperson for the past four years. Before that, I was a cashier.
2. A. How long has your daughter been in medical school?
   B. She's been in medical school for the past two years.
3. A. Have your parents always lived in a house?
   B. No. They've lived in a house for the past ten years. Before that, they lived in an apartment.
4. A. How long have you wanted to be an actor?
   B. I've wanted to be an actor since I was in college. Before that, I wanted to be a musician.
5. A. Do you and your husband still exercise at your health club every day?
   B. No. We haven't done that for a year.
6. A. Has James been a bachelor all his life?
   B. No, he hasn't. He was married for ten years.
7. A. Has your sister Jane always wanted to be a writer?
   B. Yes, she has. She's wanted to be a writer all her life.
8. A. Have you ever broken your ankle?
   B. No. I've sprained it a few times, but I've never broken it.
9. A. Have you always liked classical music?
   B. No. I've liked classical music for the past few years. Before that, I liked rock music.
10. A. Has Billy had a sore throat for a long time?
    B. He's had a sore throat for the past two days. Before that, he had a fever.
11. A. Jennifer has been the store manager since last fall.
    B. What did she do before that?
    A. She was a salesperson.

CHAPTER 5   **177**

12. A Have you always been interested in modern art?
    B No. I've been interested in modern art since I moved to Paris a few years ago. Before that, I was only interested in sports.

Answers

1.	b	7.	b
2.	b	8.	a
3.	a	9.	b
4.	b	10.	b
5.	b	11.	b
6.	a	12.	a

Text Pages 65–68: *Side by Side Gazette*

FEATURE ARTICLE
*"24/7"—24 Hours a Day/
7 Days a Week*

PREVIEWING THE ARTICLE

1. Have students talk about the title of the article and the accompanying photographs.

2. You may choose to introduce the following new vocabulary beforehand, or have students encounter it within the context of the article:

> area
> child-care center
> communication
> computer company
> daytime
> do business
> factory worker
> fax
> firefighter
> in the past
> instant
> late-night
> local
> manufacturing company
> 9 to 5
> night shift
> office worker
> photocopy center
> shift
> stay open
> switch
> 24/7
> work schedule
> World Wide Web
> worldwide

READING THE ARTICLE

1. Have students read silently, or follow along silently as the article is read aloud by you, by one or more students, or on the audio program.

2. Ask students if they have any questions. Check understanding of new vocabulary.

3. Check students' comprehension by asking the following questions:

> Why are more and more companies operating "24/7"?
> What percentage of employees work the evening and night shifts?
> What kinds of jobs did traditional night-shift workers have?
> Who are the new night-shift workers?
> How have local businesses changed to serve these night-shift workers?

4. Have students discuss the questions in small groups or as a class.

EXPANSION ACTIVITIES

1. **Dictate and Discuss** ★★★

   a. Divide the class into pairs or small groups.

   b. Dictate sentences such as the following and then have students discuss them:

   > People work more now than they did twenty years ago.
   > Technology makes life easier.
   > The 24/7 work schedule is good for families.
   > Technology makes it possible for people to take longer vacations.

   c. Call on students to share their opinions with the rest of the class.

2. **The Longest List** ★★★

   a. Divide the class into several teams. Have students brainstorm the types of businesses that operate twenty-four hours a day.

   b. Have the teams share their lists with the class. The team with the longest list wins.

3. **Advantages and Disadvantages** ★★★

   a. Have students draw two columns on a piece of paper. At the top of one column, have students write <u>Advantages</u>. At the top of the other column, have them write <u>Disadvantages</u>.

   (continued)

SIDE BY SIDE GAZETTE   179

EXPANSION ACTIVITIES (Continued)

b. Name one late-night activity—for example: *late-night shopping at a supermarket, working the 11:00 to 7:00 shift,* or *late-night shopping on the Internet.* Have students brainstorm the advantages and disadvantages of doing this at night instead of during the day. Write students' ideas in the columns and have students copy the sentences on their papers. For example:

Late-Night Shopping at a Supermarket

Advantages

There's no traffic, and there are no parking problems.
There's a short check-out lane because there are few shoppers.

Disadvantages

Tired drivers can make mistakes.
There are fewer employees to help customers.

---

4. **Survey** ★★★

Have students find out about their classmates' preferred schedules.

a. Brainstorm with the class questions students can ask each other about their preferences. For example:

When are you most active—in the morning or at night?
Do you like to stay up late at night?
When do you do your shopping?
When do you work?

b. Have each student choose one question to ask and then conduct a survey by circulating around the room, asking the others that question.

c. For homework, have students draw up the survey results in graph form (for example, a bar graph or pie chart). In class, have students share their graphs and report their results.

5. **A Perfect Work Schedule** ★★★

a. For homework, have students answer the following:

In your opinion, what is a perfect work schedule? Why?

b. Have students share their writing in pairs.

AROUND THE WORLD
Unique Jobs

1. Have students read silently or follow along silently as the text is read aloud by you, by one or more students, or on the audio program.

2. Check understanding of the words *coffee plantation worker, dog day-care worker, exist, reindeer herder, safari guide, subway pusher, tulip farmer, unique.*

3. Bring a map to class and point out the locations referred to in the photographs.

4. Have students first work in pairs or small groups, responding to the question. Then have students tell the class what they talked about. Write any new vocabulary on the board.

EXPANSION ACTIVITIES

1. **Ranking** ★★

a. Ask students: "Which of these jobs would you like to have?"

b. Have students rank these jobs from the *most interesting* to the *least interesting.*

c. As a class, in pairs, or in small groups, have students compare their lists.

2. **Unique Local Jobs** ★★

a. Divide the class into groups. Call out a city, town, or region in your area and have students brainstorm unique jobs that can be done only in that location.

b. Have the teams share their lists with the class.

INTERVIEW

1. Have students read silently, or follow along silently as the interview is read aloud by you, by one or more students, or on the audio program.

180 SIDE BY SIDE GAZETTE

2. Ask students if they have any questions. Check understanding of the words *asleep, awake, day shift, forever, normally, notes, put to bed*.

3. Check students' comprehension by asking the following questions:

   What is Mrs. Souza's work schedule?
   What is Mr. Souza's work schedule?
   Who helps them with the children?
   Do their children go to school yet?
   When do Mr. and Mrs. Souza usually see each other?
   How do Mr. and Mrs. Souza communicate during the week?
   What does Mr. Souza hope for in the future?

EXPANSION ACTIVITIES

1. The Kids' Schedule ★★

The interview describes the mother's and father's day. Have students read the interview again and write out a typical day for the Souza children.

2. Advantages and Disadvantages ★★★

a. Have students draw two columns on a piece of paper. At the top of one column, have students write <u>Advantages</u>. At the top of the other column, have them write <u>Disadvantages</u>.

b. Have students brainstorm the advantages and disadvantages of the Souzas' work schedules. Write students' ideas in the columns and have students copy the sentences on their papers. For example:

> <u>Advantages</u>
> They don't have to spend money on child care.
> The grandmother is able to spend time with her grandchildren.
>
> <u>Disadvantages</u>
> Mr. and Mrs. Souza don't get to see each other.
> It's difficult for the parents because they never have time off to relax.

3. Student Interviews ★★★

a. If possible, have students conduct an interview with parents of young children they know. Have students brainstorm the kinds of questions they want to ask.

b. Have students report their findings to the class and write up a report for homework.

FACT FILE *Vacation Time in Different Countries*

1. Before reading the Fact File, show the class a world map. Have students identify the locations of the following place names:

   > Australia
   > Denmark
   > Germany
   > Japan
   > Sweden
   > the United States

2. Have students rank the countries according to which ones they think would have the longest vacations. Write students' ideas on the board. Then have students read the table on text page 67 to check their predictions.

3. Read the table aloud as the class follows along. Ask students: "Is this list different from your list? How is your list different?"

EXPANSION ACTIVITY

Student Investigation ★★★

1. Have students conduct interviews with people from the previous generation. Have students ask:

   How much vacation time did you get thirty years ago?
   Do you think people today get more or less vacation time?
   How is vacation time different now?

2. Have students compare their notes. Ask: "Are people now getting more vacation time or less vacation time than in the past? How was vacation time different thirty years ago?"

SIDE BY SIDE GAZETTE

LISTENING Office Voice Mail

1. Check understanding of the expression *voice mail*.
2. Set the scene: "Sam works for Ms. Rivera. These are phone messages they left for each other."

LISTENING SCRIPT

Listen to the voice-mail messages between Gloria Rivera and her office assistant, Sam. Has Sam done the things on Ms. Rivera's list? Check *Yes* or *No*.

You have one message. Tuesday, 8:15 A.M.

Hello, Sam? This is Ms. Rivera. I'll be out of the office all day today. I'm not feeling well. Here's a list of things you'll need to do while I'm not here. First, please write a note to Mrs. Wilson and tell her I'm sick. Then, please call Mr. Chen and change the time of our appointment. Also, send an e-mail to everybody in the office, and tell them about next week's meeting. Don't forget to speak to the custodian about my broken desk lamp. I hope he can fix it. Hmm. Let's see. I know there are a few more things. Oh, yes. Please make a list of all the employees and give it to Ms. Baxter. She asked me for the list last week. Okay, Sam. I think that's everything. Oh . . . one more thing. Please take the package on my desk to the post office if you have time. And that's it. Thanks, Sam. I'll see you tomorrow morning.

You have reached the voice mailbox of Gloria Rivera. Please leave a message after the tone.

Ms. Rivera? This is Sam. I'm sorry you aren't feeling well. I hope you feel better tomorrow. I'm calling to tell you what I've done today, and what I haven't done yet. It's been very busy here, so I haven't had time to do everything. I wrote a note to Mrs. Wilson. I called Mr. Chen and changed the time of your appointment. I also sent the e-mail about next week's meeting. I haven't spoken to the custodian. He's been sick all week. I made a list of all the employees, but I haven't given it to Ms. Baxter yet. I'll give it to her early tomorrow morning. Finally, I haven't taken the package to the post office yet. I haven't had time. I'm going to take it to the post office on my way home.

Again, I hope you're feeling better. I'll see you in the morning.

Answers

	Yes	No
1.	✔	___
2.	✔	___
3.	✔	___
4.	___	✔
5.	✔	___
6.	___	✔
7.	___	✔

 FUN WITH IDIOMS

> a couch potato
> a real ham
> a real peach
> a smart cookie
> chicken
> the top banana

INTRODUCTION AND PRACTICE

For each idiom, do the following:

1. Have students look at the illustration.
2. Present the idiom. Say the expression and have the class repeat it chorally and individually. Check students' pronunciation of the words.

DO YOU KNOW THESE EXPRESSIONS?

Have students match the expressions with their meanings.

Answers

1. d
2. f
3. a
4. e
5. c
6. b

182 SIDE BY SIDE GAZETTE

EXPANSION ACTIVITIES

1. Line Prompts ★★

Call out one of the following line prompts and have students respond appropriately with "yes" and one of the idioms.

Is she an important person in the company.
(Yes. She's the top banana.)

Is he funny all the time?
(Yes. He's a real ham.)

Do you like your new co-worker?
(Yes. She's a real peach.)

Is he really lazy?
(Yes. He's a couch potato.)

Is she as intelligent as she looks?
(Yes. She's a smart cookie.)

Is he always afraid to try new things?
(Yes. He's chicken.)

2. Idiom Challenge! ★★★

a. Divide the class into pairs.

b. Have each pair create a conversation in which they use as many of the idioms from text page 67 as they can.

c. Have the pairs present their conversations to the class. Which pair used the most idioms?

 WE'VE GOT MAIL!

THE LETTER TO *SIDE BY SIDE*

1. Have students read silently, or follow along silently as the letter is read aloud by you, by one or more students, or on the audio program.

2. Ask students if they have any questions. Check understanding of the words *confused, past participle, perfectly*.

3. Check students' comprehension by having them decide whether these statements are true or false:

   The writers are confused about the tense in the sentence "I have driven." *(True)*
   The students have a similar tense in their own languages. *(False)*
   The students don't know when to use the present perfect tense. *(True)*
   The students think that part participles are easy to learn. *(False)*
   The students don't understand why there are so many new verb forms in the present perfect. *(True)*

4. Ask students:

   Did you ever have this question?
   Do you have a tense similar to the present perfect in your language?
   Can you explain how the present perfect is different from the present tense? How is it different from the past tense?

THE RESPONSE FROM *SIDE BY SIDE*

1. Have students read silently, or follow along silently as the letter is read aloud by you, by one or more students, or on the audio program.

2. Ask students if they have any questions. Check understanding of the words *exact, learner*.

3. Check students' comprehension by having them decide whether these statements are true or false:

   People use the present perfect tense to talk about things that happened at a specific point in the past. *(False)*
   It's correct to say in English "I have seen you yesterday morning." *(False)*
   People use the present perfect to talk about things that happened several times in the past. *(True)*
   It's correct to say in English "He's visited Tokyo three times." *(True)*
   People use the present perfect to talk about things that began in the past and continue until now. *(True)*
   It's correct to say in English "I worked here for the last two years." *(False)*

SIDE BY SIDE GAZETTE   183

EXPANSION ACTIVITY

What's Wrong? ★★★

1. Divide the class into pairs or small groups.
2. Write several sentences such as the following on the board or on a handout. Some of the sentences should be correct, and others incorrect. For example:

   I live here since 2001.
   You've been here since last Sunday.
   We tried that recipe last weekend.
   She's never saw a rainbow.
   He's read that book.
   I've already gave you a key.
   I drove a taxi for three years, and I still do.
   She knows us since 2000.
   They've went to Paris five times.
   He teaches history for several years.

3. The object of the activity is for students to identify which sentences are incorrect and then correct them. For each incorrect statement, have students identify which rule on text page 68 it breaks.
4. Have students compare their answers.

   Variation: Do the activity as a game with competing teams. The team that successfully completes the task in the shortest time is the winner.

4. Options for additional practice:
   - Have students write a response to Alex32 and share their writing in pairs
   - Have students correspond with a keypal on the Internet and then share their experience with the class.

 WHAT ARE THEY SAYING?

FOCUS

- Accomplishing Tasks

Have students talk about the people and the situation, and then create role plays based on the scene. Students may refer back to previous lessons as a resource, but they should not simply reuse specific conversations.

Note: You may want to assign this exercise as written homework, having students prepare their role plays, practice them the next day with other students, and then present them to the class.

 GLOBAL EXCHANGE

1. Set the scene: "Alex32 is writing to a keypal."
2. Have students read silently or follow along silently as the message is read aloud by you, by one or more students, or on the audio program.
3. Ask students if they have any questions. Check understanding of the expression *in a while*.

184   SIDE BY SIDE GAZETTE

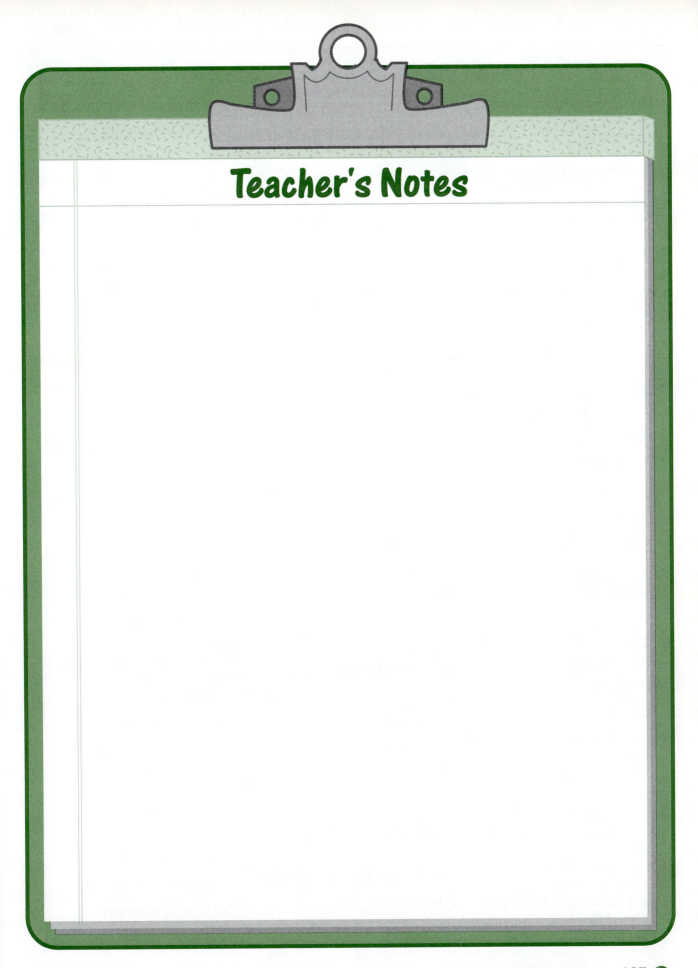
Teacher's Notes

CHAPTER 6 OVERVIEW: Text Pages 69–80

GRAMMAR

PRESENT PERFECT CONTINUOUS TENSE

(I have)	I've	
(We have)	We've	
(You have)	You've	
(They have)	They've	been working.
(He has)	He's	
(She has)	She's	
(It has)	It's	

Have	I we you they	been working?
Has	he she it	

Yes,	I we you they	have.
	he she it	has.

FUNCTIONS

ASKING FOR AND REPORTING INFORMATION

What have you been doing?
  I've been *writing letters*.
How many *letters* have you *written*?
  I've already *written fifteen letters*.

How long have you been *waiting*?
  I've been *waiting* for *two hours*.
  I've been *waiting* since *this morning*.

What *are* your neighbors *doing*?
  They're arguing.
Have *they* been *arguing* for a long time?
  Yes, *they* have. *They've* been *arguing all day*.

Where do you *live* now?
How long have you been *living* there?
Where else have you *lived*?
  I've also *lived* in _____.
How long did you *live* there?
  I *lived* there for _____.

What do you do there?

And where did you *work* before that?
  I *worked* at _____.
What did you do?

We're having a problem with *our bedroom ceiling*.
  Oh? What's the problem?
It's leaking.

Tell me, _____?

Why?

RESPONDING TO INFORMATION

Really?

INDICATING UNDERSTANDING

I see.

EXPRESSING SURPRISE–DISBELIEF

You're kidding!
No kidding!
You've got to be kidding!
I can't believe it!
That's incredible!
That's unbelievable!
That's amazing!

DESCRIBING FEELINGS–EMOTIONS

I'm nervous.

REASSURING

Don't worry!

Believe me, there's nothing to be nervous about!

PERSUADING

Believe me, . . .

EXPRESSING INTENTION

I'll *take care of it* as soon as I can.
We'll *call you* soon.

GREETING PEOPLE

Hello.
  Hello. This is *Mrs. Banks*.
Yes, *Mrs. Banks*. What can I do for you?

INITIATING A TOPIC

You look tired.

EXPRESSING GRATITUDE

Thank you.
Thank you very much.

I appreciate the opportunity to *meet with you*.

RESPONDING TO GRATITUDE

It's been a pleasure.

NEW VOCABULARY

Applying for a Job
opportunity
resume
work experience

Housing
ceiling
hallway
heating system
water heater

Verbs
appreciate
date
deliver a baby
direct traffic
do sit-ups
give *piano* lessons
leak
make noises
mend
peel
pick
ring
stand in line

Time Expressions
as soon as
lately

Adjectives
exhausted
furious
valuable

Miscellaneous
cage
chemistry
concert ticket
downtown
marathon
officer
parking ticket
pleasure
ticket

EXPRESSIONS
all right
believe me
for years
It's been a pleasure.
There's nothing to be nervous about!
What can I do for you?

You're kidding!
No kidding!
You've got to be kidding!
I can't believe it.
That's incredible!
That's unbelievable!
That's amazing!

Text Page 69: Chapter Opening Page

VOCABULARY PREVIEW

You may want to present these words before beginning the chapter, or you may choose to wait until they first occur in a specific lesson. If you choose to present them at this point, here are some suggestions:

1. Have students look at the illustrations on text page 69 and identify the words they already know.

2. Present the vocabulary. Say each word and have the class repeat it chorally and individually. Check students' understanding and pronunciation of the words.

3. Practice the vocabulary as a class, in pairs, or in small groups. Have students cover the word list and look at the pictures. Practice the words in the following ways:

   - Say a word and have students tell the number of the illustration.
   - Give the number of an illustration and have students say the word.

Text Pages 70–71: How Long Have You Been Waiting?

FOCUS

- Present Perfect Continuous Tense

CLOSE UP

RULE: The present perfect continuous tense is formed with the auxiliary verb *have* + *been* + the present participle (the *-ing* form of the verb). The auxiliary verb *have/has* is usually contracted in informal language.

EXAMPLES: I**'ve been working**.
You**'ve been working**.
He**'s been working**.
She**'s been working**.
It**'s been working**.
We**'ve been working**.
They**'ve been working**.

RULE: Like the present perfect tense, the present perfect continuous tense is associated with a period of time beginning in the past and continuing up until the present.

EXAMPLES: I**'ve been waiting** for two hours. *(I'm still waiting.)*
It**'s been barking** since this morning. *(It's still barking.)*

INTRODUCING THE MODELS

There are two model conversations. Introduce and practice each separately. For each model:

1. Have students look at the model illustration.
2. Set the scene:
   1st model: "Some people are waiting to see the doctor."
   2nd model: "One friend is asking the other about her neighbor's dog."
3. Present the model.
4. Full-Class Repetition.

Pronunciation Note

The pronunciation focus of Chapter 6 is **Reduced *for*** (text page 80). You may wish to model this pronunciation at this point *(I've been waiting for two hours)* and encourage students to incorporate it into their language practice.

5. Ask students if they have any questions. Check understanding of new vocabulary:

   1st model: *have been waiting*
   2nd model: *has been barking*

6. Group Choral Repetition.
7. Choral Conversation.

CHAPTER 6   189

8. Call on one or two pairs of students to present the dialog.

   (For additional practice, do Choral Conversation in small groups or by rows.)

9. Form sentences with the words in the box at the top of text page 70 and have students repeat chorally. For example:

   I've been working.
   We've been working.

10. Expand the first model with further practice by replacing *you* with *they, we, Mary*. For example:

    they
    A. How long have they been waiting?
    B. They've been waiting for two hours.

SIDE BY SIDE EXERCISES

Examples

1. A. How long has Yasmin been studying English?
   B. She's been studying English for eight months.
2. A. How long have Mr. and Mrs. Green been living on School Street?
   B. They've been living on School Street since 1994.

1. **Exercise 1:** Call on two students to present the dialog. Then do Choral Repetition and Choral Conversation practice.
2. **Exercise 2:** Same as above.
3. **Exercises 3–12:** Either Full Class Practice or Pair Practice.

New Vocabulary

3. ring (v)
9. date (v)

WORKBOOK

Pages 62–65

EXPANSION ACTIVITIES

1. **Match the Conversations** ★★

   a. Make up matching cards such as the following:

How long have you been reading?	I've been reading for an hour.
How long have you been eating?	I've been eating for an hour.
How long has she been driving?	She's been driving since ten o'clock.

How long has she been riding?	She's been riding since ten o'clock.
How long has he been sitting?	He's been sitting for fifteen minutes.
How long has he been knitting?	He's been knitting for fifteen minutes.
How long have you been dating?	We've been dating since last month.

190 CHAPTER 6

How long have you been waiting?	We've been waiting since last month.
How long have they been ringing?	They've been ringing for a long time.
How long have they been singing?	They've been singing for a long time.
How long have you been feeling bad?	I've been feeling bad since last Tuesday.
How long have you been feeling sad?	I've been feeling sad since last Tuesday.

b. Distribute a card to each student.

c. Have students memorize the sentences on their cards, and then have students walk around the room saying their sentences until they find their match.

d. Then have pairs of students say their matched sentences aloud to the class.

2. Create a Story ★★

Have students look at the illustration for Exercise 1 and use their imaginations to tell more about Yasmin.

a. Write the following on the board:

> study hard
> do her homework every _____
> come to class on time
> speak English with _____
> watch television programs
> see movies
> _____

b. Tell the class that Yasmin is going to take a very important English examination soon. She's been trying to get ready for the exam.

c. Have students use the cues on the board as well as ideas of their own to answer the question: "What has Yasmin been doing to get ready for the exam?" For example:

> She's been studying hard.
> She's been doing her homework every day.
> She's been coming to class on time.
> She's been speaking English with other students.
> She's been watching television programs in English.
> She's been seeing American movies.
> She's been listening to English language tapes.
> She's been talking to the teacher after class.

d. Have students pretend to be Yasmin, and ask them: "Yasmin, what have you been doing to improve your English?"

> I've been studying very hard.
> I've been doing my homework every day.
> etc.

3. Change the Sentence! ★★

a. Write a sentence on the board, underlining and numbering different portions of the sentence. For example:

> 1   2
> Paul   has been practicing
> 3   4
> the guitar   since this morning.

b. Have students sit in a circle.

c. Tell them that when you say a number, the first student in the circle makes a change in that part of the sentence. For example:

> Teacher: Two.
> Student 1: Paul *has been cleaning* the guitar since this morning.

d. The second student keeps the first student's sentence, but changes it based on the next number you say. For example:

> Teacher: Three.
> Student 2: Paul has been cleaning *the house* since this morning.

e. Continue this way with the rest of the students in the circle. For example:

> Teacher: Four.
> Student 3: Paul has been cleaning the house *for two hours.*

(continued)

EXPANSION ACTIVITIES (Continued)

4. Role Play: I've Been Very Busy ★★

a. Write the following conversation model on the board:

> A. Hi, _____. How are you?
> B. Okay. And you?
> A. Fine, thanks. I haven't spoken to you in a few days. What's new?
> B. Well, I've been very busy.
> A. Oh. What have you been doing?
> B. _____

b. Make up the following situation cards:

> You're having a big English test this week.
> You've been _____ ing.
> You've been _____ ing.
> You've been _____ ing.

> You're having a big party this weekend.
> You've been _____ ing.
> You've been _____ ing.
> You've been _____ ing.

> You're going on a vacation next week, and you've been very busy.
> You've been _____ ing.
> You've been _____ ing.
> You've been _____ ing.

c. Divide the class into pairs and have them create role plays based on the model on the board. Give one member of the pair one of the situation cards as a cue for why he or she has been so busy. That person must tell about at least three things he or she has been doing.

d. Have students rehearse their role plays, and then call on various pairs to present them to the class.

5. Question the Answers! ★★

a. Dictate answers such as the following to the class:

For two hours.
Since last week.
For several years.
Since I was a child.
For twenty minutes.

b. Have students write questions for which these answers would be correct. For example:

For two hours.	How long have you been waiting for the doctor?
Since last week.	How long has your back been hurting you?

c. Have students compare their questions with each other.

Variation: Write the answers on cards. Divide the class into groups and give each group a set of cards.

6. Find the Right Person! ★★★

a. Write the questions below on the board. Have students write their responses and hand them in to you.

> Where do you live?
> How long have you been living there?
> What do you do?
> How long have you been doing that?
> What are your hobbies?
> How long have you been doing them?

b. Put the information in the following form:

> Find someone who . . .
> 1. has been living in Westville _____ for 10 years.
> 2. has been skiing since _____ first grade.
> 3. has been working at a _____ bank for three months.
> 4. has been studying guitar _____ for two years.

c. Have students circulate around the room, asking each other the original questions on the board to identify the above people.

d. The first student to find all the people, raise his or her hand, and identify the students is the winner of the game.

7. Barry's Boring Life ★★★

a. Write the following on the board:

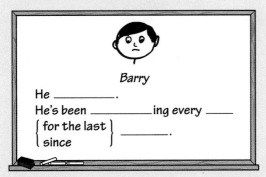

b. Set the scene: "Barry is a very nice person, but his life is a little boring. Barry's life never changes. He's been doing the same things for many, many years. For example: He works at the post office on Main Street. He's been working at the post office on Main Street since 1985."

c. Ask questions about Barry. Have students use the model on the board to tell about Barry's boring life, using any vocabulary they wish. For example:

Teacher: What does Barry eat for breakfast every morning?
Student: He eats scrambled eggs and two pieces of bread. He's been eating scrambled eggs and two pieces of bread for breakfast every morning for the past twenty years.

Possible questions:

What time does Barry get up every morning?
How does Barry get to work every day?
What does he have for lunch every day?
What does he do every evening after work?
What time does he go to bed at night?
When does he clean his apartment?
What does he do every Saturday night?
Where does he go on vacation every year?

d. Have students suggest ways in which Barry might change his life to make it less boring.

CHAPTER 6   193

Text Page 72: They've Been Arguing All Day

FOCUS

- Present Perfect Continuous Tense: Yes/No Questions and Short Answers
- Contrast: Present Perfect Continuous and Present Continuous Tenses

INTRODUCING THE MODEL

1. Have students look at the model illustration.
2. Set the scene: "Two friends are talking. One of them is upset about his noisy neighbors."
3. Present the model.
4. Full-Class Repetition.
5. Ask students if they have any questions. Check understanding of vocabulary.
6. Group Choral Repetition.
7. Choral Conversation.
8. Call on one or two pairs of students to present the dialog. Have some of the students use the alternative expressions (shown under the model) in place of *all day*.

   (For additional practice, do Choral Conversation in small groups or by rows.)

SIDE BY SIDE EXERCISES

Students can use any time expressions they wish in the exercises.

Examples

1. A. What are you doing?
   B. I'm studying.
   A. Have you been studying for a long time?
   B. Yes, I have. I've been studying all *(morning)*.

2. A. What's Gary doing?
   B. He's exercising.
   A. Has he been exercising for a long time?
   B. Yes, he has. He's been exercising all *(afternoon)*.

1. **Exercise 1:** Call on two students to present the dialog. Then do Choral Repetition and Choral Conversation practice.
2. **Exercise 2:** Same as above.
3. **Exercises 3–8:** Either Full-Class Practice or Pair Practice.

New Vocabulary

5. make noises
6. direct traffic
8. stand in line
   tickets

4. **Exercise 9:** Have students use the model as a guide to create their own conversations, using vocabulary of their choice. Encourage students to use dictionaries to find new words they want to use. This exercise can be done orally in class or for written homework. If you assign it for homework, do one example in class to make sure students understand what's expected. Have students present their conversations in class the next day.

WORKBOOK

Page 66–68

EXPANSION ACTIVITIES

1. Not Long at All! ★★

For this activity, use *Side by Side* Picture Cards for verbs (36–67, 88–90, 123–130, 158–162) or your own visuals that depict actions.

a. Write the following on the board:

> A. Has/Have ____ been _____ing very long?
> B. No. ____ hasn't/haven't been _____ing long at all. In fact, ____ just started _____ing a few minutes ago.

b. Hold up a visual and call on a pair of students to create a conversation, using the model on the board. For example:

[visual: man reading]

A. Has he been reading very long?
B. No, he hasn't been reading long at all. In fact, he just started reading a few minutes ago.

[visual: couple dancing]

A. Have they been dancing very long?
B. No, they haven't been dancing long at all. In fact, they just started dancing a few minutes ago.

2. Tic Tac Question the Answer ★★

a. Draw a tic tac grid on the board and fill it in with short answers to questions:

Yes, she has.	Yes, she is.	Yes, they are.
No, they haven't.	Yes, we have.	No, we aren't.
Yes, it is.	No, it isn't.	Yes, it has.

b. Divide the class into teams. Give each team a mark: X or O.

c. Have each team ask a question for an answer in the grid. For example:

X Team: Have you been studying English for a long time?
Yes, we have.

d. If an answer is appropriate and is stated correctly, that team may replace the answer with its team mark. For example:

Yes, she has.	Yes, she is.	Yes, they are.
No, they haven't.	X	No, we aren't.
Yes, it is.	No, it isn't.	Yes, it has.

e. The first team to mark out three boxes in a straight line—either vertically, horizontally, or diagonally—wins.

3. Miming ★★

a. Write various activities on cards. For example:

exercising	crying	jogging
looking for your wallet	waiting for the train	standing in line
studying for a test	practicing the piano	watching people
lifting weights	repairing your bicycle	paying bills

b. Have students take turns picking a card from the pile and pantomiming the action on the card.

c. Students must guess what the person is doing. Once the action has been guessed, students may then ask: "How long have you been _____?" The person answers using any time expression he or she wishes.

(continued)

CHAPTER 6   195

EXPANSION ACTIVITIES (Continued)

Variation: Do the activity as a game with competing teams.

4. Picture Clues ★★★

   a. Show the class a picture of an interesting scene.

   b. Divide the class into pairs. Have students answer the following questions:

   > What's happening?
   > What are the people doing?
   > How long have they been doing that?
   > What will happen next?

   c. Have students share their interpretations with the class.

5. Group Story ★★★

   a. Write on the board:

   > Today has been one of the worst days I can remember! _____ has/have been _____ing since/for _____.

   b. Divide the class into groups of 3 to 5 students.

   c. Begin the following story, using the model on the board:

   > Today has been one of the worst days I can remember! My upstairs neighbors have been arguing since nine o'clock this morning.

   d. Have each group continue the story by writing at least ten more things that have been happening. Encourage students to use their imaginations to tell the story of this person's terrible day.

   e. Have one person from each group present that group's story to the class.

   f. Have the class decide which group's story describes the *worst* day of all.

Text Page 73

📖 READING Apartment Problems

FOCUS

- Present Perfect Continuous Tense

NEW VOCABULARY

ceiling	leak (v)
furious	peel
hallway	water heater
heating system	

READING THE STORY

Optional: Preview the story by having students talk about the story title and/or illustration. You may choose to introduce new vocabulary beforehand, or have students encounter the new vocabulary within the context of the reading.

1. Have students read silently, or follow along silently as the story is read aloud by you, by one or more students, or on the audio program.
2. Ask students if they have any questions. Check understanding of vocabulary.
3. Check students' comprehension, using some or all of the following questions:

   What's wrong with the bedroom ceiling?
   What's wrong with the refrigerator?
   What's wrong with the paint in the hallway?
   Why have they been taking cold showers?
   Why haven't they been sleeping at night?
   Who have they been calling every day?
   What has he been promising?
   Has he fixed anything yet?

READING EXTENSION

Tic Tac Question the Answer

1. Draw a tic tac grid on the board and fill it in with the following short answers to questions:

For more than a week.	No, it hasn't.	Since last week.
No, he hasn't.	Every day.	Yes, it has.
Yes, they have.	For several weeks.	No, they haven't.

2. Divide the class into teams. Give each team a mark: *X* or *O*.
3. Have each team ask a question about the reading for an answer in the grid. For example:

   X Team: How often have Mr. and Mrs. Banks been calling their landlord? Every day.

4. If an answer is appropriate to the reading and is stated correctly, that team may replace the answer with its team mark.
5. The first team to mark out three boxes in a straight line—either vertically, horizontally, or diagonally—wins.

✓ READING CHECK-UP

Q & A

1. Call on a pair of students to present the model. Check understanding of the expressions *What can I do for you?*, *all right*, *as soon as I can*.
2. Have students work in pairs to create new dialogs.
3. Call on pairs to present their new dialogs to the class.

How About You?

Have students answer the question in pairs or as a class.

CHAPTER 6   **197**

Text Pages 74–75: No Wonder They're Tired!

FOCUS

- Contrast: Present Perfect and Present Perfect Continuous Tenses

CLOSE UP

RULE: Unlike the present perfect, the present perfect continuous cannot be used to describe an event which has ended or has been completed.

EXAMPLES: **I've been writing** letters since nine o'clock this morning.
(I'm still writing.)
I've already **written** fifteen letters.
(I've completed fifteen letters.)

GETTING READY

Contrast the present perfect continuous and present perfect tenses.

1. Write the following on the board:

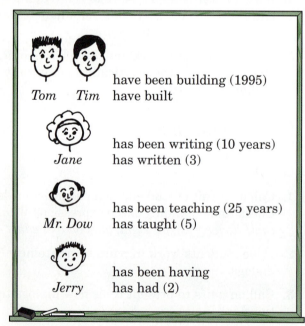

2. Have students listen as you tell the following, while pointing to the appropriate cues on the board:

   Tom and his brother Tim have been building houses since 1995. They've built twenty houses this year.

   Jane has been writing books for ten years. She's written three novels.

   Mr. Dow has been teaching languages for twenty-five years. He's taught five different languages.

   Unfortunately, Jerry isn't a very good driver. He's been having accidents since he started driving. He's already had two accidents this year.

3. Check students' understanding of the two tenses.

4. Tell each situation again and ask questions after each. For example:

   How long have Tom and Tim been building houses?
   How many houses have they built this year?

INTRODUCING THE MODELS

There are two model conversations. Introduce and practice each separately. For each model:

1. Have students look at the model illustration.

198 CHAPTER 6

2. Set the scene:

   1st model: "One friend is visiting another."

   2nd model: "Two people are talking about Anthony."

3. Present the model. (Note that the capitalized words indicate spoken emphasis.)

4. Full-Class Repetition.

5. Ask students if they have any questions. Check understanding of vocabulary.

6. Group Choral Repetition.

7. Choral Conversation.

8. Call on one or two pairs of students to present the dialog.

   (For additional practice, do Choral Conversation in small groups or by rows.)

SIDE BY SIDE EXERCISES

Students can use any time expressions and numbers they wish in the exercises.

Examples

1. A. You look tired. What have you been doing?
   B. I've been planting flowers since *(eight o'clock)* this morning.
   A. Really? How many flowers have you planted?
   B. Believe it or not, I've already planted *(fifty)* flowers.
   A. You're kidding! *(Fifty)* flowers?! NO WONDER you're tired!

2. A. Ms. Perkins looks tired. What has she been doing?
   B. She's been giving piano lessons since *(ten o'clock)* this morning.
   A. Really? How many piano lessons has she given?
   B. Believe it or not, she's already given *(seven)* piano lessons.
   A. You're kidding! *(Seven)* piano lessons?! NO WONDER she's tired!

1. **Exercise 1:** Call on two students to present the dialog. Then do Choral Repetition and Choral Conversation practice.

2. **Exercise 2:** Introduce the new expression *give piano lessons*. Same as above.

3. **Exercises 3–12:** Either Full Class Practice or Pair Practice.

> **New Vocabulary**
>
> 4. mend
> 5. pick
> 6. thank-you note
> 10. cage
> 11. do sit-ups
> 12. deliver a baby

Culture Note

Exercise 6: It's polite to write a thank-you note after receiving a gift or after spending two or more days visiting at someone's home.

Language Note

Exercise 12: To *deliver a baby* is to help the mother give birth.

WORKBOOK

Pages 69–71

EXPANSION ACTIVITIES

1. Complete the Sentence ★★

With books closed, read each of the sentences below and have students complete it with an appropriate verb.

How many thank-you notes have you . . . ?
(written)

How many flowers has she . . . ?
(planted)

How many photographs have they . . . ?
(taken)

How many sit-ups has he . . . ?
(done)

How many pictures have you . . . ?
(drawn)

How many patients has Dr. Green . . . ?
(seen)

How many lessons has your piano teacher . . . ?
(given)

How many socks has she . . . ?
(mended)

How many apples have you . . . ?
(picked)

How many apple pies have they . . . ?
(made/baked)

How many babies has Dr. Chen . . . ?
(delivered)

How many job interviews has she . . . ?
(gone to)

2. Match the Conversations ★★

a. Make up the following matching cards:

I've been writing all morning.	What have you written?
I've been riding all morning.	Where have you ridden?
I've been reading all morning.	What have you read?
I've been eating all morning.	What have you eaten?
I've been swimming all afternoon.	Where have you swum?
I've been singing all afternoon.	What have you sung?
I've been sweeping all afternoon.	What have you swept?
I've been sleeping all afternoon.	Where have you slept?
I've been chopping all day.	What have you chopped?
I've been shopping all day.	Where have you shopped?

b. Distribute a card to each student.

c. Have students memorize the sentences on their cards, and then have students walk around the room saying their sentences until they find their match.

d. Then have pairs of students say their matched sentences aloud to the class.

3. The Differences Between Steve and Bill ★★

a. Write the following on the board:

Bill has been _____ing for many years too, but he's never _____.

b. Tell about Steve by reading the statements below. After each one, call on a student to make a contrasting statement about Bill. For example:

200   CHAPTER 6

Teacher: Steve has been driving for many years, and he's had a lot of accidents.
Student: Bill has been driving for many years too, but he's never had an accident.

Statements:

Steve has been studying French for many years, and he's traveled to France many times.
Steve has been working in Washington for many years, and he's seen the president several times.
Steve has been listening to jazz on the radio for many years, and he's gone to a lot of jazz concerts.
Steve has been playing baseball for many years, and his team has won all their games.
Steve has been visiting New York for many years, and he's seen the Statue of Liberty many times.
Steve has been going skiing every winter for many years, and he's broken his leg a few times.
Steve has been going sailing every summer for many years, and he's gotten seasick a few times.
Steve has been cooking delicious meals for many years, and he's had several dinner parties.
Steve has been giving blood at the hospital every year for a long time, and he's fainted a few times.
Steve has been singing opera for many years, and he's sung at the White House two or three times.
Steve has been swimming every day for many years, and he has swum in the Mediterranean several times.
Steve has been playing the piano for many years, and he's written several songs.

4. Begin the Sentence! ★★

Give students sentence endings and have them add appropriate beginnings, paying attention to the verb tenses. For example:

Teacher: fifteen lessons
Student: The teacher has given fifteen lessons.

Teacher: pizzas since eight o'clock
Student: He's been making pizzas since eight o'clock.

Variation: This activity may be done as a class, in pairs or small groups, or as a game with competing teams.

5. Surprise Situations ★★★

a. Put a skeletal framework of the model conversation on the board:

> A. You look tired. What _____ doing?
> B. I've been _____ since _____.
> A. Really? How many _____?
> B. Believe it or not, ___ already _____.
> A. _____?! No wonder you're tired!

b. Ask for a pair of student volunteers to come to the front of the room.

c. Give them word cards such as the following and have them create a conversation based on the framework on the board, using the information on their cards. They should feel free to modify the conversation any way they wish.

Speaker A: Your friend looks tired.	Speaker B: You've been making cookies since _____.
Speaker A: Your friend looks tired.	Speaker B: You've been doing grammar exercises since _____.
Speaker A: Your friend looks tired.	Speaker B: You've been filling out job applications since _____.

(continued)

CHAPTER 6

EXPANSION ACTIVITIES (Continued)

6. Interview: Students' Hobbies ★★★

a. Brainstorm with the class questions to ask each other about hobbies and sports interests. For example:

> What hobbies do you have?
> How long have you been _____?
> Do you play any team sports?
> How long have you been playing _____?
> How many games have you played this season?
> How many awards has your team won?
> How often does your team practice?

b. Have students interview each other and then report to the class.

7. Number Facts ★★★

a. Have students complete the following sentences:

> I've _____ three _____.
> I've _____ four _____.
> I've _____ five _____.
> I've _____ ten _____.

b. Have students share their sentences in pairs or small groups. For example:

> I've skied two times this year.
> I've been to Paris four times.
> I've read five books by Agatha Christie.
> I've seen ten movies this year.

c. Have students report to the class any interesting facts they have learned about each other.

How to Say It!

Expressing Surprise: In informal spoken English, there are many ways to express surprise, such as the ones presented on text page 75.

1. Present the expressions.
2. Full-Class Repetition.
3. Ask students if they have any questions.
4. Have students practice the conversations in this lesson again, using any of these new expressions.
5. Call on pairs to present their conversations to the class.

Text Pages 76–77: There's Nothing to Be Nervous About!

FOCUS

- Contrast: Present Perfect and Present Perfect Continuous Tenses

INTRODUCING THE MODEL

1. Have students look at the model illustration.
2. Set the scene: "Two college roommates are talking. One of them is going on a trip tomorrow."
3. Present the model.
4. Full-Class Repetition.
5. Ask students if they have any questions. Check understanding of new vocabulary: *for years, believe me, There's nothing to be nervous about!*
6. Group Choral Repetition.
7. Choral Conversation.
8. Call on one or two pairs of students to present the dialog.

   (For additional practice, do Choral Conversation in small groups or by rows.)

SIDE BY SIDE EXERCISES

Examples

1. A. I'm nervous.
   B. Why?
   A. I'm going to drive downtown tomorrow, and I've never driven downtown before.
   B. Don't worry! I've been driving downtown for years. And believe me, there's nothing to be nervous about!

2. A. I'm nervous.
   B. Why?
   A. I'm going to give blood tomorrow, and I've never given blood before.
   B. Don't worry! I've been giving blood for years. And believe me, there's nothing to be nervous about!

1. **Exercise 1:** Introduce the word *downtown*. Call on two students to present the dialog. Then do Choral Repetition and Choral Conversation practice.
2. **Exercise 2:** Same as above.
3. **Exercises 3–11:** Either Full-Class Practice or Pair Practice.

New Vocabulary

4. chemistry
5. marathon

Culture Notes

Exercise 5: Long-distance running and running in marathons for amateur athletes is very popular in the United States. Some U.S. cities, such as Boston and New York, sponsor annual marathons.

Exercise 10: It is common for U.S. employers to give their workers regular salary increases. Employees may also ask for additional increases in salary if they feel they deserve more money for the work they do.

After each exercise, have students tell about their own experiences. Encourage students to ask each other questions. For example, after doing Exercise 2:

Have you ever given blood?
Were you nervous?
Tell about your experience.

4. **Exercise 12:** Have students use the model as a guide to create their own conversations, using vocabulary of their choice. Encourage students to use dictionaries to find new words they want to use. This exercise can be done orally in class or for written homework. If you assign it for homework, do one example in class to make sure students understand what's expected. Have students present their conversations in class the next day.

CHAPTER 6

INTERVIEW *Have You Ever...?*

WORKBOOK

Pages 72–75

1. Check understanding of the word *valuable*.
2. Have students interview each other about their experiences and then report back to the class.

EXPANSION ACTIVITIES

1. **Memory Chain** ★★

   a. Divide the class into groups of 5 or 6 students each.

   b. Tell each student to think of something that he or she has never done.

   c. One group at a time, have Student 1 begin. For example:

      I've never given blood.

   d. Student 2 repeats what Student 1 said and adds a statement about himself or herself. For example:

      Marco has never given blood, and I've never run in a marathon.

   e. Student 3 continues in the same way. For example:

      Marco has never given blood. Carol has never run in a marathon, and I've never ridden a motorcycle.

   f. Continue until everyone has had a chance to play the *memory chain*.

2. **Good Suggestions** ★★

   a. Write the following conversation model on the board:

      A. I've never _____ before. Do you have any suggestions?
      B. Yes. You should _____, you should _____, and most of all you should _____.
      A. Thanks. Those are good suggestions.

   b. Have pairs of students talk about how to prepare for the situations on text pages 76 and 77, using the model on the board as a guide. For example:

      Situation 2
      A. I've never gone to a job interview before. Do you have any suggestions?
      B. Yes. You should prepare a resume, you should make a list of your qualifications, and most of all you should relax.
      A. Thanks. Those are good suggestions.

3. **Grammar Chain** ★★

   a. Write the following conversation model and verbs on the board:

      A. Have you ever _____?
      B. Yes. I've been _____ for years!

      ride _____
      speak _____
      take a _____ lesson
      sing in front of _____
      ask for _____
      drive _____
      go out _____
      buy a used _____
      give _____
      fly _____

204 CHAPTER 6

b. Start the chain game by saying:

   Teacher *(to Student A):* Have you ever ridden a motorcycle?

c. Student A answers according to the model on the board, and then asks a different question to Student B, and the chain continues. For example:

   Student A: Yes. I've been riding motorcycles for years!
   (to Student B): Have you ever spoken at a meeting?

   Student B: Yes. I've been speaking at meetings for years!
   (to Student A): Have you ever taken a karate lesson?

4. Surprise Situations ★★★

a. Put the following cues for the model conversation on the board:

> A. nervous
> B. Why?
> A. going to
>   never / before
> B. Don't worry!
>   for years
>   Believe me!

b. Ask for a pair of student volunteers to come to the front of the room.

c. Give them word cards such as the following and have them create a conversation based on the model conversation from the text, using the key words on the board and the information on their cards. They should feel free to modify the conversation any way they wish.

> Speaker A:
> You're nervous! You're going to ride in a hot-air balloon.

> Speaker B:
> Your friend is nervous. Give your friend some encouragement.

> Speaker A:
> You're nervous! You're going to go water-skiing.

> Speaker B:
> Your friend is nervous. Give your friend some encouragement.

> Speaker A:
> You're nervous! You're going to sing in a karaoke club.

> Speaker B:
> Your friend is nervous. Give your friend some encouragement.

5. Pantomime Role Play ★★★

This activity is similar to Activity 4. However, this activity is done through miming.

a. Make up role-play cards such as the following:

> You're nervous. You're going to fly in a helicopter, and you've never flown in a helicopter before. Your friend tells you not to worry.

> You're nervous. You're going to ride a horse, and you've never ridden a horse before. Your friend tells you not to worry.

> You're nervous. You're going to drive a truck, and you've never driven a truck before. Your friend tells you not to worry.

> You're nervous. You're going to go scuba diving, and you've never gone scuba diving before. Your friend tells you not to worry.

b. Have pairs of students pantomime their role plays. The class watches and guesses the situation and what the two characters are saying.

(continued)

EXPANSION ACTIVITIES (Continued)

6. Which One Isn't True? ★★

a. Tell students to write three true statements and one false statement about themselves. For example:

> I've never given blood.
> I've run in several marathons.
> I called the president on the telephone last week.
> I've been studying Swahili for the past two years.

b. Have students take turns reading their statements to the class, and have the class guess which statement isn't true.

Text Page 78

 ROLE PLAY *At a Job Interview*

FOCUS

- Review: Present Perfect, Present Perfect Continuous, Simple Past

INTRODUCING THE ROLE PLAY

1. Have students look at the model.
2. Set the scene: "Someone is at a job interview."
3. Present the model dialog, using any names, places, and time expressions you wish.
4. Ask students if they have any questions. Check understanding of new vocabulary: *resume, work experience, appreciate, opportunity, It's been a pleasure.*

ROLE PLAY

1. Call on two of your stronger students to role-play the conversation, using any names, places, and time expressions they wish.
2. Divide the class into pairs and have students practice the role play. Then call on pairs to present their role plays to the class.

EXPANSION ACTIVITY

Scrambled Interview ★★

1. Complete the first 6 lines of the dialog on text page 78 any way you wish, and write each line on a separate card.
2. Scramble the cards, and give a card to six different students.
3. Have those students work together to put the lines in the correct order.
4. Those students should then come to the front of the room and present their lines in the correct order.
5. Do the same with the next 6 lines, beginning with "Okay. I see here on your resume..."
6. Do the same with the next 12 lines, beginning with "Tell me about your work experience."

CHAPTER 6   207

Text Page 79

READING *It's Been a Long Day*

FOCUS

- Present Perfect Tense
- Present Perfect Continuous Tense

NEW VOCABULARY

exhausted
officer
parking ticket

READING THE STORY

Optional: *Preview the story by having students talk about the story title and/or illustrations. You may choose to introduce new vocabulary beforehand, or have students encounter the new vocabulary within the context of the reading.*

1. Have students read silently, or follow along silently as the story is read aloud by you, by one or more students, or on the audio program.
2. Ask students if they have any questions. Check understanding of vocabulary.

   Culture Note

   Parking is a problem in many U.S. cities. Public parking garages are expensive. Street parking is difficult to find. People have to put money into parking meters for street parking. Police officers give parking tickets to cars parked in illegal spaces and at meters that have run out of money.

3. Check students' comprehension, using some or all of the following questions:

What has Frank been doing since 7 A.M.?
How many cameras has he assembled?
Has he ever assembled that many cameras in one day before?
What does he have to do before he can go home?

What has Julie been doing since 9 A.M.?
How many letters has she typed?
Has she ever typed that many letters in one day before?
What does she have to do before she can go home?

What has Officer Jackson been doing since 8 A.M.?
How many parking tickets has he written?
Has he ever written that many parking tickets in one day before?
What does he have to do before he can go home?

READING CHECK-UP

Q & A

1. Call on a pair of students to present the model.
2. Have students work in pairs to create new dialogs.
3. Call on pairs to present their new dialogs to the class.

READING EXTENSION

Tic Tac Question the Answer

1. Draw a tic tac grid on the board and fill it in with short answers to questions:

Yes, she has.	Yes, she is.	25.
No, she hasn't.	Yes, it has.	No, he hasn't.
19.	211.	Yes, he is.

2. Divide the class into teams. Give each team a mark: *X* or *O*.

3. Have each team ask a question for an answer in the grid. For example:

   X Team: Has Julie been typing letters since 9 A.M.?
   Yes, she has.

4. If an answer is appropriate and is stated correctly, that team may replace the answer with its team mark.

5. The first team to mark out three boxes in a straight line—either vertically, horizontally, or diagonally—wins.

 LISTENING

Which Word Do You Hear?

Listen and choose the correct answer.

1. He's gone to the bank.
2. I've never written so many letters in one day before.
3. She's been seeing patients all day.
4. What courses have you taken this year?
5. Is Beverly giving blood?
6. Ben has driven all night.

Answers

1. a
2. a
3. b
4. a
5. b
6. a

Who Is Speaking?

Listen and decide who is speaking.

1. What a day! All the tenants have been complaining that nothing is working.
2. I'm very tired. I've given six lessons today.
3. Thank you! You've been a wonderful audience!
4. I'm really tired. I've been watching them all day.
5. I'm very tired. I've been looking at paychecks since early this morning.
6. It's been a long day. I've been selling tickets since ten A.M.

Answers

1. a
2. b
3. a
4. b
5. b
6. a

CHAPTER 6 209

Text Page 80

 PRONUNCIATION Reduced *for*

Reduced *for*: When spoken in mid-sentence, the word *for* is commonly reduced to "fr."

Focus on Listening

Practice the sentences in the left column. Say each sentence or play the audio one or more times. Have students listen carefully and repeat.

Focus on Pronunciation

Practice the sentences in the right column. Have students say each sentence and then listen carefully as you say it or play the audio.

If you wish, have students continue practicing the sentences to improve their pronunciation.

 JOURNAL

Have students write their journal entries at home or in class. Encourage students to use a dictionary to look up words they would like to use. Students can share their written work with other students if appropriate. Have students discuss what they have written as a class, in pairs, or in small groups.

WORKBOOK

Check-Up Test: Pages 76–77

 CHAPTER SUMMARY

GRAMMAR

1. Divide the class into pairs or small groups.
2. Have students take turns forming sentences from the words in the grammar boxes. Student A says a sentence, and Student B points to the words from each column that are in the sentence. Then have students switch: Student B says a sentence, and Student A points to the words.

KEY VOCABULARY

Have students ask you any questions about the meaning or pronunciation of the vocabulary. If students ask for the pronunciation, repeat after the student until the student is satisfied with his or her own pronunciation.

EXPANSION ACTIVITIES

1. **Do You Remember the Words?** ★

   Check students' retention of the vocabulary depicted on the opening page of Chapter 6 by doing the following activity:

   a. Have students open their books to page 69 and cover the list of vocabulary words and phrases.

   b. Either call out a number and have students tell you the word or phrase, or say a word or phrase and have students tell you the number.

   Variation: You can also do this activity as a game with competing teams.

210 CHAPTER 6

2. Student-Led Dictation ★
   a. Tell each student to choose a word or phrase from the Key Vocabulary list on text page 80 and look at it very carefully.
   b. Have students take turns dictating their words to the class. Everybody writes down that student's word.
   c. When the dictation is completed, call on different students to write each word on the board to check the spelling.

3. Letter Game ★
   a. Divide the class into two teams.
   b. Say, "I'm thinking of a verb that starts with *r*."
   c. The first person to raise his or her hand and guess correctly and say its present, past, and past participle forms *[ring-rang-rung]* wins a point for his or her team.
   d. Continue with other letters of the alphabet and verbs.

   The team that gets the most correct answers wins the game.

4. Miming ★
   a. Write on cards some of the actions and activities listed on text page 80.
   b. Have students take turns picking a card from the pile and pantomiming the action on the card.
   c. The class must guess what the person is doing and say the present, past, and past participle forms of the verb.

   Variation: This can be done as a game with competing teams.

5. Tic Tac Grammar ★
   a. Have students draw a tic tac grid on a piece of paper and fill it in with the present form of any of the verbs on text page 80.
   b. Call out the past participle of any of these verbs. Tell students to cross out any present tense verb on their grid for which you have given a past participle form.
   c. The first person to cross out three verbs in a straight line—either vertically, horizontally, or diagonally—wins the game.
   d. Have the winner call out the words to check the accuracy.

6. Finish the Sentence! ★★

   Begin a sentence using the verbs listed on text page 80, and have students repeat what you said and add appropriate endings to the sentence, paying attention to the verb tenses. For example:

Teacher	Students
I've been drawing . . .	I've been drawing pictures all day.
He's written . . .	He's written ten thank-you notes.
We've been picking . . .	We've been picking flowers since early this morning.

   Variation: This activity may be done as a class, in pairs or small groups, or as a game with competing teams.

END-OF-CHAPTER ACTIVITIES

1. **Board Game** ★★★

    a. On poster boards or on manila file folders, make up game boards with a pathway consisting of separate spaces. You may use any theme or design you wish.

    b. Divide the class into groups of 2 to 4 students and give each group a game board and a die, and each student something to be used as a playing piece.

    c. Give each group a pile of cards face-down with statements written on them. Some sentences should be correct, and others incorrect. For example:

    > We've been arguing all day long.
    > They've been living on this street for 1998.
    > I've been feeling bad since five hours ago.
    > Did they been waiting in line for a long time?
    > It been making strange noises all day.
    > It's been leaking for about an hour.
    > I've been writing ten letters since nine o'clock this morning.
    > They've made already twelve cakes.
    > He's been taking photographs since ten o'clock this morning.
    > I've never been buying a used car.
    > We've been running in marathons for years.
    > She has sung never in front of an audience before.

    d. Each student in turn rolls the die, moves the playing piece along the game path, and after landing on a space, picks a card, reads the sentence, and says if it is *correct* or *incorrect*. If the statement is incorrect, the student must correct it. If the response is correct, the student takes an additional turn.

    e. The first student to reach the end of the pathway is the winner.

2. **Dialog Builder** ★★★

    a. Divide the class into pairs.

    b. Write lines on the board from conversations in Chapter 6 such as the following:

    > That's incredible!
    > Don't worry!
    > I'm nervous.
    > Believe it or not, . . .

    c. Have each pair create a conversation incorporating those lines. Students can begin and end their conversations any way they wish, but they must include those lines in their dialogs.

    d. Call on students to present their conversations to the class.

3. **Sentence Cues** ★★

    a. On separate cards, write key words that can be put together to form sentences or questions. Clip together the cards for each sentence. For example:

how long	speak	on the phone
they	argue	all day
he	never	go to a job interview	before
I	take	photographs	since this morning
they	run	in marathons	for years

    b. Divide the class into small groups and give a clipped set of cards to each group.

    c. Have each group write a sentence based on their set of cards.

    d. Have one member of each group write that group's sentence on the board, then compare everybody's sentences. Did they choose the correct tense? What words helped them choose the correct tense?

WORKBOOK ANSWER KEY AND LISTENING SCRIPTS

WORKBOOK PAGE 62

A. WHAT'S THE WORD?

1. since
2. for
3. for
4. since
5. since
6. for
7. since
8. for

B. CHOOSE

1. a
2. b
3. b
4. a
5. b
6. b

WORKBOOK PAGE 63

C. HOW LONG?

1. I've been studying since
2. She's been feeling sick for
3. He's been having problems with his car for
4. They've been arguing since
5. We've been waiting for
6. It's been ringing since
7. He's been talking for
8. They've been dating since
9. I've been teaching since
10. You've been chatting online for

WORKBOOK PAGE 64

D. WHAT ARE THEY DOING?

1. is looking
   He's been looking
2. is jogging
   She's been jogging
3. is barking
   It's been barking
4. are planting
   They've been planting
5. is doing
   He's been doing
6. is browsing
   She's been browsing
7. are assembling
   They've been assembling
8. baking
   I've been baking

9. are making
   You've been making

E. LISTENING

Listen and choose the correct time expressions to complete the sentences.

1. A. How long have you been living there?
   B. I've been living there since . . .
2. A. How long has your daughter been practicing the piano?
   B. She's been practicing for . . .
3. A. How long have I been running?
   B. You've been running since . . .
4. A. How long have you been feeling bad?
   B. I've been feeling bad for . . .
5. A. How long have they been waiting?
   B. They've been waiting for . . .
6. A. How long has your son been studying?
   B. He's been studying since . . .
7. A. How long have your sister and her boyfriend been dating?
   B. They've been dating since . . .
8. A. Dad, how long have we been driving?
   B. Hmm. I think we've been driving for . . .
9. A. How long has your little girl been crying?
   B. She's been crying for . . .

Answers

1. a
2. b
3. a
4. b
5. b
6. a
7. b
8. a
9. b

WORKBOOK PAGES 66–67

G. WHAT ARE THEY SAYING?

1. Have you been waiting
   have
   I've been waiting
2. Has it been snowing
   it has
   It's been snowing
3. Has he been taking
   he has
   He's been taking

CHAPTER 6   213

4. Have you been working
   I haven't
   been working
5. Has, been making
   it has
   It's been making
6. Have you been vacuuming
   I have
   I've been vacuuming
7. Have they been studying
   they have
   They've been studying
8. Have we been running
   have
   We've been running
9. Have you been wearing
   I haven't
   I've been wearing
10. Have you been playing
    I haven't
    I've been playing

H. LISTENING

Listen and choose what the people are talking about.

1. She's been directing it for an hour.
2. We've been rearranging it all morning.
3. I've been paying them on time.
4. He's been playing them for years.
5. Have you been bathing them for a long time?
6. They've been rebuilding it for a year.
7. She's been writing it for a week.
8. He's been translating them for many years.
9. I've been reading it all afternoon.
10. She's been knitting them for a few weeks.
11. We've been listening to them all afternoon.
12. I've been recommending it for years.
13. They've been repairing it all day.
14. She's been taking it all morning.
15. I've been solving them all my life.

Answers

1. a
2. b
3. b
4. a
5. b
6. b
7. a
8. a
9. b
10. a
11. b
12. a
13. b
14. a
15. b

214   CHAPTER 6

WORKBOOK PAGE 68

I. SOUND IT OUT!

1. interested
2. is
3. Steve's
4. in
5. history
6. sister
7. very
8. Chinese
9. Steve's sister is very interested in Chinese history.
10. receive
11. this
12. any
13. Peter
14. week
15. didn't
16. e-mail
17. Peter didn't receive any e-mail this week.

WORKBOOK PAGES 70–71

K. WHAT'S HAPPENING?

1. We've been eating
   We've, eaten
   We haven't eaten
2. She's been seeing
   She's, seen
   She hasn't seen
3. He's been swimming
   He's, swum
4. She's been going
   She's, gone
5. He's been talking
   He's, talked
   he hasn't talked
6. They've been writing
   They've, written
   they haven't written
7. he's been making
   He's, made
   He hasn't made
8. She's been studying
   She's, studied
   she hasn't studied
9. He's been reading
   He's, read
   he hasn't read
10. They've been complaining
    They've, complained
    haven't complained

L. LISTENING

Listen and decide where the conversation is taking place.

1. A. I'm really tired.
   B. No wonder! You've been chopping tomatoes for the past hour.

2. A. Mark! I'm surprised. You've been falling asleep in class all morning, and you've never fallen asleep in class before.
   B. I'm sorry, Mrs. Applebee. It won't happen again.

3. A. I've been washing these shirts for the past half hour, and they still aren't clean.
   B. Here. Try this Presto Soap.

4. A. We've been standing in line for an hour and forty-five minutes.
   B. I know. I hope the movie is good. I've never stood in line for such a long time.

5. A. What seems to be the problem, Mr. Jones?
   B. My back has been hurting me for the past few days.
   A. I'm sorry to hear that.

6. A. You know, we've been reading here for more than two hours.
   B. You're right. I think it's time to go now.

7. A. Do you want to leave?
   B. I think so. We've seen all the paintings here.

8. A. How long have you been exercising?
   B. For an hour and a half.

9. A. We've been waiting for an hour, and it still isn't here.
   B. I know. I'm going to be late for work.

10. A. I think we've seen them all. Which one do you want to buy?
    B. I like that black one over there.

11. A. We've been watching this movie for the past hour, and it's terrible!
    B. You're right. Let's change the channel.

12. A. I've got a terrible headache.
    B. Why?
    A. Customers have been complaining all morning.
    B. What have they been complaining about?
    A. Some people have complained about our terrible products, but most people have complained about our high prices.

Answers
1. a
2. b
3. b
4. a
5. a
6. b
7. b
8. a
9. b
10. b
11. a
12. b

WORKBOOK PAGE 72

M. WHICH WORD?

1. leaking
2. flying
3. run
4. made
5. have you been
6. seen
7. given
8. taken
9. gone
10. has been ringing
11. singing

WORKBOOK PAGE 74

O. A NEW LIFE

1. He's never lived in a big city
2. He's never taken English lessons
3. He's never taken the subway
4. He's never shopped in American supermarkets
5. He's never eaten American food
6. He's never played American football

8. They've been living in a big city
9. They've been taking English lessons
10. They've been taking the subway
11. They've been shopping in American supermarkets
12. They've been eating American food
13. They've been playing American football

WORKBOOK PAGES 76–77

CHECK-UP TEST: Chapters 4–6

A.

1. have, eaten
2. hasn't taken
3. haven't written
4. has, gone
5. haven't paid
6. has, had

CHAPTER 6   215

B.
1. Have you spoken
2. Has he ridden
3. Have they gotten
4. Has he, flown
5. Has she, been
6. Have you met

C.
1. It's been sunny
2. We've been browsing
3. She's had
4. He's been studying
5. They've been arguing
6. I've known
7. She's been
8. We've been cleaning

D.
1. She's been working at the bank since
2. They've been barking for
3. It's been snowing for
4. I've wanted to be an astronaut since

E.
1. He's owned
   he owned
2. I've been
   I was
3. She's liked
   she liked

F.
Listen and choose the correct answer.
1. A. How long has Janet been an actress?
   B. She's been an actress since she graduated from acting school.
2. A. Have you watched the news yet?
   B. Yes. I saw the president, and I heard his speech.
3. A. Have you always lived in Denver?
   B. No. We've lived in Denver since 1995. Before that, we lived in New York.
4. A. Has Dad made dinner yet?
   B. Not yet. He still has to make it.
5. A. How long has your ceiling been leaking?
   B. It's been leaking for more than a week.
   A. Have you called the superintendent?
   B. Yes, I have. I've called him several times.
6. A. Billy is having trouble with his homework.
   B. Has he asked anyone to help him?
   A. No, he hasn't.

Answers
1. b
2. a
3. b
4. a
5. a
6. b

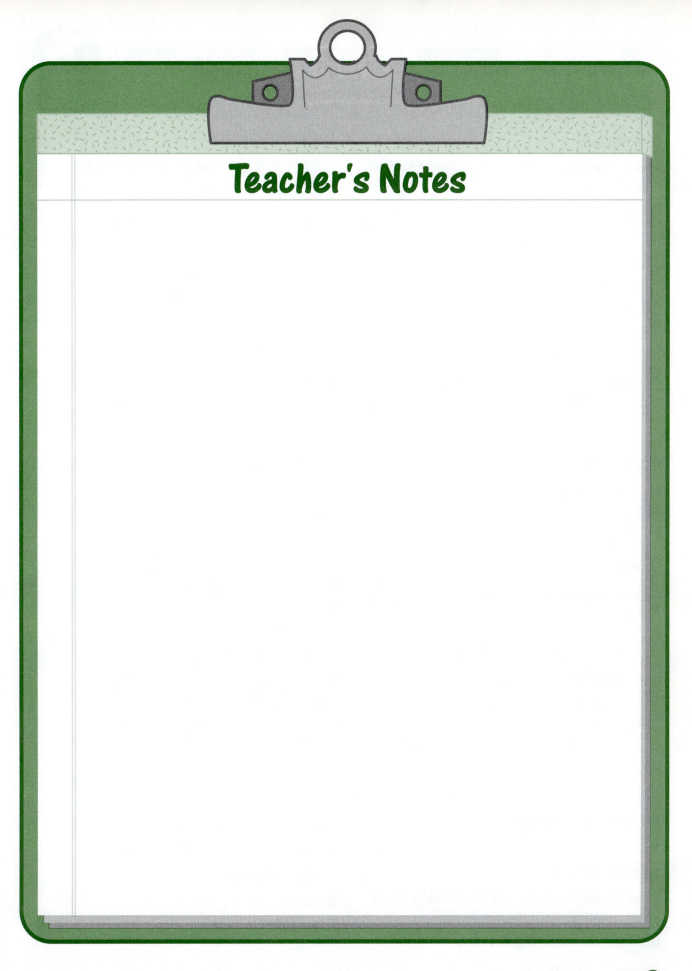

CHAPTER 7 OVERVIEW: Text Pages 81–94

GRAMMAR

Verb + Infinitive

| decide
learn | to _____ |

Verb + Gerund

| avoid
consider
enjoy
keep on
practice
quit
stop
think about | _____ing |

Verb + Infinitive / Gerund

| begin
can't stand
continue
hate
like
start | to _____
_____ing |

Gerund as Subject

Watching TV is my favorite way to relax.

Gerund as Object

I'm thinking about getting married.

FUNCTIONS

Inquiring About Likes/Dislikes

Do you like to *watch TV*?

What do you like to *read*?

Expressing Likes

I enjoy *reading short stories*.
I enjoy *watching TV* very much.
I like to *read books about famous people*.

Watching TV is my favorite way to relax.

Expressing Dislikes

I can't stand to *drive downtown*.
I can't stand *driving downtown*.

I avoid *going to the mall* whenever I can.

Inquiring About Satisfaction

Are you enjoying the *party*?

Expressing Preference

I'd rather be *reading*.

Offering Advice

I don't mean to be critical, but I really think you should *stop eating junk food*.

Getting married is a great idea.

Initiating a Topic

Guess what I've decided to do!

I've made a decision.

Asking for and Reporting Information

How about you?

I've never *swum* before.

I've decided to *get married*.

I considered *getting married* a few years ago, but never did.

How long have you been thinking about *getting married*?

How did you learn to *swim* so well?
   I started to *swim* when I was *young*, and I've been *swimming* ever since.

Have you ever tried to *stop eating junk food* before?

Responding to Information

I hope you're successful this time.

Focusing Attention

In fact, . . .

After all, . . .

218   CHAPTER 7

ADMITTING

To tell you the truth, . . .

The truth is . . .

CONGRATULATING

That's wonderful!
That's great!

EXPRESSING AGREEMENT

You're right.

EXPRESSING GRATITUDE

Thank you.
Thanks.

EXPRESSING APPRECIATION

Thank you.
I appreciate that.
That's very kind of you.
That's very nice of you.

LEAVE TAKING

Well, please excuse me.

I have to go now.

It was nice meeting you.
    Nice meeting you, too.

DESCRIBING FEELINGS–EMOTIONS

I envy you.

HESITATING

You know, . . .

ATTRACTING ATTENTION

Nancy?

NEW VOCABULARY

Verbs

avoid
box
break a habit
can't stand
consider
continue
enroll
envy
figure skate
go on a diet
go out of business
gossip
guess
hate
interrupt
keep on
make a decision
quit
surf
tap dance
tease

Miscellaneous

critical
engineering
ever since
fast-food restaurant
habit
junk food
network programming
part
rather
reporter
rest
technical school
vegetarian

EXPRESSIONS

after all
I don't mean to be critical.
I hope so.
It was nice meeting you.
Nice meeting you, too
Not at all.
the rest of
the truth is
to tell you the truth

Text Page 81: Chapter Opening Page

VOCABULARY PREVIEW

You may want to present these words before beginning the chapter, or you may choose to wait until they first occur in a specific lesson. If you choose to present them at this point, here are some suggestions:

1. Have students look at the illustrations on text page 81 and identify the words they already know.

2. Present the vocabulary. Say each word and have the class repeat it chorally and individually. Check students' understanding and pronunciation of the words.

3. Practice the vocabulary as a class, in pairs, or in small groups. Have students cover the word list and look at the pictures. Practice the words in the following ways:

   - Say a word and have students tell the number of the illustration.
   - Give the number of an illustration and have students say the word.

Text Page 82: My Favorite Way to Relax

FOCUS

- Like to _____
- Enjoy _____ ing
- Gerunds as Subject of a Sentence

CLOSE UP

RULE:	Gerunds are formed by adding *-ing* to the base form of the verb.
EXAMPLES:	watch **watching** paint **painting** swim **swimming**
RULE:	Gerunds perform the same function as nouns. They can act as subjects and as objects.
EXAMPLES:	I enjoy **watching TV**. **Watching TV** is my favorite way to relax.
RULE:	Some verbs are followed only by gerunds and others only by infinitives. Some verbs are followed by either gerunds or infinitives with no change in meaning. For a comprehensive list of each category, see text page 94.
EXAMPLES:	**like to** watch **like** watch**ing** **enjoy** watch**ing**

GETTING READY

Introduce *like* with infinitives and *enjoy* with gerunds.

1. Write on the board:

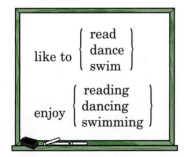

2. Form sentences with the words on the board and have students repeat chorally. For example:

   I like to read.
   I enjoy reading.

   (*George*) likes to dance.
   He enjoys dancing.

   (*Jane*) likes to swim.
   She enjoys swimming.

3. Ask students questions in order to have them practice making statements about themselves, using these verbs. For example:

   Teacher: What do you like to do?
   Student: I like to swim.

CHAPTER 7   221

Teacher: What do you enjoy doing?
Student: I enjoy playing baseball.

INTRODUCING THE MODEL

1. Have students look at the model illustration.
2. Set the scene: "Two co-workers are talking during a break at work."
3. Present the model.
4. Full-Class Repetition.

   Pronunciation Note

   The pronunciation focus of Chapter 7 is **Reduced to** (text page 94). You may wish to model this pronunciation at this point and encourage students to incorporate it into their language practice.

5. Ask students if they have any questions. Check understanding of vocabulary.
6. Group Choral Repetition.
7. Choral Conversation.
8. Call on one or two pairs of students to present the dialog.
9. Expand the model with further practice by replacing *she, he,* and *they* with names of students in the class. For example:

   Does (Anna) like to watch TV?
   Yes. She enjoys watching TV very much.
   Watching TV is her favorite way to relax.

(For additional practice, do Choral Conversation in small groups or by rows.)

SIDE BY SIDE EXERCISES

Examples

1. A. Do you like to paint?
   B. Yes. I enjoy painting very much. Painting is my favorite way to relax.
2. A. Does Beverly like to knit?
   B. Yes. She enjoys knitting very much. Knitting is her favorite way to relax.

1. **Exercise 1:** Call on two students to present the dialog. Then do Choral Repetition and Choral Conversation practice.
2. **Exercise 2:** Same as above.
3. **Exercises 3–8:** Either Full-Class or Pair Practice.

Whenever possible, after doing each exercise ask students about their own likes and dislikes. For example:

   Do you like to swim?
   Do you enjoy dancing?

4. **Exercise 9:** Have students use the model as a guide to create their own conversations, using vocabulary of their own choice. Encourage students to use dictionaries to find new words they want to use. This exercise can be done orally in class or for written homework. If you assign it for homework, do one example in class to make sure students understand what's expected. Have students present their conversations in class the next day.

WORKBOOK

Pages 78–79

EXPANSION ACTIVITIES

1. **Grammar Chain** ★★

   a. Write the following conversation model on the board:

   > A. Do you like to _____?
   > B. Yes. I enjoy _____ a lot. As a matter of fact, I've been _____ for years!

   b. Start the chain game by saying:

   > Teacher (to Student A): Do you like to skate?

   c. Student A answers according to the model on the board and then asks Student B a different question, and the chain continues. For example:

   > Student A: Yes. I enjoy skating a lot. As a matter of fact, I've been skating for years!
   > (to Student B): Do you like to run?
   > Student B: Yes. I enjoy running a lot. As a matter of fact, I've been running for years!
   > (to Student C): Do you like to knit?
   > Etc.

2. **Memory Chain** ★★

   a. Divide the class into groups of 5 or 6 students each.

   b. Have each student tell what he or she enjoys doing to relax.

   c. One group at a time, have Student 1 begin. For example:

   > I enjoy sitting in the park.

   d. Student 2 repeats what Student 1 said and adds a statement about himself or herself. For example:

   > Susan enjoys sitting in the park, and I enjoy reading.

   e. Student 3 continues in the same way. For example:

   > Susan enjoys sitting in the park, Robert enjoys reading, and I enjoy playing chess.

   f. Continue until everyone has had a chance to play the *memory chain*.

3. **Find the Right Person** ★★

   a. Write the following on the board:

   > I like to _____.
   > I enjoy _____ing.
   > _____ing is my favorite way to relax.

   b. Have students complete these sentences on a separate piece of paper with real information about themselves.

   c. Collect the papers and distribute them randomly to everyone in the class.

   d. Have students interview each other in order to find the correct person to match the information they have. For example:

   > Do you like to (ski)?
   > Do you enjoy (going to movies)?
   > Is (reading) your favorite way to relax?

   e. Have students report back to the class.

   Variation: This activity can be done as a game in which the first student to identify the correct person is the winner.

4. **Places Around Town** ★★

   a. Write the following on the board:

   > A. Have you ever gone to _____?
   > B. Yes. I really enjoy _____ing there.

   b. The object of the activity is for students to tell things people enjoy doing in different places in their community. Present the dialog with one of your students. Begin by asking about a place such as a park, a restaurant, a cafe, or a museum. For example:

   > A. Have you ever gone to (The Europa Cafe)?
   > B. Yes. I really enjoy eating there.

   (continued)

CHAPTER 7

EXPANSION ACTIVITIES (Continued)

  A. Have you ever gone to (Central Park)?
  B. Yes. I really enjoy flying my kite there.

  c. In pairs or as a class, have students talk about other places around town, using the model on the board.

5. Survey ★★

  a. Have the class brainstorm the different things people do to relax, and have students write down these activities on a sheet of paper with columns for *yes* and *no* responses. For example:

Ways to Relax	Yes	No
go to the movies listen to music read rent videos go to the mall plant flowers		

  b. Have students circulate around the room interviewing each other about their preferred relaxation activities. For example:

     Student 1: Do you like to go to the movies?
     Student 2: No, I don't.
     Student 1: Do you enjoy listening to music?
     Student 2: Yes, I do. How about you? Do you enjoy going to the movies?
              Etc.

  c. Have students report their findings to the class.

Variation: ★★ Have students also interview friends and family members and report to the class.

Option: ★★★ Have students put the results of their surveys in chart or graph form.

6. Complete the Sentences ★★★

  a. Write the following on the board or on a handout:

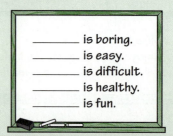

  _____ is boring.
  _____ is easy.
  _____ is difficult.
  _____ is healthy.
  _____ is fun.

  b. Divide the class into pairs or small groups.

  c. Have students complete each sentence with 5 examples.

  d. Have students compare their lists.

7. Dictate and Discuss ★★★

  a. Divide the class into pairs or small groups.

  b. Dictate sentences such as the following, and then have students discuss whether they agree or disagree:

     Watching TV is a good way to relax.
     Running is not good for you.
     Drinking coffee is a good way to stay awake.
     Swimming is healthier than jogging.
     Skiing is easier than skating.
     Going to the movies is more fun than renting videos.
     Knitting is only for women.
     Browsing the web is boring.
     Going to English movies is a good way to learn the language.
     Playing golf is only for men.

  c. Call on students to share their opinions with the rest of the class.

Variation: Divide the class into small groups, and have the groups create statements for others in the class to react to.

224 CHAPTER 7

Text Page 83

READING *Enjoying Life*

FOCUS

- Gerunds

NEW VOCABULARY

part

READING THE STORY

Optional: *Preview the story by having students talk about the story title and/or illustrations. You may choose to introduce new vocabulary beforehand, or have students encounter the new vocabulary within the context of the reading.*

1. Have students read silently, or follow along silently as the story is read aloud by you, by one or more students, or on the audio program.
2. Ask students if they have any questions. Check understanding of vocabulary.
3. Check students' comprehension, using some or all of the following questions:

    What does Howard enjoy doing?
    Where does he like to read?

    What does Patty enjoy doing?
    Where does she like to sing?

    What does Brenda enjoy doing?
    Where does she like to watch TV?

    What does Tom enjoy doing?
    Who does Tom like to talk about politics with?

✓ READING *CHECK-UP*

Q & A

1. Call on a pair of students to present the model.
2. Introduce the following expressions: *to tell you the truth, It was nice meeting you. Nice meeting you, too.*
3. Have students work in pairs to create new dialogs.
4. Call on pairs to present their new dialogs to the class.

READING EXTENSION

Guess Who!

1. Have each student think of a famous person.
2. Have a volunteer come to the front of the classroom and pretend to *be* that person.
3. The other students in the class then try to guess the person's identity by asking questions. For example:

    [*thinking of Andrea Bocelli*]

    Student 1: I'm a famous person.
    Student 2: What do you like to do?
    Student 1: I like to sing.
    Student 3: What kind of music do you enjoy singing?
    Student 1: I enjoy singing opera.
    Student 4: What language do you usually sing in?
    Student 1: I usually sing in Italian.
    Student 2: Are you Andrea Bocelli?
    Student 1: Yes, I am!

4. Have other students take a turn thinking of a celebrity for the others to guess.

CHAPTER 7   225

Text Page 84: She Hates to Drive Downtown

FOCUS

- $\begin{cases} \text{Like to \_\_\_\_} \\ \text{Like \_\_\_\_ing} \end{cases}$
- $\begin{cases} \text{Hate to \_\_\_\_} \\ \text{Hate \_\_\_\_ing} \end{cases}$
- Avoid ____ing

CLOSE UP

RULE: The verbs *like* and *hate* are followed by either gerunds or infinitives with no change in meaning.

EXAMPLES: **like to** work
like work**ing**

hate to work
hate work**ing**

RULE: The verb *avoid* is followed only by a gerund.
EXAMPLE: **avoid** driv**ing**

GETTING READY

Introduce *like, hate,* and *avoid.*

1. Write the following on the board:

2. Tell the following story about *Richard.* Point to the appropriate verb on the board as you tell each part of the story.

> Richard likes to study languages.
> He also likes meeting people from other countries.
> Unfortunately, he doesn't like to travel.
> In fact, he HATES to travel.
> He hates riding in airplanes.
> He also hates driving long distances.
> It's too bad that Richard avoids traveling.
> He could meet a lot of interesting people.

3. Point to each verb on the board as you say each sentence again. Call on students to retell that sentence.

INTRODUCING THE MODEL

In this model conversation, the verbs *like* and *hate* can be used with the infinitives *to drive* or the gerund *driving.* Present the model first with the infinitive. Then present it again with the gerund.

1. Have students look at the model illustration.

226　CHAPTER 7

2. Set the scene: "Two people are talking about Helen."
3. Present the model.
4. Full-Class Repetition.
5. Ask students if they have any questions. Check understanding of the verbs *hate* and *avoid*.
6. Group Choral Repetition.
7. Choral Conversation.
8. Call on several pairs of students to present the dialog.
9. Introduce the expression *can't stand to* _____ / *can't stand* _____ *ing*.

Call on pairs of students to present the dialog again, using *can't stand* in place of *hate*.

(For additional practice, do Choral Conversation in small groups or by rows.)

SIDE BY SIDE EXERCISES

Examples

1. A. Does Albert like to travel/traveling by plane?
   B. No. He hates to travel/traveling by plane. He avoids traveling by plane whenever he can.
2. A. Do you like to go/going to the mall?
   B. No. I hate to go/going to the mall. I avoid going to the mall whenever I can.

1. **Exercise 1:** Call on two students to present the dialog. Then do Choral Repetition and Choral Conversation practice.
2. **Exercise 2:** Same as above.
3. **Exercises 3–8:** Either Full-Class Practice or Pair Practice.

   Whenever possible, after doing each exercise ask students about their own likes and dislikes. For example:

   Do you like driving downtown?
   Do you like to travel by plane?

New Vocabulary
3. fast-food restaurant
8. reporter

Culture Note

Exercise 3: *Fast-food restaurants* serve food that is already prepared and can be served immediately. Examples of this kind of food include hamburgers, hot dogs, french fries, sandwiches, and pizza.

4. **Exercise 9:** Have students use the model as a guide to create their own conversations, using vocabulary of their own choice. Encourage students to use dictionaries to find new words they want to use. This exercise can be done orally in class or for written homework. If you assign it for homework, do one example in class to make sure students understand what's expected. Have students present their conversations in class the next day.

How About You?

Have students answer the questions in pairs or as a class.

WORKBOOK

Pages 80–81

EXPANSION ACTIVITIES

1. **Memory Chain** ★★

   a. Divide the class into groups of 5 or 6 students each.

   b. Tell each student to name something he or she *hates* or *can't stand* to do.

   c. One group at a time, have Student 1 begin. For example:

   > I hate going to the mall.

   d. Student 2 repeats what Student 1 said and adds a statement about himself or herself. For example:

   > Marco hates going to the mall, and I can't stand driving downtown.

   e. Student 3 continues in the same way. For example:

   > Marco hates going to the mall, Nancy can't stand driving downtown, and I hate to wear a tie.

   f. Continue until everyone has had a chance to play the *memory chain*.

2. **Sense or Nonsense?** ★★

   a. Divide the class into four groups.

   b. Make many sets of split sentence cards with beginnings and endings of sentences. For example:

I can't stand talking on . . .	the phone.
I don't like to talk . . .	about politics.
I try to avoid eating in . . .	expensive restaurants.
I can't stand eating . . .	fish.
I don't like taking . . .	tests.

I try to avoid taking a . . .	taxi to the office.
I can't stand traveling . . .	by bus.
I avoid shopping . . .	on the Internet.
I avoid sitting . . .	in the sun.
I really like to sit on . . .	my new living room couch.

   c. Mix up the cards and distribute sets of cards to each group, keeping the beginning and ending cards in different piles.

   d. Have students take turns picking up one card from each pile and reading the sentence to the group. For example:

I can't stand traveling . . .	about politics.

   e. The group decides if the sentence makes *sense* or is *nonsense*.

   f. After all the cards have been picked, have the groups lay out all the cards and put together all the sentence combinations that make sense.

3. **Miming** ★★

   a. Write the following on cards:

travel by plane	sit in the sun	talk on a cell phone
wear a suit and tie	eat with chopsticks	iron shirts
work overtime	baby-sit	do sit-ups

228   CHAPTER 7

| go water-skiing | browse the web | give blood |

b. Have students take turns picking a card from the pile and pantomiming the action or situation on the card. The student should decide whether he or she *likes* to do that thing or *hates* to do that thing, and mime accordingly.

c. The class must guess how the person feels about what he or she is doing. For example:

   Maria likes doing sit-ups.
   Anthony hates wearing a suit and tie.

Variation: This can be done as a game with competing teams.

4. Change the Sentence! ★★

a. Write a sentence on the board, underlining and numbering different portions of the sentence. For example:

   | 1 | 2 | 3 | 4 |
   | She | can't stand | to use | a cell phone. |

b. Have students sit in a circle.

c. Tell them that when you say a number, the first student in the circle makes a change in that part of the sentence. For example:

   Teacher: Two.
   Student 1: She <u>likes</u> to use a cell phone.

d. The second student keeps the first student's sentence, but changes it based on the next number you say. For example:

   Teacher: Three.
   Student 2: She likes <u>to talk on</u> a cell phone.

e. Continue this way with the rest of the students in the circle. For example:

   Teacher: Four.
   Student 3: She likes to talk on <u>the Internet</u>.

5. Expand the Sentence! ★★

Tell students that the object of the activity is to build a long sentence on the board, one word at a time.

a. Call on a student to write a pronoun or someone's name on the far left side of the board. For example:

Carmen

b. Have another student come to the board and add a word. For example:

Carmen enjoys

c. Have a third student add a third word. For example:

Carmen enjoys going

d. Continue until each student in the class has had one or more turns to add a word to expand the sentence into the longest one they can think of. For example:

Carmen enjoys going to the movies on the weekend because she wants to become a movie star when she grows up.

6. Category Dictation: What We Share in Common ★★★

a. Have students draw two columns on a piece of paper. At the top of one column, have students write <u>I like</u>. At the top of the other column, have them write <u>I hate</u>.

b. Dictate various activities introduced in previous chapters. For example:

speaking English	going to the bank
writing letters	using the Internet
driving in the city	swimming
doing the laundry	eating with chopsticks

(continued)

CHAPTER 7 229

EXPANSION ACTIVITIES (Continued)

giving blood
mending clothes
doing sit-ups
waiting for the bus
exercising
standing in line
running
watching the news

Have students write the activities in the appropriate column. For example:

<u>I like</u>
speaking English
watching the news

<u>I hate</u>
driving in the city
doing sit-ups

c. Divide the class into groups of four. Have students compare their lists and find at least three activities they share in common. Have each group share their common interests with the class.

7. Which One Isn't True? ★★

a. Tell students to write three true statements and one false statement about themselves, using *like*, *hate*, and *avoid*. For example:

I like going to the movies.
I hate to run in marathons.
I avoid eating in fast-food restaurants.

b. Have students take turns reading their statements to the class, and have the class guess which statement isn't true.

8. Pair Conversations ★★★

a. Write the following verbs and conversation model on the board:

watch   talk about
eat   listen to
do   talk to
play   go to
read   practice

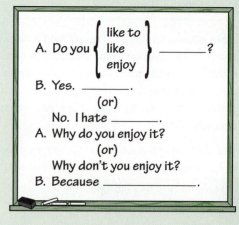

A. Do you { like to / like / enjoy } _____?
B. Yes. _____.
   (or)
   No. I hate _____.
A. Why do you enjoy it?
   (or)
   Why don't you enjoy it?
B. Because _____.

b. Have pairs of students create conversations based on the verbs and the model on the board. For example:

A. Do you enjoy talking about world politics?
B. Yes. I like it a lot.
A. Why do you enjoy it?
B. Because I think it's interesting to hear other people's opinions.

A. Do you like to practice the piano?
B. No. I can't stand practicing the piano.
A. Why don't you enjoy it?
B. Because it's boring, and it takes a lot of time.

230   CHAPTER 7

Text Page 85

READING *Bad Habits*

FOCUS

- Gerunds

NEW VOCABULARY

break a habit
gossip (v)
habit
interrupt
junk food
keep on

READING THE STORY

Optional: *Preview the story by having students talk about the story title and/or illustrations. You may choose to introduce new vocabulary beforehand, or have students encounter the new vocabulary within the context of the reading.*

1. Have students read silently, or follow along silently as the story is read aloud by you, by one or more students, or on the audio program.
2. Ask students if they have any questions. Check understanding of vocabulary.

   Culture Note

   Junk food refers to packaged snack foods such as soft drinks, potato chips, and candy.

3. Check students' comprehension, using some or all of the following questions:

   What do Jill's friends tell her?
   Why?
   Has Jill stopped eating junk food?
   Why can't she stop?

   What do Vincent's friends tell him?
   Why?

   Has Vincent stopped gossiping?
   Why can't he stop?

   What do Jennifer's parents tell her?
   Why?
   Has Jennifer stopped interrupting people while they're talking?
   Why can't she stop?

   What does Walter's wife tell him?
   Why?
   Has Walter stopped talking about business?
   Why can't he stop?

✓ READING *CHECK-UP*

Q & A

1. Call on a pair of students to present the model.
2. Introduce the following new expressions: *I don't mean to be critical, the truth is.*
3. Have students work in pairs to create new dialogs.
4. Call on pairs to present their new dialogs to the class.

READING EXTENSION

Giving Advice

1. Have groups of students create lists of advice for breaking one of the four bad habits in the reading. Their sentences can begin with:

   Avoid _____.
   Keep on _____.

2. Have students work in small groups to develop their lists of advice and then share their ideas with the class.

How About You?

Have students do the activity in pairs or as a class.

CHAPTER 7

Text Pages 86–87: How Did You Learn to Swim So Well?

FOCUS

- Start to _____
  Start _____ing
- Learn to _____
  Practice _____ing
- Review of Tenses

CLOSE UP

RULE:	The verb *start* is followed by either a gerund or an infinitive with no change in meaning.
EXAMPLES:	**start to** swim **start** swimm**ing**
RULE:	The verb *practice* is followed only by a gerund.
EXAMPLE:	**practice** swimm**ing**
RULE:	The verb *learn* is followed only by an infinitive.
EXAMPLE:	**learn to** swim

GETTING READY

Introduce *start*, *learn*, and *practice*.

1. Write on the board:

   learned to _____
   started to _____
   started _____ing
   practice _____ing

2. Tell the story below about *Bruno* one or two times. Point to the appropriate verb on the board as you tell each part of the story.

   Bruno *learned to swim* at the beach a long time ago.

   His family *started to go* to the beach every summer when he was five years old.

   And that's when Bruno *started swimming*.

   Now he *practices swimming* in the pool at school whenever he can.

3. Point to each verb on the board as you say each sentence again. Call on students to retell that sentence.

INTRODUCING THE MODEL

1. Have students look at the model illustration.
2. Set the scene: "Someone is talking to a girl who is swimming."
3. Present the model. In line 2, first say the sentence with *started to swim*. Present the sentence again, using *started swimming*.

4. Full-Class Repetition.

5. Ask students if they have any questions. Check understanding of new vocabulary: *ever since, envy, Not at all*.

6. Group Choral Repetition.

7. Choral Conversation.

8. Call on two pairs of students to present the dialog. Have one pair use *started to swim* and have the other use *started swimming*.

   (For additional practice, do Choral Conversation in small groups or by rows.)

SIDE BY SIDE EXERCISES

Examples

1. A. How did you learn to draw so well?
   B. Well, I started to draw/drawing when I was young, and I've been drawing ever since.
   A. I envy you. I've never drawn before.
   B. I'll be glad to teach you how.
   A. Thank you. But isn't drawing very difficult?
   B. Not at all. After you practice drawing a few times, you'll probably draw as well as I do.

2. A. How did you learn to box so well?
   B. Well, I started to box/boxing when I was young, and I've been boxing ever since.
   A. I envy you. I've never boxed before.
   B. I'll be glad to teach you how.
   A. Thank you. But isn't boxing very difficult?
   B. Not at all. After you practice boxing a few times, you'll probably box as well as I do.

1. **Exercise 1:** Call on two students to present the dialog. Then do Choral Repetition and Choral Conversation practice.

2. **Exercise 2:** Introduce the word *box*.

3. **Exercises 3–5:** Either Full-Class Practice or Pair Practice.

New Vocabulary
3. surf
4. figure skate
5. tap dance

4. **Exercise 6:** Have students use the model as a guide to create their own conversations, using vocabulary of their own choice. Encourage students to use dictionaries to find new words they want to use. This exercise can be done orally in class or for written homework. If you assign it for homework, do one example in class to make sure students understand what's expected. Have students present their conversations in class the next day.

How to Say It!

Expressing Appreciation: In spoken English there are many ways to express appreciation to someone. These are the most common phrases: "Thank you." "I appreciate that." "That's very kind of you." and "That's very nice of you."

1. Present the expressions.

2. Full-Class Repetition.

3. Ask students if they have any questions. Check understanding of the expressions.

4. Group Choral Repetition.

5. Have students practice the conversations in this lesson again, using any of these new expressions.

6. Have pairs of students present conversations to the class.

WORKBOOK

Page 82

CHAPTER 7   233

EXPANSION ACTIVITIES

1. Sentence Cues ★★

a. On separate cards, write key words that can be put together to form sentences or questions. Clip together the cards for each sentence. For example:

how	you	learn	do karate	so well
I	start	do karate		in 2000
I		do karate		ever since
I	never		tap dance	before
After	you	practice	tap dance	you	tap dance very well

b. Divide the class into small groups and give a clipped set of cards to each group.

c. Have each group write a sentence based on their set of cards.

d. Have one member of each group write that group's sentence on the board and compare everybody's sentences. Did they choose the correct tense? What words helped them choose the correct verb form?

2. Scrambled Dialogs ★

a. Divide the class into pairs or small groups.

b. Write each line of the model conversation on text page 86 and the exercises on text page 87 on separate cards.

c. Give each pair or group a clipped set of cards for one conversation.

d. Have students unscramble the lines to put together their conversation.

e. Call on pairs to read their unscrambled dialogs.

3. Class Interviews ★★

a. Write on the board:

> I can _____ very well.

b. Call on students to tell about something they're good at. For example:

> I can skate very well.
> I can fix cars very well.

c. Ask students the following questions:

> When did you start to _____?
>   or
> When did you start _____ing?
>
> Is _____ing very difficult?
> Why? / Why not?
>
> How often do you practice _____ing?

Encourage others in the class to ask additional questions.

Variation: ★★★ Divide the class into pairs, and have students interview each other about their skills and then report back to the class.

4. Role Play: Welcome to School! ★★★

a. Write on the board:

> A. Welcome to _____ School! We're very glad you're going to be studying here with us. Do you have any questions?
> B. Yes. What will we be learning first?
> A. First, we'll learn to _____, and we'll practice _____.
> B. And what will we be learning after that?
> A. Next, we'll practice _____, and we'll learn how to _____.
> B. And when will we start studying _____?
> A. _____.
> B. Oh, that'll be great! I'm really looking forward to starting school.

234 CHAPTER 7

b. Divide the class into pairs. Have each pair choose or make up the name of a training school. For example:

    The (*Speedy*) Secretarial School
    The (*Ace*) Driving School
    The (*Chen*) Cooking School
    (*Charlie's*) Auto Repair School
    The (*Century*) Computer Programming School
    The (*Ajax*) Accounting School

Have each pair create a role play about the school, using the model on the board. Speaker A is the director or a teacher. Speaker B is a new student. Have students use dictionaries to find new vocabulary for skills one might learn at that school.

c. Have students present their role plays to the class. For example:

  A. Welcome to (*The Speedy Secretarial School*)! We're very glad you're going to be studying here with us. Do you have any questions?
  B. Yes. What will we be learning first?
  A. First we'll learn to (*file*), and we'll practice (*filing letters*).
  B. And what will we be learning after that?
  A. Next, we'll practice (*typing*), and we'll learn how to (*type business letters*).
  B. And when will we start studying (*accounting*)?
  A. (*We'll start studying accounting in a few weeks.*)
  B. Oh, that'll be great! I'm really looking forward to starting school.

5. Mystery People! ★★

a. Write the following on the board:

```
I can _____.
I started _____ when I was _____.
I practice _____ every _____.
I enjoy _____ because _____.
```

b. Have students complete the sentences about themselves and then return them to you. For example:

    I can ski.
    I started skiing when I was twelve.
    I practice skiing every winter.
    I enjoy skiing because I think it's good exercise.

c. Distribute students' sentences to others in the class, and call on students to read them. See if the class can guess who the *mystery people* are.

6. Group Conversations ★★★

a. Write on the board:

```
I like _____.
I learned to _____ when I was young.
I've been _____ since _____.
```

b. Have students complete the sentences about their hobbies and special interests, using the model on the board.

c. Divide the class into groups. Have students share their information with one another.

Text Pages 88–89: Guess What I've Decided to Do!

FOCUS

- Decide to _____
- Consider _____ing
- Think about _____ing

CLOSE UP

RULE: The verbs *consider* and *think about* are followed by gerunds.

EXAMPLES: **consider** buy**ing**
think about buy**ing**

RULE: The verb *decide* is followed by an infinitive.

EXAMPLE: **decide to** buy

GETTING READY

Introduce the new expressions *consider _____ing*, *think about _____ing*, and *decide to _____*.

1. Write on the board:

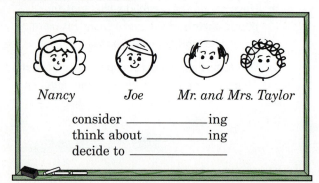

2. Have students listen for the new verbs as you tell about the people on the board one or more times:

   Nancy recently moved into a new apartment. She's *considering buying* a new TV. She saw a nice TV in a store downtown, and she's *thinking about buying* it.

   Joe graduated from high school recently. He's looking for a job. He *considered going* to college. And for a while he *was thinking about* visiting some schools. But he's *decided to work* for a few years first.

   Mr. and Mrs. Taylor are going to retire next year. They're *considering moving* after that. They're *thinking about selling* their house in the suburbs and *buying* an apartment in the city. They aren't sure what they'll do.

3. Check students' understanding of the new verbs by asking questions about each person. Have students retell as much of each story as they can. For example, after telling about Nancy, you can ask:

   What did Nancy do recently?
   What's she considering doing?

INTRODUCING THE MODEL

1. Have students look at the model illustration.

2. Set the scene: "Two co-workers are having lunch in the company cafeteria. One of them has some exciting news."

3. Present the model.

236   CHAPTER 7

4. Full-Class Repetition.
5. Ask students if they have any questions. Check understanding of new vocabulary: *guess, consider, make a decision.*
6. Group Choral Repetition.
7. Choral Conversation.
8. Call on one or two pairs of students to present the dialog.

   (For additional practice, do Choral Conversation in small groups or by rows.)

SIDE BY SIDE EXERCISES

Examples

1. A. Guess what I've decided to do!
   B. What?
   A. I've decided to get a dog.
   B. That's wonderful! How long have you been thinking about getting a dog?
   A. For a long time, actually. I considered getting a dog a few years ago, but never did.
   B. Well, I think you're making the right decision. Getting a dog is a great idea.

2. A. Guess what I've decided to do!
   B. What?
   A. I've decided to buy a new car.
   B. That's wonderful! How long have you been thinking about getting a new car?
   A. For a long time, actually. I considered getting a new car a few years ago, but never did.
   B. Well, I think you're making the right decision. Getting a new car is a great idea.

1. **Exercise 1:** Call on two students to present the dialog. Then do Choral Repetition and Choral Conversation practice.
2. **Exercise 2:** Same as above.
3. **Exercises 3–8:** Either Full-Class Practice or Pair Practice.

New Vocabulary
5. go back
8. vegetarian

As a follow-up after each pair has presented its conversation about an important decision someone has made, interview that person and ask what the reasons were for making that decision.

4. **Exercise 9:** Have students use the model as a guide to create their own conversations, using vocabulary of their own choice. Encourage students to use dictionaries to find new words they want to use. This exercise can be done orally in class or for written homework. If you assign it for homework, do one example in class to make sure students understand what's expected. Have students present their conversations in class the next day.

WORKBOOK

Pages 83–84

EXPANSION ACTIVITIES

1. Our Future Plans ★★

a. Write on the board:

> A. What are you going to do after _____?
> B. I've been { thinking about / considering } _____.
> How about you? What do YOU plan to do after _____?

b. Have pairs of students create conversations about their future plans. Encourage students to expand and vary the dialog any way they wish.

2. Advantages and Disadvantages ★★★

a. Have students draw two columns on a piece of paper. At the top of one column, have students write <u>Advantages</u>. At the top of the other column, have them write <u>Disadvantages</u>.

b. Say one of the decisions on student text page 89, and have students brainstorm its advantages and disadvantages. Write their ideas in the columns, and have students copy them on their papers. For example:

buy a new car

<u>Advantages</u>	<u>Disadvantages</u>
The car will last a long time.	The insurance is more expensive.
New cars have new technology.	You don't know if the car is reliable.

c. For homework, have students write two paragraphs: one about the advantages of a particular decision discussed in class and another about the disadvantages of that decision.

3. Role Play: Giving Advice ★★★

After doing the above activity of advantages and disadvantages, have students create role plays in which they give advice to the various characters on student text page 89.

a. Write on the board:

> Have you ever considered _____?
> You should avoid _____.
> You should start _____.

b. In pairs, have students develop a conversation with a character in the lesson based on the advantages and disadvantages identified in Activity 2. Students may wish to use the phrases on the board in their role plays.

c. Call on pairs to present their role plays to the class.

4. Role Play: That's Too Bad! ★★★

a. Write the following conversation model on the board:

> A. I'm having problems with my _____.
> B. What's the matter?
> A. _____.
> B. That's too bad.
> { Have you considered _____?
> { Have you thought about _____?
> A. That's a good idea.

b. Divide the class into pairs. Give one member of the pair a cue card with one of the following:

car	bicycle	cell phone
son	daughter	dog
cat	roof	feet
computer	back	boss
girlfriend	boyfriend	kitchen sink

c. Have pairs of students create conversations based on the cue cards and the conversation model on the board.

d. Call on pairs of students to present their conversations to the class. For example:

>   A. I'm having problems with my back.
>   B. What's the matter?
>   A. It hurts after I sit at my desk all day.
>   B. That's too bad. Have you thought about doing back exercises?
>   A. That's a good idea.

5. Big Decisions ★★★

a. Individually, have students make a list of big decisions they have made in their lives. For example:

>   I decided to go to this university.
>   I decided to major in astronomy.
>   I decided to live on campus.
>   I decided to quit my job.

b. Divide the class into small groups, and have students share their lists with each other and tell whether they think they made the right decisions.

c. Call on students to report back to the class.

6. Dialog Builder! ★★★

a. Divide the class into pairs.

b. Write the following on the board:

>   I think you're making the wrong decision!

c. Have each pair create a conversation incorporating that line. Students can begin and end their conversations any way they wish, but they must include that line in their dialogs.

d. Call on students to present their conversations to the class.

CHAPTER 7 239

Text Pages 90–91: I've Made a Decision

FOCUS

- Review: Start to _____
           Keep on _____ing
           Stop _____ing

- Introduction of New Expressions:

  { Begin to _____
  { Begin _____ing

  { Continue to _____
  { Continue _____ing

   Quit _____ing

CLOSE UP

RULE:	The verbs *begin* and *continue* are followed by either infinitives or gerunds, with no change in meaning.
EXAMPLES:	**begin to** eat **begin** eat**ing** **continue to** eat **continue** eat**ing**
RULE:	The verbs *keep on, quit,* and *stop* are followed by gerunds.
EXAMPLES:	**keep on** eat**ing** **quit** eat**ing** **stop** eat**ing**
RULE:	*Begin* and *start* are synonyms, *keep on* and *continue* are synonyms, and *quit* and *stop* are synonyms.
EXAMPLES:	begin to eat/begin eating = start to eat/start eating keep on eating = continue to eat/continue eating quit eating = stop eating

GETTING READY

1. Write the following on the board:

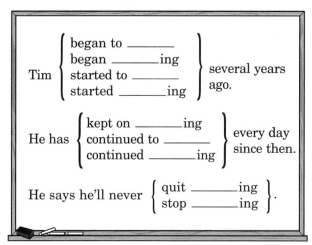

2. Tell the following story about *Tim*, pointing to the appropriate verbs on the board as you tell the story:

   Tim began to ride his bicycle to work several years ago.
   He has kept on riding his bicycle to work every day since then.
   He says he'll never quit riding his bicycle to work.

   Tell the story again, and then call on individual students to repeat each line.

3. Point to other verb forms on the board, and call on students to retell the story, using those verbs. For example:

   Tim started riding his bicycle to work several years ago.
   He has continued to ride his bicycle to work every day since then.
   He says he'll never stop riding it to work.

INTRODUCING THE MODEL

1. Have students look at the model illustration.
2. Set the scene: "Two friends are talking. One of them has made a decision."
3. Present the model.
4. Full Class Repetition.
5. Ask students if they have any questions. Check understanding of new vocabulary: *begun, I hope so, after all, the rest of.*
6. Group Choral Repetition.
7. Choral Conversation.
8. Call on one or two pairs of students to present the dialog.
9. Call on pairs of students to present the model again, using the synonyms given below the grammar boxes as replacements for the boldface verbs in the model dialog.

   (For additional practice, do Choral Conversation in small groups or by rows.)

SIDE BY SIDE EXERCISES

Examples

1. A I've made a decision.
    B. What is it?
    A. I've decided to quit biting my nails.
    B. That's great! Have you ever tried to stop biting your nails before?
    A. Yes. Many times. But every time I've stopped biting them, I've begun to bite/begun biting them again after a few days.
    B. Well, I hope you're successful this time.
    A. I hope so, too. After all, I can't keep on biting my nails for the rest of my life.

2. A. I've made a decision.
    B. What is it?
    A. I've decided to quit teasing my little sister.
    B. That's great! Have you ever tried to stop teasing your little sister before?
    A. Yes. Many times. But every time I've stopped teasing her, I've begun to tease/begun teasing her again after a few days.
    B. Well, I hope you're successful this time.
    A. I hope so, too. After all, I can't keep on teasing my little sister for the rest of my life.

CHAPTER 7   241

1. **Exercise 1:** Call on two students to present the dialog. Then do Choral Repetition and Choral Conversation practice.

2. **Exercise 2:** Introduce the word *tease*. Same as above.

3. **Exercises 3–5:** Either Full-Class Practice or Pair Practice.

    As a follow-up after each pair has presented its conversation, ask Speaker A: "What things are you going to do to help you quit?"

4. **Exercise 6:** Have students use the model as a guide to create their own conversations, using vocabulary of their own choice. Encourage students to use dictionaries to find new words they want to use. This exercise can be done orally in class or for written homework. If you assign it for homework, do one example in class to make sure students understand what's expected. Have students present their conversations in class the next day.

WORKBOOK

Pages 85–87

EXPANSION ACTIVITIES

1. Scrambled Dialog ★

a. Divide the class into five groups.

b. Make five sets of the model conversation from text page 90, writing each line on a separate card.

c. Give each group one set of the cards, and have the group members reorder the conversations.

d. Have one group read the conversation aloud while the others listen to check for accuracy.

2. Grammar Chain ★★

a. Write the following conversation model on the board:

> A. When did you start _____ ?
> B. I began _____ .
>   I've continued _____ .
>   In fact, I'll never quit _____ .
>   How about you?
>   When did you start _____ ?

b. Start the chain game by saying:

> Teacher (to Student A): When did you start studying English?

c. Student A answers according to the model and then asks a different question to Student B, and the chain continues. For example:

> Student A: I began studying two years ago. I've continued to study English. In fact, I'll never quit studying English.
> (to Student B): How about you? When did you start to use a cell phone?
> Student B: I began using a cell phone last year. I've continued to use a cell phone. In fact, I'll never quit using a cell phone.
> (to Student C): How about you? When did you start jogging every day?
> Etc.

d. Continue until everyone has had a chance to answer and ask a question.

3. In Common ★★★

a. Divide the class into pairs.

b. The object is for pairs of students to find one habit they have in common that they would like to break, and then report back to the class. For example:

> We both can't stop worrying about school.

c. Have students switch partners and again find a common habit they would like to break.

d. Continue until each student has talked with four other students. Ask the class: "What is the most common habit that people would like to break? What are ways to stop this habit?"

4. What Should You Do? ★★★

   a. Write the following on the board:

   start
   begin
   continue
   keep on
   stop
   quit

   b. Present situations such as the following and have students respond, using appropriate verbs from the list on the board:

   You're driving along a street, and you see a red traffic light. What should you do?
   You're driving down the street, and you see a green traffic light. What should you do?
   You're driving down the street, and you see a yellow traffic light. What should you do?
   You've been eating dinner, and now you're feeling full. (There's still a lot of food on your plate.) What should you do?
   You have an exam tomorrow, and you haven't opened a book yet. What should you?
   You have an exam tomorrow. You've studied for an hour, and now your friends want to go to a movie. What should you do?
   Your doctor is concerned about your blood pressure. What should you do?
   You don't think your supervisor is pleased with your work. What should you do?
   You think your neighbors are going to complain to the landlord about you. What should you do?

   c. Divide the class into small groups, and have students think of other situations.

   d. Have each group present its situations to the class, and have students respond, using the verbs on the board.

5. Chain Story ★★

   a. Begin by saying: "John made an important decision yesterday."

   b. Student 1 repeats what you said and adds another item. For example: "John made an important decision yesterday. He decided to quit worrying about his health."

   c. Continue around the room in this fashion, with each student repeating what the previous one said and adding another sentence.

   d. You can do the activity again, beginning and ending with different students.

      If the class is large, you may want to divide students into groups to give students more practice.

CHAPTER 7   243

Text Pages 92–93

READING *Important Decisions*

FOCUS

- Gerunds
- Infinitives

NEW VOCABULARY

engineering
go out of business
network programming
technical school

READING THE STORY

Optional: Preview the story by having students talk about the story title and/or illustrations. You may choose to introduce new vocabulary beforehand, or have students encounter the new vocabulary within the context of the reading.

1. Have students read silently, or follow along silently as the story is read aloud by you, by one or more students, or on the audio program.

2. Ask students if they have any questions. Check understanding of vocabulary.

    Language Note

    Network programming is the development of computer programs for computer networks that are most commonly used in businesses and schools.

3. Check students' comprehension, using some or all of the following questions:

    Why did Jim have to make an important decision recently?

What did he consider doing first?
Then what did he think about doing?
What did he finally decide to do?
How does Jim feel about his decision?

Why did Emily have to make an important decision recently?
What did she consider doing first?
Then what did she think about doing?
What did she finally decide to do?
How does Emily feel about her decision?

Why did Nick have to make an important decision recently?
What did he consider doing first?
Then what did he think about doing?
What did he finally decide to do?
How does Nick feel about his decision?

Why did Maria have to make an important decision recently?
What did she consider doing first?
Then what did she think about doing?
What did she finally decide to do?
How does Maria feel about her decision?

✓ READING *CHECK-UP*

1. True
2. Maybe
3. True
4. False
5. Maybe
6. False
7. Maybe
8. Maybe
9. False
10. True

READING EXTENSION

1. *Tic Tac Question the Answer*

    a. Draw a tic tac grid on the board and fill it in with short answers to questions about one of the stories on text pages 92–93. For example:

 244   CHAPTER 7

Wear a sweater.	Wearing a sports jacket.	A suit and tie.
Yes, he does.	The Tektron Internet Co.	Yes, he is.
Because it was the best thing to do.	Recently.	No, he didn't.

b. Divide the class into teams. Give each team a mark: *X* or *O*.

c. Have each team ask a question about the story for an answer in the grid. For example:

Story One

X Team: Why did Jim wear a suit and tie to the interview?
Because it was the best thing to do.

d. If an answer is appropriate and is stated correctly, that team may replace the answer with its team mark.

e. The first team to mark out three boxes in a straight line—either vertically, horizontally, or diagonally—wins.

f. Do the same for the other stories.

2. *Interview the Characters*

   a. Divide the class into pairs.

   b. One member of the pair is *Jim, Emily, Nick,* or *Maria* from the story. The other is a friend. The friend wants to know why that person thought his or her decision was *the best thing to do*.

   c. Have students report back to the class about their conversations, and compare everybody's reasons.

 LISTENING

Listen and choose the correct answer.

1. A. I avoid going to the mall whenever I can.
   B. Me, too.
2. A. I've decided to sell my car.
   B. Your beautiful car?
3. A. Please try to quit biting your nails.
   B. Okay, Mom.
4. A. Do you enjoy traveling by plane?
   B. Very much.
5. A. We're thinking about moving to Florida.
   B. Oh. That's interesting.
6. A. I've been considering getting married for a long time.
   B. Oh, really? I didn't know that.
7. A. Don't stop practicing.
   B. Okay.
8. A. Interrupting people is a habit I just can't break.
   B. That's too bad.

Answers

1. b
2. b
3. a
4. a
5. b
6. b
7. a
8. a

CHAPTER 7

Text Page 94

 PRONUNCIATION Reduced *to*

> **Reduced *to*:** In spoken English, the pronunciation of *to* is often reduced to [tə].

Focus on Listening

Practice the sentences in the left column. Say each sentence or play the audio one or more times. Have students listen carefully and repeat.

Focus on Pronunciation

Practice the sentences in the right column. Have students say each sentence and then listen carefully as you say it or play the audio.

If you wish, have students continue practicing the sentences to improve their pronunciation.

 JOURNAL

Have students write their journal entries at home or in class. Encourage students to use a dictionary to look up words they would like to use. Students can share their written work with other students if appropriate. Have students discuss what they have written as a class, in pairs, or in small groups

 CHAPTER SUMMARY

GRAMMAR

1. Divide the class into pairs or small groups.
2. Have students take turns forming sentences from the words in the grammar boxes. Student A says a sentence, and Student B points to the words from each column that are in the sentence. Then have students switch: Student B says a sentence, and Student A points to the words.

EXPANSION ACTIVITY

Category Dictation ★★

1. Have students draw two columns on a piece of paper. At the top of one column, have students write <u>tap dancing</u>. At the top of the other column, have them write <u>to tap dance</u>.

2. Dictate various verbs and have students write them in the appropriate column. For example:

<u>tap dancing</u>	<u>to tap dance</u>
begin	begin
start	start
like	like
avoid	learn
practice	decide
enjoy	

KEY VOCABULARY

Have students ask you any questions about the meaning or pronunciation of the vocabulary. If students ask for the pronunciation, repeat after the student until the student is satisfied with his or her own pronunciation.

EXPANSION ACTIVITIES

1. Do You Remember the Words? ★

    Check students' retention of the vocabulary depicted on the opening page of Chapter 7 by doing the following activity:

    a. Have students open their books to page 81 and cover the list of vocabulary words.

    (continued)

EXPANSION ACTIVITIES (Continued)

    b. Either call out a number and have students tell you the word, or say a word and have students tell you the number.

    Variation: You can also do this activity as a game with competing teams.

2. Student-Led Dictation ★

    a. Tell each student to choose a word or phrase from the Key Vocabulary list on text page 94 and look at it very carefully.

    b. Have students take turns dictating their words to the class. Everybody writes down that student's word.

    c. When the dictation is completed, call on different students to write each word on the board to check the spelling.

3. Complete the Sentence! ★★

Begin a sentence using the vocabulary from the first two columns on text page 94, and have students complete the sentence with the correct synonym. For example:

Teacher	Student
Another word for *begin* is . . .	start.
Another word for *quit* is . . .	stop.

Variation: This activity may be done as a class, in pairs or small groups, or as a game with competing teams.

END-OF-CHAPTER ACTIVITIES

1. Board Game ★★★

a. On poster boards or on manila file folders, make up game boards with a pathway consisting of separate spaces. You may use any theme or design you wish.

b. Divide the class into groups of 2 to 4 students, and give each group a game board and a die, and each student something to be used as a playing piece.

c. Give each group a pile of cards face-down with statements written on them. Some sentences should be correct, and others incorrect. For example:

> We avoid to drive downtown.
> They like surfing.
> She's considered to sell her house for a long time.
> I'm thinking about to move to Chicago.
> He keeps on eating junk food.
> I began biting my nail when I was a little boy.
> He enjoys to practice the piano every night.
> They decided figure skating.
> Browse the web is my favorite way to relax.
> They can't stand to talk about politics.
> Jennifer has finally stopped teasing her sister.
> Is swimming very difficult?
> Has he finally quit to argue with people?
> She started to practice to draw when she was young.

d. Each student in turn rolls the die, moves the playing piece along the game path, and after landing on a space, picks a card, reads the sentence, and says if it is *correct* or *incorrect*. If the statement is incorrect, the student must correct it. If the response is correct, the student takes an additional turn.

e. The first student to reach the end of the pathway is the winner.

2. Change the Sentence! ★★

a. Write a sentence on the board, underlining and numbering different portions of the sentence. For example:

> 1 2
> Vincent is considering going on a diet
> 3
> after he retires.

b. Have students sit in a circle.

c. Tell them that when you say a number, the first student in the circle makes a change in that part of the sentence. For example:

> Teacher: Two.
> Student 1: Vincent is considering going to Nepal after he retires.

d. The second student keeps the first student's sentence, but changes it based on the next number you say. For example:

> Teacher: Three.
> Student 2: Vincent is considering going to Nepal this summer.

e. Continue this way with the rest of the students in the circle. For example:

> Teacher: One.
> Student 3: Nancy decided to go to Nepal this summer.

3. Scrambled Sentences ★★

a. Divide the class into two teams.

b. Write individual sentences out of order on the board. Use sentences based on the lessons in Chapter 7. For example:

> has   Walter   walks   when   the
> street   decided   his   quit   he
> phone   talking   to   on   cell
> down

c. The first person to raise his or her hand, come to the board, and write the sentence in the correct order earns a point for that team. (*Walter has decided to quit talking on his cell phone when he walks down the street.*)

d. The team with the most points wins the scrambled sentence game.

Variation: Write the words to several sentences on separate cards. Divide the class into small groups, and have students work together to put the sentences into correct order.

4. Dialog Builder! ★★★

   a. Divide the class into pairs.

   b. Write several lines on the board from conversations in Chapter 7, such as the following:

   > I've made a decision.
   > I hope so, too.
   > What?
   > I envy you.
   > Not at all. I avoid doing that whenever I can.

   c. Have each pair create a conversation incorporating those lines. Students can begin and end their conversations any way they wish, but they must include those lines in their dialogs.

   d. Call on students to present their conversations to the class.

5. Class Discussion: Giving Advice ★★★

   a. Write the following on the board:

   > Avoid _____.
   > Consider _____.
   > Think about _____.
   > Continue _____.
   > Keep on _____.
   > Start _____.
   > Begin _____.
   > Stop _____.
   > Learn _____.
   > Practice _____.
   > Decide _____.

   b. Have groups of students create lists of advice for any of the following topics:

saving money	studying English
driving downtown	planning a trip
buying a computer	going to an interview
buying a car	

   The sentences must begin with any of the sentences on the board.

   c. Have students work in small groups to develop their lists of advice and then share their ideas with the class.

CHAPTER 7   249

WORKBOOK ANSWER KEY AND LISTENING SCRIPTS

WORKBOOK PAGE 78

A. WHAT DO THEY { ENJOY DOING / LIKE TO DO } ?

1. enjoy
2. likes to, Talking
3. enjoy
4. like to, Knitting
5. enjoy
6. likes to, delivering
7. enjoy, being
8. likes to, planting
9. enjoys, chatting
10. like to, playing
11. enjoy
12. likes to, going
13. enjoy

WORKBOOK PAGE 80

C. WHAT'S THE WORD?

1. complain
2. sitting
3. eat
4. clean
5. wear
6. cleaning
7. go
8. going
9. sit
10. complaining
11. eating
12. wearing

WORKBOOK PAGE 82

F. MY ENERGETIC GRANDFATHER

1. to play/playing
2. to play
3. play

WORKBOOK PAGE 83

H. CHOOSE

1. to buy
2. moving
3. going
4. changing
5. get
6. retiring

WORKBOOK PAGE 85

K. WHAT'S THE WORD?

1. rearranging
2. eating
3. worrying
4. to get/getting
5. to exercise/exercising
6. to ask/asking
7. arguing
8. to take/taking
9. paying, to pay/paying
10. to fall/falling

L. GOOD DECISIONS

1. biting
2. to do/doing
3. to cook
4. to cook/cooking
5. paying
6. cleaning
7. gossiping
8. interrupting

WORKBOOK PAGE 86

M. PROBLEMS!

1. falling
   falling
2. to lift/lifting
   to lift/lifting
   lifting
3. to tease/teasing
   teasing
   crying
   teasing
4. driving
   to drive/driving
   to drive/driving
5. dressing
   to dress/dressing
   dressing
6. stepping
   to dance/dancing
   going

WORKBOOK PAGE 87

N. LISTENING

Listen and choose the correct answer.

1. Dr. Gomez really enjoys . . .
2. Whenever possible, my wife and I try to avoid . . .
3. Next summer I'm going to learn . . .
4. Every day Rita practices . . .
5. My parents have decided . . .
6. I've considered . . .
7. Are you thinking about . . .
8. I'm going to quit . . .
9. Why do you keep on . . .
10. My doctor says I should stop . . .
11. David can't stand . . .
12. Are you going to continue to . . .
13. James doesn't want to start . . .
14. Next semester Kathy is going to begin . . .
15. You know, you can't keep on . . .

Answers

1. a	6. a	11. b
2. a	7. b	12. b
3. b	8. b	13. a
4. b	9. a	14. a
5. a	10. b	15. b

O. WHAT DOES IT MEAN?

1. b	7. b
2. c	8. a
3. a	9. c
4. b	10. b
5. c	11. b
6. a	12. c

CHAPTER 8 OVERVIEW: Text Pages 95–110

GRAMMAR

PAST PERFECT TENSE

| I / He / She / It / We / You / They | had eaten. |

| I / He / She / It / We / You / They | hadn't eaten. |

PAST PERFECT CONTINUOUS TENSE

| I / He / She / It / We / You / They | had been eating. |

FUNCTIONS

ASKING FOR AND REPORTING INFORMATION

I heard that *Arnold failed his driver's test*.

What happened?
What went wrong?

He *broke* his *leg*.
She *sprained* her *wrist*.

How did *he* do that?

He was *roller-skating* . . . and he had never *roller-skated* before.

I hadn't *swum in the ocean* in a long time.

Why didn't *Mr. and Mrs. Henderson see a movie last weekend*?
They didn't want to. *They* had *seen a movie the weekend before*.

Did you *get to the plane* on time?
No I didn't. By the time *I got to the plane, it* had already *taken off*.

What were you preparing for?
What had you done?

What had you forgotten to do?
What had you planned to do?
What had you done beforehand?
How long had you been planning to do it?
How long had you been preparing for that?
What did you accomplish?

Is it true?
 Yes, it is.

SHARING NEWS ABOUT SOMEONE

Have you heard about *Harry*?
Have you heard the news about *Harry*?
Have you heard what happened to *Harry*?

RESPONDING TO INFORMATION

That's terrible!

SYMPATHIZING

Poor *Harry*!

EXPRESSING REGRET

It's really a shame.

EXPRESSING HOPE

I hope *he feels better soon*.

INQUIRING ABOUT FEELINGS–EMOTIONS

Were you upset?
Were you disappointed?

DESCRIBING FEELINGS–EMOTIONS

I feel nostalgic when _____.
I felt foolish when _____.
I was furious when _____.
I was heartbroken when _____.

INQUIRING ABOUT SATISFACTION

Did you enjoy *swimming last weekend*?

EXPRESSING WANT–DESIRE

They didn't want to.

EXPRESSING APPRECIATION

I appreciate that.
That's very kind of you.
That's very nice of you.

252   CHAPTER 8

NEW VOCABULARY

Verbs

accomplish
break up
bring along
bring back
bump into
cancel
chew
deserve
discuss
dislocate
do card tricks
do poorly
earn
eat out
fail
fall through
fly a kite
get ready (for)
get to
give a party
go by
go canoeing
go together
injure
look through
lose *his* voice
memorize
move out
pass a test
pass by
perform
plan
play squash
purchase
rehearse
roller-skate
sail away
say hello
shine
shovel
take a course
take off
train
twist *her* wrist
water
wrestle

Time Expressions

ahead of time
beforehand
by the time
end
in advance

Performing Arts

curtain
movie hero
opera
recital
tango
voice

Entertaining

dinner party
dinner table
invitation
visit (n)

Leisure

card tricks
"hide and seek"
kite
window-shopping

Adjectives

foolish
heartbroken
homemade
imported
nostalgic
tenth-grade

Food

brownies
health food
popcorn
steak bone
strawberry shortcake

Travel

plane ticket
traveler's checks

Getting a Driver's License

driver's test
driving school
"rules of the road"

Miscellaneous

accomplishment
balcony
candy store
ceremony
childhood
computer programming
driveway
extra
field
front teeth
gymnastics
heart attack
home town
lap
lecture
love letter
memories
outskirts
oven
parade
perfectly
promotion
rules
science teacher
true
wrist

EXPRESSIONS

days gone by
from beginning to end
"get cold feet"
It's really a shame.
Poor *Harry*!

Text Page 95: Chapter Opening Page

VOCABULARY PREVIEW

You may want to present these words before beginning the chapter, or you may choose to wait until they first occur in a specific lesson. If you choose to present them at this point, here are some suggestions:

1. Have students look at the illustrations on text page 95 and identify the words they already know.

2. Present the vocabulary. Say each word and have the class repeat it chorally and individually. Check students' understanding and pronunciation of the words.

3. Practice the vocabulary as a class, in pairs, or in small groups. Have students cover the word list and look at the pictures. Practice the words in the following ways:

   - Say a word and have students tell the number of the illustration.
   - Give the number of an illustration and have students say the word.

Text Pages 96–97: They Didn't Want to

FOCUS

- Past Perfect Tense

CLOSE UP

RULE:	The past perfect tense is formed with *had* plus the past participle of the verb.
EXAMPLES:	I **had eaten**. They **had driven**. He **had gone**.

RULE:	The past perfect is used to refer to actions or events that occurred before a particular point in the past.
EXAMPLES:	They **had seen** a movie the weekend before. She **had made** eggs the morning before.

INTRODUCING THE MODEL

1. Have students look at the model illustration.
2. Set the scene:
   a. Put the following time line on the board:

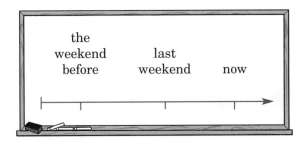

   b. "Two people are talking about Mr. and Mrs. Henderson. One of them wants to know why the Hendersons didn't see a movie last weekend."
3. Present the model. Point to the appropriate time expression on the board as you present each line of the model.
4. Full-Class Repetition.

Pronunciation Note

The pronunciation focus of Chapter 8 is **Reduced *had*** (text page 110). You may wish to model this pronunciation at this point and encourage students to incorporate it into their language practice.

5. Ask students if they have any questions. Check understanding of the expression *the weekend before*.
6. Group Choral Repetition.
7. Choral Conversation.
8. Call on one or two pairs of students to present the dialog.

   (For additional practice, do Choral Conversation in small groups or by rows.)
9. Practice other verbs in the past perfect tense.

   a. Practice verbs whose past participles are the same as the past tense forms.

CHAPTER 8 255

1.) Write on the board:

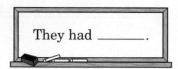

2.) Say the simple form of each verb and have students make a sentence with that verb in the past perfect tense, using the model on the board. For example:

    Teacher: walk to school
    Student: They had walked to school.

listen to music	watch TV
talk about politics	have a party
work late	wait for the bus
buy a car	visit some friends
read the newspaper	review their lessons

b. Practice verbs whose past participles differ from the past tense forms.

1.) Write on the board:

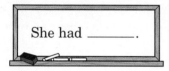

2.) Have students make sentences as above.

eat dinner	do well on the test
take the bus	fly to London
go to school	write a letter
have dinner	make pizza
give a party	drive to the airport

SIDE BY SIDE EXERCISES

Examples

1. A. Why didn't your parents eat out yesterday evening?
   B. They didn't want to. They had eaten out the evening before.

2. A. Why didn't Barry go canoeing last Saturday?
   B. He didn't want to. He had gone canoeing the Saturday before.

1. **Exercise 1:** Introduce the expression *eat out*. Call on two students to present the dialog. Then do Choral Repetition and Choral Conversation practice.

2. **Exercise 2:** Introduce the expression *go canoeing*. Same as above.

3. **Exercises 3–13:** Either Full-Class Practice or Pair Practice.

> **New Vocabulary**
> 9. opera
> 10. window-shopping
> 11. kite
> 12. discuss
>   dinner table
> 13. card tricks

Language Note

Exercise 10: *Go window-shopping* is an idiomatic expression that means *just looking around stores, store windows, and displays,* or *shopping without buying anything.*

4. **Exercise 14:** Have students use the model as a guide to create their own conversations, using vocabulary of their choice. Encourage students to use dictionaries to find new words they want to use. This exercise can be done orally in class or for written homework. If you assign it for homework, do one example in class to make sure students understand what's expected. Have students present their conversations in class the next day.

WORKBOOK

Pages 88–89

EXPANSION ACTIVITIES

1. **Grammar Chain** ★★

   a. Write the following conversation model on the board:

   > A. Did you _____ last night?
   > B. No, I didn't. I had _____ the night before.

   b. Start the chain game by saying:

   > Teacher *(to Student A)*: Did you *go out to eat* last night?

   c. Student A answers according to the model on the board and then asks a different question to Student B, and the chain continues. For example

   > Student A: No, I didn't. I had gone out to eat the night before.
   > *(to Student B)*: Did you *wear your suit* last night?
   > Student B: No, I didn't. I had worn my suit the night before.
   > *(to Student C)*: Did you *drive downtown* last night?

2. **Match the Sentences** ★★

   a. Make a set of split sentence cards such as the following:

I didn't want to have a sandwich for lunch today . . .	because I had had one yesterday.
I didn't want to wear a suit yesterday . . .	because I had worn one the day before.
I didn't want to fly a kite last weekend . . .	because I had flown one the weekend before.
I didn't want to take an astronomy course last semester . . .	because I had taken one the semester before.
I didn't want to make an omelet yesterday morning . . .	because I had made one the morning before.
I didn't want to see a play last weekend . . .	because I had seen one the weekend before.
I didn't want to drive to the beach last Sunday . . .	because I had driven there the Sunday before.
I didn't want to give a party last night . . .	because I had given one the night before.
I didn't want to write a composition yesterday . . .	because I had written one the day before.
I didn't want to ride a motorcycle last weekend . . .	because I had ridden one the weekend before.

   b. Distribute a card to each student.

   c. Have students memorize the sentence portion on their cards, then walk around the room trying to find their corresponding match.

   d. Then have pairs of students say their completed sentences aloud to the class.

3. **Concentration** ★

   a. Using the cards from the previous expansion activity, shuffle them and place them in five rows of four each.

   b. Divide the class into two teams. The object of the game is for students to find the matching cards. Both teams should be able to see all the cards, since *concentrating* on their location is an important part of playing the game.

   (continued)

CHAPTER 8 257

EXPANSION ACTIVITIES (Continued)

c. A student from Team 1 turns over two cards. If they match, the student picks up the cards, that team gets a point, and the student takes another turn. If the cards don't match, the student turns them face down, and a member of Team 2 takes a turn.

d. The game continues until all the cards have been matched. The team with the most correct matches wins the game.

Variation: This game can also be played in groups and pairs.

4. Sense or Nonsense? ★★

a. Divide the class into four groups.

b. Using the cards from Expansion Activity 2, mix up the cards and distribute sets of cards to each group, keeping the beginning and ending cards in different piles.

c. Have students take turns picking up one card from each pile and reading the sentence to the group. For example:

| I didn't want to have a sandwich for lunch today . . . | because I had given one the night before. |

d. That group decides if the sentence makes sense or is *nonsense*.

e. After all the cards have been picked, have the groups lay out all the cards and put together all the sentence combinations that make sense.

5. Student Interviews ★★★

a. Divide the class into pairs. Have students interview each other about what they did last weekend.

b. Have students report back to the class explaining what their classmate *had done* last weekend. Remind students to use the past perfect tense.

6. Where's Martha? ★★★

a. Write the following on the board or on a handout for students:

Martha

Morning
get up
wash her hair
meet a friend for breakfast
borrow some books from the library
take a math test

Afternoon
eat lunch with a friend
walk to the post office to get her mail
go to history class
talk to her English teacher about her exam
do her laundry
buy some things

A. Have you seen Martha today?

B. Yes. I saw her this { morning / afternoon }. She had just _____, and she was getting ready to _____.

---

b. Set the scene: "Martha and Sally are college students. They're roommates in a dormitory at the college. It's evening now. Sally is in her room, and she's worried because Martha isn't there. She's asking other people in the dormitory if they have seen Martha." For example, she asked Bill: "Have you seen Martha today?" And Bill said:

"Yes. I saw her this afternoon. She had just eaten lunch with a friend, and she was getting ready to walk to the post office to get her mail."

c. Role play the conversation with a few of your students. Then call on pairs of students to role play. (Speaker B decides which cue to use in the answer.)

7. **What's First?** ★★

   a. Divide the class into pairs.

   b. On a handout, write pairs of sentences such as the following:

   > She studied hard.
   > She took the test.
   >
   > He made dinner.
   > He bought the food.
   >
   > She went to work.
   > She brushed her teeth.
   >
   > He started to cook on the barbecue.
   > He made a fire.
   >
   > They practiced a lot.
   > They ran in the race.
   >
   > My parents came to visit.
   > I cleaned the house
   >
   > She returned it to the library.
   > She read the book.
   >
   > We put on our coats.
   > We went outside.
   >
   > She went to bed.
   > She ate dinner.

   c. Have students in each pair decide which sentence happened first, and then combine the sentences using the word *before*. For example:

   > She had studied hard before she took the test.
   > He had bought the food before he made dinner.

   d. Have the pairs compare their sentences.

Text Pages 98–99

READING The Most Important Thing

FOCUS

- Past Perfect Tense

NEW VOCABULARY

ahead of time	look through
bring along	memorize
curtain	oven
dinner party	perfectly
driveway	plane ticket
end (n)	purchase (v)
foolish	rehearse
from beginning to end	shine
heartbroken	shovel
imported (adj)	traveler's checks
in advance	water (v)
invitation	

READING THE STORY

Optional: Preview the story by having students talk about the story title and/or illustrations. You may choose to introduce new vocabulary beforehand, or have students encounter the new vocabulary within the context of the reading.

1. Have students read silently, or follow along silently as the story is read aloud by you, by one or more students, or on the audio program.
2. Ask students if they have any questions. Check understanding of vocabulary.
3. Check students' comprehension, using some or all of the following questions:

What had Roger done to prepare for his dinner party?
What had he forgotten to do?
Why did Roger feel foolish?

What had Mr. and Mrs. Jenkins done to prepare for their vacation?
What had they forgotten to do?
Why were they heartbroken?

What had Harold done to prepare for his job interview?
What had he forgotten?
Why was Harold furious with himself?

What had Janet done to prepare for the play?
What had she forgotten to do?
Why was she embarrassed?

✓READING *CHECK-UP*

TRUE, FALSE, OR MAYBE?

1. True
2. True
3. Maybe
4. False
5. True
6. True
7. Maybe
8. False
9. True

WHICH IS CORRECT?

Before doing the exercise, introduce the word *laptop*.

1. traveler's checks
2. an invitation
3. borrowed
4. heartbroken
5. important, imported

260   CHAPTER 8

READING EXTENSION

1. ***Time Lines***

    Have students draw a time line for the each of the characters in the four readings. In pairs, have students compare their time lines.

2. ***Chain Story***

    a. Begin by saying, "Henry was all prepared for his first interview. He had bought a new suit."

    b. Student 1 repeats what you said and adds another item. For example: "Henry was all prepared for his first interview. He had bought a new suit, and he had practiced the interview questions."

    c. Continue around the room in this fashion, with each student repeating what the previous one said and adding another sentence.

    d. You can do the activity again, beginning and ending with different students.

    If the class is large, you may want to divide students into groups to give students more practice. Here are some additional story lines:

    > Martha was all prepared for the move to a new apartment.
    > Barry and Paul were all prepared for their car trip.
    > Our neighbors were all prepared for the rainstorm.
    > Jim was all prepared for the first day of school.

How About You?

Have students answer the questions in pairs or as a class.

Text Page 100: They Didn't Get There on Time

FOCUS

- Past Perfect Tense

CLOSE UP

RULE: The time expression *by the time* establishes a point in time before which something occurred.

EXAMPLES: **By the time** I got to the concert, it had already begun.
By the time I got to the plane, it had already taken off.

INTRODUCING THE MODEL

1. Have students look at the model illustration.
2. Put the following time line on the board:

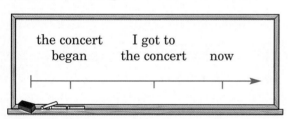

3. Set the scene: "Two friends are talking. One was late for a concert."
4. Present the model while pointing to the appropriate cues on the time line on the board.
5. Full-Class Repetition.
6. Ask students if they have any questions. Check understanding of the expressions *by the time, get to*.
7. Group Choral Repetition.
8. Choral Conversation.
9. Call on one or two pairs of students to present the dialog.

   (For additional practice, do Choral Conversation in small groups or by rows.)

SIDE BY SIDE EXERCISES

Examples

1. A. Did you get to the post office on time?
   B. No, I didn't. By the time I got to the post office, it had already closed.
2. A. Did you get to the plane on time?
   B. No, I didn't. By the time I got to the plane, it had already taken off.

1. **Exercise 1:** Call on two students to present the dialog. Then do Choral Repetition and Choral Conversation practice.
2. **Exercise 2:** Introduce the expression *take off*. Same as above.
3. **Exercises 3–9:** Either Full-Class Practice or Pair Practice.

   New Vocabulary
   5. lecture   9. parade
   8. sail away   go by

WORKBOOK

Page 90

262 CHAPTER 8

EXPANSION ACTIVITIES

1. Grammar Chain ★★

a. Write the following conversation model and verbs on the board:

> A. Did you _____?
> B. No. By the time I got to _____, _____ had already _____.

catch your plane	mail the letter
cash the check	talk to the mechanic
buy the milk	take the train
see the play	enjoy the lecture
return the book	see the doctor

b. Start the chain game by saying:

Teacher (to Student A): Did you *catch your plane*?

c. Student A answers according to the model on the board and then asks a different question to Student B, and the chain continues. For example

Student A: No. By the time I got to the airport, the plane had already taken off.
(to Student B): Did you *mail the letter*?
Student B: No. By the time I got to the post office, it had already closed.
(to Student C): Did you *cash the check*?
Etc.

2. Change the Sentence! ★★

a. Write a sentence on the board, underlining and numbering different portions of the sentence. For example:

>   1   2
> By the time <u>I got to</u> <u>the concert,</u>
>   3
>   <u>it had already begun.</u>

b. Have students sit in a circle.

c. Tell them that when you say a number, the first student in the circle makes a change in that part of the sentence. For example:

Teacher: Two.
Student 1: By the time I got to <u>the movie</u>, it had already begun.

d. The second student keeps the first student's sentence, but changes it based on the next number you say. For example:

Teacher: Three.
Student 2: By the time I got to the movie, <u>it had already ended</u>.

e. Continue this way with the rest of the students in the circle. For example:

Teacher: One.
Student 3: By the time <u>we decided to see</u> the movie, it had already ended.

3. Sentence Cues ★★

a. On separate cards, write key words that can be put together to form sentences or questions. Clip together the cards for each sentence. For example:

(continued)

CHAPTER 8   263

EXPANSION ACTIVITIES (Continued)

b. Divide the class into small groups and give a clipped set of cards to each group.

c. Have each group write a sentence based on their set of cards.

d. Have one member of each group write that group's sentence on the board and compare everybody's sentences. Did they choose the correct tense? What words helped them choose the correct verb form?

4. Finish the Sentence! ★★

Begin sentences with "By the time, . . ." and call on students to repeat what you said and then complete the sentence any way they wish. For example:

Teacher: By the time I got to the party, . . .
Student: By the time I got to the party, everybody had already left.

Teacher: By the time I got to the parade, . . .
Student: By the time I got to the parade, it had already gone by.

5. No Wonder! ★★★

a. Write the following conversation framework on the board:

> A. I saw _____ at _____ yesterday, and (he/she) looked very upset/sad/excited/happy.
> B. I know. (He/She) had just _____.
> A. No wonder (he/she) looked so _____!

b. Divide the class into pairs.

c. Have students create conversations based on the model on the board and then present them to the class. For example:

A. I saw your uncle at the supermarket yesterday, and he looked very upset.
B. I know. He had just lost his wallet.
A. No wonder he looked so upset!

A. I saw Gloria at the bank yesterday, and she looked very excited.

B. I know. She had just gotten a raise.
A. No wonder she looked so excited!

6. Class Quiz ★★★

a. Divide the class into pairs or small groups.

b. Dictate sentences about history (local, national, entertainment, or sports history) and then have students discuss whether they agree or disagree. For example:

By the time the French Revolution began, the American Revolutionary War had already ended.

c. Call on students to respond. For example:

I agree. The American Revolutionary War ended in 1783, and the French Revolution didn't begin until 1789.

7. Memory Game ★★

a. Write the following on a handout.

8:00–9:00	Alice took the bus to work.
9:00–12:00	She wrote a report.
12:00–1:00	She had lunch with a friend.
1:00–2:00	She went to the clinic for a check-up.
2:00–5:00	She gave a presentation at work.
5:00–6:00	She took the bus to the museum.
6:00–9:00	She looked at the paintings.
10:00	She came home.

b. Give the handout to students and tell them they have 30 seconds to look at it and try to remember as much information as they can.

c. Have students put the handout aside.

d. Write the following beginning of a sentence on the board:

> By 2:00, Alice had already _____.

Have students write down as many sentences as they can remember about Alice's day, using the past perfect.

e. Have students share their sentences with the class.

f. Let students look at the schedule for another 30 seconds, and then write the following sentence on the board:

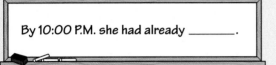

By 10:00 P.M. she had already _____.

See how many students can write down all the things Alice had done that day.

Variation: You can do this activity as a game with competing teams. The first team to write the most number of correct statements about Alice's day is the winner.

Text Page 101: He Hadn't Gone Fishing in a Long Time

FOCUS

- Past Perfect: Negatives

CLOSE UP

RULE:	To form the negative of the past perfect tense, *not* is added. The word *not* contracts with the auxiliary *had*.
EXAMPLES:	I **had not** gone. I **hadn't** gone. You **had not** gone. You **hadn't** gone. She **had not** gone. She **hadn't** gone. He **had not** gone. He **hadn't** gone. We **had not** gone. We **hadn't** gone. They **had not** gone. They **hadn't** gone.

INTRODUCING THE MODEL

1. Have students look at the model illustration.
2. Set the scene: "Two people are talking about their grandfather."
3. Present the model.
4. Full-Class Repetition.
5. Ask students if they have any questions. Check understanding of vocabulary.
6. Group Choral Repetition.
7. Choral Conversation.
8. Call on one or two pairs of students to present the dialog.

   (For additional practice, do Choral Conversation in small groups or by rows.)

SIDE BY SIDE EXERCISES

Examples

1. A. Did Natalie enjoy swimming in the ocean last weekend?
   B. Yes, she did. She hadn't swum in the ocean in a long time.

2. A. Did you enjoy seeing a movie yesterday evening?
   B. Yes, I did. I hadn't seen a movie in a long time.

1. **Exercise 1:** Call on two students to present the dialog. Then do Choral Repetition and Choral Conversation practice.
2. **Exercise 2:** Same as above.

3. Exercises 3–9: Either Full-Class Practice or Pair Practice.

> **New Vocabulary**
> 6. strawberry shortcake
> 8. hide and seek
> 9. love letter

Culture Note

Hide and seek is a favorite game of young children in which one person *hides* and the others *seek* (look for) the person who is hiding.

WORKBOOK

Page 91

EXPANSION ACTIVITIES

1. Match the Sentences ★★

a. Make a set of split sentence cards such as the following:

I enjoyed looking at the paintings because . . .	I hadn't gone to a museum in a long time.
I enjoyed going to the beach last weekend because . . .	I hadn't gone swimming in a long time.
I enjoyed going out for dinner last Friday because . . .	I hadn't eaten in a restaurant in a long time.
I enjoyed going to the symphony last night because . . .	I hadn't listened to classical music in a long time.
I enjoyed relaxing in my yard last Saturday because . . .	I hadn't stayed home on the weekend in a long time.
I enjoyed making an apple pie yesterday because . . .	I hadn't baked anything in a long time.
I enjoyed working in my garden on Sunday because . . .	I hadn't planted flowers in a long time.
I enjoyed my flight to Denver last week because . . .	I hadn't flown anywhere in a long time.

b. Distribute a card to each student.

c. Have students memorize the sentence portion on their cards, then walk around the room trying to find their corresponding match.

d. Then have pairs of students say their completed sentences aloud to the class.

2. Concentration ★

a. Using the cards from the previous expansion activity, shuffle them and place them in four rows of four each.

b. Divide the class into two teams. The object of the game is for students to find the matching cards. Both teams should be able to see all the cards, since *concentrating* on their location is an important part of playing the game.

c. A student from Team 1 turns over two cards. If they match, the student picks up the cards, that team gets a point, and the student takes another turn. If the cards don't match, the student turns them face down, and a member of Team 2 takes a turn.

(continued)

CHAPTER 8   267

EXPANSION ACTIVITIES (Continued)

d. The game continues until all the cards have been matched. The team with the most correct matches wins the game.

Variation: This game can also be played in groups and pairs.

3. Sense or Nonsense? ★★

a. Divide the class into four groups.

b. Using the cards from Expansion Activity 2, mix up the cards and distribute sets of cards to each group, keeping the beginning and ending cards in different piles.

c. Have students take turns picking up one card from each pile and reading the sentence to the group. For example:

| I enjoyed going out for dinner last Friday because . . . | I hadn't gone swimming in a long time. |

d. That group decides if the sentence makes *sense* or is *nonsense*.

e. After all the cards have been picked, have the groups lay out all the cards and put together all the sentence combinations that make sense.

4. What's the Reason? ★★

a. Write the following list of verbs and conversation framework on the board:

drive	ride
eat	run
fly	sing
give	speak

That's because ___ hadn't ___ in a long time.

b. Present the situations below and have students respond, using an appropriate verb and the sentence framework on the board. For example:

Teacher: Tom had too much pizza last night.
Student: That's because he hadn't eaten pizza in a long time.

Situations:

Tom had too much pizza last night.
Barbara was very nervous before her flight to Florida yesterday.
Richard was afraid to take his car into New York City last weekend.
Kathy was very nervous before the marathon race last Saturday.
Alan was feeling nervous before choir practice yesterday.
Gloria almost fainted yesterday when the nurse at the hospital started taking her blood.
The president practiced Spanish all weekend before the president of Colombia arrived in Washington.
Tim Flynn, the movie actor, wasn't looking forward to making a western movie last year.

5. Have You Seen Them? ★★★

a. Write the following on the board:

A. Have you seen _____ since (he/she/they) _____?
B. No, I haven't. The last time I saw ___, (he/she/they) hadn't _____ yet.

b. Write the following cues on cards:

Betty have her baby	Bill move into his new apartment
Julie run in the marathon	George take his English exam
Jane win the lottery	Ted begin studying French

Gloria become a movie star	Ron meet his new girlfriend
Sally speak to her supervisor about a raise	Brian decide to move to South America
Mr. and Mrs. Lopez buy a sports car	Judy and Tim get married
Walter had an operation on his knee	Nancy quit her job
Howard lose fifty pounds	Rita start lifting weights

c. Call on pairs of students to come to the front of the room. Have each pair pick a card and create a conversation based on that situation and the model on the board. For example:

> A. Have you seen Betty since she had her baby?
> B. No, I haven't. The last time I saw her, she hadn't had her baby yet.
>
> A. Have you seen Bill since he moved into his new apartment?
> B. No, I haven't. The last time I saw him, he hadn't moved into his new apartment yet.

6. What's Wrong? ★★★

a. Divide the class into pairs or small groups.

b. Write several sentences such as the following on the board or on a handout. Some of the sentences should be correct, and others incorrect. For example:

> I hadn't see them in a long time.
> I enjoyed swim at the beach last weekend.
> She hadn't ate there in a long time.
> By the time we got to the theater, the play had already started.
> Did you seen your friends at the party?
> They had took that course before.
> By the time they got to the meeting, it already began.
> Did they get to the airport on time?
> Why didn't he gone to class last week?
> He had ridden on a roller coaster in a long time.

c. The object of the activity is for students to identify which sentences are incorrect and then correct them.

d. Have students compare their answers.

Variation: Do the activity as a game with competing teams. The team that successfully completes the task in the shortest time is the winner.

CHAPTER 8   269

Text Pages 102–103

READING *Days Gone By*

FOCUS

- Past Perfect Tense

NEW VOCABULARY

balcony	move out
bring back	movie hero
bump into	nostalgic
candy store	outskirts
childhood	pass by
days gone by	popcorn
field	say hello
homemade	science teacher
home town	tenth-grade
memories	visit (n)

READING THE STORY

Optional: *Preview the story by having students talk about the story title and/or illustrations. You may choose to introduce new vocabulary beforehand, or have students encounter the new vocabulary within the context of the reading.*

1. Have students read silently, or follow along silently as the story is read aloud by you, by one or more students, or on the audio program.

2. Ask students if they have any questions. Check understanding of vocabulary.

3. Check students' comprehension, using some or all of the following questions:

What did Michael do last month?
Why was Michael's visit to Fullerton very special to him?
Where did he walk, and what did he remember?
What did he pass by?
Where did he stand for a while, and what did he think about?
What did he have at the ice cream shop?
What did he do in the park?
Where did he go fishing?
Why did Michael feel like a kid again?
Who did Michael visit?
Who did he say hello to?
Who did he bump into?
What did Michael remember during his visit to his home town?
Why was his trip back to Fullerton a very nostalgic experience for him?

✓ READING *CHECK-UP*

TRUE, FALSE, OR MAYBE?

1. False
2. True
3. False
4. True
5. Maybe
6. True
7. True
8. Maybe

WHICH WORD IS CORRECT?

Before doing the exercise, introduce the word *located*.

1. homemade
2. outskirts
3. spent
4. into

270   CHAPTER 8

5. back
6. nostalgic

READING EXTENSION

1. **Michael's Childhood**

   Have students compose a short paragraph describing Michael's childhood based on the information in the reading.

2. **Childhood Memories**

   a. Have students individually make a list of activities they enjoyed in their childhood.

   b. Divide the class into pairs and have students share their lists. As they talk, have them find common childhood hobbies or activities.

   c. Have students report to the class about their partners.

 LISTENING

Listen and choose the correct answer.

1. Did your parents enjoy eating at Joe's Restaurant last night?
2. Why don't you want to see the new James Bond movie with us next weekend?
3. Did you get to the play on time last night?
4. Michael, please go upstairs and do your homework.
5. Why did Carmen do so well on the history test?
6. We really enjoyed our vacation at the Ritz Hotel.

Answers

1. b
2. b
3. a
4. b
5. a
6. b

 THINK ABOUT IT! *Feelings and Experiences*

Have students complete the sentences and then share their responses in pairs or as a class.

Text Pages 104–105: Have You Heard About Harry?

FOCUS

- Contrast: Past Perfect vs. Past Continuous

INTRODUCING THE MODEL

1. Have students look at the model illustration.
2. Set the scene: "Harry had an accident recently. Two of his friends are talking about him."
3. Present the model.
4. Full-Class Repetition.
5. Ask students if they have any questions. Check understanding of the word *roller-skate*.
6. Group Choral Repetition.
7. Choral Conversation.
8. Call on one or two pairs of students to present the dialog.

    (For additional practice, do Choral Conversation in small groups or by rows.)

SIDE BY SIDE EXERCISES

Examples

1. A. Have you heard about Tom?
   B. No, I haven't. What happened?
   A. He twisted his ankle last week.
   B. That's terrible! How did he do THAT?
   A. He was flying a kite . . . and he had never flown a kite before.
   B. Poor Tom! I hope he feels better soon.

2. A. Have you heard about Peggy?
   B. No, I haven't. What happened?
   A. She injured her knee last week.
   B. That's terrible! How did she do THAT?
   A. She was skiing . . . and she had never skied before.
   B. Poor Peggy! I hope she feels better soon.

1. **Exercise 1:** Introduce the word *twist*. Call on two students to present the dialog. Then do Choral Repetition and Choral Conversation practice.
2. **Exercise 2:** Introduce the word *injure*. Same as above.
3. **Exercises 3–11:** Either Full-Class Practice or Pair Practice.

New Vocabulary

3. brownies
4. wrist
   play squash
6. wrestle
7. lose his voice
8. dislocate
   gymnastics
10. tango
11. front teeth
    chew
    steak bone

4. **Exercise 12:** Have students use the model as a guide to create their own conversations, using vocabulary of their own choice. Encourage students to use dictionaries to find new words they want to use. This exercise can be done orally in class or for written homework. If you assign it for homework, do one example in class to make sure students understand what's expected. Have students present their conversations in class the next day.

How to Say It!

Sharing News About Someone: The present perfect is used to talk about a recent event. Three common opening questions to share some news about someone are: "Have you heard about _____?" "Have you heard the news about _____?" and "Have you heard what happened to _____?"

1. Present the expressions.
2. Full-Class Repetition.
3. Ask students if they have any questions. Check understanding of the expressions.
4. Group Choral Repetition.
5. Have students practice the conversations in this lesson again, beginning with any of these new expressions.
6. Call on pairs to present their conversations to the class.

WORKBOOK

Pages 92–93

EXPANSION ACTIVITIES

1. **Can You Hear the Difference?** ★
   a. Write on the board:

Present Perfect	Past Perfect
I have seen that.	I had seen that.
You have been there.	You had been there.
We have had those.	We had had those.
They have gone.	They had gone.

   b. Choose a sentence randomly from one of the two columns and say it to the class. Have the class listen and identify whether the sentence is in the *present perfect* or in the *past perfect*.
   c. Have students continue the activity in pairs. One student pronounces a sentence and the other identifies the tense. Then have them reverse roles.
   d. Write other similar sentences on the board and continue the practice.

2. **Scrambled Dialogs** ★
   a. Write each line of Exercise 1 and Exercise 2 from text page 104 on a separate card. Scramble the cards.
   b. Give the cards to 12 students. Have them unscramble the lines and put together the two conversations.

   [Variation]
   a. Divide the class into three groups.
   b. Make three sets of Exercises 1 and 2, writing each line on a separate card.

   c. Give each group one set of the cards, and have the group members reorder the conversations.
   d. Have each group read one of the conversations aloud while the others listen to check for accuracy.

3. **Concentration** ★
   a. Write the following sentences on separate cards:

She was roller-skating . . .	and she had never roller-skated before.
He was flying a kite . . .	and he had never flown a kite before.
She was skiing . . .	and she had never skied before.
He was singing opera . . .	and he had never sung opera before.
She was doing gymnastics . . .	and she had never done gymnastics before.
He was doing the tango . . .	and he had never done the tango before.

   (continued)

CHAPTER 8

EXPANSION ACTIVITIES (Continued)

She was riding a motorcycle . . .	and she had never ridden a motorcycle before.
He was boxing . . .	and he had never boxed before.

b. Shuffle the cards and place them face down in four rows of four each.

c. Divide the class into two teams. The object of the game is for students to find the matching cards. Both teams should be able to see all the cards, since *concentrating* on their location is an important part of playing the game.

d. A student from Team 1 turns over two cards. If they match, the student picks up the cards, that team gets a point, and the student takes another turn. If the cards don't match, the student turns them face down, and a member of Team 2 takes a turn.

e. The game continues until all the cards have been matched. The team with the most correct matches wins the game.

Variation: This game can also be played in groups and pairs.

4. Telephone: Have You Heard the News? ★

a. Divide the class into large groups. Have each group sit in a circle.

b. Whisper some news to one student. For example:

   "Have you heard the news? David sprained his right ankle and broke his left arm last week. He was ice-skating and he had never ice-skated before!"

c. The first student whispers the news to the second student, and so forth around the circle.

d. When the message gets to the last student, that person says it aloud. Is it the same message you started with? The group with the most accurate message wins.

5. Do You Remember? ★★

a. Have students close their books.

b. Ask questions about the things that happened to the people on text pages 104 and 105. See if students can remember who they are and what happened to them. For example:

   Teacher: Who lost his voice?
   Student: Victor.
   Teacher: How did it happen?
   Student: He was singing opera . . . and he had never sung opera before.

   Teacher: Who got hurt in an accident?
   Student: Ann.
   Teacher: How did it happen?
   Student: She was riding a motorcycle . . . and she had never ridden a motorcycle before.

Variation: Do the activity as a game with competing teams.

6. Finish the Sentence! ★★

a. Write on the board:

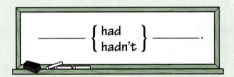

b. Begin each of the sentences below and call on different students to finish the sentence, using verbs in the past perfect. For example:

   Teacher: Martha was very tired yesterday morning because . . .
   Student 1: she had studied until midnight.
   Student 2: she hadn't slept well.
   Student 3: her neighbor's dog had barked until 2 A.M.

Sentences:

   Martha was very tired yesterday morning because . . .
   Joe was very hungry at dinner last night because . . .
   Richard didn't have any clean clothes to wear last weekend because . . .

Anita didn't get to the airport on time yesterday because . . .

Tom didn't get the job as a secretary last week because . . .

Betty was very nervous before her job interview yesterday because . . .

Brian was really excited about visiting Mexico last summer because . . .

My parents didn't go to a movie last night because . . .

7. How Did It Happen? ★★★

Text pages 104 and 105 deal with accidents or unfortunate things that happened to various people. Have students tell about similar experiences they have had.

a. Write the following questions on the board or on a handout for students:

Have you ever broken your leg or arm?
How did it happen?

Have you ever twisted your ankle?
How did it happen?

Have you ever sprained your wrist or back?
How did it happen?

Have you ever gotten into an accident?
How did it happen?

Have you ever lost your voice?
Tell about it.

b. Divide the class into pairs or small groups.

c. Have students ask each other the questions and then report to the class about the other person.

Variation: ★★★ For homework, have students write about an unfortunate experience they have had. Collect the papers and distribute them randomly to students in the class. Have those students read the papers to the class and have others try to guess who this unfortunate event happened to.

CHAPTER 8   275

Text Pages 106–107: It's Really a Shame

FOCUS

- Past Perfect Continuous Tense

CLOSE UP

RULE:	The past perfect continuous tense is formed with *had been* plus the present participle (*-ing* form) of the verb.
EXAMPLES:	I **had been eating** you **had been working** he **had been going** we **had been feeling** they **had been studying**
RULE:	Like the past perfect tense, the past perfect continuous refers to events or actions that occurred before a particular point in the past. Like other continuous tenses, the past perfect continuous focuses on the duration of activity.
EXAMPLE:	He **failed** his driver's test. *(past event)* He **had been practicing** for a long time. *(activity that lasted for a long time)*

GETTING READY

Introduce the past perfect continuous tense.

1. Write on the board:

2. Point to the appropriate cues on the board as you tell the following story: "I went to see some of my old friends at the Presto Company yesterday afternoon. Everybody was happy to see me, but they were all very tired."

   They *had been working* very hard all day.
   Bill *had been typing* all day.
   Sally *had been talking* on the telephone all day.
   And Frank and Susan *had been hiring* new employees all day.

3. Have students repeat the sentences chorally and individually.

4. Form sentences with the words in the box at the top of text page 106. Have students repeat chorally. For example:

   I had been eating.
   He had been eating.

276   CHAPTER 8

INTRODUCING THE MODEL

1. Have students look at the model illustration.
2. Set the scene: "Arnold took his driver's test last week, but he didn't do very well. Two of his friends are talking about what happened."
3. Present the model.
4. Full-Class Repetition.
5. Ask students if they have any questions. Check understanding of the words *fail, driver's test, true,* and the expression *it's really a shame.*
6. Group Choral Repetition.
7. Choral Conversation.
8. Call on one or two pairs of students to present the dialog.

   (For additional practice, do Choral Conversation in small groups or by rows.)

SIDE BY SIDE EXERCISES

Examples

1. A. I heard that Fred lost his job at the factory last week. Is it true?
   B. Yes, it is . . . and it's really a shame. He had been working there for a long time.
2. A. I heard that Larry and Jane broke up last week. Is it true?
   B. Yes, it is . . . and it's really a shame. They had been going together for a long time.

1. **Exercise 1:** Call on two students to present the dialog. Then do Choral Repetition and Choral Conversation practice.
2. **Exercise 2:** Introduce the words *break up, go together.* Same as above.

   Culture Note

   The expressions *go together* and *break up* are associated with dating customs in the United States. When two people date each other exclusively, they are *going together*. When this type of relationship ends, they *break up*.

3. **Exercises 3–10:** Either Full-Class Practice or Pair Practice.

New Vocabulary

3. cancel
   plan
6. heart attack
7. do poorly
8. train
9. perform
   recital

WORKBOOK

Pages 94–96

CHAPTER 8

EXPANSION ACTIVITIES

1. Who Is It? ★

Make statements about the people in the exercises. Have students respond by telling who you're talking about. For example:

> They had been arguing a lot.
> Larry and Jane [Exercise 2]
>
> He had been trying to lose weight.
> Walter [Exercise 6]
>
> She had been studying French.
> Mona [Exercise 3]
>
> He hadn't studied enough.
> Alex [Exercise 7]
>
> She hadn't been wearing good shoes.
> Penny [Exercise 8]
>
> He had been a good employee.
> Fred [Exercise 1]
>
> She had fallen in love with someone else.
> Pam [Exercise 4]
>
> They had found a nice house in a different city.
> Mr. and Mrs. Williams [Exercise 5]

2. Jigsaw Story ★★★

a. Divide the class into groups of six. Give each member of the group one of these cards:

• John had been feeling very nervous.
• Alice had been looking for a dress.
• John's mother had been writing invitations.
• Alice's father had been trying on new tuxedos.
• John's father had been talking to bakers about special cakes.
• Alice's mother had been looking at different churches.

b. Have students share their information to create a story. Have them answer these two questions: *What had they been preparing for? What happened?*

c. Have each group tell its story and explain its logic to the class.

3. For a Long Time ★★

a. Write the following on the board:

> Yes. _____ had been _____ing for a long time.

b. Ask students the questions below and have them answer according to the model on the board. For example:

> Teacher: Was it raining when you got up this morning?
> Student: Yes. It had been raining for a long time.

Questions:

> Was it raining when you got up this morning?
> Were the musicians playing when you arrived at the concert?
> Had Bob started working at the bank when you met him?
> Was Professor Lopez already teaching when you came to class?
> Had Nancy started driving trucks for a living when you met her?
> Had Peter started to study astronomy when he went to college?
> Had Mr. and Mrs. Miller already started to paint their house when you saw them last week?
> Did Maria speak English when she moved to Canada?
> Did you play baseball before you went to high school?
> Were your friends eating when you got to the restaurant last night?
> Were people dancing when you got to the party?

4. Chain Story ★★

a. Begin by saying, "It's really a shame Roger didn't get a raise. He had been working very hard."

b. Student 1 repeats what you said and adds another item. For example: "It's really a shame Roger didn't get the raise. He had been working very hard. He had been staying late at the office."

c. Continue around the room in this fashion, with each student repeating what the previous one said and adding another sentence.

d. You can do the activity again, beginning and ending with different students.

If the class is large, you may want to divide students into groups to give students more practice. Here are some additional story lines:

> Herbert failed his English exam and couldn't graduate.
> Mary lost her voice and couldn't perform in the Broadway show.
> There was a bad fire at the Smiths' new house.

5. Good News/Bad News ★★★

a. Write the following conversation model on the board:

```
A. Hi, _____. What's new?
B. _____.
A. That's great! ___ had been _____ing.
       or
   That's a shame! ___ had been _____ing.
```

b. Write the following situations on cards:

> You finally passed your driver's test.
>
> Your wife/husband just lost his/her job.
>
> Your wife/husband just got promoted.
>
> You just broke up with your boyfriend/girlfriend.
>
> You just got engaged.
>
> You did very badly on your (English) exam.
>
> You did very well on your (English) exam.
>
> You hurt your back and couldn't be in the school play last weekend.
>
> You had to cancel your trip to (Mexico) because you sprained your ankle.

c. Have pairs of students pick a card and create conversations based on the model on the board. Encourage them to then expand the conversation any way they wish. For example:

> A. Hi, Joe. What's new?
> B. I finally passed by driver's test.
> A. That's great! You had been preparing for it for a long time.
> B. You're right.
> A. How are you going to celebrate?
> B. I'm going to drive to the beach this weekend with my friends.

> A. Hi, Barbara. What's new?
> B. My husband just lost his job at Green's Supermarket.
> A. That's a shame! He had been working there for a long time.
> B. I know.
> A. What's he going to do?
> B. He's going to look for a job at another supermarket.
> A. I hope he finds one.

6. When Your Parents Were Young ★★★

a. Write the following on the board:

```
A. Did _____ when your parents were young?
B. Yes. _____ had been _____ing for a long time.
       or
   No. _____ hadn't started _____ yet.
```

b. Use cues such as the following to create conversations about how things have changed since your students' parents were young. Write these cues on the board or on a handout for students:

(continued)

CHAPTER 8 279

EXPANSION ACTIVITIES (Continued)

> Did people . . .
>   wear jeans?
>   watch TV?
>   drive cars?
>   travel by airplane?
>   listen to rock music?
>   eat frozen food?
>   eat a lot of junk food?
>   use computers?
>   use fax machines?
>   talk on cell phones?
>   use the Internet?
>   send e-mail?
>
> Did women . . .
>   work?
>   wear pants?
>   wear suits?
>
> Did men . . .
>   stay home and take care of their children?
>   wear their hair long?
>   wear earrings?

c. Have students think of other questions to ask and continue the activity.

Text Page 108

 READING *Their Plans "Fell Through"*

FOCUS

- Past Perfect
- Past Perfect Continuous

NEW VOCABULARY

ceremony
fall through
"get cold feet"
get ready (for)

READING THE STORY

Optional: *Preview the story by having students talk about the story title and/or illustrations. You may choose to introduce new vocabulary beforehand, or have students encounter the new vocabulary within the context of the reading.*

1. Have students read silently, or follow along silently as the story is read aloud by you, by one or more students, or on the audio program.

2. Ask students if they have any questions. Check understanding of vocabulary.

   Language Note

   The expression *get cold feet* is most often used when someone fails to follow through with an important plan, such as a wedding, asking someone out on a date, or applying for an important job.

3. Check students' comprehension, using some or all of the following questions:

   What had Patty planned to do last weekend?
   What had she done before the party?
   Why did she have to cancel the party?

   What had Michael planned to do last weekend?
   How had he been preparing to ask for a raise?
   Did he get the raise? Why not?

   What had John and Julia planned to do last month?
   What had they done before the wedding?
   Did they get married? Why not?

READING EXTENSION

Role Play

1. Divide the class into pairs.

2. Have students role-play a conversation between a friend and one of the characters in the three stories. For example:

   A. Patty, how are you?
   B. I'm sick. And I'm so disappointed! I had to cancel my party!
   A. That's a shame. You had been preparing for the party for so long.
   B. I know. I had invited everyone, I had cleaned the house, and I had cooked my favorite food. But then I got sick!
   A. Well, maybe you can have another party soon.

3. Have students present their role plays to the class.

 IN YOUR OWN WORDS

1. Make sure students understand the instructions. Check understanding of the word *beforehand*.

2. Have students do the activity as written homework, using a dictionary for any new words they wish to use.

3. Have students present and discuss what they have written, in pairs or as a class.

CHAPTER 8   281

Text Page 109

 ON YOUR OWN
Accomplishments

FOCUS

- Past Perfect Continuous Tense

ON YOUR OWN ACTIVITY

1. Set the scene: "These are situations about people who worked very hard to get something." Check understanding of the title, *Accomplishments*.

2. Have students read each situation silently, or follow along silently as the situation is read aloud by you, by one or more students, or on the audio program.

3. Ask students if they have any questions. Check understanding of new vocabulary:

    Situation 1: *health food, deserve*
    Situation 2: *pass a test, driving school, rules of the road*
    Situation 3: *computer programming, extra, earn*

4. Check students' comprehension with the following questions:

    Situation 1:
    What did Stella Karp win last week?
    What had she been doing every morning?
    What had she been doing several months?
    What had she been doing every day after work?
    Why did she deserve to win?

    Situation 2:
    What did Stuart pass the other day?
    What had he been doing for several months?
    What had he been doing the past several weeks?
    What had he been studying since he was a little boy?
    Why did he deserve to pass his driver's test?

    Situation 3:
    What did Sally Compton get last week?
    What had she been doing for several months?
    What had she been studying in the evening?
    What had she been doing on the weekends?
    Why did she deserve to get a promotion?

5. In pairs, small groups, or as a class, have students tell about their own accomplishments.

WORKBOOK

Page 97

 JOURNAL

Have students write their journal entries at home or in class. Encourage students to use a dictionary to look up words they would like to use. Students can share their written work with other students if appropriate. Have students discuss what they have written as a class, in pairs, or in small groups.

Text Page 110

PRONUNCIATION Reduced *had*

> **Reduced *had*:** In spoken English, the pronunciation of *had* in the past perfect and past perfect continuous tenses is often reduced to [həd].

Focus on Listening

Practice the sentences in the left column. Say each sentence or play the audio one or more times. Have students listen carefully and repeat.

Focus on Pronunciation

Practice the sentences in the right column. Have students say each sentence and then listen carefully as you say it or play the audio.

If you wish, have students continue practicing the sentences to improve their pronunciation.

WORKBOOK

Check-Up Test: Pages 98–99

 ## CHAPTER SUMMARY

GRAMMAR

1. Divide the class into pairs or small groups.
2. Have students take turns forming sentences from the words in the grammar boxes. Student A says a sentence, and Student B points to the words from each column that are in the sentence. Then have students switch: Student B says a sentence, and Student A points to the words.

KEY VOCABULARY

Have students ask you any questions about the meaning or pronunciation of the vocabulary. If students ask for the pronunciation, repeat after the student until the student is satisfied with his or her own pronunciation.

EXPANSION ACTIVITIES

1. **Do You Remember the Words?** ★

   Check students' retention of the vocabulary depicted on the opening page of Chapter 8 by doing the following activity:

   a. Have students open their books to page 95 and cover the list of vocabulary words.

   b. Either call out a number and have students tell you the word, or say a word and have students tell you the number.

   Variation: You can also do this activity as a game with competing teams.

2. **Student-Led Dictation** ★

   a. Tell each student to choose a word or phrase from the Key Vocabulary list on text page 110 and look at it very carefully.

   b. Have students take turns dictating their words to the class. Everybody writes down that student's word.

   c. When the dictation is completed, call on different students to write each word on the board to check the spelling.

   (continued)

CHAPTER 8   283

EXPANSION ACTIVITIES (Continued)

3. Miming ★

a. Write on cards actions from the verb list on text page 110. For example:

do the tango	do gymnastics	catch a cold
fly a kite	get married	go camping
find	box	lose
bump into	go fishing	discuss
borrow	break	injure

b. Have students take turns picking a card from the pile and pantomiming the action on the card.

c. The class must guess what the person is doing.

Variation: This can be done as a game with competing teams.

4. Chain Story ★★

a. Write some of the words in the vocabulary list on small slips of paper and distribute one to each student.

b. Have the class form a circle. Begin the story by saying, "Herbert woke up early."

c. A student repeats what you said and adds another sentences using the word on the slip. For example, "Herbert woke up early. He had caught a cold and didn't feel well."

d. Continue having students add sentences using their designated vocabulary words.

e. You can do the activity again, beginning and ending with different students.

Variation 1: If the class is large, you may want to divide students into groups to give students more practice.

Variation 2: You can do this activity on paper. Have several students begin stories with their designated words and then pass their papers along for other students to add sentences. Then read aloud the final composition to the class.

5. Categorization ★★

a. Divide the class into pairs.

b. Call out one of the following categories.

sports
love
employment
friendship
illness and injury
the outdoors
housework
school
food

Have students look through the vocabulary list on text page 110 and find all the verbs that could belong to that category.

c. Have students read their lists aloud. Who has the longest list? Does everybody agree that all those verbs belong to the category?

284 CHAPTER 8

END-OF-CHAPTER ACTIVITIES

1. Board Game ★★★

   a. On poster boards or on manila file folders, make up game boards with a pathway consisting of separate spaces. You may use any theme or design you wish.

   b. Divide the class into groups of 2 to 4 students and give each group a game board and a die, and each student something to be used as a playing piece.

   c. Give each group a pile of cards face-down with statements written on them. Some sentences should be correct, and others incorrect. For example:

   > He had been working there since a long time.
   > They had never ate there before.
   > She already had gone there.
   > He hadn't spoken to me in a long time.
   > By the time we arrived, the lecture had already began.
   > We had felt very foolish.
   > She had flew on an airplane the Sunday before.
   > By the time I already had got there, the store had closed.
   > She enjoyed seeing a movie last week. She had seen a movie in a long time.
   > We were very tired because we hadn't slept the night before.
   > He hadn't ridden on a bike since he had been a child.
   > She felt nostalgic when she visited her old home.

   d. Each student in turn rolls the die, moves the playing piece along the game path, and after landing on a space, picks a card, reads the sentence, and says if it is *correct* or *incorrect*. If the statement is incorrect, the student must correct it. If the response is correct, the student takes an additional turn.

   e. The first student to reach the end of the pathway is the winner.

2. Scrambled Sentences ★★

   a. Divide the class into two teams.

   b. Write individual sentences out of order on the board. Use sentences based on the lessons in Chapter 8. For example:

   > he he playing played soccer had was before never it and
   >
   > every had the after piano been she school practicing day
   >
   > had they already to the it by the post office time closed got

   c. The first person to raise his or her hand, come to the board, and write the sentence in the correct order earns a point for that team.

   d. The team with the most points wins the scrambled sentence game.

   Variation: Write the words to several sentences on separate cards. Divide the class into small groups, and have students work together to put the sentences into correct order.

3. Finish the Sentence ★★

   Begin a sentence and have students add appropriate endings to the sentence using the past perfect. For example:

   Teacher: He was heartbroken because . . .
   Student: his girlfriend had left him.

   Teacher: She was furious because . . .
   Student: her friend had broken her laptop.

   Teacher: They felt foolish because . . .
   Student: they had forgotten about the party.

   Teacher: He caught a cold because . . .
   Student: he had walked in the rain.

   Teacher: She lost her job because . . .
   Student: the company had decided to move.

   (continued)

END-OF-CHAPTER ACTIVITIES (Continued)

Variation: This activity may be done as a class, in pairs or small groups, or as a game with competing teams.

4. **Dialog Builder!** ★★★

   a. Divide the class into pairs.

   b. Write several lines on the board from conversations in Chapter 8 such as the following:

   > That's terrible!
   > Poor _____!
   > I was heartbroken when _____.
   > Is it true?
   > How did _____ do that?

   c. Have each pair create a conversation incorporating those lines. Students can begin and end their conversations any way they wish, but they must include those lines in their dialogs.

   d. Call on students to present their conversations to the class.

WORKBOOK ANSWER KEY AND LISTENING SCRIPTS

WORKBOOK PAGE 88

A. BEFORE

1. had eaten
2. had, gotten
3. had, visited
4. had driven
5. had, cut
6. had spent
7. had, gone
8. had made
9. had seen
10. had, left
11. had had
12. had, given
13. had lost

WORKBOOK PAGE 90

C. LATE FOR EVERYTHING

1. had, left
2. had, begun
3. had, gone
4. had, closed
5. had, started
6. had, left
7. had, arrived

WORKBOOK PAGE 91

D. IN A LONG TIME

1. hadn't listened
2. hadn't seen
3. hadn't had
4. hadn't gone
5. hadn't remembered
6. hadn't ironed, hadn't shaved
7. hadn't lost
8. hadn't skied
9. hadn't gotten
10. hadn't taken off
11. hadn't studied
12. hadn't ridden

WORKBOOK PAGES 92–93

E. WORKING HARD

1. She was studying for her science test.
2. She had already written an English composition.
3. She hadn't practiced the trombone yet.
4. She hadn't read the next history chapter yet.
5. She hadn't memorized her lines for the school play yet.
6. He was hooking up the new printer.
7. He had already sent an e-mail to the boss.
8. He had already given the employees their paychecks.
9. He hadn't written to the Bentley Company yet.
10. He hadn't taken two packages to the post office yet.
11. They were cleaning the garage.
12. They had already assembled Billy's new bicycle.
13. They had already fixed the fence.
14. They hadn't repaired the roof yet.
15. They hadn't started to build a tree house yet.
16. She was playing squash.
17. She had already done yoga.
18. She had already gone jogging.
19. She hadn't lifted weights yet.
20. She hadn't swum across the pool 10 times yet.

WORKBOOK PAGE 94

F. WHAT HAD THEY BEEN DOING?

1. had been talking
2. had been living
3. had been working
4. had been going out
5. had been planning
6. had been thinking about
7. had been getting
8. had been borrowing
9. had been eating
10. had been rehearsing
11. had been looking forward
12. had been training
13. had been arriving

WORKBOOK PAGE 96

I. MARYLOU'S BROKEN KEYBOARD

1.

> Roger,
> I'm afraid there's something wrong with the fireplace in the living room. Also, the refrigerator is broken. I've been calling the landlord for three days on his cell phone, but he hasn't called back. I hope he calls me tomorrow.
> Marylou

CHAPTER 8   287

2.

> _L_ouise,
>
> I'm te_rr_ib_l_y wo_rr_ied about my b_r_other La_rr_y's hea_l_th. He hu_r_t his _l_eg whi_l_e he was p_l_aying baseba_ll_. He had a_l_ready dis_l_ocated his shou_l_der whi_l_e he was su_r_fing _l_ast F_r_iday. Acco_r_ding to his docto_r_, he is a_l_so having p_r_ob_l_ems with his b_l_ood p_r_essu_r_e and with his _r_ight w_r_ist. He _r_ea_ll_y should t_r_y to _r_e_l_ax and take _l_ife a _l_itt_l_e easie_r_.
>
> Ma_r_y_l_ou

3.

> A_r_no_l_d,
>
> Can you possib_l_y _r_ecommend a good _r_estau_r_ant in you_r_ neighbo_r_hood? I'm p_l_anning on taking my _r_elatives to _l_unch tomo_rr_ow, but I'm not su_r_e whe_r_e.
>
> We ate at a ve_r_y nice G_r_eek _r_estau_r_ant nea_r_ your apa_r_tment bui_l_ding _l_ast month, but I haven't been ab_l_e to _r_emembe_r_ the name. Do you know the p_l_ace?
>
> You_r_ f_r_iend,
> Ma_r_y_l_ou

4.

> _R_osa,
>
> I have been p_l_anning a t_r_ip to F_l_o_r_ida. I'_ll_ be f_l_ying to O_r_lando on F_r_iday, and I'_ll_ be _r_eturning th_r_ee days _l_ater. Have you eve_r_ been the_r_e? I _r_emembe_r_ you had fami_l_y membe_r_s who _l_ived in F_l_o_r_ida seve_r_a_l_ yea_r_s ago.
>
> P_l_ease w_r_ite back.
>
> A_ll_ my _l_ove,
> Ma_r_y_l_ou

WORKBOOK PAGE 97

J. LISTENING

Listen and choose the correct answer.

1. Steve lost his voice.
2. Is Beverly one of your relatives?
3. We just canceled our trip to South America.
4. Ricky has been failing all of his tests this year.
5. Francine dislocated her shoulder.
6. What did you and your students discuss in class?
7. My girlfriend and I rode on the roller coaster yesterday.
8. Grandma can't chew this piece of steak very well.
9. Jimmy loves my homemade food.
10. Did you see the motorcycles go by?
11. Do you think Mr. Montero will take a day off soon?
12. Amy wanted to ask her boss for a raise, but she got cold feet.
13. Have you heard that Margaret sprained her wrist?
14. I have to make an important decision.
15. I envy you.
16. I feel terrible. Debbie and Dan broke up last week.
17. My ankle hurts a lot.
18. I was heartbroken when I heard what happened.
19. Michael was furious with his neighbors.
20. We went to a recital last night.
21. Tom, don't forget to shine your shoes!
22. My friend Carla is extremely athletic.
23. My husband and I have been writing invitations all afternoon.
24. Charles rented a beautiful tuxedo for his niece's wedding.

Answers

1.	c	13.	b
2.	b	14.	a
3.	c	15.	c
4.	b	16.	c
5.	c	17.	b
6.	b	18.	c
7.	a	19.	b
8.	b	20.	a
9.	c	21.	b
10.	b	22.	c
11.	a	23.	a
12.	c	24.	c

WORKBOOK PAGES 98–99

CHECK-UP TEST Chapters 7–8

A.

1. eating
2. wrestling
3. to stop
4. boxing
5. Swimming
6. to skate
7. talking
8. doing

B.
1. hadn't spoken
2. had, done
3. had, left
4. hadn't written
5. hadn't had
6. hadn't taken
7. hadn't eaten
8. hadn't gone

C.
1. had been working
2. had been training
3. had been arguing
4. had been planning

D.
Listen and choose the correct answer.

Ex. My grandfather likes to . . .
1. Susan says she's going to stop . . .
2. My wife and I are thinking about . . .
3. David is considering . . .
4. I can't stand to . . .
5. You should definitely keep on . . .

Answers
1. b
2. a
3. b
4. b
5. a

Text Pages 111-114: *Side by Side Gazette*

 FEATURE ARTICLE
The Jamaican Bobsled Team

PREVIEWING THE ARTICLE

1. Have students talk about the title of the article and the accompanying photographs.

2. You may choose to introduce the following new vocabulary beforehand, or have students encounter it within the context of the article:

> bobsled
> compete
> competition
> event
> fact
> fiction
> first time
> four-person
> give up
> group
> impossible (n)
> include
> Jamaican
> last time
> movie soundtrack
> Olympics
> place (v)
> reggae music
> represent
> skating (n)
> skiing (n)
> soundtrack
> strong
> Summer Olympics
> swimming (n)
> team
> track
> training center
> two-person
> weight train
> Winter Olympic Games
> Winter Olympics

Places Around the World
> Calgary, Canada
> Caribbean
> Jamaica
> Lake Placid, New York
> Norway

READING THE ARTICLE

1. Have students read silently, or follow along silently as the article is read aloud by you, by one or more students, or on the audio program.

2. Ask students if they have any questions and check understanding of new vocabulary. Show the class a world map and have students identify the locations of all the place names.

3. Have students read the captions under the photos silently, or follow along silently as the captions are read aloud by you or by one or more students.

4. Ask students if they have any questions. Check understanding of new vocabulary.

5. Check students' comprehension of the article and captions by having students answer the following questions:

   Feature Article

   Why was the Jamaican Bobsled Team unusual?
   How had they trained for their first Olympic event in Calgary, Canada?
   How did they do in the 1988 Olympics?
   How did they train for the 1994 Olympic Winter Games?
   How had they become famous?
   How did they do in the 1994 Olympics?

   1st Caption

   Is the movie about the Jamaican Bobsled team true?
   What kind of music was in the movie?

   2nd Caption

   When were the first modern Olympics?
   Where were the first modern Olympics?
   What are some sports in the Summer Olympics?

290 SIDE BY SIDE GAZETTE

What are some sports in the Winter Olympics?

EXPANSION ACTIVITIES

1. Making Inferences ★★★

a. In small groups, have students discuss the following questions:

> Why do you think the Jamaican athletes decided to try bobsledding?
> Why do you think their story is so popular?

b. Have the groups report back to the class.

2. Who's the Best? ★★★

a. Divide the class into small groups. Have students discuss the following questions:

> What are your favorite Olympic sports?
> Which countries do best in those sports?
> Why are those countries so good at those sports?
> What kinds of advantages do they have?

b. Have students share their ideas with the class. Write any new sports vocabulary on the board.

3. Olympic Sports Game ★★★

a. Divide the class into several teams.

b. Have the students in each team work together to make a list of all the sports that are played in the Summer Olympics.

c. Have the teams share their lists with the class. Write any new sports vocabulary on the board. The team with the longest list wins.

d. Play the game again with sports that are played in the Winter Olympics.

AROUND THE WORLD
Children and Sports Training

1. Have students read silently or follow along silently as the text is read aloud by you, by one or more students, or on the audio program.

2. Check understanding of the expressions *distance running, sports training*.

3. Have students first work in pairs or small groups to respond to the questions. Then have students tell the class what they talked about. Write any new vocabulary on the board.

EXPANSION ACTIVITY

Dictate and Discuss ★★★

1. Divide the class into pairs or small groups.

2. Dictate sentences such as the following and then have students discuss them:

> If you want to be the best, you must begin training at a very young age.
> Parents often push their children too hard to win in sports.
> Young children should not compete in sports.
> Team sports teach children many good things.

3. Call on students to share their opinions with the rest of the class.

 ## INTERVIEW

1. Have students read silently, or follow along silently as the interview is read aloud by you, by one or more students, or on the audio program.

2. Ask students if they have any questions. Check understanding of the words *dream, figure-skating, level, medal, national, over and over, regional, routine*.

3. Check students' comprehension by having them answer the following questions:

> How many hours a day had Olga been practicing for the Regional Competition?
> How old was Olga when she began skating?
> What had she done by the time she was seven?
> How old was she when she found a professional coach?
> What did Olga win recently?
> What's the next step for her?
> If she wins in the National Competition, what's the next level?

EXPANSION ACTIVITY

Student Interviews ★★★

1. Identify students in the class who are especially good at a particular sport. Have the other students form groups around these people. Then have students interview these athletes. Brainstorm with the class possible questions to ask. For example:

   What's your favorite sport?
   How long have you been doing that sport?
   When did you begin?
   Do you remember your first coach or teacher?
   Have you ever thought about competing? Why or why not?
   What's the most difficult part of your sport?
   How often do you practice?

2. Have the groups move from speaker to speaker so they may interview all the athletes in the class.

FACT FILE
Countries in the Olympics

1. Ask students: "How many countries do you think participate in the Olympics?" Write students' estimates on the board.

2. Read the table aloud as the class follows along. Ask students: "Whose number was the closest?"

3. For a comprehension activity, state the number of countries participating in the Olympics and have students tell you what year you are describing. For example:

   Teacher: 50 countries participated in the Olympics.
   Student: That was in 1924.

4. As a class, in pairs, or in small groups, have students discuss the questions posed in the fact file.

LISTENING Olympic Game Highlights

1. Set the scene: "This is a news report about the highlights of the most recent Olympics."

   Culture Notes

   When covering large and complex sporting events, such as the Olympics, television reporters often report just the *highlights*, the most interesting moments.

   Three medals are awarded in an Olympic event. A *gold medal* is awarded to the first-place winner, a *silver medal* to the second-place winner, and a *bronze medal* to the third-place winner.

   Language Note

   The simple present tense is often used to describe an ongoing action. Sports commentators use it to narrate the actions in the sports event they are describing.

2. There is a lot of new vocabulary in the listening. Encourage students to listen for key words that will help them identify which sport is being described. For example:

   basketball: game, team, basket
   swimming: water
   gymnastics: fell, graceful
   running: run, move
   skating: ice, move, gracefully, music

NEW VOCABULARY

Basketball	*Running*
basket	a time of *two hours*
shoot	finish line
Swimming	lead (n)
even (adj)	race
lane	*Skating*
move through	*five* point *eight*
speed	judge
Gymnastics	marks
balance beam	score
floor routine	

292 SIDE BY SIDE GAZETTE

LISTENING SCRIPT

Listen to the Olympic Game highlights. Match the highlight and the sport.

And now, sports fans, let's finish today's program with highlights of the Olympic Games. Here are five of my favorite moments in the most recent summer and winter games:

There are three seconds left in the game. Number 38 gets ready to shoot again. His team needs this point to win the game. He shoots, and it's in the basket! [*Buzzer*] That's it! The game is over! And the United States wins 99 to 98. The U.S. gets the gold medal!

Kirshner is still in front. But wait! Look at Tanaka in the next lane! What speed! Look at him move through the water! Tanaka is even with Kirshner. Now Tanaka is ahead! And Tanaka wins the event! Japan wins the gold medal, Germany gets the silver, and Hungary gets the bronze.

Natasha knows she must do this floor routine perfectly to win the gold medal. She had problems today when she fell off the balance beam, and that's usually her best event. She's doing very well. What a strong and graceful athlete! And here's the most difficult part of her routine. Beautiful! But, oh . . . she falls! Natasha has fallen at the very end of her routine. What a shame! There will be no gold for Natasha this year.

What a race! Anderson is still in first place and Sanchez is right behind him in second place. Look at Sanchez run! He's moving ahead of Anderson. The lead has changed! Sanchez is now in front! He crosses the finish line! Sanchez wins with a time of two hours, ten minutes, and eleven seconds. So Mexico wins the gold, Canada gets the silver, and France gets the bronze.

And Tamara leaves the ice after a beautiful long program! I think that's one of the best programs I've ever seen at the Olympics. She moved so gracefully to the music. Let's see what the judges think. Look at these marks! Five-point-eight, five-point-nine, five-point-nine, five-point-eight, five-point-seven, five-point-nine, five-point-nine, six-point-oh, five-point-eight. Excellent scores! Tamara wins the gold medal! Look at all the flowers people are throwing on the ice! I'm sure this is the happiest day of Tamara's life!

Answers

1. b
2. e
3. d
4. c
5. a

EXPANSION ACTIVITIES

1. **Listening Comprehension** ★★★

   Have students listen to the audio program again and answer the following questions:

   Basketball
   How many seconds were left in the game?
   Who won?
   By how many points did they win?

   Swimming
   Who was in the lead in the swimming competition?
   What happened at the end of the competition?
   Where is Tanaka from?

   Gymnastics
   How has Natasha's day been?
   In what event did she fall?
   Did Natasha win the gold medal?

   Running
   Who won the running competition?
   Where is Sanchez from?
   Where is Anderson from?

   Ice-skating
   Did Tamara skate alone?
   How many judges were watching her?
   Why were people throwing flowers on the ice?

2. **Association Game** ★★

   a. Divide the class into pairs or small groups.

   b. Call out a sport and tell students to write down all the words they associate with that sport. For example:

   running: lanes, sneakers, fast, finish line
   baseball: ball, uniforms, run, throw

   c. Have a student from each pair or group come to the board and write their words.

   Variation: Do the activity as a game in which you divide the class into teams. The team with the most number of associations is the winner.

SIDE BY SIDE GAZETTE 293

FUN WITH IDIOMS

> Break a leg!
> Get off my back!
> Hold your tongue!
> Keep your chin up!
> Keep your eye on the ball!
> Put your best foot forward!

INTRODUCTION AND PRACTICE

For each idiom, do the following:

1. Have students look at the illustration.
2. Present the idiom. Say the expression and have the class repeat it chorally and individually. Check students' pronunciation of the words.

DO YOU KNOW THESE EXPRESSIONS?

Have students match the expressions with their meanings.

Answers

1. c
2. f
3. a
4. d
5. b
6. e

EXPANSION ACTIVITIES

1. **Mystery Conversations** ★★★

   a. Divide the class into pairs.

   b. Have each pair choose an idiom

   c. Write roles such as the following on word cards and give one to each pair of students:

   | a parent and a child |
   | a teacher and a student |
   | two teammates |
   | two athletes competing against each other |
   | a boss and an employee |
   | a coach and an athlete |
   | a fan and an athlete |
   | a brother and a sister |

   d. Have each pair create a short dialog that uses one of the idioms. The dialogs should be appropriate for the roles the students have on their cards.

   e. Have each pair present their dialog to the class. Then have the other students guess who the people are: Are they a parent and a child? Are they two competing athletes?

2. **Idiom Challenge!** ★★★

   a. Divide the class into pairs.

   b. Have each pair create a conversation in which they use as many of the idioms from text page 113 as they can.

   c. Have the pairs present their conversations to the class. Which pair used the most idioms?

294 SIDE BY SIDE GAZETTE

WE'VE GOT MAIL!

THE 1ST LETTER TO *SIDE BY SIDE*

1. Have students read silently, or follow along silently as the letter is read aloud by you, by one or more students, or on the audio program.

2. Ask students if they have any questions. Check understanding of the words *gerund, infinitive, rule, verb*.

3. Check students' comprehension by having them decide whether these statements are true or false:

    The writer wants to know the rules for using gerunds and infinitive. *(True)*
    The writer uses incorrect examples of gerunds and infinitives. *(False)*

4. Ask students:

    Are you ever confused about gerunds and infinitives?
    Can you think of another example of a verb that takes a gerund?
    Can you think of another example of a verb that takes an infinitive?
    Can you think of another example of a verb that takes a gerund and an infinitive?

THE RESPONSE FROM *SIDE BY SIDE*

1. Have students read silently, or follow along silently as the letter is read aloud by you, by one or more students, or on the audio program.

2. Ask students if they have any questions. Check understanding of vocabulary.

3. Check students' comprehension by having them decide whether these statements are true or false:

    There are rules about how to use gerunds and infinitives. *(False)*
    The best way to learn how to use gerunds and infinitives is to practice using the verbs. *(True)*

4. Ask students: "How do you memorize these verbs and their forms?"

THE 2ND LETTER TO *SIDE BY SIDE*

1. Have students read silently, or follow along silently as the letter is read aloud by you, by one or more students, or on the audio program.

2. Ask students if they have any questions. Check understanding of the words *grammar, past perfect tense, present perfect, present perfect continuous*.

3. Check students' comprehension by having them decide whether these statements are true or false:

    The writer understands when to use this tense: "I have been." *(True)*
    The writer understands when to use this tense: "She has been playing." *(True)*
    The writer understands when to use this tense: "We had written." *(False)*

4. Ask students: "Have you ever had this question?"

THE RESPONSE FROM *SIDE BY SIDE*

1. Have students read silently, or follow along silently as the letter is read aloud by you, by one or more students, or on the audio program.

2. Ask students if they have any questions. Check understanding of the word *difference*.

3. Check students' comprehension by having them decide whether these statements are true or false:

    People use the present perfect to speak about an event in the past. *(True)*
    People use the present perfect to speak about an event before another event in the past. *(False)*

4. Ask students:

    Do you have a tense like the past perfect in your language?
    Can you explain how the present perfect is different from the past perfect?

SIDE BY SIDE GAZETTE   **295**

EXPANSION ACTIVITY

What's Wrong? ★★★

1. Divide the class into pairs or small groups.
2. Write several sentences such as the following on the board or on a handout. Some of the sentences should be correct, and others incorrect. For example:

   I began skating when I was three.
   You should avoid to eat eggs.
   By the time I was seven, I had been skiing for four years.
   She can't stand to eat fish.
   He practiced to do the routine for ten hours.
   She decided become a figure skater.
   We want to learn to speak English well.
   He didn't stop running after he fell.
   They had been study for it for a long time.
   Before we left, we have already cleaned the house.
   I had looked forward to the trip.
   She had been swimming . . . and she had never swam before.
   When we arrived, they had already started eating.
   They've read the book before they saw the movie.

3. The object of the activity is for students to identify which sentences are incorrect and then correct them.
4. Have students compare their answers.

   Variation: Do the activity as a game with competing teams. The team that successfully completes the task in the shortest time is the winner.

GLOBAL EXCHANGE

1. Set the scene: "Stamp4 is writing to a keypal."
2. Introduce the words *collect, envelope, penpal, stamp, stamp collection*.
3. Have students read silently or follow along silently as the message is read aloud by you, by one or more students, or on the audio program.

4. Ask students if they have any questions. Check understanding of vocabulary.
5. Options for additional practice:
   - Have students write a response to Stamp4 and share their writing in pairs
   - Have students correspond with a keypal on the Internet and then share their experience with the class.

 WHAT ARE THEY SAYING?

FOCUS

- Preparing for an Important Event

Have students talk about the characters and the situation, and then create role plays based on the scene. Students may refer back to previous lessons as a resource, but they should not simply reuse specific conversations.

Note: You may want to assign this exercise as written homework, having students prepare their role plays, practice them the next day with other students, and then present them to the class.

296 *SIDE BY SIDE* GAZETTE

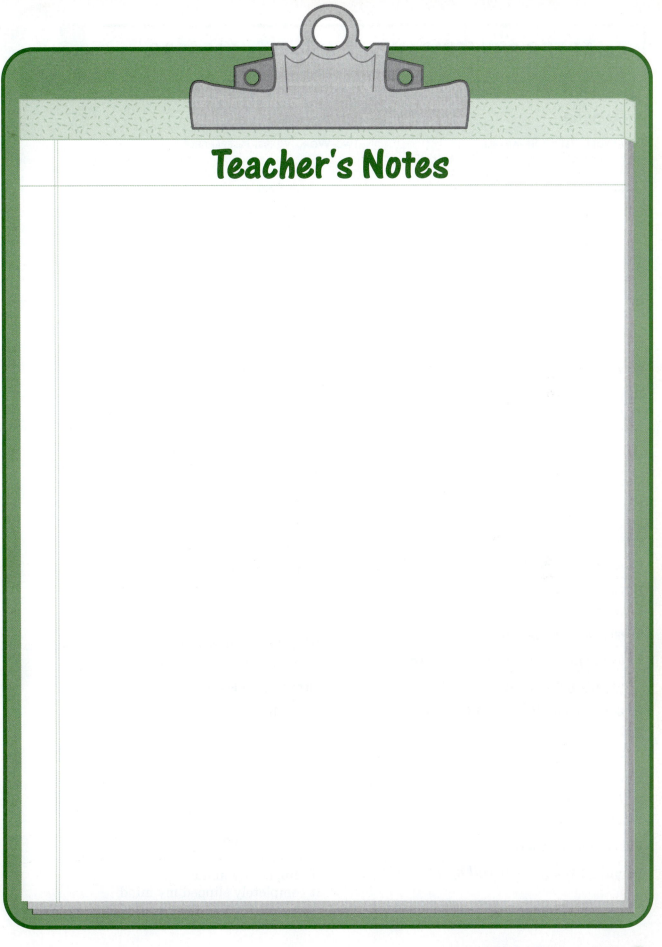

CHAPTER 9 OVERVIEW: Text Pages 115–130

GRAMMAR

Two-Word Verbs: Separable

| I'm going to | **put on** my boots.
put my boots **on**.
put them **on**. |

Two-Word Verbs: Inseparable

| I | **hear from** Aunt Betty
hear from her
~~hear Aunt Betty from~~
~~hear her from~~ | very often. |

FUNCTIONS

Extending an Invitation

Would you like to *play tennis with me this morning*?
Would you like to *get together today*?
Are you free *after you take them back*?

Declining an Invitation

I'd like to, but I can't.
I'd really like to, but I can't.
I'm afraid I can't.

Expressing Inability

I can't.
I'm afraid I can't.

Expressing Obligation

I have to *fill out my income tax form*.
I've really got to do it.

Asking for and Reporting Information

What size do you wear?
  Size 32.
How much *does it* cost?
  The *usual* price is _____ dollars.

Inquiring About Intention

Will you *take it back*?
When are you going to *call up your uncle*?

Expressing Intention

I'm going to *call him up next week*.
I'll *call you in the morning*.
I'll *turn it off* right away.

Inquiring About Remembering

Did you remember to *turn off the oven*?

Asking for Advice

Do you think I should *keep these old love letters*?

Offering Advice

I think you should *throw them away*.

Offering a Suggestion

Let's *get together tomorrow instead*.
Why don't you *look through all of our suits and pick out the one you like*?

Offering to Help

May I help you?

Expressing Want–Desire

I'm looking for a *suit*.
Do you have any *suits* that are *a little darker*?

Remembering and Forgetting

I forgot all about it!
I completely forgot!
It slipped my mind!
It completely slipped my mind!

298 CHAPTER 9

NEW VOCABULARY

Adjectives

baggy
concerned
discouraged
final
free
loose
narrow
plaid
plain
regular
tight
usual

Verbs

accept
check
erase
fit
go with
kiss
notice
refuse

Separable Two-Word Verbs

bring back
call up
clean up
cross out
do over
drop off
figure out
fill out
give back
hand in
hang up
hook up
leave on
look up
pick out
pick up
put away
put on
take back
take down
take out
think over
throw away
throw out
try on
turn down
turn on
turn off
use up
wake up
write down

Inseparable Two-Word Verbs

call on
feel like
get along with
get over
go with
hear from
leave on
look through
look up to
pick on
run into
run out of
take after

Celebrations

Christmas decorations
New Year's decorations
wedding guest
wedding invitation

Places Around the US

Arizona
Colorado
Denver
Phoenix

Clothing

button
trousers
zipper

Clothing Sizes

extra large
medium
size

Money

on sale
refund

Adverbs

accidentally
apparently
constantly
eventually
incorrectly
simply

Time Expressions

so far
within

Miscellaneous

accident report
alarm
answer (n)
child rearing (n)
cleaner's
college application form
definition
dressing room
during the week
ex-boyfriend
ex-girlfriend
garbage
happiness
heat
hospital bill
insurance form
library book
modem
paper
portrait
selection
toy

EXPRESSIONS

I'd like to, but I can't.
in the first place
Maybe some other time.
No problem at all.
Walk home
You're in luck!

CHAPTER 9 299

Text Page 115: Chapter Opening Page

VOCABULARY PREVIEW

You may want to present these words before beginning the chapter, or you may choose to wait until they first occur in a specific lesson. If you choose to introduce them at this point, here are some suggestions:

1. Have students look at the illustrations on text page 115 and identify the words they already know.

2. Present the vocabulary. Say each word and have the class repeat it chorally and individually. Check students' understanding and pronunciation of the words.

3. Practice the vocabulary as a class, in pairs, or in small groups. Have students cover the word list and look at the pictures. Practice the words in the following ways:
   - Say a word and have students tell the number of the illustration.
   - Give the number of an illustration and have students say the word.

Text Page 116: Sometime Next Week

FOCUS

- Separable Two-Word Verbs:

bring back	*pick up*
call up	*take back*
fill out	*take down*
hang up	*throw out*
hook up	*turn on*

- Separating Two-Word Verbs with Pronouns

CLOSE UP

RULE:	A two-word verb consists of a main verb plus a particle. In most cases, the addition of the particle changes the meaning of the verb.
EXAMPLES:	I'm going to **take** the bus. She's going to **take back** her books. We're going to **take down** the Christmas tree.
RULE:	In some cases, the two-word verb is interchangeable with the main verb.
EXAMPLES:	I'm going to **call** my uncle. I'm going to **call up** my uncle.
RULE:	Some two-word verbs are *separable*. The noun object can follow the two-word verb or the two-word verb can be separated by a noun object.
EXAMPLES:	He's going to **throw out** his old newspapers. He's going to **throw** his old newspapers **out**.
RULE:	When the noun object of a two-word verb is replaced by a pronoun, the pronoun *must* be placed between the two parts of the verb.
EXAMPLES:	She's going to **fill out** her college application forms. She's going to **fill** them **out**. I'm going to **hook up** my new computer. I'm going to **hook** it **up**.

See text page 130 for a list of separable two-word verbs introduced in Chapter 9.

INTRODUCING THE MODEL

1. Have students look at the model illustration.
2. Set the scene: "A husband and wife are talking. He's upset because a repairman has just taken the TV set from their house."
3. Present the model.
4. Full-Class Repetition.
5. Ask students if they have any questions. Check understanding of the two-word verb *bring back*.
6. Group Choral Repetition.
7. Choral Conversation.
8. Call on one or two pairs of students to present the dialog.

   (For additional practice, do Choral Conversation in small groups or by rows.)
9. Read the verbs in the box at the top of text page 116, which show how other two-word verbs can be separated by a pronoun:

   bring back the TV
   bring it back

   call up Sally
   call her up

   throw out the newspapers
   throw them out

SIDE BY SIDE EXERCISES

Examples

1. A. When are you going to call up your uncle in Ohio?
   B. I'm going to call him up sometime next week.
2. A. When is Ted going to throw out his old newspapers?
   B. He's going to throw them out sometime next week.

1. **Exercise 1:** Introduce the verb *call up*. Call on two students to present the dialog. Then do Choral Repetition and Choral Conversation practice.
2. **Exercise 2:** Introduce the verb *throw out*. Same as above.
3. **Exercises 3–9:** Either Full-Class Practice or Pair Practice.

New Vocabulary

3. fill out college application form
4. pick up cleaner's
5. take back library book
6. hook up
7. hang up portrait
8. take down Christmas decorations
9. turn on heat

WORKBOOK

Page 100

302   CHAPTER 9

EXPANSION ACTIVITIES

1. **Grammar Chain** ★★

   a. Write the following conversation model and phrases on the board:

   > A. When are you going to _____?
   > B. I'm going to _____ sometime tomorrow.

   > pick up the groceries
   > fill out the income tax form
   > take back the computer
   > hang up the photograph
   > turn on the heat
   > throw out that old couch
   > call up Aunt Bertha
   > hook up the computer
   > take down that ugly portrait

   b. Start the chain game by saying:

   Teacher *(to Student A)*: When are you going to pick up the groceries?

   c. Student A answers according to the model on the board and then asks a different question to Student B, and the chain continues. For example

   Student A: I'm going to pick them up sometime tomorrow.
   (to Student B): When are you going to throw out that old couch?

   Student B: I'm going to throw it out sometime tomorrow.
   (to Student C): When are you going to call up Aunt Bertha?

   Etc.

2. **What's Missing?** ★★

   a. Write on the board:

   > I'm going to _____ soon.

   > bring back   pick up
   > call up   take back
   > fill out   take down
   > hang up   throw out
   > hook up   turn on

   b. Say each of the object cues below. For each one, have students choose a two-word verb that fits that object and make a sentence using the model on the board. For example:

   Teacher: Uncle Bill
   Student: I'm going to call up Uncle Bill soon.

   Object Cues:

   > the college application form *(fill out)*
   > some friends at the airport *(pick up)*
   > these old shoes *(throw out)*
   > the TV at the repair shop *(pick up)*
   > my new photographs *(hang up)*
   > the hammer and screwdriver you borrowed *(bring back)*
   > the heat *(turn on)*
   > the library books *(take back)*
   > tickets at the symphony *(pick up)*
   > the garbage *(throw out)*
   > the new fax machine *(hook up)*
   > the Christmas decorations *(take down)*
   > the air conditioner *(turn on)*
   > my income tax form *(fill out)*
   > these old souvenirs we don't want anymore *(throw out)*
   > my sister at the dentist's office *(pick up)*
   > the videos *(take back)*
   > this portrait of my grandmother *(hang up)*
   > Mr. and Mrs. Garcia *(call up)*

3. **Finish the Sentence Line-Up** ★★

   a. Write the following two-word verbs on the board:

   (continued)

CHAPTER 9   303

EXPANSION ACTIVITIES (Continued)

bring back	pick up
call up	take back
fill out	take down
hang up	throw out
hook up	turn on

b. Have students line up in two rows opposite each other.

c. Have the first student in the *left* row begin a sentence with one of the verbs on the board. The opposite student in the *right* row must complete the sentence. For example:

   Student 1: I turned on . . .
   Student 2: the heat.

d. Then have the next student in the *right* row begin a sentence with another verb, and the opposite student in the *left* row complete it. For example:

   Student 3: He hung up . . .
   Student 4: the picture.

e. Continue going back and forth until all the students have had an opportunity to either begin or complete a sentence.

4. Miming ★★

a. Write the following on cards:

fill out a form	turn on the heat	hang up a portrait
pick up clothes at the cleaner's	call up your girlfriend/boyfriend	hook up a computer and a printer
take down decorations	throw out old newspapers	take back videos to the video store

b. Have students take turns picking a card from the pile and pantomiming the action on the card.

c. The class must guess what the person is doing.

Variation: Do the activity as a game with competing teams.

5. Match the Sentences ★

a. Make a set of split sentence cards such as the following:

Every Sunday we call . . .	up the family.
We have to throw . . .	out the old newspapers.
She is going to fill . . .	out the application form.
They haven't brought . . .	back the TV yet.
You can hook . . .	up the DVD player with the computer.
You should take . . .	down that horrible portrait of yourself.
Please turn . . .	on the TV.
She likes to hang . . .	up Christmas decorations around the house.
I've got to pick . . .	up my car at the repair shop.

b. Distribute a card to each student.

c. Have students memorize the sentence portion on their cards, then walk around the room trying to find their corresponding match.

d. Then have pairs of students say their completed sentences aloud to the class.

6. Sense or Nonsense? ★★

   a. Divide the class into small groups.
   b. Make multiple sets of cards from Activity 5, mix them up, and distribute them to each group, keeping the beginning and ending cards in different piles.
   c. Have students take turns picking up one card from each pile and reading the sentence to the group. For example:

   | I've got to pick . . . | on the TV. |

   d. That group decides if the sentence makes sense or is nonsense.
   e. After all the cards have been picked, have the groups lay out all the cards and put together all the sentence combinations that make sense.

7. Tomorrow! ★★

   a. Write on the board:

   > I never have the time to _____.
   > I think I'll _____ tomorrow.

   b. Call out a two-word verb from text page 116 and have students complete the sentence, drawing on their own experiences. For example:

   Teacher: call up
   Student: I never have the time to call up my Uncle William. I think I'll call him up tomorrow.

   c. Have students share their sentences in groups or pairs. Ask the class: What do you avoid doing? Why?

CHAPTER 9   305

Text Page 117: Oh, No! I Forgot!

FOCUS

- Separable Two-Word Verbs:
    hand in
    put on
    take off
    take out
    turn off
- Separating Two-Word Verbs with Pronouns and Nouns

INTRODUCING THE MODEL

This model should be presented twice: once with the object noun after the verb *(turn off the oven)* and once with the noun between the two parts of the verb *(turn the oven off)*.

1. Have students look at the model illustration.
2. Set the scene: "A husband and wife are having dinner together. They turned on the oven while they were cooking dinner, and it's still on."
3. Present the model.
4. Full-Class Repetition.

    Pronunciation Note

    The pronunciation focus of Chapter 9 is **Linking "t" Between Vowels** (text page 130). You may wish to model this pronunciation at this point and encourage students to incorporate it into their language practice.

    I'll turn **it off** right away.

    I'll fill **it out** right away.

5. Ask students if they have any questions. Check understanding of the verb *turn off*.
6. Group Choral Repetition.
7. Choral Conversation.
8. Call on one or two pairs of students to present the dialog.
9. Expand the model with further practice. Call on pairs of students to present the model, using *the lights, the radio*.

    (For additional practice, do Choral Conversation in small groups or by rows.)

SIDE BY SIDE EXERCISES

Examples

1. A. Did you remember to take back the videos/take the videos back?
   B. Oh, no! I forgot! I'll take them back right away.
2. A. Did you remember to fill out the accident report/fill the accident report out?
   B. Oh, no! I forgot! I'll fill it out right away.

1. **Exercise 1:** Call on two students to present the dialog. Then do Choral Repetition and Choral Conversation practice.
2. **Exercise 2:** Introduce the phrase *accident report*. Same as above.
3. **Exercises 3–9:** Either Full-Class Practice or Pair Practice.

    New Vocabulary
    3. alarm
    4. put away
       toy
    5. hand in
    6. wake up
    7. put on
    8. take off
    9. take out
       garbage

306 CHAPTER 9

How to Say It!

Remembering and Forgetting: In spoken English there are many ways to express forgetting something.

1. Present the expressions.
2. Full-Class Repetition.
3. Ask students if they have any questions. Check understanding of the new expressions: *I forgot all about it! I completely forgot! It slipped my mind! It completely slipped my mind!*
4. Group Choral Repetition.
5. Have students practice again the conversations in this lesson using any of these new expressions.
6. Call on pairs of students to present their conversations to the class.

WORKBOOK

Pages 101–102

EXPANSION ACTIVITIES

1. Finish the Verb! ★

Say each of the verbs below and have students add any particles they have learned to make them into two-word verbs:

Teacher	Student
bring	bring back
call	call up
fill	fill out
hand	hand in
hang	hang up
hook	hook up
pick	pick up
put	put away
	put on
throw	throw out
turn	turn on
	turn off
take	take back
	take down
	take off
	take out
wake	wake up

2. Associations ★

a. Divide the class into pairs or small groups.
b. Call out a two-word verb, and tell students to write down all the words they associate with that verb. For example:

  take back: the videos/the books
  fill out: the form/the application/the report
  turn on: the TV/the radio/the alarm

c. Have a student from each pair or group come to the board and write their words.

Variation: Do the activity as a game in which you divide the class into teams. The team with the most number of associations is the winner.

3. What's the Word? ★★

a. Write the following verbs on the board:

bring back	take back
call up	take down
fill out	take out
hand in	take off
hang up	throw out
hook up	turn off
pick up	turn on
put away	wake up
put on	

A. Have you _____ yet?
B. Yes. I _____ yesterday.

(continued)

CHAPTER 9   307

EXPANSION ACTIVITIES (Continued)

b. Point to a verb and call on a pair of students to create a conversation, using the model on the board. For example:

call up
A. Have you called up Uncle Marvin yet?
    or
   Have you called Uncle Marvin up yet?
B. Yes. I called him up yesterday.

hand in
A. Have you handed in your English homework yet?
    or
   Have you handed your English homework in yet?
B. Yes. I handed it in yesterday.

4. Scrambled Sentences ★★

a. Divide the class into teams.

b. Write individual sentences out of order on the board. For example:

> it   away   off   I'll   turn   right
> you   your   yesterday   in   homework   handed
> going   off   to   his   he's   shoes   take

c. The first person to raise his or her hand, come to the board, and write the sentence in the correct order earns a point for that team.

d. The team with the most points wins the *scrambled sentence game*.

Variation: Write the words to several sentences on separate cards. Divide the class into small groups, and have students work together to put the sentences into correct order.

5. Finish the Sentence ★★

a. Write the following verbs on the board:

> bring back   take back
> call up   take down
> fill out   take out
> hand in   take off
> hang up   throw out
> hook up   turn off
> pick up   turn on
> put away   wake up
> put on

b. Begin the sentences below, and have students complete them with an appropriate two-word verb. For example:

Teacher: I've already read these library books, so I think I'll . . .
Student: take them back.

Questions:

My clothes are ready at the cleaner's. I think I'll . . . *(pick them up).*
I haven't spoken to Aunt Clara for a while, so I think I'll . . . *(call her up).*
I've already completed my homework, so I think I'll . . . *(hand it in).*
I love this new portrait. I'm going to . . . *(hang it up).*
Is the heat too high? I'll . . . *(turn it off).*
My new printer doesn't work. I'm having trouble . . . *(hooking it up).*
My income tax forms are on the kitchen table. It's time to . . . *(fill them out).*
I don't want these old magazines anymore. I think I'll . . . *(throw them out).*
I'm upset. It's very hot, and my air conditioner is broken. I can't . . . *(turn it on).*
I'm unhappy without my TV. When is the repairman going to . . . *(bring it back)?*
It's July, and my Christmas decorations are still in my living room. I think it's time to . . . *(take them down).*
It's late, and the children are still sleeping. It's time to . . . *(wake them up).*
The garbage is still in the kitchen. Please . . . *(take it out).*
Do you want to see my new coat? I'll . . . *(put it on).*

I've already watched all these videos. I think
I'll . . . *(take them back).*
Is the oven still on? You should . . . *(turn it off).*
Billy, your toys are in the living room, and
guests are coming for dinner. Please . . .
(put them away).

6. Listen for the Right Answer ★★

a. Write the following on the board:

> A. Have you _____ yet?
> B. _____ ? Yes. I _____ a few
>   minutes ago.

b. Have pairs of students create conversations based on the model. Give Student A a *verb cue* and Student B a card with two *object cues*. Based on the verb he or she hears, Student B must choose the correct object to complete the dialog. For example:

<u>Student A</u> <u>Student B</u>

| turn it on | my coat the heat |

A. Have you turned it on yet?
B. The heat? Yes. I turned it on a few
   minutes ago.

Cue cards:

turn it on	my coat / the heat
turn it off	my jacket / the stove
fill it out	the accident report / a new suit
throw it out	the garbage / my new raincoat
hand it in	the telephone / my homework
put them away	my books / my children
take it off	the oven / my coat
hang them up	the portraits / the magazines

CHAPTER 9   309

Text Page 118

READING *A Busy Saturday*

FOCUS

- Separable Two-Word Verbs

NEW VOCABULARY

during the week
feel like
modem

READING THE STORY

Optional: *Preview the story by having students talk about the story title and/or illustrations. You may choose to introduce new vocabulary beforehand, or have students encounter the new vocabulary within the context of the reading.*

1. Have students read silently, or follow along silently as the story is read aloud by you, by one or more students, or on the audio program.
2. Ask students if they have any questions. Check understanding of vocabulary.
3. Check students' comprehension, using some or all of the following questions:

    Why is everybody in the Peterson family going to be busy today?
    What does Mr. Peterson have to do? Why?
    What does Mrs. Peterson have to do? Why?
    What does Steve have to do? Why?
    What does Michael have to do? Why?
    What does Stacey have to do? Why?
    What does Abigail have to do? Why?

✓ READING *CHECK-UP*

Q & A

1. Call on a pair of students to present the model.

2. Introduce the new expressions: *I'd like to, but I can't. Maybe some other time.*
3. Have students work in pairs to create new dialogs.
4. Call on pairs to present their new dialogs to the class.

READING EXTENSION

Tic Tac Question Formation

1. Draw a tic tac grid on the board and fill it with question words. For example:

Why?	Does?	What?
Which?	When?	Do?
Is?	Are?	Where?

2. Divide the class into two teams. Give each team a mark: *X* or *O*.
3. Have each team ask a question about the reading that begins with one of the question words, then provide the answer to the question. If the question and answer are correct, the team gets to put its mark in that space. For example:

    X Team: Does Abigail have to take the
    library books back?
    No, she doesn't.

Why?	X	What?
Which?	When?	Do?
Is?	Are?	Where?

4. The first team to mark out three boxes in a straight line—vertically, horizontally, or diagonally—wins.

How About You?

Have students do the activity in pairs or as a class.

Text Page 119: I Don't Think So

FOCUS

- Separable Two-Word Verbs:

cross out	think over
do over	throw away
give back	throw out
leave on	turn down
look up	write down

INTRODUCING THE MODEL

1. Have students look at the model illustration.
2. Set the scene: "Two friends are looking through some old things. One of them has found some old letters from a boyfriend. She doesn't know what to do with them."
3. Present the model.
4. Full-Class Repetition.
5. Ask students if they have any questions. Check understanding of the two-word verb *throw away*.
6. Group Choral Repetition.
7. Choral Conversation.
8. Call on one or two pairs of students to present the dialog.

   (For additional practice, do Choral Conversation in small groups or by rows.)

SIDE BY SIDE EXERCISES

Examples

1. A. Do you think I should hand in my homework?
   B. No, I don't think so. I think you should do it over.
2. A. Do you think I should use up this old milk?
   B. No, I don't think so. I think you should throw it out.

1. Exercise 1:
   a. Set the scene: "This person has made a lot of mistakes on his homework. He's asking what he should do."
   b. Introduce the verb *do over*.
   c. Call on two students to present the dialog. Then do Choral Repetition and Choral Conversation practice.

2. Exercise 2:
   a. Set the scene: "There's a little more milk in the carton. It's old, but it might be okay to drink."
   b. Introduce the verb *use up*.
   c. Same as above.

3. Exercises 3–9: Either Full-Class Practice or Pair Practice.

New Vocabulary

3. erase	7. think over
cross out	8. ex-boyfriend
4. leave on	give back
5. write down	9. accept
6. definition	ex-girlfriend
look up	turn down

Language Note

Exercises 8 and 9: *Ex-boyfriend* and *ex-girlfriend*. The prefix *ex-* means *former*. Other examples of this are *ex-husband* and *ex-wife*.

As you introduce the new two-word verb in each exercise, set each of the following scenes:

3. "This person made a lot of mistakes on his homework. He isn't going to do it over, but he wants to fix the mistakes."
4. "It's very hot today. The air conditioner has been on, but now it's too cold."
5. "This person can't remember Amy's telephone number."
6. "Some students use a dictionary when they don't know the definition of a word. Other students like to ask the teacher."

CHAPTER 9 311

7. "When you have an important decision to make, it's a good idea to think about it for a while before you make your decision."

8. "This person has broken up with her boyfriend, but she still has the ring he gave her."

9. "This person has been invited to the wedding of an old girlfriend and can't decide what to do."

WORKBOOK

Page 103

EXPANSION ACTIVITIES

1. Finish the Sentence! ★★

Read the following incomplete sentences and have students complete each with an appropriate two-word verb. For example:

Teacher: I didn't ask anyone the definition of that word. I . . .
Student: looked it up.

Sentences:

I didn't ask anyone the definition of that word. I . . .
I didn't accept the invitation. I . . .
I didn't erase my mistakes. I . . .
I didn't keep those old letters. I . . .
I didn't use up the old milk in my refrigerator. I . . .
I didn't try to remember their phone number. I . . .
I didn't leave on the air conditioner. I . . .
I didn't keep the hammer I borrowed from my neighbor. I . . .
I didn't hand in my homework. I . . .
I didn't make my decision right away. I . . .

Variation: Divide the class into teams and do the activity as a game. Say a sentence, and the first person to raise his or her hand and complete the sentence correctly gets a point for that team. The team with the most points wins the game.

2. Match the Conversations ★★

a. Make up the following matching cards:

| Don't keep those letters! | Throw them away! |

Don't drink this old milk!	Throw it out!
Don't hand in that terrible composition!	Do it over!
Don't erase your mistakes!	Cross them out!
Don't leave the heat on!	Turn it off!
Don't try to remember their address!	Write it down!
Don't ask me the definition of this word!	Look it up!
Don't make your decision right away!	Think it over!
Don't accept that invitation!	Turn it down!
Don't keep the screwdriver you borrowed!	Give it back!

b. Distribute a card to each student.

c. Have students memorize the sentences on their cards, and then have students walk around the room saying their sentences until they find their match.

312   CHAPTER 9

d. Then have pairs of students say their matched sentences aloud to the class.

3. Concentration ★

   a. Shuffle the cards from Activity 2 above and place them face down in four rows of 5 each.

   b. Divide the class into two teams. The object of the game is for students to find the matching cards. Both teams should be able to see all the cards, since *concentrating* on their location is an important part of playing the game.

   c. A student from Team 1 turns over two cards. If they match, the student picks up the cards, that team gets a point, and the student takes another turn. If the cards don't match, the student turns them face down, and a member of Team 2 takes a turn.

   d. The game continues until all the cards have been matched. The team with the most correct matches wins the game.

   Variation: This game can also be played in groups and pairs.

4. Question the Answers! ★★

   a. Write the following two-word verbs on the board:

bring back	take back
call up	take down
cross out	take off
do over	take out
fill out	think over
give back	throw away
hand in	throw out
hang up	turn down
hook up	turn off
look up	turn on
pick up	wake up
put away	write down
put on	

   b. Dictate answers and have students write questions for which these answers would be correct. For example:

   Answer: His brother's dictionary.
   Question: What did he give back?

   Answer: A new recipe.
   Question: What did you write down?

   Answer: Her computer.
   Question: What did she turn on?
   What did she hook up?

   c. Have students compare their questions with each other.

   Answers and possible questions:

   His brother's dictionary.
   (What did he give back?)

   A new recipe?
   (What did you write down?)

   Her computer.
   (What did she hook up?)
   (What did she turn on?)

   His shoes.
   (What did he put on?)

   Her old letters.
   (What did she throw out?)

   Your homework.
   (What did you do over?)
   (What did you hand in?)

   Their mistakes.
   (What did they cross out?)

   The invitation.
   (What did they turn down?)

   His old milk.
   (What did he throw out?)

   My TV.
   (What did you turn on?)
   (What did you turn off?)

   The definition.
   (What did you look up?)

   The decision.
   (What did she think over?)

   Their photographs.
   (What did they hang up?)

   (continued)

CHAPTER 9   313

EXPANSION ACTIVITIES (Continued)

Her tax forms.
(What did she fill out?)

Variation: Write the answers on cards. Divide the class into groups and give each group a set of cards.

5. Synonyms ★★

a. Write on the board:

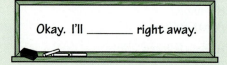

call up	pick up
cross out	take back
do over	think over
fill out	throw away
give back	turn down
hand in	turn off
hang up	use up
look up	write down

Okay. I'll _____ right away.

b. Read each of the statements below. Have students respond with an appropriate two-word verb synonym from the list on the board. For example:

    Teacher: Don't forget to phone her.
    Student: Okay. I'll call her up right away.

Situations:

Don't forget to phone her. *(call her up)*
Don't forget to return this book. *(take it back)*
Please complete the form. *(fill it out)*
Don't forget to find the meaning of this word.
    (look it up)

Please get off the telephone. *(hang up)*
Please write these exercises again.
    (do them over)
Don't forget to copy Mr. Franklin's address.
    (write it down)
Don't forget to get my shirt at the cleaner's.
    I need it this morning. *(pick it up)*
Please fix your mistakes. *(cross them out)*
Don't forget to give the teacher your
    homework. *(hand it in)*

6. What's Wrong? ★★★

a. Divide the class into pairs or small groups.

b. Write several sentences such as the following on the board or on a handout. Some of the sentences should be correct, and others incorrect. For example:

  I think you should leave the heat on.
  He's going to bring back it soon.
  He should think over it.
  They forgot to hand their homework in.
  She'll take the old garbage out right away.
  It slipped out of my mind!
  I forgot all about it!
  They should use up it.
  We try to every address write down.
  He should turn them down.

c. The object of the activity is for students to identify which sentences are incorrect and then correct them.

d. Have students compare their answers.

Variation: Do the activity as a game with competing teams. The team that successfully completes the task in the shortest time is the winner.

314   CHAPTER 9

Text Pages 120–121

READING Lucy's English Composition

FOCUS

- Separable Two-Word Verbs

NEW VOCABULARY

accidentally
apparently
check (v)
discouraged
in the first place
incorrectly
paper
simply
throw away

READING THE STORY

Optional: *Preview the story by having students talk about the story title and/or illustration. You may choose to introduce new vocabulary beforehand, or have students encounter the new vocabulary within the context of the reading.*

1. Have students read silently, or follow along silently as the story is read aloud by you, by one or more students, or on the audio program.
2. Ask students if they have any questions. Check understanding of vocabulary.
3. Check students' comprehension, using some or all of the following questions:

    Why is Lucy discouraged?
    Why did her English teacher tell her to do her English composition over?
    What had she done with her mistakes?
    Why had she used several words incorrectly?
    Why hadn't she written her homework on the correct paper?

✓ READING CHECK-UP

TRUE, FALSE, OR MAYBE?

1. True
2. False
3. Maybe
4. True
5. False
6. Maybe

WHAT'S THE WORD?

1. give it back
2. hand it in
3. do it over
4. throw it away
5. look it up
6. cross them out

READING EXTENSION

Good Study Habits

1. Have pairs of students write a list of good study habits. For example:

    Look up new words in the dictionary.
    Write down the new word and its definition in a special place.
    Write down all homework assignments in a special place so you don't forget.

2. Have pairs of students share their lists with the class. As they talk, write their ideas on the board. According to students in the class, what are the most important study habits?

CHAPTER 9   315

COMPLETE THE LETTERS

Before doing the activity, show students on a map the locations of *Denver, Colorado,* and *Phoenix, Arizona.*

"Discouraged Donald" Letter

1. gave it back
2. thrown them away
3. thought it over
4. turned me down
5. call her up

"Frustrated Fran" Letter

1. turns it off
2. turns it on
3. hung it up
4. took it down
5. put them away
6. took them out

For homework, have students write letters of advice to "Discouraged Donald" and "Frustrated Fran". Have students share their letters in class.

Text Pages 122–123: Would You Like to Get Together Today?

FOCUS

- Review: Separable Two-Word Verbs
- Introduction: *clean up, drop off, figure out*

INTRODUCING THE MODEL

1. Have students look at the model illustration.
2. Set the scene: "Two friends are talking on the telephone."
3. Present the model.
4. Full-Class Repetition.
5. Ask students if they have any questions. Check understanding of the words *free, drop off*.

   ### Language Notes

   The expression *Are you free?* means *Are you available?* or *Do you have free time?*

   In *I'd really like to*, the word *I'd* is a contraction of *I would*. The expression *I'd really like to* and similar expressions with *I'd* are often used in polite language for expressing one's wants and needs.

6. Group Choral Repetition.
7. Choral Conversation.
8. Divide the class into pairs and have students practice the model conversation.
9. Call on pairs of students to present the dialog.

   (For additional practice, do Choral Conversation in small groups or by rows.)

SIDE BY SIDE EXERCISES

Examples

1. A. Would you like to get together today?
   B. I'm afraid I can't. I have to clean up my living room.
   A. Are you free after you clean it up?
   B. I'm afraid not. I also have to throw out all my old newspapers.
   A. Would you like to get together after you throw them out?
   B. I'd really like to, but I can't. I ALSO have to pick my brother up at the train station.
   A. You're really busy today! What do you have to do after you pick him up?
   B. Nothing. But by then I'll probably be exhausted. Let's get together tomorrow instead.
   A. Fine. I'll call you in the morning.

2. A. Would you like to get together today?
   B. I'm afraid I can't. I have to figure out my hospital bill
   A. Are you free after you figure it out?
   B. I'm afraid not. I also have to fill out my insurance form.
   A. Would you like to get together after you fill it out?
   B. I'd really like to, but I can't. I ALSO have to call the doctor up.
   A. You're really busy today! What do you have to do after you call him/her up?
   B. Nothing. But by then I'll probably be exhausted. Let's get together tomorrow instead.
   A. Fine. I'll call you in the morning.

1. **Exercise 1:** Introduce the verb *clean up*. Call on two students to present the dialog. Then do Choral Repetition and Choral Conversation practice.

CHAPTER 9   317

2. **Exercise 2:** Introduce the words *figure out, hospital bill, insurance form.* Same as above.

3. **Exercises 3–5:** Either Full-Class Practice or Pair Practice.

> **New Vocabulary**
> 3. New Year's decorations
> 4. pick out
>   wedding guest
>   wedding invitation

4. **Exercise 6:** For homework, have students write a new conversation using any two-word verbs they wish. Have students present their dialogs in the next class.

WORKBOOK

Pages 104–105

EXPANSION ACTIVITIES

1. Scrambled Dialog ★

a. Write each line of the model conversation on text page 122 or any of the exercises on text page 123 on a separate card. Scramble the cards.

b. Give the cards to 9 students. Have them unscramble the lines and put together the conversation.

2. What's the Word? ★★

a. Write on the board:

```
call up        look up       take off
clean up       pick out      take out
figure out     pick up       think over
hand in        put on        turn off
hang up        take down
```

b. Read the sentences below and have students respond with an appropriate two-word verb from the list on the board. For example:

Teacher: Your coat is on the floor.
Student: I'll pick it up.

Sentences:

Your coat is on the floor. *(pick it up) (hang it up)*
Which tie should I wear with this suit?
   (pick it out)
We're supposed to write our name, address,
   and phone number on this form. *(fill it out)*
What does "edible" mean? *(look it up)*
How much is 2436 and 8941? *(figure it out)*
There's a lot of garbage in the kitchen.
   (take it out)
What are you going to do, stay or leave?
   (think it over)
The basement is really dirty! *(clean it up)*
Those pictures on the wall look terrible!
   (take them down)
You should wear those new gloves I gave you.
   (put them on)
That black tie doesn't look very good with your
   brown suit. *(take it off)*
Who's watching TV? Nobody. *(turn it off)*
I have to talk to you this weekend about
   something very important. *(call you up)*

3. That's a Good Idea ★★★

a. Write on the board:

```
A. _____.
B. Why don't you _____ ?
A. That's a good idea. I think I'll _____
   _____ _____ right now.
```

318   CHAPTER 9

b. Write the following on cue cards:

> I'd like to hear some good music.

> This coat is too warm.

> My living room is so dirty, I can't stand it.

> I can never remember your phone number.

> I really don't need these boots during the summer.

> The birthday party was a week ago. These decorations are starting to look terrible.

> I'd really like to talk to my friend Bob in New York.

> I'd really like to know the definition of that word.

> My homework looks terrible! It has too many mistakes.

> I really want to wear my blue suit, but it's at the cleaner's.

> I'd really like to watch the news on TV.

> I'll never be able to remember the directions to Amanda's house.

c. Divide the class into pairs and give each pair a card. Have Speaker A begin a conversation by reading a cue. Speaker B continues the conversation using any two-word verb and the model on the board. For example:

  A. I'd like to hear some good music.
  B. Why don't you turn on the CD player?
  A. That's a good idea. I'll turn it on right now.

4. Mysteries ★★★

   a. Divide the class into pairs.

   b. Write the following question on the board:

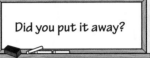

   c. Have each pair create a short dialog that begins with "Did you put it away?" The dialogs should elaborate about *it* without revealing what *it* is.

   d. Have each pair present their dialog to the class. Then have the other students guess what *it* is. For example:

   A. Did you put it away?
   B. Yes. I put it in the closet, under some shoes. I don't think she can find it.
   A. I hope she likes it.
   B. We'll give it to her after we have the cake tomorrow.

   [a birthday gift]

5. Chain Story ★★

   a. Tell students they're going to construct a story about preparing for a party, using two-word verbs. Ask: "What two-word verbs have you learned?" Make a list of the verbs on the board as they name them.

   b. Begin the story by saying: "Today is a busy day. First, I have to clean up my apartment."

   c. Have each student take a turn in which he or she repeats or rewords the last sentence of the previous person and then adds a new line using one of the two-word verbs. For example:

   Student 1: First I have to clean up my apartment. After I clean it up, I have to put up some decorations.

   (continued)

CHAPTER 9   319

EXPANSION ACTIVITIES (Continued)

Student 2: After I put them up, I have to pick up some flowers.

Student 3: After I pick them up, I have to hang up some decorations.

Etc.

6. **Student Lists** ★★

   a. Write the following events on the board:

   > a job interview
   > a play performance
   > a wedding
   > a marriage proposal
   > a New Year's Eve party
   > a vacation in Tahiti

   b. Divide the class into pairs.

   c. Have each pair choose one of the events on the board and make up a list of all the things to do before that event. Encourage students to use their newly learned two-word verbs.

   d. Have students share their lists with the class.

   Variation: ★★★ Have students read their lists, but not say what the event is, and the class has to guess the event based on the list.

7. **Group Story Game** ★★★

   a. Divide the class into small groups.

   b. Have each group write a story in which they use as many two-word verbs as they can.

   c. The group that includes the most number of two-word verbs is the winner of the *story game*.

320   CHAPTER 9

Text Page 124: I Heard from Her Just Last Week

FOCUS

- Inseparable Two-Word Verbs

    call on *look up to*
    get along with *pick on*
    get over *run into*
    hear from *run out of*
    look through *take after*

CLOSE UP

RULE: Some two-word verbs are inseparable. The noun or pronoun object must always follow the two-word verb.

EXAMPLES: I **heard from** Aunt Betty last week.
I **heard from** her last week.

See text page 130 for a list of inseparable two-word verbs introduced in Chapter 9.

INTRODUCING THE MODEL

1. Have students look at the model illustration.
2. Set the scene: "A brother and a sister are talking. They usually get a letter from their aunt every month."
3. Present the model.
4. Full-Class Repetition.
5. Ask students if they have any questions. Check understanding of the verb *hear from*.
6. Group Choral Repetition.
7. Choral Conversation.
8. Call on one or two pairs of students to present the dialog.

    (For additional practice, do Choral Conversation in small groups or by rows.)

SIDE BY SIDE EXERCISES

Examples

1. A. Have you run into Mr. Clark recently?
   B. Yes, I have. I ran into him just last week.
2. A. Have you run out of paper recently?
   B. Yes, I have. I ran out of it just last week.

1. **Exercise 1:** Introduce the verb *run into*. Call on two students to present the dialog. Then do Choral Repetition and Choral Conversation practice.
2. **Exercise 2:** Introduce the verb *run out of*. Same as above.

CHAPTER 9   321

3. **Exercises 3–6:** Either Full-Class Practice or Pair Practice.

> **New Vocabulary**
> 3. get over
> 4. call on
> 5. look through
> 6. pick on

How About You?

Introduce the new expressions *get along with, take after, look up to.* Write these new expressions on the board. Then point to each one as you tell the following situations:

> "Mary *gets along with* her sister very well. They never argue, and they like each other very much. They enjoy spending time together."

> "John *takes after* his father. John's father is good at mathematics. John does very well in math, too. His father can sing very well, and John sings well, too."

> "Mr. and Mrs. Smith have a son named Mark. Mark really *looks up to* his parents. He thinks they're wonderful people, and he hopes he'll be like them when he grows up."

Have students answer the questions in pairs or as a class.

WORKBOOK

Pages 106–107

EXPANSION ACTIVITIES

1. Scrambled Sentences ★

a. Divide the class into teams.

b. Write individual sentences out of order on the board. For example:

> week last over got it she
> looked we yesterday them through
> our into yesterday ran neighbor we

c. The first person to raise his or her hand, come to the board, and write the sentence in the correct order earns a point for that team.

d. The team with the most points wins the scrambled sentence game.

Variation: Write the words to several sentences on separate cards. Divide the class into small groups, and have students work together to put the sentences into the correct order.

2. Finish the Sentence Line-Up ★★

a. Write the following two-word verbs on the board:

> hear from
> pick on
> take after
> run into
> call on
> get along with
> look through
> get over
> look up to

b. Have students line up in two rows opposite each other.

c. Have the first student in the *left* row begin a sentence with one of the verbs on the board. The opposite student in the *right* row must complete the sentence. For example:

322   CHAPTER 9

Student 1: I heard from . . .
Student 2: my grandmother.

d. Then have the next student in the *right* row begin a sentence with another verb, and the opposite student in the *left* row complete it. For example:

Student 3: He called on . . .
Student 4: the student.

e. Continue going back and forth until all the students have had an opportunity to either begin or complete a sentence.

3. Match the Sentences ★★

a. Make a set of split sentence cards such as the following:

We don't have enough flour to make bread. We ran . . .	out of it.
I see my neighbor all the time. Every day I run . . .	into her.
My house is very messy. I'm going to clean . . .	it up.
I'm confused by my insurance form. I can't figure . . .	it out.
Every morning I take my son to school. I drop . . .	him off.

I don't like this new chair. I'm going to take . . .	it back.
My daughter fights with my son. She always picks . . .	on him.
They were very sick. I hope they got . . .	over it.
He's just like his mother. He takes . . .	after her.
I miss my Aunt Clara. I'd like to hear . . .	from her.
Sam usually gives the correct answer. Teachers like to call . . .	on him.

b. Distribute a card to each student.

c. Have students memorize the sentence portion on their cards, then walk around the room trying to find their corresponding match.

d. Then have pairs of students say their completed sentences aloud to the class.

(continued)

CHAPTER 9   323

EXPANSION ACTIVITIES (Continued)

4. Sense or Nonsense? ★★

Use the cards from Activity 3.

a. Mix up the cards and distribute sets of cards to each group, keeping the beginning and ending cards in different piles.

b. Have students take turns picking up one card from each pile and reading the sentence to the group. For example:

| I miss my Aunt Clara. I'd like to hear . . . | after her. |

c. That group decides if the sentence makes *sense* or is *nonsense*.

d. After all the cards have been picked, have the groups lay out all the cards and put together all the sentence combinations that make sense.

5. Category Dictation ★★

a. Have students draw two columns on a piece of paper. At the top of one column, have students write <u>Separable</u>, and at the top of the other column, have them write <u>Inseparable</u>.

b. Dictate various two-word verbs from the chapter and have students write them in the appropriate column. For example:

<u>Separable</u>	<u>Inseparable</u>
hang up	hear from
look up	look through
pick out	pick on
take out	take after

6. Synonyms: Guess Who? ★★

a. Write the following two-word verbs on the board:

call on	look up to
get along with	pick on
get over	run into
hear from	run out of
look through	take after

I don't know. Who _____ ?

b. Read the sentences below and have students respond with an appropriate two-word verb from the list on the board. For example:

Teacher: Guess who I met downtown!
Student: I don't know. Who did you run into?

Sentences:

Guess who I met downtown! *(run into)*
Guess who my little brother was fighting with! *(pick on)*
Guess who wrote me a letter! *(hear from)*
Guess which student Ms. Thomas asked about two-word verbs *(call on)*
Guess who I admire! *(look up to)*
Guess who doesn't have any more paper! *(run out of)*
Guess which of my parents I'm similar to! *(look like/take after)*
Guess who my favorite friends are! *(get along with)*
Guess who doesn't have the flu any more! *(get over)*

7. Create a Story ★★★

a. Put the following on the board:

b. Set the scene: "Julie is twelve years old. She's a healthy, happy young girl."

c. Ask the following questions about *Julie*. Have students use their imaginations to make up answers.

1. Julie has two younger brothers. Does she pick on them? (When? Why?)
2. Julie is the best student in her class. Does she get embarrassed when the teacher calls on her?

324   CHAPTER 9

3. How does she get along with the other students in her class?
4. Julie likes to get letters and phone calls. Who does she like to hear from?
5. Who does Julie look up to? Who looks up to Julie?
6. After school Julie likes to go to the drug store and buy a soda. Who does she hope she runs into there?
7. Last year Julie had a boyfriend, but they broke up. Has she gotten over it yet?

8. What's Wrong? ★★★

   a. Divide the class into pairs or small groups.

   b. Write several sentences such as the following on the board or on a handout. Some of the sentences should be correct, and others incorrect. For example:

   > I ran into Herbert yesterday.
   > I ran them into yesterday.
   > She'll drop them off at 2:00.
   > I'll fill out it at home.
   > He doesn't get along with them.
   > You should write down it.
   > She doesn't take him after.
   > The teacher always calls me on.
   > She got over the flu.
   > They did their homework over.

   c. The object of the activity is for students to identify which sentences are incorrect and then correct them.

   d. Have students compare their answers.

Variation: Do the activity as a game with competing teams. The team that successfully completes the task in the shortest time is the winner.

Text Page 125

READING A Child-Rearing Problem

FOCUS

- Inseparable Two-Word Verbs

NEW VOCABULARY

answer (n)
child rearing (n)
concerned
constantly
eventually
so far

READING THE STORY

Optional: *Preview the story by having students talk about the story title and/or illustration. You may choose to introduce new vocabulary beforehand, or have students encounter the new vocabulary within the context of the reading.*

1. Have students read silently, or follow along silently as the story is read aloud by you, by one or more students, or on the audio program.
2. Ask students if they have any questions. Check understanding of vocabulary.
3. Check students' comprehension, using some or all of the following questions:

    How do Timmy and his little sister Patty get along with each other?
    What do they constantly do?
    When does he pick on her?
    When does she pick on him?
    Why are their parents concerned?
    How have they looked for an answer to their problem?
    Have they been successful so far?
    What are they hoping?

READING EXTENSION

Child-Rearing Advice

1. Divide the class into pairs and ask them to write a list of advice for the parents.
2. Have the pairs share their lists with the class. As they talk, write their ideas on the board and discuss them as a class.

✓ READING CHECK-UP

TRUE, FALSE, OR MAYBE?

1. False
2. True
3. True
4. False
5. Maybe

CHOOSE

Before doing the exercise, introduce the word *kiss*.

1. a
2. a
3. b
4. b
5. a
6. b
7. a
8. b

326   CHAPTER 9

Text Pages 126–127

ROLE PLAY *May I Help You?*

FOCUS

- Review: Separable and Inseparable Two-Word Verbs

ROLE PLAY

1. Set the scene: "A salesman in a department store is talking to a customer."

2. Go over the conversational model. Introduce the following new vocabulary:

baggy	regular
dressing room	selection
extra large	size
fit	tight
loose	try on
medium	usual
narrow	within
No problem at all.	You're in luck.
plain	

Language Note

May I help you?, *I think I'll take (it/them)*, and *Thanks for your help* are expressions that are typically used in shopping situations.

3. Present Exercise 1 at the bottom of text page 127 with a student. Then do Choral Repetition practice.

4. Divide the class into pairs, and have students practice Exercises 1–3.

5. Call on pairs of students to present their role plays.

Example

1. A. May I help you?
   B. Yes, please. I'm looking for a suit.
   A. What size do you wear?
   B. *(Size 40.)*
   A. Here. How do you like this one?
   B. Hmm. I think it's a little too *(dark)*. Do have any suits that are a little *(lighter)*?
   A. Yes. We have a wide selection. Why don't you look through all of our suits on your own and pick out the one you like?
   A. Can I try it on?
   B. Of course. You can try it on in the dressing room over there.

   [5 minutes later]
   A. Well, how does it fit?
   B. I'm afraid it's a little too *(short)*. Do you have any suits that are a little *(longer)*?
   A. Yes, we do. I think you'll like THIS suit. It's a little *(longer)* than the one you just tried on.
   B. Will you take it back if I decide to return it?
   A. Of course. No problem at all. Just bring it back within *(10)* days, and we'll give you your money back.
   B. Fine. I think I'll take it. How much does it cost?
   A. The usual price is *(200)* dollars. But you're in luck! We're having a sale this week, and all of our suits are *(20)* percent off the regular price.
   B. That's a real bargain! I'm glad I decided to buy a suit this week. Thanks for your help.

6. **Exercise 4:** For homework, have students write a new role play with any article of clothing they wish. Encourage students to use dictionaries to find new words they wish to use. Have students act out their role plays in the next class.

WORKBOOK

Page 108

CHAPTER 9 327

Text Pages 128–129

READING *On Sale*

FOCUS

- Separable and Inseparable Two-Word Verbs

NEW VOCABULARY

button	notice	trousers
final	on sale	walk home
go with	plaid	zipper
happiness	refund (n)	
men's clothing store	refuse (v)	

READING THE STORY

Optional: Preview the story by having students talk about the story title and/or illustrations. You may choose to introduce new vocabulary beforehand, or have students encounter the new vocabulary within the context of the reading.

1. Have students read silently, or follow along silently as the story is read aloud by you, by one or more students, or on the audio program

2. Ask students if they have any questions. Check understanding of vocabulary.

3. Check students' comprehension, using some or all of the following questions:

   Why did Gary go to a men's clothing store yesterday?
   What did he look through?
   What did he pick out first?
   How did it fit?
   What did he pick out next?
   How did it fit?
   Finally, what did he pick out?
   How did it fit?
   Then what did he decide to buy?
   What did he look through?
   What did he pick out first?
   How did they fit?
   What did he pick out next?
   How did they fit?
   Finally, what did he pick out?
   How did they fit?
   Why was Gary especially happy?
   Why didn't Gary's happiness last very long?
   What did he do the next day?
   Why did the people at the store refuse to give him his money back?
   What will Gary do the next time he buys something on sale?

✓ READING CHECK-UP

WHAT'S THE SEQUENCE?

1. Gary went shopping for clothes yesterday.
2. Gary picked out a few jackets he really liked.
3. The brown jacket seemed to fit perfectly.
4. He picked out several pairs of trousers.
5. A pair of plaid pants fit very well.
6. He paid only half of the regular price.
7. He walked home feeling very happy.
8. But then, Gary noticed problems with the jacket and the pants.
9. Gary went back and asked for a refund.
10. The store refused to give him back his money.
11. He walked home feeling very upset and angry.

328   CHAPTER 9

READING EXTENSION

Consumer Advice

1. Have pairs of students write a list of advice for Gary (or any other consumer). For example:

    Always read the signs next to the cashier.
    Always ask about the store's return policy.
    Look for holes in the clothes.
    Keep your receipt.

2. Have pairs of students share their lists with the class. As they talk, write their ideas on the board.

How About You?

Have students do the activity in pairs or as a class.

 LISTENING

Listen and choose what the people are talking about.

1. A. Where can I try them on?
   B. The dressing room is over there.
2. A. Now remember, you can't bring them back!
   B. I understand.
3. A. Have you filled it out yet?
   B. No. I'm having some trouble. Can you help me?
4. A. Please drop them off at the school by eight o'clock.
   B. By eight o'clock? Okay.
5. A. Where should I hang them?
   B. What about over the fireplace?
6. A. Have you thought it over?
   B. Yes, I have.
7. A. It's cold in here.
   B. You're right. I'll turn it on.
8. A. Should we use it up?
   B. No. Let's throw it out.
9. A. What are you going to do?
   B. I'm going to turn it down.

Answers

1. a
2. a
3. a
4. b
5. a
6. b
7. b
8. a
9. b

CHAPTER 9 329

Text Page 130

 PRONUNCIATION *Linking "t" Between Vowels*

> The consonant "t" is pronounced with a flapped [d] sound when it occurs between vowels.

Focus on Listening

Practice the sentences in the left column. Say each sentence or play the audio one or more times. Have students listen carefully and repeat.

Focus on Pronunciation

Practice the sentences in the right column. Have students say each sentence and then listen carefully as you say it or play the audio.

If you wish, have students continue practicing the sentences to improve their pronunciation.

 ## JOURNAL

Have students write their journal entries at home or in class. Encourage students to use a dictionary to look up words they would like to use. Students can share their written work with other students if appropriate. Have students discuss what they have written as a class, in pairs, or in small groups

 ## CHAPTER SUMMARY

GRAMMAR

1. Divide the class into pairs or small groups.
2. Have students take turns forming sentences from the words in the grammar boxes. Student A says a sentence, and Student B points to the words from each column that are in the sentence. Then have students switch: Student B says a sentence, and Student A points to the words.

EXPANSION ACTIVITY

Verb Quiz ★★

1. Divide the class into teams.
2. Call out a two-word verb and a pronoun. Have the teams take turns producing a correct and complete sentence using the verb and pronoun. For example:

   Teacher: hook up, it
   Team 1: I'm going to hook it up tomorrow.

3. A team wins a point every time it produces a correct sentence. The team with the most points wins.

KEY VOCABULARY

Have students ask you any questions about the meaning or pronunciation of the vocabulary. If students ask for the pronunciation, repeat after the student until the student is satisfied with his or her own pronunciation.

EXPANSION ACTIVITIES

1. **Do You Remember the Words? ★**

   Check students' retention of the vocabulary depicted on the opening page of Chapter 9 by doing the following activity:

   a. Have students open their books to page 115 and cover the list of two-word verbs.

   b. Either call out a number and have students tell you the verb, or say a verb and have students tell you the number.

   Variation: You can also do this activity as a game with competing teams.

2. **Student-Led Dictation ★**

   a. Tell each student to choose a two-word verb from the Key Vocabulary list on text page 130 and look at it very carefully.

---

 330   CHAPTER 9

b. Have students take turns dictating their words to the class. Everybody writes down that student's word.

c. When the dictation is completed, call on different students to write each word on the board to check the spelling.

3. Miming ★

   a. Write on cards actions from the verb list on text page 130.

   b. Have students take turns picking a card from the pile and pantomiming the action on the card.

   c. The class must guess the verb and then produce a correct sentence using it.

   Variation: This can be done as a game with competing teams.

4. Chain Story ★★

   a. Write some of the two-word verbs in the vocabulary list on small slips of paper and distribute one to each student.

   b. Have the class form a circle. Begin the story by saying: "Sandra has a lot of things to do today."

   c. A student repeats what you said and adds another sentence using the word on the slip. For example: "Sandra has a lot of things to do today. She has to figure out a problem."

   d. Continue having students add sentences using their designated vocabulary words.

   e. You can do the activity again, beginning and ending with different students.

   Variation 1: If the class is large, you may want to divide students into groups to give students more practice.

   Variation 2: You can do this activity on paper. Have several students begin stories with their designated words and then pass their papers along for other students to add sentences. Then read aloud the final composition to the class.

CHAPTER 9

END-OF-CHAPTER ACTIVITIES

1. **Scrambled Sentences** ★

   a. Divide the class into teams.

   b. Write individual sentences out of order on the board. Use sentences based on the lessons in Chapter 9. For example:

   > you think throw should I away them
   >
   > it completely off to I turn forgot
   >
   > few ran we into ago days a them
   >
   > up to afternoon pick he this them has
   >
   > me teacher called recently my hasn't on English

   c. The first person to raise his or her hand, come to the board, and write the sentence in the correct order earns a point for that team.

   d. The team with the most points wins the scrambled sentence game.

   Variation: Write the words to several sentences on separate cards. Divide the class into small groups, and have students work together to put the sentences into correct order.

2. **Dialog Builder!** ★★★

   a. Divide the class into pairs.

   b. Write several lines on the board from the conversations in Chapter 9 such as the following:

   > It completely slipped my mind!
   > I'm afraid not.
   > No, I don't think so.
   > Oh, no!

   c. Have each pair create a conversation incorporating those lines. Students can begin and end their conversations any way they wish, but they must include those lines in their dialogs.

   d. Call on students to present their conversations to the class.

3. **Finish the Sentence** ★★

   Begin a sentence using one of the two-word verbs on text page 130 and have students repeat what you said and add appropriate endings to the sentence.

Teacher	Student
He's going to pick . . .	me up at 8:00.
We have to fill . . .	out the insurance forms.
Can you look . . .	up the word in the dictionary?
She hopes to hear . . .	from her boyfriend tonight.

   Variation: This activity may be done as a class, in pairs or small groups, or as a game with competing teams.

WORKBOOK ANSWER KEY AND LISTENING SCRIPTS

WORKBOOK PAGE 100

A. WHAT ARE THEY SAYING?

1. pick him up
2. turned it on
3. take them back
4. fill them out
5. hang it up
6. hook it up
7. throw them out
8. took it back
9. took them down
10. call her up

WORKBOOK PAGE 101

B. WHAT ARE THEY SAYING?

1. turn on
   turn it on
2. hand, in
   hand it in
3. wake up
   wake them up
4. turn, off
   turn it off
5. take off
   take them off
6. put, away
   put them away
7. Put, on
   put them on
8. bring, back
   bring her back

WORKBOOK PAGE 103

D. WHAT ARE THEY SAYING?

1. do it over
2. gave it back
3. hook it up
4. think it over
5. look it up
6. turn him down
7. throw them away
8. written it down
9. cross them out
10. turned it off

WORKBOOK PAGE 104

E. WHAT'S THE WORD?

1. put away
2. hook up
3. take back
4. wake up
5. call up
6. write down
7. clean up
8. put away
9. throw out
10. hang up

WORKBOOK PAGE 105

F. WHAT SHOULD THEY DO?

1. think it over
2. give it back
3. used it up
4. look it up
5. figure it out
6. wake them up
7. turn it off
8. throw them out

G. LISTENING

Listen and choose the correct answer.

1. A. I looked in the refrigerator, and I can't find the orange juice.
   B. That's because we . . .
2. A. I'm frustrated! My computer isn't working today.
   B. I think you forgot to . . .
3. A. What should I do with the Christmas decorations?
   B. I think it's time to . . .
4. A. Should I take these clothes to the cleaner's?
   B. Yes. You should definitely . . .
5. A. Hmm. What does this word mean?
   B. You should . . .
6. A. I have to return this skateboard to my cousin.
   B. When are you going to . . .

CHAPTER 9

7. A. This math problem is very difficult.
   B. Maybe I can . . .
8. A. I'll never remember their new telephone number.
   B. You should . . .
9. A. I just spilled milk on the kitchen floor!
   B. Don't worry. I'll . . .

Answers

1. b
2. b
3. a
4. b
5. b
6. a
7. b
8. a
9. b

WORKBOOK PAGE 106

H. COME UP WITH THE RIGHT ANSWER

1. take after
   take after him
2. heard from
   hear from him
3. called on
   call on me
4. looking through
   looked through them
5. got over
   got over it
6. look up to
   look up to me
7. ran into
   ran into her
8. get along with
   get along with her
9. picks on
   picks on them

WORKBOOK PAGE 107

J. CHOOSE

1. b
2. a
3. b
4. b
5. a
6. b
7. b
8. a
9. a
10. b
11. a
12. a
13. b
14. b

WORKBOOK PAGE 108

K. WHAT DOES IT MEAN?

1. b
2. c
3. b
4. c
5. a
6. a
7. b
8. c

L. LISTENING

Listen and choose the correct answer.

1. I really look up to my father.
2. My brother picks on me all the time.
3. Did you throw away the last can of paint?
4. I still haven't gotten over the flu.
5. Have you heard from your cousin Sam recently?
6. Why did you turn him down?
7. Did your French teacher call on you today?
8. George picked out a new suit for his wedding.
9. I have to drop my sister off at the airport.
10. Everything in the store is 20 percent off this week.
11. This jacket fits you.
12. Did you try on a lot of shoes?

Answers

1. c
2. b
3. c
4. a
5. b
6. c
7. a
8. c
9. c
10. b
11. a
12. b

334 CHAPTER 9

CHAPTER 10 OVERVIEW: Text Pages 131–144

GRAMMAR

CONNECTORS:

Too/So

I'm hungry.	I am, too. / So am I.
I can swim.	I can, too. / So can I.
I've seen that movie.	I have, too. / So have I.
I have a car.	I do, too. / So do I.
I worked yesterday.	I did, too. / So did I.

Either/Neither

I'm not hungry.	I'm not either. / Neither am I.
I can't swim.	I can't either. / Neither can I.
I've haven't seen that movie.	I haven't either. / Neither have I.
I don't have a car.	I don't either. / Neither do I.
I didn't work.	I didn't either. / Neither did I.

But

I don't sing, **but** my sister does.
She didn't know the answer, **but** I did.
He can play chess, **but** I can't.
We're ready, **but** they aren't.

I'm tired,	and he is, too. / and so is he.
He'll be busy,	and she will, too. / and so will she.
She's been sick,	and he has, too. / and so has he.
They sing,	and she does, too. / and so does she.
She studied,	and I did, too. / and so did I.

I'm not tired,	and he isn't either. / and neither is he.
He won't be busy,	and she won't either. / and neither will she.
She hasn't been sick,	and he hasn't either. / and neither has he.
They don't sing,	and she doesn't either. / and neither does she.
She didn't study,	and I didn't either. / and neither did I.

FUNCTIONS

ASKING FOR AND REPORTING INFORMATION

How do you know *Mr. and Mrs. Randall*?

Have you heard *tomorrow's weather forecast*?

Where were you when *the accident happened*?
  I was *standing on the corner*.

Tell me about *your skills*.

Have you had any *special vocational training*?

When can you *start*?

SHARING NEWS ABOUT SOMEONE

Have you heard about *Harry*?
Have you heard the news about *Harry*?
Have you heard what happened to *Harry*?

EXPRESSING LIKES

I like *peppermint ice cream*.

He enjoys *sports*.

EXPRESSING DISLIKES

I don't like *macaroni and cheese*.

I don't like *fairy tales* very much.

INQUIRING ABOUT WANT–DESIRE

Why do *you and your husband* want to *enroll in my dance class*?

What *do you and Greg* want to *talk to me about*?

Why don't *you and your friends* want to *come to the game*?

EXPRESSING WANT–DESIRE

He wants *this parking space*.

She doesn't want to *take the garbage out*.

336　CHAPTER 10

Inquiring About Ability

Can you *baby-sit for us tomorrow night?*

Expressing Ability

I can *speak four languages fluently.*

Expressing Inability

I can't *skate* very well.
I won't be able to *go bowling next Saturday.*

Inquiring About Intention

What *are you and your brother* going to do *when you grow up?*

Expressing Intention

I'm going to *start an Internet company.*

Extending an Invitation

Are you interested in *seeing a movie tonight?*

Describing

My sister and I are exactly the same.
My sister and I are very different.
I'm *tall and thin.*
I have *brown eyes and black curly hair.*

She's very *outgoing and popular.*

Inquiring About Feelings–Emotions

Why *do you and your sister* look so frightened?
Why were *you and your wife* so nervous?

Expressing Appreciation

I appreciate that.
That's very kind of you.
That's very nice of you.

NEW VOCABULARY

Verbs

afford
allow
behave
commute
expect
explain
help (someone) with
hide
lay off
major (in)
offer
pay attention
prefer
respect
support
tend (to)
walk *their* dog

Adjectives

academic
allergic (to)
available
certain
compatible
conservative
cultural
equal
frightened
hopeful
lenient
liberal
main
opposed to
pessimistic
philosophical
similar
strict
vocational
willing

People

salesman
school nurse

Performing Arts

dance class
theater group

Politics

defense
energy
equal rights
government
minorities
nuclear energy
rights

Schooling

assignment
educational
background
homework assignment
training
vocational training

Employment

job opening
layoff (n)
skill
typing skills
want ad

Food

macaroni and cheese
peppermint ice cream

Miscellaneous

act (n)
background
business trip
coincidence
collection
despite
fairy tale
far (adv)
fluently
group
ice skating (n)
Internet company
lately
lightning
neither
outlook
overseas
parking space
personality
reason
surprise (n)
thunder
use (n)
winter sport
whatever

EXPRESSIONS

an hour a day
as the days go by
by any chance
for the past few days
go through some difficult times
have a lot in common
"made for each other"
on the weekend
out of town
outlook on life
"touchy subject"
What a coincidence!
you can see why

CHAPTER 10 337

Text Page 131: Chapter Opening Page

VOCABULARY PREVIEW

You may want to introduce these words before beginning the chapter, or you may choose to wait until they first occur in a specific lesson. If you choose to introduce them at this point, here are some suggestions:

1. Have students look at the illustrations on text page 131 and identify the words they already know.

2. Present the vocabulary. Say each word and have the class repeat it chorally and individually. Check students' understanding and pronunciation of the words.

3. Practice the vocabulary as a class, in pairs, or in small groups. Have students cover the word list and look at the pictures. Practice the words in the following ways:
   - Say a word and have students tell the number of the illustration.
   - Give the number of an illustration and have students say the word.

Text Page 132: What a Coincidence!

FOCUS

- *So, Too* in 1st person Expressions:

$$I \begin{Bmatrix} am \\ can \\ have \\ do \\ did \end{Bmatrix}, too.$$

$$So \begin{Bmatrix} am \\ can \\ have \\ do \\ did \end{Bmatrix} I.$$

CLOSE UP

RULE:	The expressions *so* and *too* are interchangeable in meaning, but they require different word orders. *Too* comes at the end of the sentence and is preceded by a comma. *So* reverses the word order, with the verb preceding the subject.

EXAMPLES:	I'm tired.
	    I am, too.
	    So am I.

RULE:	The auxiliary verb replaces and agrees with the initial verb phrase.
EXAMPLES:	(To Be) I **am** happy. So **am** I. I **am**, too. (Past Continuous) I **was** watching. So **was** I. I **was**, too. (Future: Will) I**'ll be** busy. So **will** I. I **will**, too. (Present Perfect) I**'ve been** sick. So **have** I. I **have**, too. (Simple Present) I **have** an exam. So **do** I. I **do**, too. (Simple Past) I **missed** the bus. So **did** I. I **did**, too.

INTRODUCING THE MODEL

1. Have students look at the model illustration.
2. Set the scene: "Two friends are talking about a problem they both have."
3. Present the model twice, once with each expression in the brackets.
4. Full-Class Repetition.
5. Ask students if they have any questions. Check understanding of the expressions *allergic (to), What a coincidence!*
6. Group Choral Repetition.
7. Choral Conversation.
8. Call on one or two pairs of students to present the dialog. Have students practice both of the expressions with the model.

(For additional practice, do Choral Conversation in small groups or by rows.)

9. Practice the expressions in the boxes at the top of the page. There are five short dialogs (each with a statement and a response). For each:

   a. Present the dialog, and have students repeat chorally. Then call on pairs of students to present the dialog.

   b. Write on the board:

   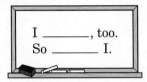

   Have students close their books. Read each statement. Then, point to the expressions on the board and call on students to form correct responses. For example:

   Teacher: I'm hungry.
   Student: I am, too.

   Teacher: I'm hungry.
   Student: So am I.

SIDE BY SIDE EXERCISES

Examples

1. A. I'm a vegetarian.
   B. What a coincidence!
      I am, too./So am I.

2. A. I like peppermint ice cream.
   B. What a coincidence!
      I do, too./So do I.

1. **Exercise 1:** Call on two pairs of students to present the dialog. Have each pair use a different expression of agreement.

2. **Exercise 2:** Introduce the expression *peppermint ice cream*. Same as above.

3. **Exercises 3–8:** Either Full-Class Practice or Pair Practice. Have students practice both possible expressions for each exercise.

   New Vocabulary
   3. fluently
   5. business trip
   6. lately

4. **Exercise 9:** Have students use the model as a guide to create their own conversations, using vocabulary of their choice. Encourage students to use dictionaries to find new words they want to use. This exercise can be done orally in class or for written homework. If you assign it for homework, do one example in class to make sure students understand what's expected. Have students present their conversations in class the next day.

WORKBOOK

Pages 109–110

340 CHAPTER 10

EXPANSION ACTIVITIES

1. **Match the Sentences** ★★

   a. Make a set of split sentence cards such as the following:

I went to the ballgame.	So did I.
I'll be on vacation next week.	I will, too.
I had already done that.	I had, too.
I can play tennis very well.	I can, too.
I've got to leave now.	So do I.
I'm going to see the play.	I am, too.
I was at a play last night.	So was I.
I've worked hard this week.	So have I.

   b. Distribute a card to each student.

   c. Have students memorize the sentences on their cards, then walk around the room trying to find their corresponding match.

   d. Then have pairs of students say their matching sentences aloud to the class.

2. **Concentration** ★

   a. Using the cards from Activity 1, place the first sentences face down in two rows of 4 each. In a different area, place the second sentences face down in two rows of 4 each.

   b. Divide the class into two teams. The object of the game is for students to find the matching cards. Both teams should be able to see all the cards, since *concentrating* on their location is an important part of playing the game.

   c. A student from Team 1 turns over a card from each group (first sentences and second sentences). If they match, the student picks up the cards, that team gets a point, and the student takes another turn. If the cards don't match, the student turns them face down, and a member of Team 2 takes a turn.

   d. The game continues until all the cards have been matched. The team with the most correct matches wins the game.

   Variation: This game can also be played in groups and pairs.

3. **Grammar Chain** ★★

   a. Write the following conversation model on the board:

   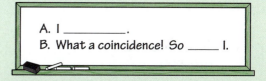

   A. I _____.
   B. What a coincidence! So _____ I.

   b. Start the chain game by saying:

   Teacher (to Student A): I like to watch scary movies.

   c. Student A answers according to the model on the board and then makes a different statement to Student B, and the chain continues. For example

   Student A: What a coincidence! So do I.
   (to Student B): I've studied the guitar for two years.

   Student B: What a coincidence! So have I.
   (to Student C): I went to the Baxter Boys concert last night.

   Etc.

   (continued)

CHAPTER 10   341

EXPANSION ACTIVITIES (Continued)

4. So Do I! ★★

a. Have each student write one sentence about a favorite weekend activity beginning with *I like...*

b. Have students take turns reading their sentences aloud to the class—for example, "I like to go camping." Any other students in the class who genuinely like to do the same thing on the weekend respond by saying "I do, too."

c. Count the number of students who agree with each statement. What are the most popular weekend activities in the class?

Text Page 133: What a Coincidence!

FOCUS

- *Either, Neither* in 1st Person Expressions:

  $\left.\begin{array}{l}\text{I'm not}\\ \text{I can't}\\ \text{I haven't}\\ \text{I don't}\\ \text{I didn't}\end{array}\right\}$ either.   Neither $\left\{\begin{array}{l}\text{am}\\ \text{can}\\ \text{have}\\ \text{do}\\ \text{did}\end{array}\right\}$ I.

CLOSE UP

RULE: The expressions *either* and *neither* are interchangeable in meaning, but they require different word orders. *Either* comes at the end of the sentence. *Neither* reverses the word order, with the verb preceding the subject.

EXAMPLES: I'm not hungry.
   I'm not either.
   Neither am I.

RULE: A negative verb is used with *either*, and an affirmative verb is used with *neither*.

EXAMPLES: I didn't work.
   I didn't either.
   Neither did I.

PRESENTING THE MODEL

1. Have students look at the model illustration.
2. Set the scene: "Two people are dancing."
3. Present the model twice, once with each expression in the brackets.
4. Full-Class Repetition.
5. Ask students if they have any questions. Check understanding of vocabulary.
6. Group Choral Repetition.
7. Choral Conversation.
8. Call on one or two pairs of students to present the dialog. Have students practice both of the expressions with the model.

(For additional practice, do Choral Conversation in small groups or by rows.)

9. Practice the expressions in the boxes at the top of the page. There are five short dialogs (each with a statement and a response). For each:

   a. Present the dialog, and have students repeat chorally. Then call on pairs of students to present the dialog.

   b. Write on the board:

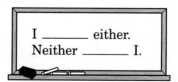

Have students close their books. Read each statement. Then, point to the expressions on the board and call on students to form correct responses. For example:

Teacher: I'm not hungry.
Student: I'm not either.

Teacher: I'm not hungry.
Student: Neither am I.

SIDE BY SIDE EXERCISES

Examples

1. A. I don't like macaroni and cheese.
   B. What a coincidence!
      I don't either./Neither do I.

2. A. I didn't see the stop sign.
   B. What a coincidence!
      I didn't either./Neither did I.

1. **Exercise 1:** Introduce the expression *macaroni and cheese*. Call on two students to present the dialog. Then do Choral Repetition and Choral Conversation practice.

Culture Note

Macaroni and cheese is a common food served to children in school cafeterias.

2. **Exercise 2:** Same as above.

3. **Exercises 3–8:** Either Full Class Practice or Pair Practice. Have students practice both possible expressions for each exercise.

4. **Exercise 9:** Have students use the model as a guide to create their own conversations, using vocabulary of their choice. Encourage students to use dictionaries to find new words they want to use. This exercise can be done orally in class or for written homework. If you assign it for homework, do one example in class to make sure students understand what's expected. Have students present their conversations in class the next day.

WORKBOOK

Pages 111–112

EXPANSION ACTIVITIES

1. **Match the Sentences** ★★

   a. Make a set of split sentence cards such as the following:

I didn't like the movie.	Neither did I.
I won't be in class tomorrow.	Neither will I.
I had never done that.	I hadn't either.
I wasn't feeling well yesterday.	I wasn't either.
I can't ski very well.	Neither can I.
I'm not going to get there on time.	Neither am I.
I don't have to work tonight.	I don't either.
I haven't been to Moscow.	I haven't either.

   b. Distribute a card to each student.

   c. Have students memorize the sentences on their cards, then walk around the room trying to find their corresponding match.

   d. Then have pairs of students say their matching sentences aloud to the class.

2. **Concentration** ★
   a. Using the cards from Activity 1, place the first sentences face down in two rows of 4 each. In a different area, place the second sentences face down in two rows of 4 each.
   b. Divide the class into two teams. The object of the game is for students to find the matching cards. Both teams should be able to see all the cards, since *concentrating* on their location is an important part of playing the game.
   c. A student from Team 1 turns over a card from each group (first sentences and second sentences). If they match, the student picks up the cards, that team gets a point, and the student takes another turn. If the cards don't match, the student turns them face down, and a member of Team 2 takes a turn.
   d. The game continues until all the cards have been matched. The team with the most correct matches wins the game.

   Variation: This game can also be played in groups and pairs.

3. **Grammar Chain** ★★
   a. Write the following conversation model on the board:

   > A. I _____.
   > B. What a coincidence!
   >   Neither ____ I.
   >   or
   >   So ____ I.

   b. Start the chain game by saying:

   > Teacher *(to Student A)*: I didn't sleep well last night.

   c. Student A answers according to the model on the board and then makes a different statement (either positive or negative) to Student B, and the chain continues. For example:

   > Student A: What a coincidence! Neither did I.
   > *(to Student B):* I've been studying very hard.
   >
   > Student B: What a coincidence! So have I.
   > *(to Student C):* I didn't eat a big breakfast this morning.
   >
   > Etc.

4. **Neither Do I!** ★★
   a. Choose a category (for example: foods, celebrities, household chores) and have each student write one negative sentence beginning with *I don't like . . .*
   b. Have students take turns reading their sentences aloud to the class—for example, "I don't like eggs." Any other students in the class who genuinely agree with that statement respond by saying: "Neither do I."
   c. Count the number of students who agree with each statement. What are the least popular *(foods/celebrities/household chores)* in the class?

CHAPTER 10   345

Text Pages 134–135: And They Do, Too

FOCUS

- Expressions with *So* and *Too* with All Pronouns

GETTING READY

Practice the 3rd person singular with a variety of tenses.

1. Write on the board:

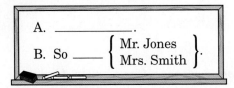

2. Set the scene: "A school needs to hire a new language teacher. Two people want the job: Mr. Jones and Mrs. Smith. Let's talk about them."

3. Read the statements below and have students respond, using line B of the model on the board.

   Mrs. Smith *studied* Spanish in Madrid and French in Paris. *(So did Mr. Jones.)*

   Mr. Jones *has studied* in many countries around the world. *(So has Mrs. Smith.)*

   By the time Mr. Jones was sixteen, he *had already studied* many languages. *(So had Mrs. Smith.)*

   Mrs. Smith *is teaching* in England now. *(So is Mr. Jones.)*

   Mr. Jones *teaches* there every summer. *(So does Mrs. Smith.)*

   Mrs. Smith *is going to write* a book soon. *(So is Mr. Jones.)*

   Mr. Jones *will send* us his new book as soon as it's ready. *(So will Mrs. Smith.)*

   Mrs. Smith *will be coming* for a job interview next week. *(So will Mr. Jones.)*

INTRODUCING THE MODEL

1. Have students look at the model illustration.
2. Set the scene: "This family has just finished eating dinner, and the father is starting to wash the dishes."
3. Present the model twice, once with each expression in the brackets.
4. Full-Class Repetition.
5. Ask students if they have any questions. Check understanding of the expression *help me with*.
6. Group Choral Repetition.
7. Choral Conversation.
8. Call on one or two pairs of students to present the dialog. Have students practice both of the expressions.

(For additional practice, do Choral Conversation in small groups or by rows.)

SIDE BY SIDE EXERCISES

Examples

1. A. Why weren't you and Bob at the meeting this morning?
   B. I missed the bus, and he did too/and so did he.

2. A. Why are you and Vanessa so nervous today?
   B. I have two final exams tomorrow, and she does too/and so does she.

346 CHAPTER 10

1. **Exercise 1:** Call on two students to present the dialog. Then do Choral Repetition and Choral Conversation practice.
2. **Exercise 2:** Same as above.
3. **Exercises 3–13:** Either Full Class Practice or Pair Practice. Have students practice both possible expressions for each exercise.

> **New Vocabulary**
>
> 3. Internet Company
> 5. walk their dog
> 6. out of town
> 7. for the past few days
> 10. parking space
> 12. act (of a play)
> 13. hide thunder and lightning

4. **Exercise 14:** Have students use the model as a guide to create their own conversations, using vocabulary of their choice. Encourage students to use dictionaries to find new words they want to use. This exercise can be done orally in class or for written homework. If you assign it for homework, do one example in class to make sure students understand what's expected. Have students present their conversations in class the next day.

WORKBOOK

Page 113

EXPANSION ACTIVITIES

1. Same and Different ★★★

a. Write the following categories on the board:

sports   school
music   home
food   family
clothes   travel

b. Divide the class into pairs.

c. The object is for pairs of students to find one thing in each of the categories that they have in common and then report back to the class. For example:

   sports: She can play tennis, and so can I.
   music: I like classical music, and she does, too.
   food: She ate cereal for breakfast, and so did I.
   clothes: I have a yellow raincoat, and she does, too.
   school: She enjoys science, and so do I.
   home: My apartment building has six floors, and hers does, too.
   family: I have a cat and a dog, and so does she.
   travel: She's been to New York City, and so have I.

2. What's Wrong? ★★★

a. Divide the class into pairs or small groups.

b. Write several sentences such as the following on the board or on a handout. Some of the sentences should be correct, and others incorrect. For example:

   I've already seen that play, and so have she.
   He's afraid of dogs, and so they are.
   They'll be back by 9:00, and we will, too.
   She's going to see it tomorrow, and are we, too.
   They missed the train, and so did he.
   I'm eating dinner right now, and she is, so.
   He'll be working overtime tonight, and will I, too.
   They've heard her sing before, and I have so.
   You were very sleepy, and too was I.

c. The object of the activity is for students to identify which sentences are incorrect and then correct them.

d. Have students compare their answers.

Variation: Do the activity as a game with competing teams. The team that successfully completes the task in the shortest time is the winner.

(continued)

CHAPTER 10   347

EXPANSION ACTIVITIES (Continued)

3. **Class Story** ★★★

   a. Write the following on the board:

   b. Begin by saying: "Jean and her sister Joan are very similar."

   c. Student 1 adds another sentence, using any verb on the board. For example: "Jean is tall and thin, and so is Joan."

   d. Continue around the room in this fashion, with each student adding another sentence.

   For example:

   Student 2: Jean has a new job, and so does Joan.
   Student 3: Jean went to college in Boston, and so did Joan.
   Student 4: Jean can swim very fast, and Joan can, too.
   Student 5: Jean will be a doctor someday, and so will Joan.
   Student 6: Jean is going to move to Miami, and Joan is, too.
   Student 7: Jean has been to San Francisco, and so has Joan.

   e. You can do the activity again, beginning and ending with different students.

   If the class is large, you may want to divide students into groups to give students more practice.

   Option: Have students tell a story about "Ned and his brother Ted."

348 CHAPTER 10

Text Pages 136–137

READING *"Made For Each Other"*

FOCUS

- Connectors:
  and . . . too
  so

NEW VOCABULARY

academic	minorities
art museum	nuclear energy
background	offer (v)
collection	opposed to
compatible	outlook on life
cultural	personality
equal rights	similar
group	support
have a lot in common	tend (to)
ice skating (n)	theater group
"made for each other"	use (n)
major in (v)	

READING THE STORY

Optional: Preview the story by having students talk about the story title and/or illustrations. You may choose to introduce new vocabulary beforehand, or have students encounter the new vocabulary within the context of the reading.

1. Have students read silently, or follow along silently as the story is read aloud by you, by one or more students, or on the audio program.

2. Ask students if they have any questions. Check understanding of vocabulary.

3. Check students' comprehension, using some or all of the following questions:

Why are Louise and Brian very compatible people?
How are their backgrounds similar?
How are their academic interests similar?
How are their athletic interests similar?
How are their cultural interests similar?
How are their personalities similar?
How are their outlooks on life similar?
What does everybody say about Louise and Brian?

✓ READING CHECK-UP

TRUE, FALSE, OR MAYBE?

1. True
2. False
3. True
4. Maybe
5. False
6. False
7. False

READING EXTENSION

1. **Same and Different**

   a. Write the following categories on the board:

   > background
   > cultural interests
   > sports
   > academic interests
   > personalities
   > outlooks on life

   b. Divide the class into pairs.

   c. The object is for pairs of students to find one thing in each of the categories that they have in common and then report back to the class.

CHAPTER 10   349

2. *A Close Friend*

a. Have students write about a close friend and ways in which they are similar to their close friend. Have students consider the categories mentioned in the above activity.

b. Have students share their writing in small groups.

 LISTENING

Before you do the exercise, check understanding of the word *scientific*.

Listen and choose what people are talking about.

1. A. To tell the truth, I'm a little shy.
   B. What a coincidence! I am, too.

2. A. I enjoy going to plays and concerts.
   B. We're very compatible. So do I.

3. A. I'm enjoying this course.
   B. I am, too.

4. A. I'm from Minnesota.
   B. That's interesting. So am I.

5. A. I go swimming three times a week.
   B. What a coincidence! I do, too.

6. A. I'm opposed to using animals in scientific experiments.
   B. I am, too.

Answers

1. a
2. b
3. a
4. b
5. a
6. b

350 CHAPTER 10

Text Pages 138–139: And She Hasn't Either

FOCUS

- Expressions with *Either* and *Neither* with All Pronouns

GETTING READY

Practice expressions with *either* and *neither*.

1. Write on the board:

2. Set the scene: "Tim, Tom, and Ted are triplets.* May 27th is Tim's birthday. It's Tom and Ted's birthday, too."

3. Read the following statements about *Tim*. Have students make statements about *Tom* and *Ted*, using the model on the board. For example:

    Teacher: Tim isn't a very good student.
    Student: Tom isn't either, and neither is Ted.

    Statements about Tim:

    Tim hadn't studied Spanish before this year.
    Tim won't be finishing high school next year.
    Tim isn't going to go to college.
    Tim can't dance very well.
    Tim doesn't like Italian food.
    Tim didn't like sports when he was young.
    Tim couldn't come to meet us today.

*Triplets are three children born at a single birth.

INTRODUCING THE MODEL

1. Have students look at the model illustration.
2. Set the scene: "Someone is talking to a brother and sister on a roller coaster."
3. Present the model.
4. Full Class Repetition.
5. Ask students of they have any questions. Check understanding of the word *frightened*.
6. Group Choral Repetition.
7. Choral Conversation.
8. Call on one or two pairs of students to present the dialog.

    (For additional practice, do Choral Conversation in small groups or by rows.)

SIDE BY SIDE EXERCISES

Examples

1. A. Why haven't you and your roommate hooked up your new DVD player?
   B. I don't understand the instructions, and he doesn't either/neither does he.
2. A. Why didn't you or your parents answer the telephone all weekend?
   B. I wasn't home, and they weren't either/neither were they.

1. **Exercise 1:** Call on two students to present the dialog. Then do Choral Repetition and Choral Conversation practice.
2. **Exercise 2:** Same as above.
3. **Exercises 3–13:** Either Full Class Practice or Pair Practice. Have students practice both possible expressions for each exercise.

CHAPTER 10   351

New Vocabulary
- 5. dance class
- 6. school nurse
- 12. afford
- 13. fairy tale

Language Note

Exercise 13: *Fairy tales* are short stories about magical creatures that are told to young children.

4. Exercise 14: Have students use the model as a guide to create their own conversations, using vocabulary of their choice. Encourage students to use dictionaries to find new words they want to use. This exercise can be done orally in class or for written homework. If you assign it for homework, do one example in class to make sure students understand what's expected. Have students present their conversations in class the next day.

WORKBOOK

Pages 114–115

EXPANSION ACTIVITIES

1. Same and Different ★★★

a. Write the following categories on the board:

b. Divide the class into pairs.

c. The object is for pairs of students to find one *negative* thing in each of the categories that they have in common and then report back to the class. For example:

- sports: He can't play golf, and neither can I.
- music: I don't like classical music, and he doesn't either.
- food: He didn't have eggs for breakfast, and neither did I.
- clothes: I don't own a tuxedo, and he doesn't either.
- school: He doesn't like mathematics, and neither do I.
- home: I don't live on the first floor, and neither does he.
- family: I don't have a sister, and he doesn't either.
- travel: He's never been on a boat, and I haven't either.

2. What's Wrong? ★★★

a. Divide the class into pairs or small groups.

b. Write several sentences such as the following on the board or on a handout. Some of the sentences should be correct, and others incorrect. For example:

I've never gone on a safari, and neither he has.
She isn't going to the party, and I'm not neither.
They won't arrive soon, and she won't either.
I'm not going to call them, and they are neither.

352 CHAPTER 10

He doesn't read that newspaper, and I don't neither.
She can't figure skate very well, and either can't I.
He won't do that, and neither will they.
They've never heard her sing before, and I haven't neither.
You weren't very tired, and neither I was.

c. The object of the activity is for students to identify which sentences are incorrect and then correct them.

d. Have students compare their answers.

Variation: Do the activity as a game with competing teams. The team that successfully completes the task in the shortest time is the winner.

3. Class Story ★★★

   a. Write the following on the board:

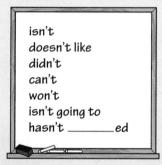

```
isn't
doesn't like
didn't
can't
won't
isn't going to
hasn't _____ed
```

b. Begin by saying, "Ned and his brother Ted are very similar."

c. Student 1 adds another sentence, using any verb on the board. For example: "Ned isn't a very good athlete, and neither is Ted."

d. Continue around the room in this fashion, with each student adding another sentence. For example:

   Student 2: Ned doesn't like to cook, and Ted doesn't either.
   Student 3: Ned didn't do well in school, and neither did Ted.
   Student 4: Ned can't type, and Ted can't either.
   Student 5: Ned won't be able to help you, and neither will Ted.
   Student 6: Ned isn't going to be very successful, and Ted isn't either.
   Student 7: Ned hasn't taken many vacations, and neither has Ted.

e. You can do the activity again, beginning and ending with different students.

   If the class is large, you may want to divide students into groups to give students more practice.

Option: Have students tell a story about "Jean and her sister Joan."

CHAPTER 10   353

Text Page 140

READING *Laid Off*

FOCUS

- Connectors:
  and . . . either
  neither

NEW VOCABULARY

as the day goes by	layoff (n)
at the same time	main
available	on the weekend
certain	pessimistic
commute	prefer
despite	skill
expect	surprise (n)
far (adv)	training
go through some difficult times	typing skills vocational
hopeful	want ad
job opening	willing
lay-off (v)	

READING THE STORY

Optional: *Preview the story by having students talk about the story title and/or illustrations. You may choose to introduce new vocabulary beforehand, or have students encounter the new vocabulary within the context of the reading.*

1. Have students read silently, or follow along silently as the story is read aloud by you, by one or more students, or on the audio program.

2. Ask students if they have any questions. Check understanding of vocabulary.

   Culture Note

   Companies lay off people when there are too many employees and too little work for them. Workers who are laid off can collect a part of their salary while they are waiting to be called back to work or until they find a new job.

3. Check students' comprehension, using some or all of the following questions:

   Why are Jack and Betty Williams going through some difficult times?
   Why are they becoming more and more concerned about their futures?
   Were the layoffs a surprise?
   Why not?
   What hadn't they expected?
   What have they been doing ever since they were laid off?
   Have they been successful?
   What's the main reason they're having trouble finding work?
   Have the want ads been helpful?
   Have there been many job openings?
   Have their friends been helpful?
   What's another reason they're having trouble finding work?
   What do Jack and Betty know about computers?
   How are their typing skills?
   Have they had any special vocational training?
   What's a third reason they're having trouble finding work?
   What do they think about working at night?
   What do they think about working on weekends?
   What do they think about commuting far to work?
   Are Jack and Betty completely discouraged? Why not?

✓ READING *CHECK-UP*

TRUE, FALSE, OR MAYBE?

1. False
2. False
3. Maybe
4. True
5. Maybe

354   CHAPTER 10

READING EXTENSION

What Can They Do?

1. Have the class discuss the following questions:

    What is one problem Jack and Betty Williams have?
    (They don't have any vocational skills.)

    What is one possible solution?
    (Betty can take a typing class.)

    What will happen if she does that?
    (Betty will get some good job skills, but she might have to wait to find a job.)

2. Write students' ideas on the board. Be sure to discuss several different problems and several different solutions.

3. Have students write two or three paragraphs in which they give advice to Jack and Betty, using the ideas generated from this class discussion.

A JOB INTERVIEW

1. Check understanding of the expression *educational background*.

2. Have students role-play a job interview using the questions suggested on text page 140. One student is the job interviewer. The other is the job applicant. Have pairs of students practice their role plays and then present them to the class.

Text Page 141: You Should Ask Them

FOCUS

- Contrasting Statements with *But*

INTRODUCING THE MODEL

1. Have students look at the model illustration.
2. Set the scene: "A woman is talking to the girl who lives next-door."
3. Present the model.
4. Full-Class Choral Repetition.

   Pronunciation Note

   The pronunciation focus of Chapter 10 is **Contrastive Stress** (text page 144). Model this pronunciation at this point and encourage students to incorporate it into their language practice.

   I can't, but my SISTER can.
   You should ask HER.

5. Ask students if they have any questions. Check understanding of the word *baby-sit*.
6. Group Choral Repetition.
7. Choral Conversation.
8. Call on one or two pairs of students to present the dialog.

   (For additional practice, do Choral Conversation in small groups or by rows.)

9. Read the statements in the box at the top of the page, and have students repeat chorally.

SIDE BY SIDE EXERCISES

Examples

1. A. Have you heard the weather forecast?
   B. No, I haven't, but my FATHER has. You should ask HIM.

2. A. Do you have a hammer?
   B. No, I don't, but my upstairs NEIGHBORS do. You should ask THEM.

1. **Exercise 1:** Call on two students to present the dialog. Then do Choral Repetition and Choral Conversation practice.
2. **Exercise 2:** Same as above.
3. **Exercises 3–6:** Either Full-Class Practice or Pair Practice.

> **New Vocabulary**
>
> 4. homework assignment
> 5. by any chance
> 6. pay attention
>   salesman

How to Say It!

> **Offering a Suggestion:** There are many ways to offer a suggestion. "You should ask HER," "Why don't you ask HER?" and "How about asking HER?" are equally polite. *How about* is followed by a gerund.

1. Present the expressions.
2. Full-Class Repetition.
3. Ask students if they have any questions. Check understanding of the expressions: *Why don't you . . .? How about . . . ?*
4. Group Choral Repetition.
5. Have students practice again the conversations in this lesson using any of these new expressions.
6. Call on pairs to present their conversations to the class.

WORKBOOK

Pages 116–117

356   CHAPTER 10

EXPANSION ACTIVITIES

1. Places Around the World ★★★

a. Write on the board:

> How are they similar?
> How are they different?

b. Divide the class into small groups of 3 to 5 students. Have each group choose two cities (either local cities or world cities). Have the students work together to write five ways these cities are similar and five ways they're different. Encourage students to use dictionaries if they need to.

c. Have one student from each group present the findings to the class. For example:

> London and Rome
> (similar)
> London isn't a small city, and neither is Rome.
> Rome has some very old buildings, and London does, too.
>
> (different)
> People in London speak English, but in Rome people speak Italian.
> The weather in London is very cold in the winter, but the weather in Rome isn't.

2. Our Differences ★★★

a. Write the following categories on the board:

sports   school
music   home
food   family
clothes   travel

b. Divide the class into pairs.

c. The object is for pairs of students to find one thing in each of the categories that they don't have in common and then report back to the class. For example:

> sports: She can't play soccer, but I can.
> music: I like rock music, but she doesn't.
> food: She enjoys Italian food, but I don't.
> clothes: Her shoes are red, but mine aren't.
> school: I'm taking history this year, but she isn't.
> home: My apartment has a jacuzzi, but hers doesn't.
> family: Her sister is in college, but mine isn't.
> travel: She's never flown in an airplane, but I have.

3. Telephone ★

a. Divide the class into large groups. Have each group sit in a circle.

b. Set the scene: "A couple is in a restaurant. They're ordering spaghetti and meatballs, but they have very special instructions!"

c. Whisper the food order to one student. For example:

> "They both want spaghetti and meatballs. She wants spaghetti with butter, and he does, too. She doesn't want tomato sauce, but he does. She wants the meatballs on the spaghetti, but he doesn't. He wants them on a different plate."

d. The first student whispers the food order to the second student, and so forth around the circle.

e. When the message gets to the last student, that person says it aloud. Is it the same message you started with? The group with the most accurate message wins.

4. Comparison Shopping ★★

a. Bring to class several shopping catalogs.

b. Divide the class into pairs or small groups and give each group two catalogs selling similar merchandise.

c. Have students compare the selections and prices in their catalogs. For example:

> This catalog sells clothes and shoes, but that one doesn't. That one only sells shoes.
> This catalog sells shoes for men and women, and that one does, too.
> This catalog has good quality shoes, and so does that one.

(continued)

CHAPTER 10   357

EXPANSION ACTIVITIES (Continued)

d. Have students report back to the class and discuss which catalogs are the best for shopping.

5. Matchmaker ★★★

a. Divide the class into groups of four. Give each student in the group one of the following cards.

- John grew up in a big family in a big city.
- John doesn't like to play golf, but he likes to play tennis.
- John is a Spanish teacher.
- John is a vegetarian.
- John enjoys going to movies, but he doesn't like to dance.

- Mary grew up in a small family in a small town.
- Mary doesn't like to play golf, and she doesn't like to play tennis.
- Mary is a lawyer.
- Mary is a vegetarian.
- Mary enjoys going to movies, and she likes to dance.

- Louise grew up in a small family in a big city.
- Louise likes to play golf, and she likes to play tennis.
- Louise is a French teacher.
- Louise likes to eat meat.
- Louise enjoys going to movies, but she doesn't like to dance.

- Carla grew up in a big family in a small town.
- Carla doesn't like to play golf, but she likes to play tennis.
- Carla is a science teacher.
- Carla is a vegetarian.
- Carla doesn't enjoy going to movies, but she likes to dance.

b. The student holding the *John* card begins by reading aloud the first sentence. Students then take turns reading aloud the corresponding sentences for *Carla*, *Mary*, and *Louise*. After each round, have students compare their characters. For example:

Student 1: John grew up in a big family.
Student 2: Carla did, too.
Student 3: But John is from a big city, and so is Louise.

c. Have students continue comparing people and then decide on the best match for John.

d. Have students report back to the class and give reasons for their conclusions.

Text Page 142

READING "Touchy Subjects"

FOCUS

- But

NEW VOCABULARY

allow	defense	strict
an hour a day	government	"touchy subject"
behave	lenient	whatever
conservative	liberal	you can see why

READING THE STORY

Optional: Preview the story by having students talk about the story title and/or illustrations. You may choose to introduce new vocabulary beforehand, or have students encounter the new vocabulary within the context of the reading.

1. Have students read silently, or follow along silently as the story is read aloud by you, by one or more students, or on the audio program.
2. Ask students if they have any questions. Check understanding of vocabulary.
3. Check students' comprehension, using some or all of the following questions:

   Do Larry and his parents agree when they talk about politics?
   What are their political philosophies?
   What do Larry and his parents think about the president?
   What do Larry and his parents think about money for defense?
   Do the Greens and their next-door neighbors, the Harrisons, agree when they talk about child rearing?
   What are their philosophies of child rearing?
   When do the Greens and the Harrisons let their children watch television?
   What do the Greens and the Harrisons think about table manners?

✓ READING CHECK-UP

TRUE, FALSE, OR MAYBE?

1. True
2. Maybe
3. False
4. Maybe
5. False

READING EXTENSION

"Touchy Subject" Role Play

1. Brainstorm with the class what they think some *touchy subjects* are. Write their ideas on the board.
2. Have students think of good responses to people who begin to talk about a touchy subject. Write their ideas on the board.
3. Have students practice and then present brief role plays in which one student introduces a touchy subject and the other responds appropriately.

How About You?

1. Present the questions.
2. Have the students do the activity as written homework, using a dictionary for any new words they wish to use.
3. Have students present and discuss what they have written in pairs or as a class.

CHAPTER 10

Text Page 143

 ON YOUR OWN *Same and Different*

FOCUS

- Review: *So/Too/Either/Neither*

ON YOUR OWN ACTIVITY

1. Have students look at the illustration and cover the text with a piece of paper.

2. Have students listen as you read or play the audio about the sisters.

3. Have students look at the text and listen as you read or play the audio once more.

4. Check understanding of the words *overseas, philosophical, respect (v).*

5. Write on the board:

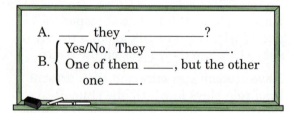

Call on pairs of students to ask and answer questions about the sisters, using the model on the board. For example:

A. Do they have black hair?
B. Yes. They both have black hair.

A. Are they married?
B. No. They aren't married.

A. Do they like classical music?
B. One of them does, but the other one doesn't.

A. Have they been to New York?
B. One of them has, but the other one hasn't.

WORKBOOK

Pages 118–119

 JOURNAL

Have students write their journal entries at home or in class. Encourage students to use a dictionary to look up words they would like to use. Students can share their written work with other students if appropriate. Have students discuss what they have written as a class, in pairs, or in small groups

360 CHAPTER 10

Text Page 144

 **PRONUNCIATION**
Contrastive Stress

Teacher:	She's a vegetarian, and . . .
Student:	so am I.
Teacher:	He won't go bowling tonight, and . . .
Student:	neither will I.
Teacher:	I don't skate well, but . . .
Student:	my sister does.

> **Contrastive Stress:** When making a contrast to something previously said, the words with new information are stressed and pronounced at a higher pitch.

KEY VOCABULARY

Have students ask you any questions about the meaning or pronunciation of the vocabulary. If students ask for the pronunciation, repeat after the student until the student is satisfied with his or her own pronunciation.

Focus on Listening

Practice the sentences in the left column. Say each sentence or play the audio one or more times. Have students listen carefully and repeat.

Focus on Pronunciation

Practice the sentences in the right column. Have students say each sentence and then listen carefully as you say it or play the audio.

If you wish, have students continue practicing the sentences to improve their pronunciation.

WORKBOOK

Check-Up Test: Pages 120–121

 CHAPTER SUMMARY

GRAMMAR

1. Divide the class into pairs or small groups.
2. Have students take turns saying the sentences from the grammar boxes. Student A says a sentence, and Student B points to the box. Then have students switch: Student B says a sentence, and Student A points to the box.

EXPANSION ACTIVITIES

1. **Do You Remember the Words?** ★

   Check students' retention of the vocabulary depicted on the opening page of Chapter 10 by doing the following activity:

   a. Have students open their books to page 131 and cover the list of vocabulary words and phrases.

   b. Either call out a number and have students tell you the word or phrase, or say a word or phrase and have students tell you the number.

   Variation: You can also do this activity as a game with competing teams.

2. **Student-Led Dictation** ★

   a. Tell each student to choose a word or phrase from the Key Vocabulary list on text page 144 and look at it very carefully.

   (continued)

EXPANSION ACTIVITY

Finish the Sentence ★★

Begin a sentence and have students add an appropriate ending. For example:

CHAPTER 10 361

EXPANSION ACTIVITIES (Continued)

   b. Have students take turns dictating their words to the class. Everybody writes down that student's word.

   c. When the dictation is completed, call on different students to write each word on the board to check the spelling.

3. Categorization ★★

   a. Divide the class into pairs.

   b. Call out one of the following categories:

family	arts and entertainment
shopping	government
employment	weather

   Have students look through the vocabulary list on text page 144 and find all the words that could belong to that category.

   c. Have students read their lists aloud. Who has the longest list? Does everyone agree all those words belong to the category?

END-OF-CHAPTER ACTIVITIES

1. **Board Game** ★★★

   a. On poster boards or on manila file folders, make up game boards with a pathway consisting of separate spaces. You may use any theme or design you wish.

   b. Divide the class into groups of 2 to 4 students and give each group a game board, and a die, and each player something to be used as a playing piece.

   c. Give each group a pile of cards face-down with statements written on them. Some sentences should be correct, and others incorrect. For example:

   > I'm not hungry, and he is.
   > She didn't like it, and neither did he.
   > He's been studying for years, and she is, too.
   > They have a boat, and I have either.
   > We can't go out now, but they can.
   > We'll go shopping tomorrow, and so will you.
   > We aren't going to see the play, but she was.
   > They eat out every night, and so do I.
   > You've been to Spain, and neither have I.
   > She doesn't have a car, but I do.
   > They'll be busy, and I will so.
   > He hasn't gone there, but my aunt has.

   d. Each student in turn rolls the die, moves the playing piece along the game path, and after landing on a space, picks a card, reads the sentence, and says if it is *correct* or *incorrect*. If the statement is incorrect, the student must correct it. If the response is correct, the student takes an additional turn.

   e. The first student to reach the end of the pathway is the winner.

2. **Scrambled Sentences** ★

   a. Divide the class into two teams.

   b. Write individual sentences out of order on the board. Use sentences based on the lessons in Chapter 10. For example:

   > does they and play don't golf father my neither
   >
   > I a and so she car do new has
   >
   > either movie haven't haven't that they we and seen
   >
   > to my not museum but going sister I'm is the
   >
   > and to week they're too Miami are next moving we

   c. The first person to raise his or her hand, come to the board, and write the sentence in the correct order earns a point for that team.

   d. The team with the most points wins the scrambled sentence game.

   Variation: Write the words to several sentences on separate cards. Divide the class into small groups, and have students work together to put the sentences into correct order.

3. **Dialog Builder!** ★★★

   a. Divide the class into pairs.

   b. Write several lines on the board from the conversations in Chapter 10 such as the following:

   > What a coincidence!
   > Why can't _____?
   > Why don't you ask _____?
   > So do I.

   c. Have each pair create a conversation incorporating those lines. Students can begin and end their conversations any way they wish, but they must include those lines in their dialogs.

   d. Call on students to present their conversations to the class.

CHAPTER 10   363

WORKBOOK ANSWER KEY AND LISTENING SCRIPTS

WORKBOOK PAGE 109

A. NOT THE ONLY ONE

1. did I
2. I do
3. can I
4. I am
5. I will
6. was I
7. am I
8. I have
9. I did
10. will I
11. do I

WORKBOOK PAGE 110

B. WHAT A COINCIDENCE!

1. do I
2. I do
3. I did
4. have I
5. I will
6. did I
7. I was
8. I did
9. I am
10. do I
11. am I

WORKBOOK PAGE 111

C. NOT THE ONLY ONE

1. did I
2. I'm not
3. was I
4. I can't
5. I won't
6. have I
7. I can't
8. am I
9. I didn't
10. do I
11. will I

WORKBOOK PAGE 112

D. LISTENING

Listen and complete the sentences.

1. I missed the bus this morning.
2. I'm allergic to nuts.
3. I'll be on vacation next week.
4. I've never flown in a helicopter.
5. I can speak Chinese.
6. I like to go sailing.
7. I'm not going to the company picnic this weekend.
8. I saw a very good movie last night.
9. I don't go on many business trips.
10. I've been to London several times.
11. I'm not a vegetarian.
12. I should lose a little weight.
13. I can't stop worrying about my health.
14. I hate to drive downtown.
15. I won't be able to go to Nancy's party this Saturday night.

Answers

1. did I
2. I am
3. will I
4. I haven't
5. I can
6. I do
7. am I
8. I did
9. do I
10. have I
11. I'm not
12. I should
13. can I
14. do I
15. I won't

WORKBOOK PAGE 113

G. WHAT ARE THEY SAYING?

1. did he
2. will she
3. he was
4. has she
5. you should
6. they were
7. so can
8. did he
9. I do
10. . . ., so has

WORKBOOK PAGE 114

H. WHAT ARE THEY SAYING?

1. can I
2. they didn't
3. is he
4. she doesn't

364 CHAPTER 10

5. were they
6. she hasn't
7. will they
8. aren't either
9. neither has
10. she hadn't

WORKBOOK PAGE 115

I. WHAT ARE THEY SAYING?

1. so did she
   she did, too
2. neither could he
   he couldn't either
3. so does he
   he does, too
4. neither does she
   she doesn't either
5. neither had she
   she hadn't either
6. so is he
   he is, too

WORKBOOK PAGE 116

J. OUR FAMILY

1. aren't, been
2. is, playing, doing
3. can, drawing, was
4. doesn't, going
5. isn't, has been taking
6. haven't, lived, for, lived
7. doesn't, hasn't spoken
8. won't, hasn't
9. does, sung, since
10. aren't, up, away
11. doesn't, for
12. aren't, skating, had, skated

WORKBOOK PAGE 117

K. LISTENING

Listen and complete the sentences.

1. I missed the bus today, . . .
2. I'm allergic to cats, . . .
3. I'll be on vacation next week, . . .
4. You've never seen a rainbow, . . .
5. I can speak Italian, . . .
6. I like to go sailing, . . .
7. I've been on television several times, . . .
8. I saw an exciting movie last weekend, . . .
9. I won't be in the office tomorrow, . . .
10. We were late, . . .
11. I'm not a vegetarian, . . .
12. I saw the stop sign, . . .
13. I can't swim very well, . . .
14. They have to work overtime this weekend, . . .
15. I won't be able to go to Sam's party this Friday night, . . .
16. I'm not afraid of flying, . . .
17. I haven't eaten breakfast yet, . . .
18. The other students weren't bored, . . .

Answers

1. didn't
2. isn't
3. won't
4. have
5. can't
6. doesn't
7. haven't
8. didn't
9. will
10. wasn't
11. is
12. didn't
13. can
14. don't
15. will
16. is
17. have
18. was

WORKBOOK PAGE 118

M. SOUND IT OUT!

1. cooks
2. too
3. shouldn't
4. put
5. cookies
6. good
7. sugar
8. Good cooks shouldn't put too much sugar in their cookies.
9. two
10. books
11. bookcase
12. who
13. took
14. afternoon
15. Susan's
16. Who took two books from Susan's bookcase this afternoon?

WORKBOOK PAGE 119

N. WHAT DOES IT MEAN?

1. j
2. c
3. q
4. s
5. n
6. h
7. i
8. x
9. m
10. v
11. w
12. y
13. b
14. a
15. u
16. l
17. p
18. e
19. o
20. k
21. f
22. t
23. z
24. g
25. d
26. r

WORKBOOK PAGES 120–121

CHECK-UP TEST: Chapters 9-10

A.
1. it in
2. up to him
3. from her
4. it over
5. it up
6. out of it
7. for it
8. them up
9. them out
10. it down
11. over it

B.
1. so is
2. neither will
3. were, too
4. can't either
5. so have
6. did, too
7. neither has
8. so do
9. neither is

C.

Listen and complete the sentences.

Ex. Nancy knows how to her type, . . .
1. I'm interested in science, . . .
2. I won't be home this evening, . . .
3. I own my own business, . . .
4. I've never hooked up a computer, . . .
5. You just got a raise, . . .

Answers
1. isn't
2. will
3. doesn't
4. has
5. didn't

Text Pages 145–148: *Side by Side* Gazette

 FEATURE ARTICLE *From Matchmakers to Dating Services*

PREVIEWING THE ARTICLE

1. Have students talk about the title of the article and the accompanying photograph.

2. You may choose to introduce the following new vocabulary beforehand, or have students encounter it within the context of the article:

> agreement
> approve
> arrange
> arrangement
> astrologer
> astrological
> birth
> choose
> custom
> dating service
> education
> freedom
> horoscope
> information
> marriage
> match (n)
> matchmaker
> matchmaking service
> modern-day
> newlywed
> occupation
> partner
> personal ad
> questionnaire
> rural
> tradition
> traditionally
> valuable
> version

READING THE ARTICLE

1. Have students read silently, or follow along silently as the article is read aloud by you, by one or more students, or on the audio program.

2. Ask students if they have any questions. Check understanding of vocabulary.

3. Check students' comprehension by having them answer these questions:

> How do families in India traditionally arrange a marriage?
> What does a matchmaker do?
> How are marriage traditions and customs changing in modern cities?
> What is the modern-day version of a matchmaker?

EXPANSION ACTIVITIES

1. **Dictate and Discuss** ★★★

   a. Divide the class into pairs or small groups.

   b. Dictate sentences such as the following and then have students discuss them:

   > A husband and wife in an arranged marriage can learn to love each other.
   > Parents know best who their child should have as a husband or wife.
   > An astrologer can help people decide if they are a good match.

   c. Call on students to share their opinions with the rest of the class.

2. **How People Meet** ★★

   a. Divide the class into several groups. Have students brainstorm different ways people meet marriage partners in their culture.

   b. Have the groups report back to the class.

3. **Advantages and Disadvantages** ★★★

   a. Have students draw two columns on a piece of paper. At the top of one column, have students write <u>Advantages</u>. At the top of the other column, have them write <u>Disadvantages</u>.

   b. Have students brainstorm the advantages and disadvantages of having an arranged marriage.

   (continued)

SIDE BY SIDE GAZETTE 367

EXPANSION ACTIVITIES (Continued)

Write their ideas in the columns and have students copy the list on their papers.

c. Have students repeat the exercise, naming the advantages and disadvantages of choosing one's own partner.

4. Interviews ★★★

In this activity, students interview their elders to find out how they met their marriage partners.

a. Have students brainstorm questions they would like to ask in their interviews.

b. Have students conduct their interviews outside the classroom and then write a report of the interview to share in class.

FACT FILE
When People Get Married

1. Before reading the Fact File, show the class a world map. Have students identify the locations of the following place names:

   > Australia
   > Brazil
   > Greece
   > India
   > Japan
   > Korea
   > Mexico
   > Russia
   > Saudi Arabia
   > Swaziland
   > Sweden

2. Ask students: "In which of these countries do you think people marry at a young age?" Have students rank the countries according to what they believe. Write students' ideas on the board. Then have students read the table on student text page 145 to check their predictions.

3. Read the table aloud as the class follows along. Ask: "Is this list different from your list? How is your list different?"

368   SIDE BY SIDE GAZETTE

EXPANSION ACTIVITY

Making Inferences ★★★

1. In small groups, have students discuss the following questions:

   Why do you think people marry younger in some countries?
   Why do you think they marry older in other countries?
   This fact file gives the average age of the woman (the bride). Do you think the age of the man (the groom) is older or younger? Why?

2. Have groups report back to the class.

AROUND THE WORLD
Wedding Customs and Traditions

1. Before reading the text, show the class a world map. Have students identify the locations of the following places:

   > Colombia
   > Cyprus
   > India
   > Japan
   > Korea
   > Romania
   > the Slovak Republic
   > the United States

2. Have students read silently, or follow along silently as the text is read aloud by you, by one or more students, or on the audio program.

3. Ask students if they have any questions. Check understanding of new vocabulary.

bouquet	light (v)
bride	pin (v)
candle	private
catch	reception hall
confetti	throw
couple	veil
crown	wedding procession
flower petal	wish
groom	worship
involve	

4. Have students first work in pairs or small groups to respond to the question. Then have students tell the class what they talked about. Write any new vocabulary on the board.

EXPANSION ACTIVITIES

1. Categorization ★★

a. Write the following categories on the board: <u>Clothes</u>, <u>Places</u>, <u>Special Customs</u>, <u>Throwing Things</u>.

b. Have students read the text and captions again, and have them put the information into the appropriate categories on the board. For example:

<u>Clothes</u>
silver crown
veil

<u>Places</u>
in a church
in homes
outdoors

<u>Special Customs</u>
pinning money
lighting candles
cutting the cake

<u>Throwing Things</u>
confetti
flower petals
rice

c. Have the class then brainstorm other traditions they know and add them to the categories on the board (or if necessary, create new categories).

2. Wedding Pictures ★★★

If possible, have students bring in pictures of a wedding they attended. Have students share their pictures in small groups. Have students tell the following:

What did the bride wear? How about the groom?
What special food was there at the wedding?
Where was the wedding ceremony?
What did the guests do to bring good luck to the bride and groom?
Tell about the music and dancing.
How did the bride and groom arrive? How did they leave?

INTERVIEW

1. Have students read silently, or follow along silently as the interview is read aloud by you, by one or more students, or on the audio program.

2. Ask students if they have any questions. Check understanding of the expression *blind date*.

EXPANSION ACTIVITIES

1. Ranking ★★★

a. Have the class brainstorm several different places to meet a marriage partner. Write their ideas on the board.

b. Have students rank these place from the *best* to the *worst* places to meet a marriage partner.

c. As a class, in pairs, or in small groups, have students compare their lists and explain their reasoning.

2. Student Interviews ★★★

a. Have students interview each other about ways they have met a boyfriend or a girlfriend, and perhaps even their marriage partners.

b. Have the class compile its results. Ask: "What is the most common way to meet a partner? Which of these ways is more successful? Which ways resulted in marriage?"

 FUN WITH IDIOMS

to be nuts about (someone)
to fall for (someone)
to give (someone) the cold shoulder
to stand (someone) up

SIDE BY SIDE GAZETTE   369

INTRODUCTION AND PRACTICE

For each idiom do the following:

1. Have students look at the illustration.
2. Present the idiom. Say the expression and have the class repeat it chorally and individually. Check students' pronunciation of the words.

DO YOU KNOW THESE EXPRESSIONS?

Have students match the expressions with their meanings.

Answers

1. b   3. a
2. d   4. c

EXPANSION ACTIVITIES

1. **Idiom Challenge!** ★★★

   a. Divide the class into pairs.
   b. Have each pair create a conversation in which they use as many of the idioms from text page 147 as they can.
   c. Have the pairs present their conversations to the class. Which pair used the most idioms?

2. **Dialog Builder** ★★★

   a. Divide the class into pairs.
   b. Write several idioms and other new vocabulary words from this Gazette on the board. For example:

   > to be nuts about someone
   > to stand someone up
   > to fall for someone
   > to give someone the cold shoulder
   >
   > matchmaker
   > partner
   > background
   > bouquet of flowers
   > choose

   c. Have each pair create a conversation incorporating at least six of the items. Students can begin and end their conversations any way they wish, but they must include at least six items in their dialogs.
   d. Call on students to present their conversations to the class.

 ## WE'VE GOT MAIL!

THE 1ST LETTER TO *SIDE BY SIDE*

1. Have students read silently, or follow along silently as the letter is read aloud by you, by one or more students, or on the audio program.
2. Ask students if they have any questions. Check understanding of the words *inseparable, separable, two-word verb*.
3. To check students' comprehension, have students answer the following question:

   What does the writer want to know?

4. Ask students:

   Did you ever have this question?
   Can you think of an example of a separable two-word verb?
   Can you think of an example of an inseparable two-word verb?

THE RESPONSE FROM *SIDE BY SIDE*

1. Have students read silently, or follow along silently as the letter is read aloud by you, by one or more students, or on the audio program.
2. Ask students if they have any questions. Check understanding of the words *circle, sentence, separately, suggestion*.
3. Check students' comprehension by having them decide whether these statements are true or false:

   There's a rule that explains which two-word verbs are separable and which two-word verbs are inseparable. *(False)*

370   SIDE BY SIDE GAZETTE

The best way to learn about two-word verbs is to memorize them all. *(True)*

It's correct to say "Hear you from soon." *(False)*

4. Ask students: How do *you* remember which two-word verbs are separable and which are inseparable?

EXPANSION ACTIVITIES

1. Class Game ★★

a. Divide the class into teams.

b. Give the teams five minutes to make a list of the two different types of two-word verbs: separable and inseparable.

c. Have the teams share their lists. The team with the longest list of correct verbs wins.

2. What's Wrong? ★★★

a. Divide the class into pairs or small groups.

b. Write several sentences such as the following on the board or on a handout. Some of the sentences should be correct, and others incorrect. For example:

> She will bring back it next week.
> He didn't cross out his mistakes.
> The teacher always calls me on in class.
> They never hear her from.
> We almost ran out milk of yesterday.
> He has hooked the computer up.
> She has taken off it.
> They wrote down all their notes.
> My big brother always picks on me.
> They don't take their father after.
> We plan to look through our books tonight.
> He can't figure out it.

c. The object of the activity is for students to identify which sentences are incorrect and then correct them.

d. Have students compare their answers.

Variation: Do the activity as a game with competing teams. The team that successfully completes the task in the shortest time is the winner.

THE 2ND LETTER TO *SIDE BY SIDE*

1. Have students read silently, or follow along silently as the letter is read aloud by you, by one or more students, or on the audio program.

2. Ask students if they have any questions. Check understanding of the word *expressions*.

3. Check students' comprehension by having them decide whether these statements are true or false:

    "Turn on" has a similar meaning to "turn down." *(False)*

    The meaning of two-word verbs is different from the meaning of each verb separately. *(True)*

    The writer doesn't understand why English uses the same verbs again and again. *(True)*

4. Ask students:

    Did you ever have this question?
    Can you think of other verbs that change their meaning when they are part of a two-word verb?

THE RESPONSE FROM *SIDE BY SIDE*

1. Have students read silently, or follow along silently as the letter is read aloud by you, by one or more students, or on the audio program.

2. Ask students if they have any questions. Check understanding of the words *decline, formal, informal, resemble, speaker, unhappy*.

3. Check students' comprehension by having them decide whether these statements are true or false:

    When people want to speak formally, they use two-word verbs. *(False)*

    There are many verbs that have the same meaning as many two-word verbs. *(True)*

    "Decline" means the same as "turn on." *(False)*

    "Resemble" means the same as "take after." *(True)*

GLOBAL EXCHANGE

1. Set the scene: "PedroJ is writing to a keypal."
2. Have students read silently or follow along silently as the message is read aloud by you, by one or more students, or on the audio program.
3. Ask students if they have any questions. Check understanding of the words *alike*, *originally*.
4. Options for additional practice:
   - Have students write a response to PedroJ and share their writing in pairs
   - Have students correspond with a keypal on the Internet and then share their experience with the class.

LISTENING *"Telephone Tag" True or False?*

1. Set the scene: "Jim and Mary are trying to make plans for the weekend. They keep missing each other's calls, and they leave messages for each other."
2. Introduce the expression *telephone tag*.

LISTENING SCRIPT

Listen to the messages on Mary and Jim's answering machines. Answer true or false.

[Monday, 6:15 P.M.]
Hi, Mary. It's Jim. Are you by any chance interested in going to a jazz concert this Friday night? Please call me and let me know. Talk to you later.

[Monday, 9:13 P.M.]
Hi, Jim. It's Mary. I'm returning your call. Thanks for the invitation. I know you like jazz, and I do, too. And I'd really like to go to the concert with you, but I have to work this Friday night. Do you want to play tennis on Saturday afternoon? Let me know. 'Bye.

[Tuesday, 3:40 P.M.]
Hi, Mary. It's Jim. I'm sorry I missed your call last night. I was at the laundromat, and I got home very late. I'm free on Saturday, but unfortunately, I really don't like to play tennis. Actually, I'm a very bad tennis player. Do you want to go to the ballet with me on Saturday night? Let me know and I'll order tickets. Talk to you soon.

[Wednesday, 5:50 P.M.]
Hi, Jim. It's Mary. I got your message. Believe it or not, I've already gone to the ballet this week. I went with my sister last night. I have an idea! Let's see the new Steven Steelberg movie. I hear that it's great. Call and let me know.

[Thursday, 6:30 P.M.]
Hi, Mary. It's Jim. Sorry I missed your call again. I guess we're playing "telephone tag!" The movie sounds great. I haven't seen it yet. Do you want to have dinner before the movie? There's a wonderful new Italian restaurant downtown. Let me know. 'Bye.

[Friday, 5:17 P.M.]
Hi, Jim. Guess who! You won't believe it! I just found out that I have to work this Saturday night. It's a shame because I really wanted to see that movie. I'm not busy on Sunday. Are you free on Sunday afternoon? Let me know. By the way, I don't really like Italian food very much. There's a very good Greek restaurant in my neighborhood. Maybe we can have dinner there after the movie. What do you think? Talk to you later.

Answers

1. True
2. False
3. True
4. True
5. False

372 SIDE BY SIDE GAZETTE

WHAT ARE THEY SAYING?

FOCUS

- Things People Have (or Don't Have) in Common

Have students talk about the people and the situation, and then create role plays based on the scene. Students may refer back to previous lessons as a resource, but they should not simply reuse specific conversations.

Note: You may want to assign this exercise as written homework, having students prepare their role plays, practice them the next day with other students, and then present them to the class.

SIDE BY SIDE PICTURE CARDS

Numerical List

1. pen
2. book
3. pencil
4. notebook
5. bookshelf
6. globe
7. map
8. board
9. wall
10. clock
11. bulletin board
12. computer
13. table
14. chair
15. ruler
16. desk
17. dictionary
18. living room
19. dining room
20. kitchen
21. bedroom
22. bathroom
23. attic
24. yard
25. garage
26. basement
27. restaurant
28. bank
29. supermarket
30. library
31. park
32. movie theater
33. post office
34. zoo
35. hospital
36. read
37. cook
38. study
39. eat
40. watch TV
41. sleep
42. play the piano
43. play the guitar
44. play cards
45. play baseball
46. drink
47. teach
48. sing
49. listen to music
50. plant
51. listen to the radio
52. swim
53. fix ___ sink
54. fix ___ car
55. fix ___ TV
56. fix ___ bicycle
57. clean ___ apartment
58. clean ___ yard
59. feed ___ cat
60. feed ___ dog
61. paint
62. do ___ exercises
63. wash ___ clothes
64. wash ___ windows
65. wash ___ car
66. brush ___ teeth
67. wash ___ hair
68. tall – short
69. young – old
70. heavy/fat – thin
71. new – old
72. married – single
73. handsome – ugly
74. beautiful/pretty – ugly
75. large/big – small/little
76. noisy – quiet
77. expensive – cheap
78. easy – difficult
79. rich – poor
80. sunny
81. cloudy
82. raining
83. snowing
84. hot
85. warm
86. cool
87. cold
88. ride ___ bicycle
89. bake
90. dance
91. school
92. hotel
93. gas station
94. bus station
95. clinic
96. fire station
97. bakery
98. video store
99. barber shop
100. laundromat
101. drug store
102. church
103. department store
104. police station
105. hair salon
106. book store
107. health club
108. cafeteria
109. train station
110. sad
111. happy
112. angry
113. nervous
114. thirsty
115. hungry
116. hot
117. cold
118. sick
119. embarrassed
120. tired
121. scared
122. cry
123. smile
124. shout
125. bite ___ nails
126. perspire
127. shiver
128. blush
129. yawn
130. cover ___ eyes
131. mechanic
132. secretary
133. teacher
134. baker
135. truck driver
136. chef
137. singer
138. dancer
139. actor
140. actress
141. have lunch
142. have dinner
143. go swimming
144. go shopping
145. go dancing
146. go skating
147. go skiing
148. go bowling
149. headache
150. stomachache
151. toothache
152. backache
153. earache
154. cold
155. fever
156. cough
157. sore throat
158. work
159. type
160. shave
161. wait for the bus
162. sit
163. apples
164. bananas
165. bread
166. cake
167. carrots
168. cheese
169. chicken
170. eggs
171. fish
172. grapes
173. ketchup
174. lemons
175. lettuce
176. mayonnaise
177. meat
178. mustard
179. onions
180. oranges
181. pears
182. pepper
183. potatoes
184. salt
185. soy sauce
186. tomatoes
187. butter
188. coffee
189. cookies
190. flour
191. ice cream
192. milk
193. orange juice
194. rice
195. soda
196. sugar
197. tea
198. yogurt
199. airport
200. baseball stadium
201. concert hall
202. courthouse
203. flower shop
204. hardware store
205. ice cream shop
206. motel
207. museum
208. parking garage
209. pet shop
210. playground
211. shoe store
212. toy store
213. university
214. high school

374 PICTURE CARDS Numerical List

Alphabetical List

actor 139
actress 140
airport 199
angry 112
apples 163
attic 23

backache 152
bake 89
baker 134
bakery 97
bananas 164
bank 28
barber shop 99
baseball stadium 200
basement 26
bathroom 22
beautiful 74
bedroom 21
big 75
bite ___ nails 125
blush 128
board 8
book 2
book store 106
bookshelf 5
bread 165
brush ___ teeth 66
bulletin board 11
bus station 94
butter 187

cafeteria 108
cake 166
carrots 167
chair 14
cheap 77
cheese 168
chef 136
chicken 169
church 102
clean ___ apartment 57
clean ___ yard 58
clinic 95
clock 10
cloudy 81
coffee 188
cold 117
cold 154
cold 87
computer 12
concert hall 201
cook 37
cookies 189
cool 86
cough 156
courthouse 202
cover ___ eyes 130
cry 122

dance 90
dancer 138

department store 103
desk 16
dictionary 17
difficult 78
dining room 19
do ___ exercises 62
drink 46
drug store 101

earache 153
easy 78
eat 39
eggs 170
embarrassed 119
expensive 77

fat 70
feed ___ cat 59
feed ___ dog 60
fever 155
fire station 96
fish 171
fix ___ bicycle 56
fix ___ car 54
fix ___ sink 53
fix ___ TV 55
flour 190
flower shop 203

garage 25
gas station 93
globe 6
go bowling 148
go dancing 145
go shopping 144
go skating 146
go skiing 147
go swimming 143
grapes 172

hair salon 105
handsome 73
happy 111
hardware store 204
have dinner 142
have lunch 141
headache 149
health club 107
heavy 70
high school 214
hospital 35
hot 116
hot 84
hotel 92
hungry 115

ice cream 191
ice cream shop 205

ketchup 173
kitchen 20

large 75

laundromat 100
lemons 174
lettuce 175
library 30
listen to music 49
listen to the radio 51
little 75
living room 18

map 7
married 72
mayonnaise 176
meat 177
mechanic 131
milk 192
motel 206
movie theater 32
museum 207
mustard 178

nervous 113
new 71
noisy 76
notebook 4

old 69, 71
onions 179
orange juice 193
oranges 180

paint 61
park 31
parking garage 208
pears 181
pen 1
pencil 3
pepper 182
perspire 126
pet shop 209
plant 50
play baseball 45
play cards 44
play the guitar 43
play the piano 42
playground 210
police station 104
poor 79
post office 33
potatoes 183
pretty 74

quiet 76

raining 82
read 36
restaurant 27
rice 194
rich 79
ride ___ bicycle 88
ruler 15

sad 110
salt 184

scared 121
school 91
secretary 132
shave 160
shiver 127
shoe store 211
short 68
shout 124
sick 118
sing 48
singer 137
single 72
sit 162
sleep 41
small 75
smile 123
snowing 83
soda 195
sore throat 157
soy sauce 185
stomachache 150
study 38
sugar 196
sunny 80
supermarket 29
swim 52

table 13
tall 68
tea 197
teach 47
teacher 133
thin 70
thirsty 114
tired 120
tomatoes 186
toothache 151
toy store 212
train station 109
truck driver 135
type 159

ugly 73, 74
university 213

video store 98

wait for the bus 161
wall 9
warm 85
wash ___ car 65
wash ___ clothes 63
wash ___ hair 67
wash ___ windows 64
watch TV 40
work 158

yard 24
yawn 129
yogurt 198
young 69

zoo 34

PICTURE CARDS Alphabetical List 375

Categories

Adjectives
angry 112
beautiful 74
big 75
cheap 77
cold 117
difficult 78
easy 78
embarrassed 119
expensive 77
fat 70
handsome 73
happy 111
heavy 70
hot 116
hungry 115
large 75
little 75
married 72
nervous 113
new 71
noisy 76
old 69, 71
poor 79
pretty 74
quiet 76
rich 79
sad 110
scared 121
short 68
sick 118
single 72
small 75
tall 68
thin 70
thirsty 114
tired 120
ugly 73, 74
young 69

Ailments
backache 152
cold 154
cough 156
earache 153
fever 155
headache 149
sore throat 157
stomachache 150
toothache 151

Classroom
board 8
book 2
bookshelf 5
bulletin board 11
chair 14
clock 10
computer 12
desk 16
dictionary 17
globe 6
map 7
notebook 4
pen 1
pencil 3
ruler 15
table 13
wall 9

Community
airport 199
bakery 97
bank 28
barber shop 99
baseball stadium 200
book store 106
bus station 94
cafeteria 108
church 102
clinic 95
concert hall 201
courthouse 202
department store 103
drug store 101
fire station 96
flower shop 203
gas station 93
hair salon 105
hardware store 204
health club 107
high school 214
hospital 35
hotel 92
ice cream shop 205
laundromat 100
library 30
motel 206
movie theater 32
museum 207
park 31
parking garage 208
pet shop 209
playground 210
police station 104
post office 33
restaurant 27
school 91
shoe store 211
supermarket 29
toy store 212
train station 109
university 213
video store 98
zoo 34

Foods
apples 163
bananas 164
bread 165
butter 187
cake 166
carrots 167
cheese 168
chicken 169
coffee 188
cookies 189
eggs 170
fish 171
flour 190
grapes 172
ice cream 191
ketchup 173
lemons 174
lettuce 175
mayonnaise 176
meat 177
milk 192
mustard 178
onions 179
orange juice 193
oranges 180
pears 181
pepper 182
potatoes 183
rice 194
salt 184
soda 195
soy sauce 185
sugar 196
tea 197
tomatoes 186
yogurt 198

Home
attic 23
basement 26
bathroom 22
bedroom 21
dining room 19
garage 25
kitchen 20
living room 18
yard 24

Occupations
actor 139
actress 140
baker 134
chef 136
dancer 138
mechanic 131
secretary 132
singer 137
teacher 133
truck driver 135

Verbs
bake 89
bite ___ nails 125
blush 128
brush ___ teeth 66
clean ___ apartment 57
clean ___ yard 58
cook 37
cover ___ eyes 130
cry 122
dance 90
do ___ exercises 62
drink 46
eat 39
feed ___ cat 59
feed ___ dog 60
fix ___ bicycle 56
fix ___ car 54
fix ___ sink 53
fix ___ TV 55
go bowling 148
go dancing 145
go shopping 144
go skating 146
go skiing 147
go swimming 143
have dinner 142
have lunch 141
listen to music 49
listen to the radio 51
paint 61
perspire 126
plant 50
play baseball 45
play cards 44
play the guitar 43
play the piano 42
read 36
ride ___ bicycle 88
shave 160
shiver 127
shout 124
sing 48
sit 162
sleep 41
smile 123
study 38
swim 52
teach 47
type 159
wait for the bus 161
wash ___ car 65
wash ___ clothes 63
wash ___ hair 67
wash ___ windows 64
watch TV 40
work 158
yawn 129

Weather
cloudy 81
cold 87
cool 86
hot 84
raining 82
snowing 83
sunny 80
warm 85

376 PICTURE CARDS Categories

GLOSSARY

The number after each word indicates the page where the word first appears in the text.
(adj) = adjective, (adv) = adverb, (n) = noun, (v) = verb.

a little later 25
a little while 25
a long time 27
academic 136
accent 59
accept 119
accident report 117
accidentally 120
accomplish 109
act 135
adjust 29
afford 139
Africa 33
after *midnight* 35
agreement 145
ahead of time 98
alarm 117
alarm clock 131
Albania 33
Alcatraz prison 49
alike 148
all right 73
allergic 131
allow 142
already 42
amazing 75
an hour a day 142
ankle 14
answer (n) 125
apparently 78
appreciate 78
approve 145
area 65
army 8
arrange 145
arrangement 145
art 57
art museum 136
as soon as 73
Asia 33
ask for a raise 67
asleep 66
aspirin 44
assistant manager 61
astrologer 145
astrological 145
astronaut 51
astronomy 23
at the last minute 108
at the same time 140
at this point 44

audience 16
Austria 33
Austria-Hungary 33
available 140
avoid 81
awake 66
aware 59
awesome 48

baby-sit 141
baby-sitter 79
bachelor 60
background 136
baggy 127
balance beam 113
balcony 102
ball 113
ballet dancer 5
ballet instructor 5
barber 62
basket 113
Batman 23
been 52
Beethoven 2
beforehand 108
beginning (n) 44
behave 142
best friend 43
bet 17
bill 8
Bingo 43
biology 23
birth 145
black and blue 54
black eye 15
blind date 147
boat 18
bobsled 111
body 54
bookkeeper 47
bottom 61
bouquet 146
box (v) 87
break up 106
bride 146
bring along 98
bring back 102
Broadway show 39
Broadway show tune 23
bronze 113
brownies 104

browse 26
browse the web 26
Bulgaria 33
bump into 102
business trip 132
button 128
by the time 100

cable car 49
cage 75
Calgary 111
call back 27
call on 124
call up 116
campfire 35
Canada 30
cancel 107
candle 146
candy store 102
canoeing 95
Caribbean 111
cashier 51
catch 146
ceiling 73
cello 56
ceremony 108
certain 140
chance 141
channel 23
check 33
chemistry 76
chew 105
child rearing 125
child-care center 65
childhood 102
chin 113
Chinatown 34
choose 145
chop 15
chopsticks 38
Christmas decorations 116
circle 148
clean up 123
cleaner's 116
clerk 47
clothing 19
clothing department 61
coach 5
coffee plantation worker 66

coincidence 132
collect 114
collection 136
college application form 116
Colombia 66
Colosseum 19
come back 30
come through 33
come to work 108
communication 65
commute 140
compatible 136
compete 111
competition 111
compose 2
composition 29
computer company 65
computer lab 35
computer programmer 51
computer programming 109
concerned 125
concert tickets 72
confetti 146
confused 68
conservative 142
consider 81
constantly 125
continue 81
cook (n) 4
cotton candy 40
count 57
couple 146
critical 85
cross out 115
crown 146
cruise 39
Cuban 34
cultural 136
curtain 99
custom 145
Cyprus 146

daily 15
Dallas 61
dance class 139
dance lesson 37
date (v) 69
dating service 145

GLOSSARY 377

day care 66
day off 31
day shift 66
daytime 65
decline 148
decorations 123
dedicated 54
defense 142
definite 35
definition 119
deliver a baby 75
demonstrator 16
Denmark 67
Denver 49
department 61
deserve 109
despite 140
difference 114
dinner party 98
dinner table 97
direct traffic 69
discouraged 120
discuss 95
dislocate 105
distance running 112
dizzy 54
do business 65
do card tricks 97
do gymnastics 105
do over 119
do poorly 107
do research 26
do sit-ups 69
do the tango 105
document 33
dog day-care worker 66
downtown 76
draw 38
dream 112
dressing room 126
driver's test 106
driveway 98
driving school 109
drop off 122

earn 109
earthquake 33
eat out 96
economic 33
education 145
educational background 140
electric bill 46
e-mail 8
emotional 30
Empire State Building 49
end 99

energy 137
engaged 56
engineer 58
engineering 92
enroll 92
envelope 114
envy 86
equal rights 137
Esquilino 33
Europe 23
event 35
eventually 125
ever 40
ever since 86
exact 68
example 33
ex-boyfriend 119
excited (adj) 30
exercise bike 37
ex-girlfriend 119
exhausted 79
exist 66
expect 140
explain 41
expression 148
extra 109
extra large 126
extremely 44

fact 111
factory worker 65
fail 106
fairy tale 139
fall for 147
fall through 108
family reunion 35
far 140
fast-food restaurant 84
favor 28
fax (n) 65
feel dizzy 54
feel like 118
fiction 111
field 102
fight 15
figure out 123
figure skate 87
figure skating 112
final 129
final exam 35
finish line 113
firefighter 65
first time 111
first-aid course 40
Fisherman's Wharf 49
fit 127
flight 25
flood (n) 33

flow 33
flower petal 146
fluently 132
fly a kite 95
folk song 23
foolish 98
foreign 33
foreign born 33
forever 66
formal 148
former 33
fortunate 60
four-person 111
free 122
free time 9
freedom 145
frightened 131
front teeth 105
furious 73
future tense 35

garbage 117
Georgia 59
Germany 33
gerund 114
get a promotion 109
get a raise 39
get along with 124
get around 19
get over 124
get ready (for) 108
get rid of 44
get stuck 40
get to 100
give a party 97
give back 119
give blood 42
give *piano* lessons 75
give *the kids* a bath 27
give up 111
go back 89
go by 100
go canoeing 95
go kayaking 45
go scuba diving 40
go to bed 46
go together 106
go water-skiing 24
go window-shopping 95
go with 128
gold 113
Golden Gate Bridge 49
gossip 85
government 142
graduate 56
grammar 114
groom 146
group 111

growl 17
guess 88
guidance counselor 51
guitarist 51
gymnastics 105

habit 85
Halloween 23
hallway 73
ham 67
hand in 115
hang up 115
happily 60
happiness 128
harbor 33
hate 81
have the time 45
health food 109
hear from 124
heart attack 107
heartbroken 98
heat 116
heating system 73
helicopter 39
help (n) 127
help with 134
hide 131
high fever 54
highlight 113
hike 14
Hindu 146
historic 33
hold 113
Holland 66
home town 102
homemade 102
homework assignment 141
hook up 115
hopeful 140
horoscope 145
horse 38
hospital bill 123
hot-air balloon 39
Hungary 33

ice cream shop 102
ice skate 26
ice skating 136
imagine 30
immigrant 33
immigrate 34
immigration 33
imported 98
impossible 111
in advance 99
in love 55
in one day 79

378   GLOSSARY

in the past 65
in the past 24 hours 55
in years 62
include 111
income tax form 26
incorrectly 120
incredible 75
India 145
infinitive 114
informal 148
information 145
injection 38
injure 104
inseparable 148
instant 65
instructor 1
insurance form 123
interested (in) 53
interests 9
Internet company 134
interrupt 85
interview (v) 112
inventory 41
invitation 98
involve 146
Ireland 33

jack 28
jail 25
Jamaica 111
Jamaican 111
jazz 57
jealous 39
job opening 140
joy 17
judge 113
jump 17
junk food 85

keep on 81
Kenya 112
kid (v) 74
kid (n) 15
kimono 40
kiss 131
kite 96

lake 35
Lake Placid 111
lap 109
laptop 98
last January 22
last spring 22
last Sunday 22
last time 111
last week/month/year 22
lately 132
late-night 65

Latin America 33
lay off (v) 140
layoff (n) 140
leader 59
leak (n) 135
leak (v) 69
learn 81
learner 68
leave for school 46
leave on 119
lecture 100
lenient 131
level 112
liberal 142
library book 116
light (v) 146
lightning 131
limousine 39
lines 13
Little Red Riding Hood 8
living conditions 33
local 65
located 103
lonely 30
look forward to 31
look through 98
look up 119
look up to 124
loose 127
lose his voice 105
lottery 59
love letter 101

macaroni and cheese 133
Madagascar 9
magic trick 15
magician 15
mail room 47
main 140
major (in) 136
make a decision 88
make a list 67
make noises 72
manager 51
manufacturing company 65
marathon 76
marks 113
marriage 145
marry 33
match (n) 145
matchmaker 145
matchmaking service 145
medal 112
medical 33
medical examination 33

medical school 60
medicine 46
Mediterranean 19
medium 126
meeting 26
Melbourne 34
memories 102
memorize 95
mend 69
men's clothing store 128
merry-go-round 102
Middle East 33
mind 117
minorities 137
modem 118
modern art 57
modern-day 145
Moldova 33
Monopoly 45
more than a week 54
move out 102
move through 113
movie hero 102
movie soundtrack 111
Mozart 97
music school 56
music teacher 5
musician 51

narrow 127
national 112
native 33
natural 33
natural disasters 33
neck 54
neither 133
network programming 93
New Year's decorations 123
newlywed 145
next January 22
next spring 22
next Sunday 22
night shift 65
normally 66
North Africa 33
Norway 111
nostalgic 102
note (n) 66
notice (v) 128
nuclear 137
nuclear energy 137

occupation 145
offer 136
office clerk 47
office party 67

office worker 65
officer 79
official 33
Olympics 111
on sale 128
once 7
onion soup 23
opera 97
opportunity 34
opposed to 137
opposite 121
originally 148
Orlando 8
outlook on life 137
outskirts 102
oven 98
over and over 112
overseas 143
own (v) 53

pain 54
paper 120
parade 100
parking space 131
parking ticket 79
part 83
past 54
participant 113
partner 145
pass 33
pass a test 109
pass by 102
past 54
past participle 68
past perfect tense 114
patient (n) 54
pay attention 113
paycheck 41
pea soup 23
peach 67
peel 69
penpal 114
peppermint 132
perfect 114
perfectly 68
perform 95
perhaps 30
permanently 30
personal 57
personal ad 145
personal computer 57
personality 137
pessimistic 140
phenomenal 48
philosophical 143
photo album 124
photocopy center 65
photography 53

GLOSSARY 379

physician 51
piano recital 107
Picasso 57
pick 69
pick on 124
pick out 115
pin (v) 146
place (v) 111
plaid 128
plain 126
plan (n) 24
plan (v) 107
plane 13
plane ticket 98
plantation 66
play Monopoly 45
play Scrabble 3
play squash 105
pleasure 78
point 113
political 33
politics 83
poorly 107
popcorn 102
portrait 116
possibly 28
prefer 140
prepare 14
prepared (adj) 13
present (adj) 59
present perfect
   continuous tense 114
present perfect tense 41
present tense 35
presentation 41
principal 16
prison 49
private 146
professional 5
promotion 109
psychology 97
public school 33
purchase 95
put away 115
put on 99
put to bed 66

questionnaire 145
quietly 142
quit 81

race 113
rainbow 40
raise (n) 39
realize 16
reason 33
receive 67
recently 34

reception hall 146
refund 129
refuse 129
reggae music 111
regional 112
registration hall 33
regular 35
rehearse 95
reindeer 66
reindeer herder 66
relax 31
report 38
reporter 84
represent 111
republic 33
resemble 148
respect 143
resume 78
retirement 31
ring (v) 69
rip (v) 15
roller-skate 104
routine 112
rule 114
rules of the road 109
run away 99
run into 124
run out of 124
rural 145

safari 66
safari guide 66
sail away 100
sale 127
salesman 141
satellite 53
satisfaction 48
Saudi Arabia 33
saxophone 62
say good-bye 30
say hello 102
schedule 35
school nurse 139
science 102
science teacher 102
score 113
Scrabble 3
screwdriver 29
selection 126
semester 23
sentence 148
separable 148
separately 148
seven days a week 34
shift 65
shine 95
shoot 113
shoulder 16

shovel 98
show tune 23
Siberia 66
silver 113
similar 136
simple 121
simply 120
sincerely 35
Singapore 60
skater 1
skating (n) 111
skiing (n) 111
sleep well 12
slip 117
Slovak Republic 146
snowboard 14
so far 125
some other time 118
soundtrack 111
souvenir 19
Soviet republic 33
space 53
speaker 148
speech 40
speed 113
sports training 112
sprain 14
square 49
squash 105
stamp 114
stamp collection 114
stand in line 69
stand up 147
Statue of Liberty 49
stay after 5
stay open 65
stay with 30
steak bone 105
stereo system 121
stiff 54
stop 81
store manager 58
strawberry shortcake
   101
strict 131
strong 111
stuck 40
subway pusher 66
successful 60
suggestion 148
Summer Olympics 111
summer vacation 31
Superman 23
support 137
surf 87
surprise (n) 140
surprised (adj) 47
Swahili 38

Swaziland 145
Sweden 67
sweetheart 147
swimmer 1
swimming (n) 111
switch 65
swollen 54
Sydney 34

take a course 97
take a ride 39
take a tour 49
take after 124
take back 116
take down 115
take home 109
take off 100
take out 121
take time 54
take your medicine 46
talk show 8
tango 105
tap dance 87
taxi driver 50
tease 91
technical school 93
telephone bill 8
tend (to) 137
tennis coach 5
tense (adj) 35
tense (n) 35
tenth-grade 102
term paper 46
termites 57
terrific 48
Texas 57
the rest of 90
theater group 136
think about 81
think over 119
this Friday night 23
this January 22
this spring 22
this Sunday 22
this weekend 24
throw 146
throw away 115
throw out 116
thunder 135
ticket 72
tied up 36
tight 127
tongue 113
tonight 21
top 49
Toronto 30
total 33
tour 49

380   **GLOSSARY**

tourist 19
toy 117
track 111
tradition 145
traditionally 145
train (v) 107
training 111
training center 111
traveler's checks 98
tree house 24
trousers 128
try on 115
tulip 66
tulip farmer 66
Turkish 34
turn down 119
turn off 35
turn on 98
TV program 35
twice 7
twist 104
two hours later 121
two-person 111
two-word verb 148
typist 1

Ukraine 33
unbelievable 75
unhappy 148
unique 66
United Nations 49
use (n) 137
use up 119
usual 127

valuable 77
Vatican 19
vegetarian 89
veil 146
verb 114
version 145
vice president 51
violinist 1
visit (n) 102
vocational training 140
voice 105
voice mail 67

waiting room 54
wake up 115
walk home 128
walk the dog 131
want ad 131
war 33
water (v) 95
water heater 73
wave 16
weather forecast 24

wedding guest 123
wedding invitation 123
wedding procession 146
weight train 111
Western Europe 97
wharf 49
whatever 142
whenever 3
whole milk 59
willing 140
window-shopping 97
window washer 79
Winter Olympic Games 111
winter sport 136
wish 146
woods 14
work experience 78
work out 26
work schedule 65
World Wide Web 65
worldwide 65
worship 146
wrestle 95
wrist 105
write down 119

yet 46

zipper 128

Expressions

"24/7" (twenty-four hours a day/seven days a week) 65
9 to 5 65
"a couch potato" 67
"a piece of cake" 36
"a real ham" 67
"a real peach" 67
"a smart cookie" 67
Absolutely! 88
after all 90
as for me 47
as the days go by 140
as you can imagine 30
at the back of 16
at the last minute 108
at the same time 140
believe me 76
break a habit 85
"Break a leg!" 113
by any chance 141
can't stand 84
"chicken" 36
Could I ask you a favor? 29

Could you do a favor for me? 29
Could you do me a favor? 29
Could you possibly do me a favor? 29
days gone by 102
do a lot of things 49
Don't you think so? 85
"fall for" someone 147
Fine. 27
for a long time 30
from beginning to end 99
"get cold feet" 108
"Get off my back!" 113
give it right back 120
"give someone a ring" 36
"give someone the cold shoulder" 147
go out of business 93
go through some difficult times 140
Good idea. 62
happily married 60
have a good life 30
Have a good weekend. 47
have a lot in common 136
Have a nice weekend. 24
have a party for 31
have the time 45
"hide and seek" 101
"Hold your tongue!" 113
I appreciate that. 87
I bet. 17
I completely forgot! 117
I don't mean to 85
I forgot all about it! 117
I hope so. 90
I see . . . 47
in the first place 120
It completely slipped my mind. 117
It slipped my mind. 117
It was nice meeting you. 83
It's been a long time. 62
It's been a pleasure. 78
It's raining cats and dogs. 36
It's really a shame. 106
"Keep your chin up!" 113

"Keep your eye on the ball!" 113
Look! 44
look over *his* shoulder 16
"made for each other" 137
Nice meeting you, too. 83
"no picnic" 36
No problem. 127
Not at all. 86
"nuts" about someone 147
on pins and needles 17
once a *day* 7
out of town 135
outlook on life 137
please excuse me 83
Poor *Harry*! 104
"Put your best foot forward!" 113
"rules of the road" 109
So . . . 55
Speak to you soon. 27
"stand someone up" 147
start at the bottom 61
Thanks for your help. 127
That's very kind of you. 87
That's very nice of you. 87
"the birds and the bees" 57
the facts of life 57
"the top banana" 67
the truth is 85
There's nothing to be nervous about. 76
three times a *day* 7
"tied up" 36
to tell you the truth 83
"touchy subject" 142
twice a *day* 7
Well, . . . 47
What a coincidence! 132
What can I do for you? 73
"What's cooking?" 36
work *his* way up to the top 61
you can see why 142
You're in luck! 127

GLOSSARY 381

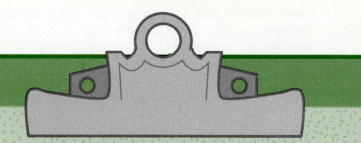

Teacher's Notes

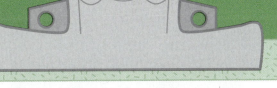

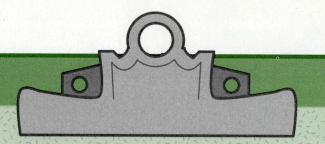

Teacher's Notes

Teacher's Notes

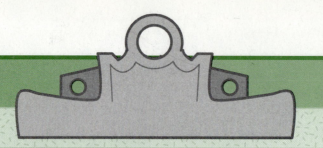
Teacher's Notes